ntina

Scobie, James R., 1929-1981.
Argentina: a city and a nation

LATIN AMERICAN HISTORIES

JAMES R. SCOBIE, EDITOR

JAMES R. SCOBIE *Argentina: A City and a Nation*
SECOND EDITION
ROLLIE E. POPPINO *Brazil: The Land and People*
CHARLES C. CUMBERLAND *Mexico: The Struggle for Modernity*

Argentina

A CITY AND A NATION
SECOND EDITION

JAMES R. SCOBIE

New York
OXFORD UNIVERSITY PRESS
London   1971   *Toronto*

Copyright © 1964, 1971 by Oxford University Press, Inc.
Library of Congress Catalogue Card Number: 78-166005
printing, last digit: 10
Printed in the United States of America

Foreword

In dealing with the complex and highly individual societies of Latin America we can no longer be content merely with political history. This volume is the first in a series which will stress the area's social and economic environment. The consideration of how people lived, what forces molded their existence, and how society and government evolved can explain much of present-day Latin America. In these studies we will be concerned with city and countryside, immigrant and native, industry and agriculture, boom and depression, and will examine the class structure, settlement patterns, customs, and arts of emerging nations.

In *Argentina: A City and a Nation** principal emphasis is placed on the country's formative years—the nineteenth century. The first chapter introduces the geography and the final chapter summarizes the contemporary scene. Other chapters explore the Spanish origins, the economies of the interior and the coast, the growth of cities and industry,

---

* I acknowledge my indebtedness to the title of René Marill (pseud., René Albérès), *Argentine, un monde, une ville* (Paris, Hachette, 1957) for the idea implied in the title of the present volume.

the predominance of Buenos Aires, the struggles for political unity, and the achievement of nationhood. A political chronology and statistical tables are provided for reference, and the annotated bibliography is intended as a guide to further study.

This work is derived from research in Argentina during 1949, 1952-54, 1959-60, and 1961 and from several years of teaching Latin American history. Extensive financial support made these studies possible. Without making institutions responsible for the outcome of their generosity, I thank the Doherty Foundation, the Social Science Research Council, the Organization of American States, and the Institute for International Studies, the Institute of Social Sciences, and the History Department of the University of California, Berkeley. The Rockefeller Foundation generously provided funds for my appointment as visiting scholar at the Institute of Latin American Studies of Columbia University in 1962-63. I appreciate the invaluable help given me by many institutions in Argentina and by the staffs of the New York Public Library, the Library of Congress, the Columbus Memorial Library, the Widener Library at Harvard, and the General Library of the University of California. Finally, I admit to a bias—a deep sense of *simpatía* and friendship for Argentina.

Berkeley, California   J. R. S.
August 1963

Foreword to Second Edition

Substantial additions to the Argentine bibliography together with the political events since 1963 require an updating of this socio-economic interpretation of Argentine development. I have added new materials to the final chapter, The Crisis of Contemporary Argentina, and have included significant new works, events, and statistics in the supporting sections.

Recent events in Argentina, especially when taken in the context of rising discontent and disillusionment among laborers, students, and average citizens, forecast continued problems and conflicts for that nation in the 1970's. I am optimistic, nevertheless, that my conclusion in the first edition—that Argentina stands on the threshold of a great future—will eventually prove accurate. This leads me to hope that I will be able to return in the next few years to the often puzzling political events of the past several decades and provide a synthesis of the post-1930 Argentine scene that will somewhat revise this edition's emphasis on the nineteenth-century formation of that nation.

Bloomington, Indiana   J. R. S.
April, 1971

Contents

Maps

Tables and Graph, 303-309

Argentina

Introduction

The sixteenth-century conquistadors dreamed of the Río de la Plata —the land and river of silver. The dream of Italian immigrants in the nineteenth century was *hacer la América*—to pick money off the streets of Buenos Aires. Such were the dreams, however illusory, which underlay the complex development of Argentina. Indians, Spaniards, and other foreigners settled this country. Cattle, sheep, and wheat contributed to its prosperity. From metropolis and village, *porteño* (of the port, hence, of Buenos Aires) and provinces, finally emerged a nation.

Today twenty-four million Argentines live in a country of one million square miles—four times larger than Texas, five times larger than France—reaching from Antarctic wastes in the south to tropical jungles and towering Andean plateaus and peaks in the north. One-third of the people cluster in Greater Buenos Aires, economic core of the nation and one of the largest metropolitan areas in the world. The remaining population is spread across the barren plateau of Patagonia, the mountain valleys of the northwest, the lowlands of the northeast, and the fertile plains of the pampas. This is the most urbanized nation of Latin America. Three-quarters of the people live in towns and cities. Industry, commerce, and government provide them with a livelihood and a way of life. Despite the major exports of beef, mutton, hides, wool, and corn, agriculture absorbs less than 25 per cent of the economically active population. On the borders of Bolivia, Chile, and Paraguay a few Indian villages recall the past, but elsewhere Argentines boast of racial homogeneity, a national literacy rate of more than 90 per cent, and a close relationship to Europe. Yet the gap between dream and reality haunts the modern Argentine as much as it did the sixteenth-century Spaniard who hoped to find silver in the Río de la Plata. The statesman deplores the scant population in comparison with Brazil's rapidly expanding nearly one hundred million, or the recent declines in per capita gross national product compared with Mexico's yearly increase of 3 per cent. The white-collar worker, unable to clothe and feed his family decently despite two jobs and a fourteen-hour day, experiences a similar frustration in a land which again seems to have deceived men's expectations.

What lies behind the illusion? What is this land? Who are these people?

In the European mind of the sixteenth century the image of the continental masses of the New World came into focus gradually. Exploration painfully sketched in the coast lines, then the rivers, the mountains, and the plains, while European nations struggled to extend their control over new lands and peoples. Temperate North America was inherited by the latecomers, France and England. The south fell clearly within Spain's orbit, but the region of the Río de la Plata aroused little interest, at least in contrast to Peru and Mexico with their mineral wealth and flourishing Indian civilizations. In the Spanish Empire the Río de la Plata soon assumed the role of supplying mules, food, and textiles to the rich mining areas of Upper Peru (Bolivia). Settlement therefore was oriented toward the interior of the continent, and the area which became Argentina vegetated as the stepchild of the empire for more than two centuries.

Europe's Industrial Revolution had radically changed the world into which the new countries of the Americas emerged. As the Spanish Empire in America tottered and collapsed in the decade following

1810, England and industrial powers on the Continent stood ready to export goods, talent, capital, and people. Under such new influences Argentina increasingly turned toward England. No longer were its people and its economy harnessed to a mercantilist empire. The industrialization of Europe created a demand for raw materials, not bullion. The production of hides and animal fats, long the mainstay of coastal settlements in the Río de la Plata area, was spurred by new incentives in the export trade. Argentina's share of the benefits of the Industrial Revolution at first appeared negligible, at least when compared with that reaped by the precocious United States. Remoteness from Europe, sparse population, inadequate transportation facilities, technological backwardness, unsettled political conditions, and continued depredations by hostile Indians—all served to retard the rise of the coastal region around Buenos Aires and to prevent a more dramatic readjustment to the world economy. Yet the direction for change had been indicated.

Argentina finally consolidated itself as a nation in the 1870's and 1880's. The last decades of the nineteenth century marked the country's boom years, with the transformation of a rude pastoral economy into a European outpost of order and prosperity. Technology revolutionized and expanded cattle and sheep raising. Crop farming suddenly acquired importance, and Argentina became a major producer and exporter of cereals. Processing of raw materials for export, the manufacture of foods, beverages, and textiles, and the construction of railroads and buildings absorbed steadily increasing amounts of labor and capital. The surging flow of European immigration, attracted by economic opportunities, submerged the original Spanish-mestizo stock, at least in the coastal zones. Population swelled from 1,800,000 in 1869, the date of the first national census, to 8,000,000 by 1914. Five million immigrants, largely Italian and Spanish, poured into the coastal cities, towns, and farms, and more than half of these remained to make Argentina their new homeland.

Thus the orientation toward the Atlantic and toward Europe became an accomplished fact. The coastal region, especially the city and province of Buenos Aires, dominated Argentine development—a dominance forcibly emphasized by the railroads. The British-built lines, which spread out from Buenos Aires and to a lesser degree from Rosario and

Bahía Blanca, encouraged a vast expansion of Argentina's agricultural realm. But they also served to drain products, people, talent, and money toward the coast. In 1869 less than half the national population lived in the coastal region, comprising the provinces of Entre Ríos and Buenos Aires and the southern portions of Santa Fe and Córdoba. By 1914 the proportion rose to more than two-thirds. No longer were the ambitious and the capable satisfied to remain on the land or in the interior. For native and the immigrant alike, the cities and towns of the littoral promised progress and success, and the city of Buenos Aires more than any other. The growth of industry and commerce further accentuated this imbalance. Investors, merchants, and tradesmen all gravitated toward this area where population and transport facilities were concentrated. Buenos Aires continued to grow as a metropolis until, by 1970, Greater Buenos Aires claimed a population of more than eight million.

The introduction of Italian immigrants, pedigreed livestock, British railroads, and Yankee plowshares stimulated other changes. The booms of the late nineteenth century and early twentieth brought vast wealth to a few and some slight benefits to the great majority. Education, the ballot, and hope for decent living were no longer the monopoly of a small elite; now these were taken for granted by most city dwellers. A new generation, developed from the immigrant and native heritages, advanced into government, business, and the professions, and, in accord with the age, adopted materialism and blatant nationalism as its creed. But accelerating industrialization and urbanization created serious pressures. In an economy where concern with consumption took precedence over production, there was little margin or surplus to satisfy rising aspirations. The middle classes comprised as much as half the population, but many of these white-collar workers, government employees, and professional people found little opportunity for advancement. As migrants from the interior drifted toward the littoral and toward the cities, the lower classes increasingly made their presence felt. Dark-skinned mestizo peasants from the north appeared on the wharves of Rosario and in the factories of Buenos Aires and reminded Argentines that the Indian heritage and the poverty-stricken masses were still realities in the twentieth century. The city slums absorbed these new arrivals, introduced them to economic and social wants, but failed to provide them with the means to fulfill their ambitions.

It is evident that Argentina has changed enormously during the past four hundred years: from a rudimentary pastoral economy has developed an urbanized, industrial society. But the head outgrew the body. The world economy fostered the prosperity of the coastal region while the rest of the country stood still. This very development has placed limits on economic growth and expansion. It falls to the present Argentine generations, therefore, to create more industrial centers as in Córdoba and Mendoza, to extend agricultural investments as in Misiones and Río Negro, to provide the urban and rural dweller with the opportunity and incentive to produce as well as to consume—to realize, in a word, the potentials of this land of silver.

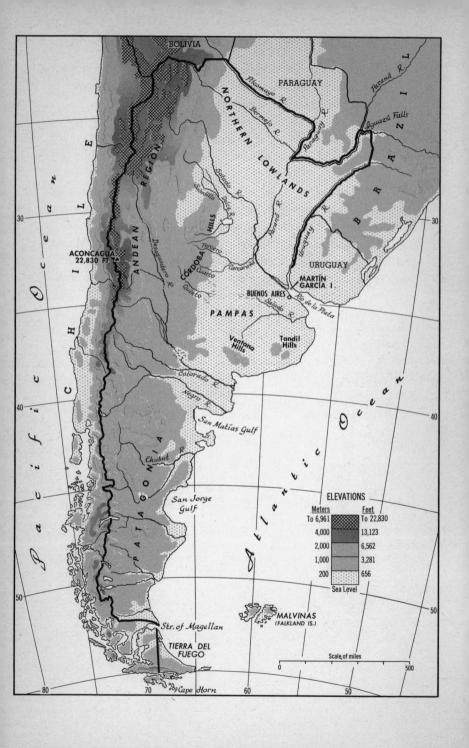

BOLIVIA

PARAGUAY

B R A Z I L

Campo Durán

JUJUY

Jujuy
Zapla Mines
Salta

SALTA

FORMOSA

CHACO

Asunción

Formosa

MISIONES

CATAMARCA

San Miguel de Tucumán
TUCUMÁN
Santiago del Estero

SANTIAGO DEL ESTERO

Resistencia
Corrientes
Posadas

CORRIENTES

Catamarca

LA RIOJA

La Rioja

SANTA FE

SAN JUAN

Córdoba

CÓRDOBA

Rafaela
Esperanza
Santa Fé

ENTRE RÍOS

Concordia

San Juan

Cañada de Gomez
Casilda
Villa Constitución
San Nicolás

Paraná
Rosario

Concepción del Uruguay

URUGUAY

Santiago

MENDOZA

Mendoza

SAN LUIS

San Luis

Pergamino

Junín
Chivilcoy

FED. DIST.

Buenos Aires

Montevideo

La Plata
Chascomús

Río de la Plata

Trenque Lauquen

Santa Rosa

LA PAMPA

BUENOS AIRES

Olavarría

Juárez

Tres Arroyos

Mar del Plata

Bahía Blanca

NEUQUÉN

Plaza Huincal
Neuquén
Chocón

RÍO NEGRO

Viedma

O c e a n

San Carlos de Bariloche

Sierra Grande

42°

42°

Rawson

CHUBUT

P a c i f i c   O c e a n

C H I L E

Comodoro Rivadavia

SANTA CRUZ

A t l a n t i c

MALVINAS
(FALKLAND IS.)

Río Turbio
Río Gallegos

TIERRA DEL FUEGO

Ushuaia

80   ARGENTINA   40
CHILE   MALVINAS
(FALKLAND IS.)
TIERRA DEL FUEGO   S. Georgia I.

60°   S. Sandwich Is.

74°   CLAIMED BY ARGENTINA

120   80

ANTARCTICA
South Pole

★ National capitals
◉ Provincial capitals

Scale of miles

0   500

Chapter 1 • The Land

The political and geographical unit we speak of today as Argentina took several centuries to achieve its present shape. As the colonial period progressed, the scattered Spanish settlements—in the northwest close to the mines of Upper Peru, in the west across the Andes from central Chile, and in the east adjacent to the river system of the coast —gradually acquired a vague sense of cohesion. In the late eighteenth century the Spanish crown unified these several regions under the Viceroyalty of the Río de la Plata based at Buenos Aires—an administrative area which embraced major portions of present-day Argentina, Uruguay, Paraguay, and Bolivia. It was from this unit of the empire that an independent country developed in the first decades of the nineteenth century. Local movements for independence and international complications soon split off Uruguay, Paraguay, and Bolivia, while the southern half of Argentina and much of the northeast remained firmly in the grasp of nomadic, warlike Indians. Not until the late nineteenth century were the present boundaries properly defined. Even then the Malvinas, or Falkland Islands, which Great Britain forcibly occupied in 1833, and the icy, deserted wedge of Antarctica lay beyond Argentine exploitation.

11

The country which emerged is an inverted and tapering triangle embracing the major portion of South America's Temperate Zone. Argentina's northern boundary with Bolivia and Paraguay, nearly a thousand miles long, is the base. To the south, the Strait of Magellan and the eastern half of the chilly island of Tierra del Fuego form the apex. Between these two extremes stretch twenty-three hundred miles, or thirty-three degrees of latitude, lying almost entirely within the temperate belt. Argentina thus shares with Australia the major portion of the southern hemisphere's Temperate Zone, but at the same time this location emphasizes the country's remoteness from the world's major centers of population and economic activity. Seven thousand miles of ocean separate the estuary of the Río de la Plata from New York or the English Channel, and, although the air age has turned weeks into hours, the handicap of distance has not been completely overcome.

As a land of temperate climate, Argentina invites comparison with the United States, at least with that portion between the Mississippi River and the Rocky Mountains. Argentina, like the United States Midwest, possesses a certain geographical unity. The barrier of the Andes, while infringing deeply on the northwestern provinces, provides one natural limit. The scrub forests, flood plains, and swamps of the Chaco create another boundary to the north. To the east the Río de la Plata river system defines political frontiers, yet facilitates communications and contact with neighboring Paraguay, Brazil, and Uruguay. Between these natural boundaries lies a vast plain sloping gently toward the east.

The map of Argentina inverted and superimposed on the similar latitudes of the central United States demonstrates a striking coincidence in climate and topography between the two areas. The humidity of the Mississippi valley is reproduced all along the Río de la Plata system. The grassy savannas and swamps of coastal Louisiana and Texas find their parallel in Corrientes and in portions of the Chaco. Just as the well-watered Mississippi valley gives way to range land and finally to desert, so do Buenos Aires and Santa Fe merge into La Pampa and Córdoba and then into the arid west broken only by the irrigated vineyards and gardens of Mendoza and San Juan. Even the wind howling across the North Dakota prairies finds its match in the fiercer gales of Patagonia. And, although the Rockies cannot approach the effectiveness of the Andes as a barrier, they mark the end of the Great Plains.

Just as with the Great Plains in the United States, Argentina's geographical unity results largely from the absence of major obstacles on this vast plain. A closer look at the area's terrain, climate, and economy reveals several natural divisions: Patagonia, the Andean region, the northern lowlands, and the pampas.

Patagonia, the area south of the Río Colorado, is still nearly unoccupied—a quarter of the nation's territory settled by a bare 3 per cent of the population. Not until the 1950's were its four major subdivisions —Neuquén, Río Negro, Chubut, and Santa Cruz—elevated from territorial to provincial status.* Although this area contains some of the world's most spectacular scenery, other characteristics have discouraged settlement. Lava flows and the action of wind and glaciers have created a succession of plateaus on a cracked and broken granite base. The plateaus rise in regular steps to the west, but the granite hills formed by the broken edges of the ancient crystalline base and the canyons or riverbeds cut by glaciers and surface water have made a chaotic jumble of the terrain. Except in the south, where water and glaciers have gouged out depressions and formed a vast lake region, the Andes rise abruptly from the western edge of the plateaus. The prevailing westerly winds leave a haze of dust in the air as they sweep violently and incessantly across these plateaus. The proximity of the Atlantic has some moderating effect on temperature variations. Cold weather and occasional snow occur over the length of Patagonia, but only in the south does the average temperature dip to the freezing point during the winter months of June, July, and August. The mountainous western region receives enough rainfall to support forest growth, but the rest of Patagonia is arid, and the few inches of moisture usually fall as snow in the winter season.

* Today the southern tip of the continent, Tierra del Fuego, is Argentina's only territory.

For centuries Patagonia appeared too remote and barren to warrant settlement or even exploration. Only an occasional Jesuit missionary intruded on the sparse and warlike Indian population. Then in the 1860's a colony of Welsh settlers on the Chubut coast demonstrated that Europeans could survive in this region. Two decades later, after a campaign of extermination had removed the Indians, sheepherders began to move southward. The short grass of the plateaus afforded good grazing, and water and shelter could be found along the streams and in the canyons. Fears that an aggressive Chile might appropriate some of the area hastened further measures of occupation: the establishment of military outposts, the building of railroads, and the survey and final arbitration of the boundary. Crop farming and some cattle raising gained a foothold in the north along the two major rivers, the Río Colorado and the Río Negro, and near the mouth of the Río Chubut. When a British railroad company completed irrigation works in the 1920's, the valley of the Río Negro became a center for fruit production, especially of apples, grapes, and pears. Yet remoteness from major population centers and absence of easily navigable rivers discouraged the development which the climate and fertility of this valley seemed to warrant. Westward along the Andean chain an increasing flow of tourists to the beautiful Argentine-Chilean lake district underwrote the modest expansion of San Carlos de Bariloche. Active exploitation of natural gas and oil deposits at Comodoro Rivadavia on the Gulf of San Jorge and at Plaza Huincal in Neuquén, the development of coal resources at Río Turbio in the Andes and of iron ore at Sierra Grande, and other government investments and programs promise further economic expansion and prosperity. But the major occupation of Patagonia remains sheep raising, with ranches that cover thousands of square miles, pasture millions of animals, yet employ only a handful of men.

The Andean region forms both the western frontier and a second major area of modern Argentina—a broad band of provinces stretching from Mendoza, San Luis, and western La Pampa in the south to Salta and Jujuy in the north. Here lie reminders of past glories, of the Spanish and Indian heritage. But this area today provides livelihood for only 15 per cent of Argentina's population, and most of the region's economic activity is concentrated in the sugar production of Tucumán and the vineyards of Mendoza.

The northern half of the Andean region—Jujuy, Salta, and northern Catamarca and La Rioja—is a continuation of Bolivia, an area of mountains and plateaus, two hundred and fifty miles wide, with elevations ranging from six to eighteen thousand feet. North-south mountain ranges interspersed with dry basins form the main Andean chain: at its edge lies the bleak *puna*, or plateau, whose eastern side is scalloped with broad valleys and paralleled by a lower series of ranges and foothills. The *puna* supports a sparse growth of thorny, drought-resistant shrubs. Along the ridges at the eastern side is a narrow forest belt, and in the valleys crops can be grown without irrigation. Although the northern tip of this land falls within the tropics, elevation and dryness moderate the effects of temperatures; even in the valleys summer nights are apt to be cool.

Population has always been concentrated in the valleys at the eastern edge of the *puna*, where rainfall and streams provide an adequate water supply. Long before the arrival of the Spaniards, sizable Indian communities existed in this region, and the long arm of the Inca Empire had penetrated as far south as Tucumán. From the sixteenth to the eighteenth centuries the mining area of Upper Peru, located in the high, arid Bolivian *puna*, came to depend on these valley settlements for food, mules, and clothing. But with the decline of the silver mines, the region lost its major economic support. Flocks of sheep still ranged the highlands, and the valleys, especially irrigated lands, continued to produce corn, wheat, and cattle. But only the local markets remained to absorb the agricultural products and the output of craftsmen. The area found itself isolated from the growing core of population and wealth on the coast, surpassed in crop farming and livestock, and overshadowed by imports from Europe and the United States. Not until the mid-twentieth century have mining of copper, lead, tungsten, and borax in Catamarca, La Rioja, and Jujuy and the recent exploitation of oil deposits at Campo Durán on Salta's northern border promised diversification and development of the region's economy.

Tucumán, although also a part of the Andean region, stands out in

BOLIVIA

PARAGUAY

BRAZIL

Pacific Ocean

CHILE

L
B
M
T

Sugar cane

Lumber

Cotton

CATTLE

C
C
L

Cotton

C
M
T

Wine Grapes

Apples
Pears
Peaches
Cherries
Grapes

Olives

Peanuts
Wheat

T

ALFALFA

FLAX

HORSES

CATTLE

Wheat

M

Wheat

Apples
Pears
Grapes

Quebracho

Tobacco
Rice

Oranges
Grapefruit

Dairy
Cattle

CATTLE
Horses

Flax

Oranges

CORN

Hogs

Sunflowers

Peaches

Flax
Sheep

Oats

Lumber
Tung
Tea
Tobacco
Lemons
Rice

Yerba Mate

SHEEP

URUGUAY

Dairy
Cattle

Cattle

Atlantic Ocean

SHEEP

CATTLE

Sheep

Iron

Oil

Natural Gas

Coal

B Borax

C Copper

M Manganese

T Tungsten

L Lead

MALVINAS
(FALKLAND IS.)

Scale of miles

0   500

sharp contrast to the mountains, the *puna,* and even to the other valleys of the northwest. The foothills that parallel the eastern side of
the *puna* end just north of Tucumán, and to the west the edge of the
puna is accentuated by the high, snow-covered ridge of Aconquija. The
result is that the winds which sweep across the lowlands from the east
drop their moisture on Tucumán and create the headwaters of the Río
Dulce and several other streams. Mild winter temperatures and fertile
alluvial soil complement the rainfall, factors that made Tucumán an
agricultural zone for Indian and Spaniard alike.

Initially Tucumán prospered from the production of cotton, rice,
wheat, and corn for the mining area of Upper Peru. As Spanish settlement spread out to the coastal areas, Tucumán also became an important trade center linking the coast with the interior. The decline of
Upper Peru's mining economy in the late eighteenth century depressed
Tucumán's industries, and nearly a hundred years passed before a new
basis for prosperity was found in sugar cane. In the last decades of the
nineteenth century the railroad brought the coastal markets within
Tucumán's reach, and large sugar interests favored by tariff protection
monopolized the national market. Sugar underwrote the region's wealth,
but unfortunately it did not assure well-being or balanced development. Tucumán achieved a high concentration of rural population, and
seasonal work in the cane fields and factories attracted migrant Indians
and peasants from the depressed northwest, from the Chaco, and from
the Bolivian *puna.* For the mass of the population, though, dependence
on one crop brought misery and even starvation.

Opposite the central valley of Chile lies the final portion of Argentina's Andean region, traditionally known as the area of Cuyo—the
three provinces of San Juan, San Luis, and Mendoza. The Andes chain
is narrower here although still a formidable barrier: behind the city
of Mendoza the 22,830-foot Aconcagua peak is surrounded by its towering sisters. The *puna* and foothills of the northwest, however, no
longer border these mountains. In their place one encounters an arid
landscape of salt flats and north-south ranges similar to that of the
Great Basin of the western United States. Crops, animals, and human
settlement depend on water that comes from the snow-capped peaks.

These streams fan out across the alluvial desert and gradually disappear through evaporation or absorption into the porous soil. Only infrequently do the sloughs and depressions toward the southeast flood sufficiently to drain into that northern boundary of Patagonia, the Río Colorado.

The proximity of Chile dominated this area's early settlement and economy. Spaniards from across the Andes established the first towns, and for many years political administration and communications linked Cuyo principally to Chile rather than to the Atlantic coast. The Spaniards soon improved on the rudimentary irrigation developed by the Indians and built a modest agricultural economy of vineyards and wheat fields in Mendoza and San Juan. In addition, Mendoza, like Tucumán, benefited throughout the colonial period from its location: west of the city, Uspallata Pass at 12,600 feet was the major and most direct route to Santiago and the central valley of Chile. The agricultural and commercial prosperity of Mendoza and San Juan did not extend as far as San Luis where a sparse population eked out a bare subsistence from weaving and pastoral industries.

The collapse of the silver-mining economy and of the Spanish commercial system contributed to Cuyo's decline in the nineteenth century. The link with Chile grew weaker. Administrative changes late in the colonial period had brought the provinces of Cuyo under the control of Buenos Aires. After the nations became independent, the Argentine and Chilean economies drew even further apart. With the exception of cattle, products on the two sides of the Andes became increasingly competitive, and Mendoza lost much of its vitality as a commercial center. The promise of wealth from copper, silver, and lead deposits proved largely illusory. Even the vineyards fell on hard times. The formerly prosperous outlets in the northwest had dried up, and costs of oxcart freight made it cheaper for the coast to secure its wines from France, Spain, or Italy than from Cuyo.

As in the case of Tucumán, however, the railroads provided the basis for economic adjustment which once again placed Mendoza's wines and grapes within reach of coastal markets. Italian immigrants, new techniques, increased investments, and tariff protection furthered the impetus given by the railroads. In an expanding agricultural economy, alfalfa and fruit trees—apples, pears, peaches, and cherries—now occupy large extensions of irrigated land, and olives thrive in the drier zones. The recent exploitation of oil deposits south of the city of Mendoza and the increasing industrial capacity of this urban center forecast the area's continued development. Neither San Juan nor San Luis have shared Mendoza's recovery—a recovery that is even more striking because of the total destruction of that city by earthquake in 1861. San Juan, although eclipsed by Mendoza, also produces wines, grapes, and fruits, and San Luis depends largely on livestock industries reinforced by a limited production of alfalfa.

The northern lowlands form another frontier and the third major geographical region of Argentina. The provinces of Santiago del Estero, Chaco, Formosa, and the northern parts of Córdoba and Santa Fe occupy the western portion of this lowland—a part of the Gran Chaco which extends northward into Paraguay, Bolivia, and Brazil. The eastern portion lies between the Paraná and Uruguay rivers—the traditional Argentine mesopotamia of Entre Ríos, Corrientes, and the northeastern province of Misiones. These northern lowlands contain some of the oldest Spanish settlements in the Río de la Plata and some of the country's newest and most rapidly developing agricultural wealth. In population, with 13 per cent of the national total, they lag only slightly behind the Andean region.

Argentina's portion of the Gran Chaco is a land of scrub forest alternating with grassy savanna and flood plains. Located in or near the tropics, the region has clearly defined seasons of hot, rainy summers and mild, dry winters. Westward toward Santiago del Estero, however, the heavy rainfall (forty inches) of the eastern Chaco decreases until irrigation is needed to support agriculture. Numerous streams water rather than drain this lowland. Major watercourses such as the Pilcomayo and Bermejo in the north and the Salado in the south follow vague and shifting channels and can be navigated by launches only near their junctures with the Paraguay and Paraná rivers. The Dulce (from its headwaters in Tucumán) and the Saladillo never do reach the Paraná but instead empty into a large salt lake in northeastern

Córdoba. Each summer these rivers and their many tributaries flood vast areas of the eastern Chaco, usually to a depth of only a few feet. Thus gravel and silt from the Andes continue the slow building of this alluvial plain.

Settlement, as in the northwest, has depended on the availability of water. Indians cultivated crops of corn, squash, and beans on these flood plains. Spanish expeditions from Upper Peru, following an old Inca route, established the first permanent town in the Argentine area at Santiago del Estero in 1553. From here the course of the Salado to the Paraná outlined an early trade route to the coast by way of the town of Santa Fe. But to the north, warlike tribes discouraged further penetration into the Chaco and limited Spanish exploitation to the existing agricultural communities along the Salado, Saladillo, and Dulce. Santiago del Estero found itself increasingly relegated to a frontier position of defense rather than of commerce or of expansion into the uninviting wilderness of the Chaco. The main trade routes to the coast soon moved westward and southward to pass through Córdoba, and the sparse, shifting population at the Chaco's southern edge was left to garner a meager existence from flood-plain crops of wheat and corn, livestock production, weaving of ponchos, and the collection of wild beeswax and honey.

The potential of the Chaco's forest products renewed interest in this forgotten frontier during the second half of the nineteenth century. From the bank of the Paraná, woodcutters pushed inland along the tributaries in search of quebracho, a hardwood containing a high percentage of tannin, essential to the leather industries. In the western Chaco a similar species of quebracho, lower in tannin content, had long been in demand for the axles and wheels of the lumbering carts that carried all inland freight. Later, this durable wood became a necessity for railroad ties, fence posts, telephone poles, and firewood in the virtually treeless coastal region. The increased exploitation of forests brought with it the subjugation of hostile Indian tribes and established nominal occupation of even the northern Chaco, but it did not bring any permanent or sizable settlement. An agricultural base was provided in the 1920's when it was discovered that the north of this deserted land was admirably suited to cotton cultivation. Colonists, many of east European origin, who migrated from the Argentine coastal region, have gradually expanded this cotton zone westward from the towns of Resistencia and Formosa.

Argentina's mesopotamian provinces form a second section of the northern lowlands, possessing as much regional character and distinction as do the northwest or Cuyo within the Andean region. Misiones is a continuation of the Paraná plateau of southern Brazil, a land of heavy rains, dense forests, and spectacular falls, and an area of recent economic expansion. Corrientes and Entre Ríos have rolling, grassy plains with small knolls usually no more than thirty feet above the surrounding land. Rain forests and extensive swamps cover a large part of northeastern Corrientes, and a somewhat similar landscape in the form of islands and deltas is found in southwestern Entre Ríos. The climate is subtropical to temperate, but, unlike the Chaco and western Argentina, there is no pronounced dry season in the winter. Rainfall is more than adequate for agriculture, varying from seventy inches in parts of Misiones to an average of forty to fifty inches for Corrientes and thirty-five to forty for Entre Ríos. Water transportation reaches almost everywhere, and no area is more than fifty miles from this cheap conveyer of freight and people. Several tributaries of the Paraná and Uruguay can be navigated by launches. Ocean vessels can go upstream as far as Concepción del Uruguay on the Uruguay and Corrientes on the Paraná, while large river boats provide service on the upper Paraná and Uruguay.

Before the arrival of Europeans in the New World, Indians of the Tupí-Guaraní stock, predominant in most of southern and central Brazil and Paraguay, had spread along both banks of the Paraná River. Luckily for Spanish fortunes in the Río de la Plata, the easy absorption of these peaceful, agrarian people enabled the conquerors to establish a viable economy at Asunción, after the initial attempts to settle at Buenos Aires had been rudely upset by the warlike, pampa tribes. When these Spaniards pushed back downstream to settle Santa Fe and refound Buenos Aires in the last decades of the sixteenth century, they also established way stations among friendly Indians. As the seventeenth century advanced, Jesuit missions, in reality Indian communities, steadily expanded into present-day Corrientes and Misiones and into Brazil's southern province of Rio Grande do Sul and began producing cotton, tobacco, and *yerba mate* (Paraguayan tea).

In the eighteenth century, however, the economic activity shifted from the Paraná side of this mesopotamia to the banks of the Uruguay. Commerce along the Paraná above the town of Santa Fe and along the Paraguay to Asunción decreased sharply. The Jesuits, pressured by Portuguese raiding expeditions from São Paulo, had already moved many of their missions southward and were devoting their attention increasingly to livestock. In the 1760's both the Spanish and the Portuguese crowns expelled the Jesuits from their territories, and the Indian communities, agriculture, and industries disintegrated. In their place arose a rudimentary pastoral economy with nomadic herdsmen tending vast herds of half-wild cattle.

The major activity in Corrientes and Entre Ríos is still the raising of livestock. During the last hundred years the rolling, grassy countryside has provided pasture for 20 to 25 per cent of Argentina's horses and cattle. Sheep, introduced in the mid-nineteenth century to Entre Ríos, have also thrived and today provide an important part of Argentine wool exports. Wheat cultivation developed in central Entre Ríos in the latter decades of the nineteenth century. This area today grows the wheat for most of Argentina's macaroni flour, although flax is now the province's leading crop. Oranges, grapefruit, tobacco, and corn do well along the deltas and in the humid, subtropical north. Lowlying areas of Corrientes give excellent rice yields, a crop which expanded rapidly with tariff protection in the 1930's.

After the decline of the Jesuit missions, Misiones, like the Chaco and Patagonia, had to await the twentieth century for its economic awakening. When the Jesuits were expelled, the forest reclaimed the *yerba mate* plantations, and the leaves, the region's principal product, were once more collected in their wild state. Even the political status of Misiones remained vague, first disputed by Spaniards and Portuguese and subsequently by Brazilians, Paraguayans, and Argentines. Argentina inherited the region as a by-product of the Paraguayan War in the 1860's. The reintroduction of *yerba mate* plantations along the upper Paraná from Posadas northward dates from the turn of the century. Since demand for *yerba mate* has never spread beyond southern South America and Brazil and Paraguay are also major growers, the government found it necessary to limit production in the 1930's in order to maintain prices. Urban development on the coast, however, stimulated exploitation of another Misiones resource, its large and rapidly growing rain forest. The Misiones pine provided pulpwood for the paper industry, while huge cedar rafts carried a rich variety of hardwoods downstream for use in the construction and furniture industries. As in the Chaco, agricultural colonists have followed in the wake of the woodcutters. In the 1950's and 1960's immigrants from Germany and eastern Europe, migrants of similar origins already established in coastal Argentina, and Brazilians have increasingly concentrated along the banks of the Paraná and the Uruguay. These are largely homesteaders and small proprietors and represent an important variation from the seasonal labor force needed by the *yerba mate* plantations. In addition to growing crops common to neighboring Corrientes, such as oranges, grapefruit, tobacco, rice, and corn, these colonists have turned Misiones into Argentina's principal producer of tea, lemons, cassava or manioc, and tung oil. Increasing numbers of tourists are drawn to the spectacular beauty of Iguazú Falls located on the northern border with Brazil.

The three major land divisions already discussed—Patagonia, the Andean region, and the northern lowlands—form the frontiers of modern Argentina and enclose the nation's economic core, the pampas. This fertile plain includes all or part of four provinces: Buenos Aires, southern Santa Fe, southeastern Córdoba, and eastern La Pampa. This area, comprising less than one-fifth of the land, supports two-thirds of the population and contains the country's major industries, urban centers, educational facilities, and wealth.

The pampas rest on the shattered and broken granite base of one of the world's oldest land masses, distinct from the granite base underlying Patagonia. Erosion by wind and water has gradually piled up hundreds of feet of sediment, fine clay, sand, and dust to create these

vast, temperate-zone plains. Around the edge of the pampas some granite breaks through to the surface: the island of Martín García in the
estuary north of the city of Buenos Aires; the hills of Tandil and those
of Ventana, with several four-thousand-foot peaks, in southern Buenos
Aires; the hills of Córdoba, with some elevations of six thousand feet;
and the low hills of the arid, western extension of the pampas in Córdoba and La Pampa. The apparent flatness of these plains has repeatedly evoked comments about their monotony and comparisons to
unruffled oceans. In reality long slopes and vast swells are perceptible,
especially where they form washes or lagoons. Along the Paraná River
between the cities of Buenos Aires and Rosario a geological upheaval
has slightly raised a hundred-mile band of the pampas and formed a
rolling countryside with very gradual contours. In southern Buenos
Aires the Tandil and Ventana hills accentuate a similarly rolling terrain. Between these two regions and extending west and north for
more than four hundred miles lie the low pampas—an area of broad
depressions, sloughs, and rain-filled lagoons.

The pampas region possesses no major rivers, largely because of
the terrain and soil. Small streambeds and gullies cut the edges of
the rolling pampas along the Paraná River and along the Atlantic
coast of southern Buenos Aires, but on the larger area of the low
pampas surface drainage is poor. In the north, of the several streams
that rise from the Córdoba hills, only the Río Tercero and the Río
Cuarto, by joining forces as the Carcarañá, manage to reach the Paraná.
The others flow north into a large salt lake of northeastern Córdoba or,
like the Río Quinto, merely disappear into the sandy soil of southeast
Córdoba. The raised rim around the low pampas affords but one outlet
to the Atlantic, the slough of the Río Salado (not to be confused with
the Salado of Santiago del Estero which empties into the Paraná), and,
to reach that, surface water must cross hundreds of miles of alternating
swells and depressions, aided by only the slightest slope eastward.
Thus, the streams which flow north from the Tandil and Ventana hills
form a series of small salt lakes. Or, where the water table is close to
the surface and where the clay content reduces the soil's absorbency,
the rains frequently create huge, shallow lakes. Similarly, the Salado

itself provides floods rather than drainage. Man-made canals which supplement it to the south have reduced but not completely eliminated the periodic inundations.

As in the rest of Argentina, rainfall on the pampas decreases as one approaches the Andes. At the eastern edge the annual average is thirty-six to thirty-nine inches. At the western edge it approximates twenty inches, the minimum for nonirrigated crops, and as a result drought periodically threatens crops and livestock throughout large areas of La Pampa, southern Córdoba, and western Buenos Aires. Summer temperatures (January) average 75° F. on the coast but may cover a range of twenty to thirty degrees during a twenty-four-hour period. Winters are mild, and rarely does the temperature fall as low as 20° F. At Bahía Blanca on the pampas' southern edge the July average is 36° F. Inland, temperatures are several degrees higher in summer and a few degrees lower in winter. Humidity is high along the Paraná River and the estuary of the Río de la Plata, reaching an average of 85 to 90 per cent in the winter months, but drops sharply beyond the coastal fringe. Snow is an extreme rarity on most of the pampas, although La Pampa and southern Buenos Aires can expect one brief snowfall per year. The winds, less fierce and constant than those of Patagonia, contribute to the erosion of the dry western area of the pampas and strongly affect the climate. Violent pamperos from the southwest bring cool, dry air from the Andes and also occasionally cause serious damage to crops, animals, buildings, and even to ships in the estuary. From the other quarter, southeasters accompanied by spectacular thunderstorms often drive river water onto the lowlying banks of Buenos Aires and Entre Ríos and cause wind and hail damage to large areas of the pampas.

The pampas attracted only the barest population of nomadic, hunting Indians. For the sixteenth-century Spaniards these grasslands offered no riches, and the subjugation of the native inhabitants soon proved both unprofitable and impossible. Conquistadors who had ranged over a hemisphere in search of gold and souls carefully skirted the rim of the pampas. But if the Spaniards were repulsed by the pampas, the contrary was true of the cattle and horses they had so laboriously brought with them across the Atlantic. Within decades a handful of escaped animals multiplied into hundreds of thousands on this fertile, well-watered plain.

The impulse for founding settlements at the pampas' edge came from the interior, not from the Atlantic. Santa Fe, settled by Spaniards returning downstream from Asunción, and Córdoba, built as an extension of the conquest from Upper Peru, were both established in 1573. After several attempts to colonize the Río de la Plata from the Atlantic failed at the beginning of the century, the permanent settlement of Buenos Aires was delayed until 1580 and then occurred as a continuation of Spanish colonization from Asunción and Santa Fe. The interior dominated the economy of these new towns almost to the same degree that it had their establishment. Córdoba expanded rapidly and became a center for woolen industries, sheep and mule raising, and trade with Upper Peru. Prosperity fostered other endeavors, and by the seventeenth century the city of Córdoba was the religious and intellectual leader of the Río de la Plata. Buenos Aires and Santa Fe received less stimulus from trade with Upper Peru; yet their economies also faced inland rather than toward the Atlantic. Royal restrictions, deliberately sought after by merchants in Lima and Panama, virtually closed Buenos Aires as a legal port of entry in the seventeenth century, and only contraband trade kept the town's commerce alive. Raising mules and hunting wild horses and cattle for their hides provided only a meager existence, and, as a result, Buenos Aires and Santa Fe remained little more than villages for nearly two centuries.

Although the rapid growth of Buenos Aires as a port city had to await the nineteenth century and the pampas were conquered only in the second half of that century, the late colonial period showed the direction for the impending changes. Declining silver production in the late seventeenth century reduced Upper Peru's predominance in Spanish South America. The demand of the Spanish crown for increased revenues and the very real danger of Portuguese and English encroachment on the Río de la Plata drew royal attention southward. As the crown gradually loosened commercial restrictions on Buenos Aires, the town's potential as a major point of access to the interior was reflected in trade statistics and customs revenues. Population and wealth rose in proportion to the influx of Negro slaves, European imports, and Brazilian sugar, tobacco, and cotton. In 1776 the creation of the Viceroyalty of the Río de la Plata centralized in Buenos Aires the fiscal and administrative control over the regions of present-day Argentina, Paraguay, Uruguay, and part of Bolivia. Military expeditions expelled the Portuguese from the left bank of the Uruguay River and attempted to drive back the Indians from the right bank of the Paraná. At the end of the century, introduction of the *saladero*, or meat-salting plant, increased the value of the vast herds of cattle on the pampas. These establishments not only salvaged the previously wasted beef but also efficiently disposed of the whole carcass—hide, hair, tallow, fats, bones, horns, and gelatin. Livestock products and exposure to world trade gradually liberated the coastal settlements from subservience to the interior and gave an economic basis to the political leadership conferred on Buenos Aires by the crown.

Independence, strongly supported by certain commercial and cattle interests at Buenos Aires, intensified the economic advance of the coast and accentuated the interior's decline. Argentina exchanged the tutelage of Spain for that of European industries—a potent stimulus to the production of raw materials. Nevertheless, adjustment of the Argentine economy to this new state of affairs proceeded slowly. The coastal area still lacked sufficient population, capital, technology, and talents to exploit the agricultural resources of the pampas. Hides, salted meat, and tallow might support Buenos Aires' commercial prosperity, but they limited Argentina to a rudimentary economy.

The second half of the nineteenth century saw the radical transformation of the pampas. The change commenced with sheep raising on lands close to the port of Buenos Aires. By 1860 wool and sheepskins joined hides and salted meat as Argentina's major exports. The completion of a rail link between Rosario and Córdoba in 1870 ushered in several decades of rapid railroad construction by British companies. Soon all of the pampas lay within easy reach of Buenos Aires and world markets. Crop farming, previously limited to lands surrounding urban settlement, followed the railroads. Immigrants, particularly from depressed areas of Italy, poured into the coastal region to raise ex-

tensive crops of wheat, corn, and flax. At the same time, closely related
changes occurred in the livestock industries. With processing by the
frigorífico, or packing plant, Argentine mutton and beef could reach
European markets. But in order to sell this meat, a revolution was
needed in breeding, care, and pasturage, and the sinewy native cattle
slaughtered in the *saladeros* had to be replaced by herds of Shorthorn
and Angus livestock. The physical area needed for this agricultural
expansion was secured in the late 1870's when the national government finally launched a campaign against the Araucanian Indians.
Within two years the Indians were pushed beyond the Río Negro and
effectively eliminated as a liability to Argentine development.

The economic conquest of the pampas underwrote the rapid rise of
coastal cities, of Rosario and Bahía Blanca as well as of Buenos Aires.
Immigrants, frequently drawn to Argentina by the hope of owning
land, found the land already monopolized by huge estates and consequently beyond their reach. Many farmed as tenants, but far more
sought employment and a future in the cities as stevedores, mechanics,
bricklayers, clerks, servants, or factory laborers. Although the economic
base was agricultural, the products of the land had to be processed,
goods manufactured and exchanged, buildings and railroads constructed, and services provided.

The pampas region today rests on just such an agricultural and urban
base. Of the more than twenty Argentine cities with a population over
one hundred thousand, all but five are in the pampas. At the time of the
last industrial census in 1954, this area included 80 per cent by number
and 86 per cent by value of Argentina's industrial establishments, largely
concentrated along the right bank of the Paraná River between Buenos
Aires and Rosario. Its ports handle almost 100 per cent of the country's
imports and exports. Within this region are located 60 per cent of the
railroad network, 70 per cent of the paved highways, and five of Argentina's eight national universities. At the same time agriculture continues
to be a major source of wealth. Land use in the pampas shifts easily between crop farming and pasturage in accord with market demand and
prices. Production includes wheat, alfalfa, flax, beef cattle, and peanuts
in southeastern Córdoba; corn, flax, hogs, and dairy cattle in southern

Santa Fe and northern Buenos Aires; vegetables and dairy cattle around Greater Buenos Aires; beef and dairy cattle in southeastern Buenos Aires; wheat, flax, oats, and sheep in southern Buenos Aires; and alfalfa, beef cattle, and wheat in western Buenos Aires and eastern La Pampa. These various areas provide nearly 90 per cent of Argentina's exports and cultivated acreage, 50 per cent of the country's cattle and horses, and 80 per cent of the hogs. As a result of the region's economic predominance, the pampas today represent the nation. So much wealth and population has been drawn into the pampas, especially since 1900, that the other three regions of Argentina appear to serve only as frontiers.

Four centuries have seen as much change in the Argentine people as in the use and occupation of the land. The modern Argentine, like the modern Argentina, is largely a product of the late nineteenth century, but vestiges of earlier centuries are evident in his culture.

The Spanish conquest and settlement of this sizable triangle of the South American continent gave rise to many of the same human relationships found in other areas of that sixteenth-century empire of the Americas. Unlike the later English expansion in North America, which expelled the original Indian occupants in order to make room for the white man, the Spaniards, wherever possible, subdued, exploited and absorbed the Indians. The conquistador did not come to the New World in order to grub the land, tend sheep, or labor in the mines— this he could have done easily enough at home. It was not hunger for land or desire for a new home that drove him through staggering hardships. Not even the love of adventure or of religion explains the incredible feats of the conquest. Basic to this golden era of Spain's empire was the ambition to become a lord over others, a dream which bore fruit in the disdain of future generations for manual labor.

In comparison with the Aztec and Inca empires and the concentrated populations of central Mexico and the Peruvian highlands, the Argentine area afforded only modest opportunities for the absorption and exploitation of native cultures. In Patagonia, the pampas, and the northern lowlands there lived at least ten distinct Indian groups, but only the Guaraní along the Paraguay and Paraná rivers possessed an agricultural economy. The others were nomadic hunters, fishermen, or gatherers of wild roots and fruit. In the valleys and foothills of the Andes, however, the Spaniards found more advanced civilizations, Indians who could provide the labor force so necessary to Spanish settlement. The conquistadors therefore based their principal towns and major economic centers on Indian agricultural communities: the Guaraní of Paraguay, Corrientes, and Misiones; the Huarpes of Cuyo; the Comechingones of the Córdoba hills; the Tonocotés of the Río Salado in Santiago del Estero; and the Diaguitas of Tucumán and the northwest.

As elsewhere in the Spanish Empire, the arrival of the conquering Spaniard among Indian peoples resulted in extensive miscegenation. Spanish policy discouraged marriage with religiously "impure" individuals such as Moors and Jews. Custom also excluded Indians and Negroes, at least for the upper classes, so that ideally Spaniards married Spaniards. By the second half of the sixteenth century, when the conquest of the Argentine area occurred, enough Spanish women had arrived in or had been born in the New World to provide the basis for some pure Spanish families. From these developed the creole (Spanish, born in the New World) elite. But the natural proclivities of the Spanish male found a more expansive outlet among the conquered Indian women. Their mestizo offspring formed a social group which aspired to the dominant Spanish culture but was not fully accepted within it. Some mestizos were recognized by their fathers, inherited wealth and position, and disappeared into the ranks of the creole elite. But the majority became the artisans and laborers of the colonial towns, or the gauchos, herdsmen, and wagoners of the countryside.

The Negro soon added another strain to these cultural-racial groupings in the Río de la Plata. Proximity to the Portuguese possessions in Brazil, growing contraband trade through Buenos Aires, and the need for laborers in the coastal regions encouraged substantial imports of slaves throughout the seventeenth and eighteenth centuries. Negroes constituted much of the artisan and servant class in the towns of the interior as well as of the coast. They planted and harvested crops and became proficient in livestock care. Many by their industry purchased freedom, but as a class they were relegated to the lowest status in the towns. The creole male might find momentary sexual pleasure or even a mistress within this group but never a wife. Yet, as with the mestizo, miscegenation gradually absorbed the Negro within the lower class.

Population statistics of the colonial period are little more than educated guesses, but they serve to give a vague idea of the relative size of the various racial groups in the Argentine area. Contemporary reports and subsequent investigation indicate that the sixteenth-century Indian population probably did not exceed three hundred thousand, and a third of these lived in Patagonia, the pampas, and the Chaco beyond the effective reach of Spanish exploitation. For the middle of the seventeenth century, estimates reduce the Indian total to two hundred and fifty thousand and add ninety thousand Spanish, creole, mestizo, Negro, and mulatto inhabitants in the Argentine area. A series of royal censuses in the 1760's and 1770's include only Christianized or peaceful Indians in their counts but reveal interesting details on the composition of other groups in various provincial areas:

	Spanish, creoles, and mestizos	Indians	Negroes and mulattoes
Jujuy	500	11,000	2,000
Tucumán	8,000	—?—	12,000
Cuyo	15,500	4,000	4,000
Misiones	—?—	80,000	—?—
Buenos Aires	26,000	2,000	9,000

From the censuses and accounts of travelers in the first decades of the nineteenth century emerges a rough average of five hundred thousand to six hundred thousand as the total population of Argentina at the time of independence. Of this figure probably 30 per cent were Indian and 10 per cent were Negro and mulatto. The remainder were creole and mestizo, but, at least within the urban and coastal areas, the creole had begun to absorb the mestizo. By the 1820's, therefore, the creole-mestizo stock predominated, and the darker shadings of mestizo and Indian elements became pronounced only in the countryside or in the interior. The Negro and mulatto strain was evident in the towns, accounting for more than a quarter of the population in Buenos Aires, but even here miscegenation was gradually absorbing the Negro into the mestizo ranks.

The changes in Argentina's rudimentary economy during the late nineteenth century were paralleled by a total transformation of the Argentine population: the rapid increase in total numbers, the disappearance of the Negro and the Indian, the apparent absorption of the mestizo, the concentration of peoples in the coastal region, the Europeanization of the cities, and a significant shift from the countryside to the urban centers.

From an estimated 500,000 at the time of independence, total population rose to 1,800,000 by 1869, 4,000,000 in 1895, 8,000,000 in 1914, 16,000,000 in 1947, and 20,000,000 in 1960, the date of the fifth national census. As the nation grew, estimates of Indian population declined precipitously. The national censuses failed to record as a distinct group Indians living within settled areas and estimated only those Indians who remained beyond the effective economic and political control of the nation: 100,000 in 1869, 30,000 in 1895, 20,000 in 1914, and in 1947 the classification disappeared completely. Today a generally accepted figure for the Indian population in Argentina is 100,000 —a figure which may approximate the population of pure Indian racial stock but assuredly exaggerates the number who maintain an Indian way of life and culture remote from modern influences. Along Argentina's borders with Chile, Bolivia, and Paraguay, and especially in rural Jujuy and Salta, communities composed largely of pure-blooded Indians still exist. But internal migration and economic development constantly reduce these vestiges and promise their eventual absorption.

The disappearance of the Negro from the Argentine scene has puzzled demographers far more than the vanishing of the Indian, probably because the more pronounced Negroid racial characteristics might have been expected to maintain this group as an easily recognizable segment of the population. By 1810 Negroes and mulattoes constituted a significant element of the urban population and probably numbered 60,000 By 1895 this total had decreased to 5,000, and, although this figure is taken as a current estimate of the Negro element in Argentina, it is probably too high. The struggles for independence and the subsequent civil wars, as well as tuberculosis and other diseases, carried off an inordinately high percentage of Negroes and mulattoes, but even more effective was their gradual absorption into the dominant creole-mestizo population.

The mestizo has followed this same route of absorption, accelerated by the massive influx of European immigrants from 1880 to 1914 and by the internal migration to the coastal cities in the 1940's and 1950's. Mestizos still predominate in many of the rural zones of the Andean region and northern lowlands and perhaps form 10 per cent of the total Argentine population. But the significance of such a racial distinction has little meaning in the contemporary cultural amalgam of creole, mestizo, and immigrant.

European immigration caused the sharp population rise of the late nineteenth century and the "whitening" of Argentina's coastal zone. In the 1860's the European population—Basque, Irish, English, French, and Italian—numbered only one hundred thousand and was concentrated wholly in the province of Buenos Aires and in the river ports of the Paraná and Uruguay. The massive influx during the next one hundred years added four and a half million Europeans. In the decades before World War I, Italians (55 per cent of the immigrants) and Spaniards (26 per cent) submerged the creole-mestizo stock of the cities and the pampas. By 1914 foreigners outnumbered native Argentines two to one in most of Santa Fe, Córdoba, and Buenos Aires, and constituted three-fourths of the adult population in the city of Buenos Aires. After each of the world wars there was a sizable renewal of European immigration, lasting in both cases for nearly a decade. Some new groups, such as Syrians, Poles, and various Slavic nationalities, appeared, but the South European continued to predominate. In 1960 Italians with 34 per cent and Spaniards with 27 per cent still composed the bulk of the 2,600,000 foreign-born residing in Argentina.

In recent decades immigration from neighboring countries and internal migration have also contributed to the concentration of population in the coastal area and in the cities. The traditional flow of Chil-

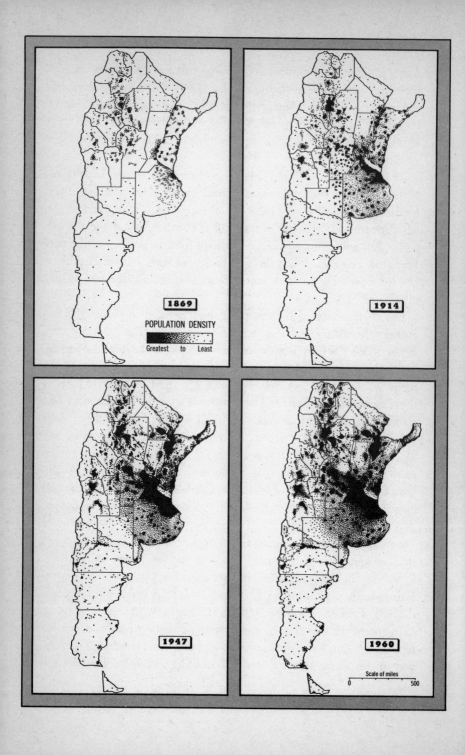

POPULATION DENSITY

Greatest   to   Least

1869

1914

1947

1960

Scale of miles

0   500

eans, Bolivians, Paraguayans, Brazilians, and Uruguayans into frontier zones in search of seasonal work, political asylum, or better economic opportunities increasingly reached Greater Buenos Aires. Migrants from the countryside, particularly from Santiago del Estero, La Rioja, Catamarca, La Pampa, San Luis, and Corrientes, likewise sought employment and a new life in the coastal cities.

Increasingly the population of Argentina has become an urban one. The proportion of those living in towns with more than two thousand inhabitants rose from 25 per cent in 1869, to 53 per cent in 1914, to an estimated 75 per cent in 1970. Today Argentines view the cities and the coastal region as the vital center of their nation, and, if an "average" Argentine exists, he is the white-collar employee in the coastal cities. But such emphasis on one area has long since ceased to foster healthy national development. The differences which separate the Basque dairyman in Santa Fe and the Indian cane cutter in Tucumán, the grocer in Rosario and the storekeeper in Catamarca, the factory worker in Buenos Aires and the weaver of ponchos in Jujuy serve only to divide and impoverish Argentina. The cities can no longer live from their size alone or from the agricultural wealth of the pampas. Progress now depends on how well all the resources of this rich and diversified land can be used and how thoroughly all the heritages of the past—creole and European, coast and interior, city and countryside—can be blended together.

Chapter 2 • Spanish Towns

The Spanish conquistadors were not frontiersmen or farmers, but rather soldiers, administrators, and masters. Therefore, they turned to the institution of the city, so deeply rooted in their own history, for the means to settle and control these new lands and peoples. The estimated three hundred thousand Indians in the Argentine area hardly provided the incentive for conquest offered by the millions in the mountain valleys of Mexico or the highlands of Peru. Yet the conquistadors of this area used much the same methods of colonization as in Mexico and Peru, establishing towns that could administer and control the Indian cultures already tied to the cultivation of the land. In the last analysis, the location of Spanish towns and the success of Spanish colonization were determined by the presence of agrarian Indian cultures. The northwest, Cuyo, and the mesopotamian provinces supported Spanish towns because the Indians who inhabited those regions cultivated crops and lived in villages. Patagonia, the pampas, and the Chaco remained Indian territory throughout the colonial period and during much of the nineteenth century primarily because these areas contained no settled, agrarian cultures.

Although the differences among Indian groups in the Argentine area determined the location and importance of Spanish towns, the sixteenth-century Spaniard was unaware of the complex variations later discovered by anthropologists. Rather than the twenty major groups of Indians and their numerous subdivisions now known to have existed at the time of the conquest, the Spaniards saw two: agrarian Indians and hunting Indians. Any further distinction was considered useless; in fact, so useless that until the late nineteenth century no one recognized the significant cultural change that had taken place among the nomadic Indians of the pampas—the replacement in the eighteenth century of the primitive inhabitants by bands of warlike Araucanians from southern Chile.

The tribes at the southern tip of the continent were immortalized by Magellan for their big feet to which the name *Patagonia* refers. The myth of gianthood has been exploded, although the average male height of 5 feet 10 inches no doubt impressed the smaller-statured Spanish, Portuguese, and Italian sailors. Well-developed physical specimens, they lived by hunting the rhea, or American ostrich, the seal, and a larger cousin of the llama, the guanaco, with bow and arrow and by collecting mollusks from the rocky shores. Their economy determined their way of life: their homes were mere windbreaks; their clothes a few furs; and their implements made from sea shells, stone, or wood. Ignored for centuries, they saw their way of life destroyed by the intrusion of the modern world, and eventually they disappeared as a distinct group.

In the sixteenth century several equally primitive hunting groups occupied northern Patagonia and the pampas. The Spanish soon discovered how impossible it was to reduce one such group, the Querandí of the Paraná's right bank, to any agricultural pursuits. These were true nomads; in the words of an early Jesuit missionary:

> . . . to live here today, tomorrow elsewhere; now I want to enjoy the pleasant shores of this stream, and tiring of it find another; now I want the shelter of woods, the solitudes, or the wide expanse of grassy plains; here to hunt and there to fish; here to pick the wild fruit and then to move with the season to new harvests; I roam as I will, leaving nothing behind to call or torment me; tragedy cannot reach me for I have nothing to lose; everything is with me and I have no other needs.

These were hardly the people to supply a docile labor force. They literally ran down their principal source of food and clothing, the small pampas deer, by pursuing a herd at a steady dog trot for two or three days, never letting them rest or drink until finally the exhausted animals could no longer stay out of the range of primitive weapons. In addition to the bow and arrow and the sling, these Indians had developed the *boleadoras,* two or three stones fastened together by long leather thongs. These, accurately thrown at distances up to one hundred yards, wrapped themselves around the legs of any fleeing animal, thus permitting the hunter to overtake his entangled game. Guanaco, rhea, roots, and berries supplemented the basic diet of venison; the Querandí's closest approach to bread was made from a flour of roasted locusts. Skins and furs provided the material for dress and shelter. Even in the eyes of the not overly fastidious sixteenth-century European, these were untamed and untamable savages; the Querandí had already earned their name, meaning "eaters of grease," from the more advanced Guaraní because of their inordinate fondness for animal fats and blood and the overpowering odor of rancid grease which emanated from their tents and bodies.

Unbeknown to the Spanish, offshoots of the more advanced Araucanian culture from southern Chile gradually pushed into northern Patagonia and the pampas, eliminating or absorbing the earlier occupants. By the end of the eighteenth century the inhabitants of the Spanish towns on the edge of the pampas no longer faced primitive hunting peoples but a culture which had adopted the horse as its own and developed the means to resist Spanish conquest in Chile. These Indians, although called Araucanians, brought with them none of the agricultural techniques developed in Chile. Rather they introduced raids and plunder by small, highly mobile bands and added the lance to the very effective *boleadoras,* arrows, and slings. To the Spaniards and then to the Argentines, these Araucanians appeared to be a continuation of the earlier nomadic cultures of the pampas. Theirs, however, was a more complex economy: the wild horses and cattle of the pampas not only provided them with all their necessities but also brought considerable profits from animals and hides sent back through the passes to Chile. From numerous semi-nomadic villages, bands of one or two hundred warriors, accompanied by women and children, roamed the plains and frequently struck at the scattered Spanish settlements. The horse formed the center of their existence. Even the gaucho had to bow to their superior skill, for they were horsemen who often rode bareback and who, by constant changing of mounts, covered untold miles. Venison or sun-dried beef nourished them, while horsemeat and rancid fat ranked as great delicacies. The hide from a colt's hind leg drawn over the foot and left to dry made a superb boot. Tents of horsehide or cowhide sheltered them from the elements. In addition to these equine aspects of their culture, the ornate silver work found on bridles and saddles and the woolen blankets and ponchos woven by the women indicated their skill as craftsmen. So effectively did these Araucanians dominate the broad expanse of the pampas that systems of defensive forts repeatedly collapsed before their onslaught. Not until the national government—armed with the telegraph and the Remington rifle —took the offensive late in the nineteenth century, destroyed their villages, and scattered the survivors, did these warriors of the pampas cease to be a distinct element of the population.

Another nomadic people, the Charrúas, supreme in the area of future Uruguay, spread across the Uruguay River to Entre Ríos. Like the Araucanians, their adoption of the horse and their effective use of *boleadoras,* slings, and arrows made them formidable adversaries. Their fondness for raiding Spanish towns, however, aroused an immediate reaction from the Spaniards. By the mid-eighteenth century expeditions had expelled them from Entre Ríos, and within another century the remaining Indians of the Uruguayan countryside had been either eliminated or absorbed into the creole-immigrant amalgam.

In the savannas and forests of the Chaco were still other nomadic tribes which successfully resisted Spanish conquest and exploitation and whose descendants today maintain a separate racial and cultural identity. In the eastern Chaco, one such group—collectors of wild fruits, nuts, and honey—rivaled the Araucanians in the skills needed for war and plunder. After adopting the horse, they forced the Spaniards to abandon several settlements along the Bermejo and Salado rivers.

The mountain valleys of the Andean region boasted the largest and most advanced groups of Argentina's sparse Indian population. By the time of the Spanish conquest, the cultural and political influence of the Inca Empire had started to expand into this area, but none of the varied groups had progressed beyond a primitive agricultural economy. They lived in permanent villages and built their dwellings of stone, branches, or straw thatch. On terraced or irrigated fields they cultivated crops of corn, squash, beans, and, in the north, potatoes. They domesticated the llama, both as a beast of burden and for its wool, and they possessed well-developed skills in weaving cloth and making pottery and baskets. Some groups surrendered readily to Spanish exploitation and soon disappeared into the lower classes: by the end of the eighteenth century, the Huarpes of Cuyo, the Comechingones of Córdoba, and the Tonocotés of Santiago del Estero had all but vanished. Others, despite their agrarian cultures, more strongly resisted the Spaniard. The Diaguitas of the northwest and scattered tribes in La Rioja and Jujuy succumbed only when brutally transplanted, in imitation of practices by earlier Inca conquerors, to new areas. But, since resistance was eventually crushed, the relatively advanced Indians of the Andes provided the labor necessary for the colonial economy.

Along the upper Paraná existed another agrarian culture, the Guaraní, whose related branches extended to the Amazon and throughout all of central Brazil. On jungle plots a slash-and-burn system of agriculture supported crops of corn, sweet potatoes, squash, and cassava. The dwellings often took the form of large communal houses built of logs and thatched with leaves. They were adept canoemen and fishermen and demonstrated considerable skill in the ceramic arts. Though in general they wore little or no clothing, their women wove the fibers of wild cotton into coarse textiles. It was among these Guaraní that the Spaniards found the only source of labor in the coastal regions. At Asunción, in the Jesuit missions, and in settlements along the Paraná, these Indians and their mestizo offspring provided a principal basis for the development of the littoral.

Spain's conquest of the New World in the sixteenth century ranks as one of history's most dramatic events, the victory of man over un-

believable obstacles. Just how "new" this western hemisphere was at
the moment of conquest can never quite be recaptured. The outline of
the continents appeared quickly enough. But over each hill, around
each bend, across each forest or swamp, lay the unknown—vast treasure,
pagan cities, or horrible death. Yet the search for power, wealth, souls,
or adventure relentlessly drove the conquistador and missionary toward
their goals and Spain toward dominion over half the New World and
over four-fifths of its native population.

Spain first approached Argentina from the Atlantic—in that same
tremendous surge of energy that enveloped the Caribbean islands, carried the red and gold banner of Castile across Panama to the Pacific
in 1513, overthrew the might of the Aztecs at Mexico City in 1521,
and toppled the Inca reign at Cuzco in 1532. In Europe the existence
of a large estuary in the southern part of the continent was already
known or at least strongly suspected. Royal anxiety to discover a new
and shorter route to Asia and to forestall southward probing by Portuguese ships that might enlarge that country's toehold on the Brazilian
coast brought the first Spaniards to the mouth of the Río de la Plata
in January 1516. Juan Díaz de Solís, one of the crown's chief navigators, had set forth four months earlier in an unusual command—in
charge of an expedition equipped and manned at royal expense but, for
reasons of state secrecy, reported as a private endeavor. The three ships,
a flagship of sixty tons and two others of twenty-five tons, carried provisions for two and a half years: a long voyage, for Solís had instructions to find a passage to the Pacific around the southern tip of the
continent, then to coast northward to Panama, and finally to attempt
the return to Spain by a northern route. As with his illustrious successor, Magellan, his life ended in an ambush by natives, and before he
accomplished the mission which might have given us instead the Strait
of Solís. Attracted by the broad, fresh-water estuary which bore his
name for a few years until it was hopefully renamed the Río de la
Plata, he took one ship upstream as far as the island of Martín García
and perhaps for a distance along the Uruguay River. Desirous of establishing contact with the natives and perhaps of enticing or captur-
ing a few to send to his sovereign, he finally landed with a handful of
men at some spot on the future Uruguayan coast. The apparently

friendly Indians immediately overpowered the small party and, according to the chroniclers, devoured the unfortunate captives before the eyes of their horrified and powerless shipmates anchored offshore.

Three years later, the Spanish crown dispatched the well-known Portuguese pilot and explorer, Ferdinão de Magalhães, or Magellan, with five ships and instructions to find a route to the Far East around the southern tip of the American continents and to define Spain's territorial claims westward in the Pacific to the Moluccas. Wiser for Solís' adventure, he only briefly entered the estuary of the Río de la Plata and then coasted southward to winter on the barren Patagonian shores of Santa Cruz. That spring, in the last months of 1520, the expedition passed on through the wind-torn strait to the Pacific, having firmly established Spain's claim to these southern lands.

For two more decades, conquistadors followed the route of Solís and Magellan and probed Argentina's Atlantic approaches. The disasters of Cabot in 1526-29 and Mendoza in 1535-37 finally emphasized the total absence of minerals or Indian cultures, at least in contrast to the dazzling wealth of Peru. Thereafter Spain's energies were directed toward the inland regions rather than toward the coast.

Solís' successor as chief navigator, Sebastian Cabot, had already been exposed to the dreams of Cathay while a member of his father's expedition in 1497-98 to find a northern route to the Far East for England. He therefore quickly won commercial support and the approval of his new sovereign for another such venture, now to follow Magellan's southern route. Cabot had the misfortune, however, to pick up and believe the rumor of great silver wealth from a sailor abandoned on the north Brazilian coast by the Solís expedition. Several other companions, abandoned farther south and similarly rescued by Cabot, reinforced the report of "a mountain two hundred leagues inland containing many mines of gold and silver and other metals." The promise of immediate riches soon displaced the visions of Cathay, and Cabot diverted his expedition to a search for the metal which would give the estuary its permanent name of Río de la Plata. After several explorations along the Uruguay and Paraná, he established his base of operations north of present-day Rosario, in a straw-thatched hut, surrounded by low breastworks and a palisade of sticks, named the fort of Sancti Spiritus (1527). From here small parties reached the Paraguay, the upper Paraná, and the hills of Córdoba. Four Spaniards even arrived several years later in Peru and there told a fantastic tale of a lost city of unparalleled wealth—a myth which drove expeditions across the remotest interior of the continent for several more decades. As the members of Cabot's force dragged their small boats upstream, struggled across swamps, and battled their way out of ambushes, the mirage of silver remained just beyond their reach. Punitive measures finally aroused the local Indian inhabitants, and during Cabot's absence a surprise attack destroyed the fort at Sancti Spiritus. Demoralized and starving, the remnants of the expedition straggled back to Spain, bearing as their only prizes the persistent rumor of silver and the new name of Río de la Plata.

In the 1530's the dream of silver and the threat posed by Portuguese claims to the Río de la Plata were sufficient to mount the largest expedition ever to be used in Spain's conquest of the New World. Cortés had seized Mexico City with five hundred men; Pizarro had toppled the Inca Empire with two hundred; and previous expeditions to the Río de la Plata had never numbered more than two hundred and fifty men. But Pedro de Mendoza, one of the leading noblemen of the Spanish court, sailed forth with fourteen ships and fifteen hundred men. The main object was to assert Spain's military claim to the area and to provide a base from which to explore the interior. In February 1536, after a brief reconnaissance of both shores of the Río de la Plata's estuary, Mendoza planted his colony on the right bank where branches of a small stream, the Riachuelo, and a large sand bar formed a somewhat protected harbor. Legend credits the name of Buenos Aires to the fresh air and healthy atmosphere of the location, but the name actually came from an Italian patron saint popular with navigators throughout the Mediterranean, Nuestra Señora Santa María del Buen Aire. Unfortunately, however, the site provided few other necessities for Spanish colonization, least of all a settled Indian population. When carefully laid plans for the dispatch of supply ships from Spain failed, starvation haunted the colony. Scouting parties were sent up the

Paraná River, but in face of increasing Indian hostility they found little
food to support the sizable Spanish population. The Querandí Indians,
meanwhile, pressed in on the sod breastworks and thatch huts of
Buenos Aires. That secret weapon of the Spaniards, the horse, which
had terrified so many powerful Indian nations in prior conquests, presented no threat to pampas warriors wielding *boleadoras,* and fire,
launched by arrow onto thatch roofs or roaring through dry grass,
further harassed the defenders. The Querandí, nevertheless, lacked
organization. After reducing the Spaniards to eating rats, snakes, thistles, shoes, horsehides, and even each other, they merely withdrew.
Efforts to reach the rumored silver of the interior killed off several
parties, but explorations upstream finally revealed to the weary Spaniards the presence of the Guaraní, the only agrarian people in the
whole coastal area. In 1537 most of Mendoza's expedition (the ailing
leader having died at sea on his return to Spain) moved up the Paraná
and Paraguay to settle Asunción, followed four years later by the remaining Spaniards from Buenos Aires.

Thus the basis for the colonial development of Argentina was laid:
the inhospitable coast was neglected while the interior fell to conquistadors from Peru and Chile. By the end of the century, when the descendants of Mendoza's expedition once more pushed downstream to
establish Spanish towns on the coast and to rebuild the Atlantic approaches to Argentina, they were several decades too late. A tortuous
but established route to Argentina ran from Spanish settlements in Peru,
through the Andean passes, to the thriving agricultural communities
of the northwest. For the next two centuries the commercial centers of
Lima and Panama successfully prevented any permanent reopening of
a legal port of entry at Buenos Aires.

In the northwest the Spaniards were able to use their traditional
methods of establishing urban settlements and exploiting native populations. By the 1540's the ambitious leaders and soldiers of Peru's conquest turned their energies southward, many of them still searching for
the mythical lost city of gold and silver. Some colonized the central
valley of Chile and matched themselves against the Araucanians.
Others moved in on the Indian settlements of the Bolivian *puna* and

in 1545 discovered the enormous silver wealth of the Potosí mines. Still others followed streams into the valleys and Indian communities of northwest Argentina. For several decades small bands of fifty or a hundred men crisscrossed this Andean region, established their armed camps, lived off and fought the native peoples, and quarreled among themselves about claims and jurisdictions.

As these Spaniards sought more permanent exploitation than that of mere marauding bands, they founded urban settlements, or, in the contemporary language, cities, always in strict accord with Spanish tradition. The conquistador carefully chose a site with an eye to its defense, its water supply, and the presence of friendly Indians. He laid out a rectangular gridwork of streets and a central plaza on which faced lots for a church and a municipal building. Then, in a ceremony invoking the names of the Holy Trinity, the Virgin Mary, several saints, the king, and the local governor and setting forth the convenience and desirability of colonizing this location, the conquistador officially named and founded the city. The formalities included the creation of a *cabildo,* or town council, composed of several magistrates and councilors, the erection of a pillory and a stake in the center of the principal plaza, the definition of municipal boundaries and jurisdictions, and the survey and assignment of city lots and surrounding garden plots to all *vecinos,* or settlers. At this stage, relations with the native population assumed vital importance to the settlement's survival. The Spaniards needed Indian labor, but the crown and Church refused to recognize enslavement of the natives. The solution, in part inherited from Spain's reconquest of the Iberian peninsula from the Moors, had already evolved in the Caribbean, Mexico, and Peru—the *encomienda,* or royal grant of Indians to the tutelage, protection, and Christianizing influence of the conquistador, in return for which the *encomendero* was entitled to a certain portion of their labor. Thus, upon establishment of a city, Indians were assigned to the principal Spanish leaders.

On this basis the towns of the Argentine interior took shape during the second half of the sixteenth century. Those that were fortunately situated endured to become capitals of present-day provinces whose boundaries outline the extensive jurisdictions of the colonial cities.

Such was the future of the first permanent Spanish town on Argentine soil, a ragged camp moved back from the flooding Río Dulce and transformed into the city of Santiago del Estero in 1553; or of the city of San Miguel de Tucumán, finally established in 1565 after two previous failures; or of the cities of Mendoza (1561) and San Juan (1562), founded by expeditions from Chile; or of Córdoba (1573), Salta (1582), La Rioja (1591), Jujuy (1592), and San Luis (1596). It was in these widely scattered towns that the society and economy which would dominate the interior of colonial Argentina began to emerge.

These were small towns with clearly divided social classes and modest tastes. The original *vecinos* and their descendants formed the upper class. Indian blood ran in some of their veins, for the first conquistadors occasionally recognized their mestizo offspring and endowed them with wealth, power, and position. But as a group they were creole, prided themselves on their pure origins, and increasingly married only within their own circle. In their hands they held the control of land and labor. The town lots and garden plots had been divided among the *vecinos*, and, although the crown strictly forbade hereditary *encomiendas*, in practice an Indian village continued to supply laborers for sons and even grandsons of the same family. The *vecinos* also occupied the principal commercial, municipal, and Church positions. In the eighteenth century Spain would send peninsular officials to fill administrative posts, but the sixteenth-century Argentine towns were still too unimportant to need such supervision. On the shoulders of the creole families, therefore, rested the administration, defense, and welfare not only of the town but also of a vaguely defined area sometimes extending as much as two hundred miles beyond the urban limits. Yet numerically this upper class was small, ranging in the early seventeenth century from twenty-four *vecinos* in San Juan and forty in Mendoza to four hundred in Santiago del Estero and five hundred in Córdoba.

Below the creole group extended the masses of the population, of many racial shades and economic levels. As the towns expanded, an urbanized laboring class developed, distinct from the Christianized, or "tamed," Indians of the surrounding villages. Negro slaves, imported by way of the coast, began to appear in the interior during the last decade of the sixteenth century. Slaves, along with Negroes who had purchased their freedom, mestizos, mulattoes, and all imaginable combinations thereof, performed household chores and all manual labor. By 1600 this laboring class probably outnumbered the creole element two to one and was rapidly expanding.

Beyond the town lay the villages of *encomienda* Indians, who were primarily occupied in raising crops. At the beginning of the seventeenth century, rough estimates placed this Indian population at twelve thousand in Mendoza, twenty thousand in Santiago del Estero, and fifteen thousand in Córdoba. But these numbers declined rapidly during the following decades—partly due to exploitation and the European diseases of smallpox and measles, but also due to the loss of distinct cultural and racial identity and the gradual blending into the all-embracing lower class.

Almost invariably, as has been pointed out, the town reflected the form of a Spanish city—a rectangular gridiron dominated by a central plaza with an imposing church, a municipal hall, and sometimes a building for the crown official. This and a few shops and warehouses near the plaza comprised the central district. Beyond stretched the residences of the creoles, substantial houses made of stone or adobe and built around patios. Frequently a single home, with its fruit trees and gardens, occupied an entire town block. Servants usually formed part of these creole households, while others of the lower class built their mud and straw shacks on the town's outskirts.

In comparison with the wealth and elegance of Mexico City or Lima, the *vecinos* of the Argentine towns led modest lives. Many settlements waged constant war with "untamed" Indians. Salta, Jujuy, Catamarca, and La Rioja knew no rest until Indian communities were broken up and the natives were transplanted to new regions, some as remote as Buenos Aires. The Church also placed severe demands on the resources of small towns. Religion formed an integral part of sixteenth-century Spanish existence: the Church provided not only religious guidance and ceremonies but also all of the community's educational and social services and a considerable portion of its political and economic prestige. A contemporary description of Córdoba reported: ". . . there is a very fine cathedral as well as the monasteries of Santo Domingo, San Francisco, and La Merced and two rich houses of the Company of Jesus. The latter have a college patterned on university standards . . . and there is also another small college . . . three convents . . . and a hospital for the sick and indigent." Even La Rioja boasted "a parish church and the monasteries of Santo Domingo and San Francisco and a Jesuit establishment." Yet despite the frontier existence and the relative poverty, the *vecinos* proudly maintained their upper-class status. They shared food, amusements, and everyday dress with the lower class, although mestizos, Indians, and Negroes were expressly forbidden to wear finery or rich jewelry. They fought campaigns and engaged in administration of government, religion, and commerce, but they never sullied their hands with manual labor. They chose mistresses from the lower class, but they zealously guarded their family institutions and lineage. As a group they were deeply traditionalistic and jealous of their hard-won position—a closed, small-town society.

Economically the interior towns developed to supply the mining region of Upper Peru. The Bolivian *puna* supported little livestock, and the heavy toll of laborers taken by the mines left few hands to raise crops. Consequently, the Andean region provided the closest source of animals, food, and textiles. By 1650, within sixty to ninety years of the founding of these Argentine towns, the lines of supply were clearly established. Córdoba, well situated for agricultural production, soon displaced Santiago del Estero as Argentina's major urban center. The Comechingones of the Córdoba hills already possessed a semi-agricultural economy and were easily absorbed as a labor force for raising sheep and mules, weaving woolen textiles, and cultivating crops. In addition to exports of mules and flour, Córdoba's central location on the major colonial trade routes between Cuyo, Buenos Aires, and the northwest insured commercial prosperity. Unwieldy oxcarts moved impressive quantities of textiles, wines, brandies, tallow, sugar, wheat, corn, rice, dried fruits, *yerba mate,* leather, bullion, and European imports through this emporium. From Mendoza and San Juan came wines, brandies, and cereals—although remoteness and the tend-

ency of *encomenderos* to remove their Indian charges across the Andes
to the flourishing central valley of Chile retarded the development of
Cuyo. Santiago del Estero, although eclipsed as a trade center during
the seventeenth century, still exported large quantities of cloth. Tucumán, which replaced Santiago del Estero as a major link on the route
to the mines, produced rice, cotton, mules, and oxcarts. Here Negro
slaves supplemented Indian labor, giving rise to the interior's largest
concentration of Negroes. From La Rioja came wines, wheat, textiles,
and mules, while to the north Salta and Jujuy expanded rapidly as way
stations for the valuable flow of trade. The annual fair at Salta where
thousands of mules were collected for sale in the mines became one
of the great markets of the Spanish Empire.

The urban settlement of coastal Argentina lagged several decades
behind that of the interior. In the mid-sixteenth century a few expeditions from Asunción struggled through the wilderness of the Chaco to
Upper Peru, but they found Spaniards from Peru already in possession
of the land and mineral wealth. Nature's obstacles, savage tribes, and
the lack of economic incentives conspired to block a direct trade route
from Asunción to Upper Peru along the meandering, shallow watercourses of the Bermejo or Pilcomayo. When the colony at Asunción
finally acquired sufficient population and vitality to conquer new frontiers, it turned its energies downstream and established settlements at
Santa Fe (1573), Buenos Aires (1580), Concepción del Bermejo
(1585), and Corrientes (1588).

Our modern knowledge of geography sometimes obscures the reasons for the struggle between Argentina's coast and interior and for the
predominance of the interior regions during much of the colonial period. Why did Spain conquer the South American continent along its
most formidable barrier, the Andes? Why did Spanish commerce cross
staggering obstacles, from Panama through Guayaquil and Lima, to
reach the interior cities such as Potosí and Córdoba? Why did Spain
shut the door on trade through the obvious route of the Río de la Plata
and not open it again until the end of the eighteenth century?

In order to comprehend this seemingly illogical situation we must
look at the conquest through the eyes of the sixteenth-century Span-

iard. The centers of overseas power and wealth were located at Mexico
City and Lima. The deserted southern flank of the empire hardly attracted commerce and fleets, and ships in the South Atlantic had to
venture far beyond the protection of Spanish bases. The safest and
most direct route to the American empire remained that taken by
Columbus, for, despite the harassments of French, English, and Dutch
buccaneers, the Caribbean was still a Spanish sea. Dependence on native labor also guided Spanish conquest and settlement to areas where
there were advanced Indian civilizations. Finally it must be remembered that mountains presented few obstacles to mule caravans loaded
with silver bullion, compact foodstuffs, and European luxuries, especially when the caravans followed the excellent, paved paths of the
Incas. Therefore, the conquest of Upper Peru and the interior of Argentina merely extended the Spanish Empire southward from Lima
along the best routes available.

The coastal region of the Río de la Plata, meanwhile, had rejected
several colonization attempts. Yet, in the same year that Spaniards from
Peru founded Córdoba, Juan de Garay, leading an expedition from
Asunción, established a town at Santa Fe, and several years later the
Atlantic approach was reopened with a permanent settlement at the
port of Buenos Aires. Why then did the area of the Río de la Plata
continue to face inland rather than becoming a main artery linking
Spain with the silver mines of Potosí? One reason was that precedence
gave the Panama-Lima route commercial predominance: merchants,
shipping, and capital refused to surrender their established positions.
Strategic interests were also at stake: security dictated that silver bullion and valuable merchandise not be sent by way of the sparsely settled pampas and the exposed South Atlantic.

The settlers who pushed downstream from Asunción found themselves, therefore, on a remote rim of the Spanish Empire rather than on
a principal commercial route to the mother country. This very isolation
tended to develop the distinct character of these people. The absence of
large numbers of "tamed" Indians, the limited possibilities for crop
farming, the vast numbers of wild horses and cattle on the pampas, the
closeness to the Portuguese sphere of influence in Brazil, the facilities

and incentives for contraband trade on the broad estuary—all placed
their stamp on the coastal towns.

When Garay led his small expedition of ninety men southward to
found Santa Fe and subsequently enlisted a party of sixty to establish
Buenos Aires, the mestizo element participated to a degree unprecedented in the conquest. More than thirty years had passed since the
remains of Mendoza's expedition had withdrawn to Asunción. Although several other expeditions from Spain had added roughly fourteen hundred men to the original Mendoza contingent of fifteen hundred, the short life expectancy of sixteenth-century man, combined with
the rigors of nature and Indian fighting, left few peninsular Spaniards
on their feet by the 1570's. Women from the Iberian peninsula were
an even greater rarity—not more than fifty ever reached the Río de la
Plata in these early decades. Due to the resultant scarcity of Spanish,
or even of strictly-defined creole, manpower and leadership, the mestizo offspring of the Guaraní women became the soldiers and often the
leaders in Asunción. At Santa Fe and Buenos Aires these mixed-bloods
contributed 80 to 90 per cent of the *vecinos,* and through identification with Spanish customs and culture these mestizo *vecinos* were considered creole and upper-class. Emphasis on Spanish lineage which
characterized the rigid class structure of the interior towns consequently
did not develop so quickly on the coast.

Conditions of life also contributed to a more egalitarian type of society. While *vecinos* certainly did not become day laborers, the absence
of servile Indian masses reduced economic and social differences among
the population. Corrientes could draw on a limited supply of Guaraní
labor, but at Concepción del Bermejo, Santa Fe, and Buenos Aires *encomiendas* were meaningless. Indeed, the impossibility of subjugating
the native inhabitants was underlined by the abandonment of Concepción del Bermejo in the 1630's and the transplanting of Santa Fe several miles southward in the 1650's. Some Guaraní Indians accompanied
expeditions downstream, and in the seventeenth century Buenos Aires
received several contingents of Indians forcibly transplanted from the
Andean region. Negro slaves added considerably to the number of
urban workers, although the majority were shipped to towns of the

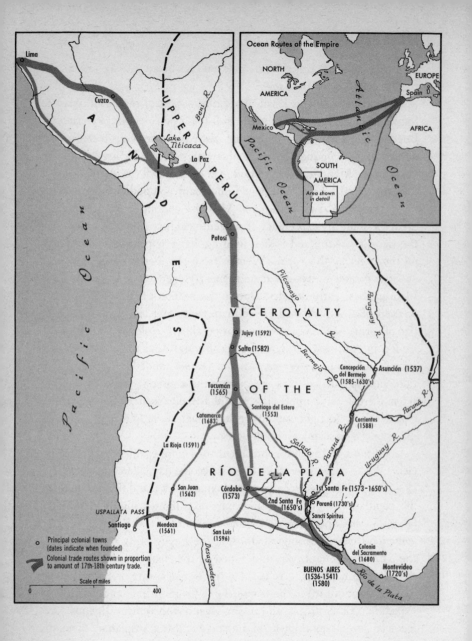

Lima

Cuzco

A

N

D

E

S

UPPER PERU

Beni R.

Lake
Titicaca

La Paz

Potosí

Pilcomayo R.

Paraguay R.

VICEROYALTY

Jujuy (1592)

Salta (1582)

Bermejo R.

Concepción
del Bermejo
(1585-1630's)

Asunción (1537)

Tucumán
(1565)

OF THE

Santiago del Estero
(1553)

Paraná R.

Catamarca
(1683)

Corrientes
(1588)

Uruguay R.

La Rioja (1591)

Salado R.

Paraná R.

RÍO DE LA PLATA

San Juan
(1562)

Córdoba
(1573)

1st Santa Fe (1573-1650's)

USPALLATA PASS

Santiago

Mendoza
(1561)

San Luis
(1596)

2nd Santa Fe
(1650's)

Paraná (1730's)

Sancti Spíritus

Pacific Ocean

Desaguadero R.

Colonia
del Sacramento
(1680)

Montevideo
(1720's)

BUENOS AIRES
(1536-1541)
(1580)

Río de la Plata

○ Principal colonial towns
(dates indicate when founded)

◢ Colonial trade routes shown in proportion
to amount of 17th-18th century trade.

Scale of miles

0   400

Ocean Routes of the Empire

NORTH
AMERICA

EUROPE

Atlantic Ocean

Spain

Mexico

AFRICA

Pacific Ocean

SOUTH
AMERICA

Area shown
in detail

Ocean

interior. The cattle, horses, and mules fortunately required little care or attention, but the shortage of laborers prevented the development of textile and handicraft industries or extensive crop farming.

The principal motive for settling the coastal towns, however, had not been production but rather commerce: to provide Asunción, and perhaps Córdoba and Potosí, with an Atlantic outlet. Yet after four decades of limited trade through the Río de la Plata, the Panama-Lima merchants destroyed this competition, at least on paper. The crown established a customs barrier at Córdoba to prevent imports from reaching the northwest and Upper Peru by way of Buenos Aires (1618) and withdrew permission to trade with Brazil (1622). All that was left for Buenos Aires was an annual ship from Seville. But enforcement of such restrictions was another matter, and the coastal economy continued to develop, although at a slower rate, on the basis of contraband trade. The areas of land and water involved were too vast and the profits were too high to prevent smuggling. Often the annual ship became a floating fair, repeatedly restocking its wares from cargoes of other, frequently foreign, ships. The drainage of silver bullion eastward from Potosí to pay for these smuggled goods cost the crown dearly, for usually this was silver on which the royal fifth, or tax, had not been paid. One merchant who made the round trip from Buenos Aires to Potosí under royal license in the 1650's reported his simple and commonly used procedure: "After a voyage of four months with oxcarts, I happily reached the Río Lujan, five leagues from Buenos Aires, where I met my partner, who had arrived first. He brought with him a small launch which we used to transport most of the silver secretly to our ship." Smuggling increased through the venality of poorly paid royal officials and the ease with which merchant ships of any flag could hide in the channels and tributaries of the Río de la Plata; it was climaxed by the establishment in 1680 of a Portuguese emporium directly opposite Buenos Aires at Colonia del Sacramento (Spanish capture in the eighteenth century changed the spelling from the Portuguese version, Colônia do Sacramento). Thus, despite the combined efforts of the crown and of Lima merchants, an increasing volume of Negro slaves, ironware, sugar, and textiles entered the Río de la Plata to be sold all along the route to Upper Peru.

The Spanish towns conquered Argentina for the crown. From these widely scattered settlements, the conquistador, *vecino,* friar, merchant, mestizo, and creole imposed Spanish values and culture on the Andean region and the fringes of the northern lowlands and the pampas. By 1650—the middle of the colonial period's so-called forgotten century— a traditionalistic class society and an economy of small industries, crop raising, and trade dominated the interior. On the coast a somewhat younger, more egalitarian society was rapidly developing on the basis of smuggling and the production of cattle, horses, and mules. The following decades witnessed the expansion of both regions. Population multiplied with the gradual assimilation of the Indian to form the mestizo peasantry and the urban lower class. Spaniards increasingly emigrated to the New World, but in a stabilized society few of them could aspire to the rank of *vecino* and thus many fitted into the economy as artisans, shopkeepers, millers, tailors, herdsmen, and even servants. Contributing to the growth of modest cities were the imports of Negro slaves, the development of large landed estates, and the importance of stock raising.

The conquistador never became an agriculturist, nor initially, for that matter, did the creole, the ambitious mestizo or mulatto, or the Negro. Argentina's rural population came from those who were already on the land—the Indians. A century of serving or fighting the Spaniard had forcibly assimilated the native population into the dominant Spanish culture. Only in the Chaco, on the pampas, and in Patagonia did nomadic tribes hold their own. Elsewhere the native agrarian civilizations succumbed to the *encomienda,* to the friar and missionary, or to relentless war and transplanting of communities. Since the missionary and conquistador came to Argentina from Peru after two decades' exposure to the Quechua tongue of the Incas, they tended to impose this common language on the diverse groups of the Andean region, further robbing these natives of their linguistic identity. The *encomienda* also broke down the separate Indian groups: the Huarpes of Cuyo were given in service to *encomenderos* from Córdoba or taken across the Andes to Chile; Indians from the northwest were sent to Upper Peru; and, after the Indian wars in La Rioja and Tucumán from 1630 to 1670, some eleven thousand Diaguitas were resettled in new areas.

From the remains of disintegrated Indian communities emerged a lower class which ethnically was heavily Indian but which possessed few indigenous cultural traits. Even racially, miscegenation gradually turned the Indian into a mestizo. The Indian village still existed in the eighteenth century, but its religious and political functions had been taken over by the Church and the crown. Its economic life, once dominated by the *encomendero,* increasingly came under the control of the nearest large landowner, who took advantage of his power to provide himself with laborers for cultivation, harvesting, or pastoral industries. Indian dress, amusements, and food were influenced, if not replaced, by Spanish customs. Even where the sword did not reach, missionaries carried forward the task of absorbing the Indians into the Christian, Europeanized world. In that vague, shifting frontier area along the upper Paraná and Uruguay, the Jesuits organized Guaraní Indians into mission communities. Less successful were Jesuit attempts to plant missions among nomadic tribes in the pampas or in Patagonia, but the missionary effort served as a first step in the absorption of several tribes in the northwest and in the Chaco.

By 1700 the continuous arrival of Spaniards who were attracted by opportunities in commerce and by the demand for artisans, tradesmen, and laborers also contributed to social change. Few penetrated inland beyond Córdoba, since the coastal region needed workers and the opportunity for advancement or even marriage to some rich creole's daughter was far better here than in the closed society of the interior towns. Some foreigners, despite royal prohibition, joined this immigration—especially Portuguese merchants from Brazil and a few Germans, Dutch, or Italians who passed for Spanish subjects. The result of this influx was that Spaniards and creoles no longer necessarily received upper-class status. Mestizo, mulatto, Negro, and white often rubbed shoulders at the same manual tasks, and from this economic and social contact came further miscegenation and mixed marriages.

The Negro added appreciably to the racial mixture. During the first two decades of the seventeenth century nine thousand Negro slaves were confiscated at Buenos Aires for illegal entry—an indication not only of the importance of smuggling but also of the volume of slave trade. By 1680 twenty-three thousand Negroes had been imported on royal licenses, and an untold number had entered as contraband. The majority of these human imports were sent inland, where they remained concentrated in urban centers. As contrasted with the reputed sullenness of Indians or the crafty ambition of mestizos, the docile cheerfulness of Negroes placed them in high demand as servants and as workmen in the trades and small industries. Within the lower class they blended readily with the mestizo, Indian, and white elements. By the early eighteenth century, Negroes, both slaves and those who had purchased their freedom, contributed 10 to 30 per cent of the population of the Argentine towns and were particularly in evidence at Tucumán, Córdoba, and Buenos Aires.

As the economy and population expanded, private ownership of large landholdings began to acquire importance as a means of exploitation and a symbol of prestige and position. The conquest had secured the New World as royal domain for the crown. In this early period private ownership of land meant little, since wealth and power were represented by exploitation of minerals or of Indian labor. In the towns established by the conquistadors, urban lots, garden plots, and occasionally grazing lands were distributed to *vecinos,* but the extensions were relatively small. By means of the *encomienda* the Spanish crown sought to Christianize the Indians, utilize their labor, and yet prevent usurpation of their lands. Intensely aware of the threat of feudalism to a national state or empire, Spain's rulers repeatedly restricted and limited the *encomendero*'s power. But, confronted in the seventeenth century with a pressing need for funds and with creole demands for seignorial status, the crown began to sell or grant large extensions of land to private owners. In the Argentine area the result was the *estancia*—vast estates of ten thousand, a hundred thousand, or a million acres, sometimes bought by the descendants of *encomenderos,* sometimes by wealthy merchants, but inevitably ending up in the hands of creoles. This land contained little of value: in the coastal region, wild cattle and horses; in the interior, sheep, Indian villages, grazing and crop lands. But by replacing the *encomienda* as the basis for rural exploitation, the *estancia* created a creole landholding class which lived in the towns but drew its prestige and subsistence from the land.

The foundations for Argentina's principal cities were laid in the sixteenth century. During the ensuing decades there were only a few additions or adjustments: in the northwest, the establishment of Catamarca (1683), the move of Tucumán several miles eastward (1685), and the abandonment of Talavera de Esteco, a flourishing town on the route between Tucumán and Salta, due to earthquake (1692); and on the coast, the previously mentioned abandonment of Concepción del Bermejo (1630's) and the move of Santa Fe (1650's), the establishment of a small settlement across the estuary at Montevideo (1720's), and the creation of parishes at Paraná across the river from Santa Fe and at Rosario farther down the Paraná River (1730's). Even more significant than the creation of new towns was the growth of the old: Buenos Aires from 1,000 inhabitants in 1600, to 3,000 by 1650, to 12,000 by 1750; Córdoba from 3,000 in 1600, to 5,000 in 1650, to 8,000 by 1750; Tucumán from 2,000 in 1600, to 4,000 by 1650, to 7,000 by 1750.

Gradually during the eighteenth century towns lost the aspect of rural villages. Offices, stores, and the shops of tradesmen and artisans filled the blocks adjoining the central plaza and sometimes spread out to secondary plazas. Warehouses, butchers, and markets moved to the outskirts. The number of churches, monasteries, convents, and residences for royal officials increased sharply. In the central district fewer homes occupied entire blocks. Second stories occasionally appeared; churches and royal buildings became more imposing; and in Córdoba and the towns of the Andean region cobblestone streets were laid. Distinct urban zones began to develop: the wealthy tended to congregate around the central plaza, while outlying areas became known for the concentration of Negroes and mulattoes or for certain trades.

The town also expanded its administrative and commercial functions and extended its influence over the countryside. No longer was urban settlement merely a nucleus of Spaniards dedicated to the exploitation of Indian labor and gathered in one center for purposes of defense. Both crown and Church now occupied a primary position in the Argentine towns: bishops, governors, lieutenants, priests, and clerks came from Spain in increasing numbers, sent across the Atlantic to control the far-flung empire. The flow of commerce, both overseas and local, enriched a substantial merchant class and contributed to a rising spirit of capitalism and progress.

Education, the arts, society, and amusements likewise found their principal expression in the towns. The Church's efforts to instruct its clergy and to teach Christian doctrine to the Indians led to a considerable emphasis on education. Convents, parish schools, and Dominican, Franciscan, and Jesuit seminaries—one of the latter developing into the University of Córdoba in 1622—educated countless creoles and not a few mestizos. The Church provided the only medical care or assistance for the indigent—services necessarily concentrated in the towns. Art found its major expression in urban surroundings where artisans made altars, images, doors, furnishings, silver ornaments, religious paintings, and embroidered altar coverings, tapestries, and clothes. Colonial pastimes, imported from the Old World, were modified in new surroundings. Mass, siesta, and evening strolls in the plaza became part of the town's daily routine. Men patronized the horse races, cock fights, bull fights, and billiard games. Those of the upper class frequently gathered in some home to listen to a recital or to discuss philosophy, poetry, or politics. The entire town joined in Church fiestas and attended the religious allegories, dramas, and puppet shows.

Perhaps most important to Argentina's future orientation was the growth of the coast, and particularly of the port of Buenos Aires, in the late seventeenth and in the eighteenth centuries. The Spanish mercantilist system, with its extended trade routes and convoyed fleets, faced serious strains. As the empire grew, the efforts of the Panama-Lima merchants to maintain their monopoly of the southern continent's trade became more and more anachronistic. The ineffectiveness of the customs barrier established at Córdoba resulted in its removal northward to Salta and Jujuy (1676), thus extending royal recognition to

Buenos Aires' control of Argentina's interior markets. The creation of a Portuguese port and trade center at Colonia del Sacramento in 1680 significantly added to the flow of Negroes and contraband into the Río de la Plata. Even the Chilean markets began to slip away from Lima's sphere and to receive shipments sent by oxcart from Buenos Aires to Mendoza and then on mules over the passes to Santiago. The costly convoys to the Caribbean, the transshipment by land or sea to Lima, and the twelve hundred miles of mountain trails to Potosí could no longer compete with the licensed annual ship, the smuggler, or the slave trader bound for the Río de la Plata. When the crown abandoned the system of convoyed fleets in the mid-eighteenth century, it was a final blow to the Panama-Lima route. The Seville merchants, once staunch supporters of the fleets, were now the first to capitalize on licensed sailings to Buenos Aires. The crown, faced with the illegal drain of silver eastward from Potosí and the consequent loss of revenue, accepted the inevitable and extended permission for individual shipments of imports from Buenos Aires to Upper Peru and for the export of silver that had paid the royal fifth.

During this same period the silver production of Upper Peru began to decline. Failure to apply modern mining techniques, heavy mortality among Indian laborers, and the exhausting of previously rich veins contributed to increasing depression in the Andean region. In contrast, the cattle and horses of the coast provided an attractive alternative for developing the Río de la Plata.

Thus the economic foundation was ready for the creation of the last great administrative subdivision of the empire in 1776, the Viceroyalty of the Río de la Plata with headquarters at Buenos Aires. The actual establishment of the Viceroyalty occurred under the guise of military and strategic considerations, related not only in date but also in fact to the emergence of the United States on the northern continent. The eighteenth century witnessed the spread of European dynastic struggles from the Continent to the overseas empires: Canada, Florida, Louisiana, India, and the Río de la Plata had become pawns on the international chessboard. The Río de la Plata now represented more than a southern frontier of the Spanish Empire. The estuary and the plains beyond promised access to the commerce and perhaps the political control of half a continent. Colonia del Sacramento, repeatedly captured from the Portuguese and twice restored to their hands by European treaties (1713, 1763), was Portugal's advance base in the Río de la Plata. Although Spain had concentrated half its regular troops on the southern continent at Buenos Aires, Portuguese battalions still outnumbered them. The situation demanded decisive action, and the opportunity presented itself when England became embroiled with its own rebellious colonies and consequently could not aid its ally, Portugal. Spain's reform-minded Charles III immediately sent a major expedition and a viceroy to expel the Portuguese from the Río de la Plata.

But the military objective only momentarily obscured the fundamental adjustments brought about by the presence of a viceroy at Buenos Aires. The reforms envisaged by Charles III and carried out by his viceroy in the Río de la Plata set the stage for the predominance of Buenos Aires in the nineteenth century. And, as in the British colonies of North America, the Spanish crown's sudden concern with profits and revenues sowed the seeds for independence.

Not only strategic concerns but also a reorientation of commercial and political policy motivated the viceregal expedition of 1776. Belatedly the crown thought it saw the error of the sixteenth century and sought to recapture from smugglers and slave traders the Atlantic approach to its southern domains. In one of his first letters the new viceroy spelled out the position of Buenos Aires: "This is our most important bastion in America, whose development we must encourage by every means possible, for here we will win or lose South America." Only economic growth could provide the desired security. With this objective in mind, the viceroy authorized the export of silver bullion via Buenos Aires and forbade the shipment of uncoined silver northward from Potosí to Lima. This extraordinary reversal of traditional trade policy was complemented by decrees permitting goods imported at Buenos Aires to circulate freely throughout the viceregal domain. The system of trade licenses was gradually expanded to permit exchange between any port in Spain and the overseas ports of the empire and finally to allow trade among the overseas ports themselves. By the 1790's, because of the pressures of renewed European conflict and the consequent shortage of shipping, trade privileges were extended to include even neutral vessels. Accompanying these commercial reforms came other royal measures aimed at stimulating production and settlement in the coastal region: administrative changes in the collection of taxes; granting of licenses to import Negro slaves; efforts to extend the frontier of the pampas to the Río Salado in Buenos Aires; reoccupation of the Malvinas, or Falkland Islands, seized by England in the 1760's; creation of outposts on Patagonia's barren coast; and economic incentives for the cultivation of wheat, flax, and hemp and the development of a salted meat industry.

The crown's policies contributed to a sudden increase in population and prosperity in the new viceregal capital. Buenos Aires grew in size from 12,000 inhabitants in 1750, to 25,000 in 1780, to 50,000 by the end of the century. By the 1780's regular Spanish troops at Buenos Aires numbered between 3,000 and 4,000 men, in addition to naval units stationed in the estuary. Legal trade, defense expenditures, and livestock production tripled and quadrupled the stimulus that the coast formerly received from contraband. Royal revenues at Buenos Aires, largely derived from import and export taxes, rose from 100,000 pesos in 1774 to 300,000 in 1776 and reached 1,000,000 in 1780. By the latter date there were porteño merchants whose fortunes exceeded half a million pesos—a commercial prosperity previously common only in Lima and Mexico City. The pampas yielded a wealth never dreamed of by the early conquistadors: the average annual export of hides from Buenos Aires increased from 150,000 in the 1750's to 700,000 in the 1790's.

Buenos Aires' progress was reflected in much more modest terms in the interior towns, sharpening the division between the interior's small local industries and crop production and the coast's commercial and livestock economy. Although the empire's mercantilist system was liberalized by Charles III, he did not throw open the doors to international trade. Consequently, not until after independence was achieved were the effects of such a divided economy fully felt: one region seeking to import its consumer goods from abroad in exchange for its agricultural products, the other demanding internal markets for the output of its industries and farms.

More immediate and certainly more disastrous for Spain was the development of Buenos Aires as a center of royal administration, for here emerged the creole demand for independence. The arrival of substantial numbers of churchmen, bureaucrats, and officers from Spain brought the long-standing division between creole and Spaniard to the Río de la Plata. Regardless of royal sentiments on the hotly debated issue of the inferiority (variously interpreted as laziness, stupidity, or disloyalty) of creoles, the crown had consistently chosen its high officials from the homeland rather than from the overseas empire. As long as Argentina remained a forgotten frontier, the need for royal control had been slight, and creoles in the municipal councils handled many of the matters of administration, finance, and defense. Establishment of the Viceroyalty changed all that. Creoles suddenly found themselves reduced to a minor political role. Royal judges, intendants, governors, commanders, and clerks usurped all but the most negligible functions. Even more galling to creole pride and pocketbooks were Charles III's reforms which charged these peninsula-born officials with more efficient collection of royal taxes. Yet, at the same time that the creoles were effectively disfranchised, as a group they remained important in the economic sphere, controlling land and local industries and threatening the commercial monopoly maintained by Spanish merchants. The resultant friction did not immediately manifest itself in demands for representation or independence or in disloyalty to the crown. But when in the early nineteenth century Napoleon momentarily overthrew the Spanish monarchy, it was the creoles at Buenos Aires who seized the political reins and led Argentina to independence.

By the end of the eighteenth century the urban settlements, and particularly the city of Buenos Aires, had completed the conquest of Argentina. Fourteen centers scattered at intervals of fifty to four hundred miles across the Andean region and along the Paraná River asserted Spain's control of a sparsely settled agricultural frontier and provided strategic and commercial access to the South American continent.

Indians now numbered less than 200,000, and the mestizo-creole population approached 400,000. The countryside contained more than three-fourths of the population, but in the urban centers were found the leadership and resources which had created a Spanish colony and which now foreshadowed the future nation. Yet the towns had failed to overcome the divisions of the land. The antagonisms of the interior versus the coast and of the creole versus the non-creole originated in the colonial towns and were to become central themes in the country's history during the nineteenth century.

Chapter 3 • The Rural Economy
of Buenos Aires

For three hundred years, from the seventeenth until the late nineteenth century, livestock provided the principal products and exports of the pampas region. The rudimentary economy progressed gradually, from the hunting of wild cattle and horses for their hides (1600-1750), to the formation of large herds of semi-tamed animals (1700-1850), to the production of fats and salted meat by the *saladero* (1800-1890), and finally to extensive sheep raising (1830-1900). At each stage the rift between the interior and the coast widened, until at last the coast achieved predominance. In the end only one city throve—the port of Buenos Aires which, by the nineteenth century, monopolized all trade. In this process hides, meat, and wool became more than mere products; for much of Argentina they determined landownership, population distribution, political events, way of life, and social customs.

At the time of the Spanish conquest the native peoples of the Argentine area cultivated corn, squash, beans, cassava, and potatoes. Less had been done to tame the animals useful to man. Only in the Andean regions had Indians domesticated the llama and occasionally its cousins, the alpaca and guanaco, for wool and as beasts of burden. On the grasslands of the coast the sparse native population depended almost entirely on deer. With the arrival of the Spaniards, however, the area began to draw on Europe's animal resources. These naturally spread with the conquest from Asunción and the Andean region, into the northern lowlands, the pampas, and finally to Patagonia. In coastal Argentina the horse, cow, sheep, mule, goat, and pig made possible the development of an economy and a society in a region devoid of crops, Indian villages, and mineral wealth.

Seventy horses and some pigs arrived with Mendoza's expedition. Five years later, upon abandoning Buenos Aires, the Spaniards left behind seven stallions and five mares, the basis for the wild horses of the pampas. In the 1540's another expedition to the Río de la Plata brought more horses and some jackasses to Asunción, while the first parties into the Argentine northwest introduced horses from Peru. In the next decade one of the infrequent Spanish expeditions across the Chaco returned to Asunción from Upper Peru with goats and sheep. During the 1550's cattle, sheep, and goats entered the Andean region with Spaniards from Peru and Chile, and a small herd of seven cows and one bull was driven overland from the Brazilian coast to Asunción. Cattle and jackasses reached the pampas in 1573—both at Córdoba and at Santa Fe. When Garay re-established a settlement at Buenos Aires, sheep, pigs, goats, five hundred cattle, and one thousand horses accompanied the expedition from Asunción. In the surrounding plains as far south as present-day Mar del Plata were found the wild descendants of the handful of horses left by Buenos Aires' first settlers.* Since there were no Indians to distribute, Garay turned to this unique resource and granted wild horses to the *vecinos*. Cattle which escaped from the herds introduced to Buenos Aires by Garay's expedition prospered equally well on these grasslands. By the early seventeenth century large herds of wild cattle had joined the bands of wild horses in this vast natural pasture.

During the initial years of the conquest, animals brought by ship

* Livestock can be expected to double in number every three years. Since they had few natural enemies and were not exploited by the Indians, the original twelve horses abandoned in 1541, aside from others that may have escaped, could have increased to one hundred thousand by 1580.

from Spain or across the Andes from Peru or Chile represented valuable investments. Herdsmen closely guarded the livestock on common grazing lands outside the small settlements, and at night they drove them into enclosures, usually within the town itself. As population, crop farming, and herds expanded, however, the animals gradually had to move farther afield. From this moment, the agricultural economies of the interior and the coast took divergent paths.

In the interior the livestock industries developed only as complements to crop and textile production for the mines of Upper Peru. As a result, cattle, sheep, mules, and horses never became the dominant elements in the economy. Crop farming demanded that animals be controlled, and wild or stray animals were quickly incorporated into domestic herds or killed. An ample supply of mestizo, Indian, and Negro labor provided the hands needed to tend flocks, build stone fences, dig wells, shear sheep, train mules and oxen, dry meat, weave woolen goods, and work the leather.

On the coast the shortage of labor and the remoteness from Upper Peru combined with the existence of large herds of wild horses and cattle to create an economy in which commercial and grazing interests reigned supreme over artisan industries or cultivation of the soil. Crop farming was limited to gardens sheltered within the confines of the towns. Sheep were useless on the pampas, for there were no laborers to tend flocks or to weave woolens, and here, where beef carcasses were left to dogs and vultures, not even beggars would look at mutton. In a land that offered wild animals almost for the taking, tame herds soon lost their value and livestock care became meaningless. *Estancias* in Santa Fe and Buenos Aires bred mules only to send them off as yearlings to Córdoba and Tucumán where they were acclimatized and trained for use in the mines. In the seventeenth century, at least, no attempt was made to dry or salt meat for export. The hides of wild horses and cattle consequently provided the area's principal exploitable product, for this was both an economy and a society based on leather. Furniture, hammocks, and every conceivable type of container were fashioned from hides. Leather was universally used in the construction of roofs, walls, and carts. Hides were also in great demand for export to the mines of Upper Peru or, by contraband trade, to Brazil and Europe.

This type of economy endowed the coastal area with some character-istics it would never lose. Outstanding in the heritage of song and leg-end was the gaucho—Argentina's colorful counterpart of the American cowboy. His background is still a mystery. He emerged first in the seventeenth century as a mestizo vagabond of the coastal countryside. But he also appeared in the interior, particularly during that region's nineteenth-century decline and the shift of certain areas to a rudimen-tary grazing economy. In Salta gauchos formed the scarlet-clad cavalry hordes of the independence hero, Martín Güemes. The gaucho pro-vided a central theme for Domingo F. Sarmiento's masterful biography, *Facundo,* written in the 1840's to present the struggle between bar-barism and civilization in the interior. In La Rioja gauchos fought a war to the death with national troops in the 1860's. And in the 1870's José Hernández' epic poem *Martín Fierro* immortalized their final agonies in the face of settlement and fences on the pampas.

The gaucho was Argentina's frontiersman. But rather than serving as a harbinger of civilization, he remained outside society and on the fringes of the economy. His labors made possible the exploitation of the animal wealth of the pampas, but he avoided the towns and scorned crop farming. He warred relentlessly with the nomadic Indian tribes, but he shared their drifting existence and their desire to remain beyond the reach of urban law and order.

He was, above all, a horseman. His food was meat, freshly hacked from the warm carcass of a wild cow or sun-dried to the color and con-sistency of Cordovan leather. An occasional handful of roasted maize and the convivial *mate*—a strong brew of Paraguayan tea passed from hand to hand in any gaucho gathering—provided the only variation from the steady diet of meat. Like the Araucanian, he used the hide from a colt's hind leg for a boot. Loose baggy trousers, a wide strip of cloth passed between the legs in the form of a breech cloth, and a pon-cho sufficed for protection from the elements. His principal tools of trade also served as weapons. The double-edged dagger made him a formidable opponent on foot as well as an effective butcher. On horse-back he adopted the Indian *boleadoras* to throw cattle, horses, rheas,

and mounted enemies; or, when more care was required, he depended
on a short lariat of braided leather. Brutality and disregard for life or
limb became his trademarks. In an environment where human life had
little value, his skill and agility with a knife endowed him with a fear-
some reputation for courage and lawlessness. He never tamed his
mounts, as did the Indian, by patient handling, but in one or two
savage gallops he literally broke a wild horse to the saddle. Twenty or
thirty such animals formed his string: his speed and mobility depended
on constant changing of horses, made all the more necessary by the
heavy, cumbersome saddle, a veritable traveling bed. He sank no roots
and had few needs. Somewhere in a mud hut a mestizo or Indian girl
raised his children and awaited his occasional visit. But usually his
home was his saddle and poncho.

His amusements and pleasures grew likewise from his surroundings:
gambling and horses. The *taba,* made from a cow's knuckle bone and
thrown for "heads or tails," substituted for cards or dice. To supplement
the excitement of horse racing, a gaucho would often gallop through a
double line of horsemen, to land on his feet when a lucky throw of the
lariat snagged his horse from under him. As the economy expanded and
country stores, or *pulperías,* appeared across the pampas, he indulged in
some luxuries—a few tiny black cigars and a glass of pale rum, or *caña.*
Equine sports became more sophisticated while losing nothing of their
roughness. One rural pastime still occasionally played as a national
sport, *el pato,* consisted of a pitched battle among several horsemen for
possession of a cooked duck that had been sewed into a hide. In its
rules, speed, dexterity, and violence it resembled another national sport,
polo, which the British introduced late in the nineteenth century.
Among his gentler accomplishments, the gaucho played the guitar
and sang ballads. Poetic competitions became an integral part of all
rural social gatherings, with endless queries and riddles answered in
spontaneous and rather monotonous verse.

Beyond this bare outline, fact and myth blend together. As with all
historical figures which become national symbols, the true gaucho must
have been something between the brave and honorable hero of legend
and the dirty, vicious vagabond painted by skeptics.

The rural economy as it developed in the coastal region drew its workers from the gaucho ranks. Towns might despise or distrust the gaucho, but he provided the one means to exploit the wild herds. Initially this meant expeditions of horsemen and dogs to hunt down the cattle and horses. Armed with a long lance tipped with a thin curving steel blade, the gaucho skillfully hamstrung the fleeing beasts at full gallop. The fact that Negro slaves, representing substantial investments, never were used on these hunts indicates the dangers from hostile Indians, infuriated herds, or simply from breaking a mount's leg. After crippling a few dozen animals, the gaucho returned to kill his fallen prey. He took only the hide and sometimes the kidney and intestinal fats for tallow, while often cutting out the tongue to roast as a delicacy. The carcass remained where it fell, to provide carrion for dogs and vultures.

The initial grants to the Buenos Aires *vecinos* had included licenses to hunt or capture wild horses. The subsequent spread of wild cattle gave rise to a somewhat different division of pastoral wealth. Since these animals originated from herds brought by settlers from Asunción, the same settlers or their descendants were given the privilege of hunting the wild cattle. But wild animals tended to move away from the towns and thus increased the difficulties of transporting the wet or green hides to the coast. As wild herds drifted deeper into the pampas, hunting parties often faced hostile Indians—by the eighteenth century the redoubtable Araucanians. The solution to these problems was found in semi-tamed animals which could be driven and yet required little attention. The owners of small tame herds consequently used their licenses not only to kill but also to capture wild cattle, thereby creating the basis for cattle *estancias*. Municipal regulations set aside summer months for the cattle hunt, and this also became the period for branding captured cattle as well as calves. Since cattle could be trained to stay in one particular area, the *estanciero* selected well-drained land with a dependable water supply from streams or rain-filled lakes and gathered his herd under the supervision of a few gauchos—one gaucho per thousand head of cattle. Ideally he sought areas where the juncture of streams or swamps imposed natural limits on wandering animals.

The simple expedient of an occasional hardwood post driven into the ground provided a powerful attraction for cattle, something to rub against in the treeless plains. Three or four months of constant rodeo accustomed even the wildest herds to their several square miles of pampas and to man's presence. In return for the chores of roundup, castration, and branding, the cattle owner could enlarge his possessions to include huge herds of semi-tamed cattle. The *estancia* also permitted a more thorough preparation of products: there the hides could be dried and sent by oxcart to the towns, and the intestines and fatty portions of the carcasses could be boiled to remove the tallow.

As the coast's prosperity and production increased, landownership replaced ownership of semi-tamed herds. *Estancias* measured in terms of thousands of cattle now became landholdings of thousands of acres. Since the scrawny range animals were individually of slight value, large-scale exploitation was an economic necessity. Roughly two acres of grassland around Buenos Aires or Santa Fe were needed per head, and the annual yield of hides could be estimated at 10 per cent of the herd. Even an *estancia* with twenty thousand acres and ten thousand animals yielded only modest income. The complexities of the land tenure system further encouraged large holdings. Royal sales or grants of land inevitably demanded substantial expenses in litigation or bribery. The crown might sell fifty thousand acres for a trifle, equivalent perhaps to four hundred head of cattle. But subsequent costs to define and retain ownership frequently amounted to twenty or thirty times the original purchase price. The fact that such charges were apt to be as high on fifty acres as on fifty thousand virtually eliminated the small property owner.

Land tenure thus required financial resources and political influence. Some descendants of the first settlers managed to acquire vast holdings, but most of the *estancias* in the eighteenth century were developed by wealthy merchants and occasionally by Church institutions. The result was to reinforce absentee ownership by individuals who acquired land for prestige and income but who left administration and labor to foremen and gauchos. Few landowners chose to foresake the towns and to accept the hardships and dangers of rural life. The *estancia* headquarters was not the palatial weekend or summer retreat which it would become at the end of the nineteenth century. Those eccentrics who managed their own properties shared the existence of their gauchos. Their diet was meat and *mate*. They wore simple clothing suited to wind, rain, dust, and equestrian activity. Their home was a mud hut, or rancho, furnished with a cot made of hides, some ox skulls for chairs, and a few pegs from which to hang the heavy silver spurs and ornate bridles. Twenty or thirty miles separated neighbors, and the charred remains of more than one rancho bore eloquent testimony to raids by marauding Indians. Little wonder then if the average *estanciero* satisfied himself with an infrequent visit to his holdings or an occasional accounting by his foreman.

For most of the rural population this type of economy meant a drifting, squatter existence. The gaucho born on the pampas or the peasant newly arrived from Spain lacked the resources to acquire land. Small units, be they fifty or a thousand acres, dedicated to cattle production would not sustain a man, much less a family. Crops could not be raised on the open range where fences were unknown and cattle and horses roamed at will. Yet, although legal title to the land might be vested in some absentee owner, the rural dweller was able to satisfy his modest needs from the countryside. The seasonal labors of the roundup provided the gaucho with a few silver coins. He could drop his saddle or build a rude rancho almost anywhere. No one would notice or object if he occasionally appropriated a horse for his string, killed a cow for a hunk of roasted meat, or sold a hide to some rural storekeeper.

Despite limitations imposed by the crown and the Lima merchants, the economy and population of the coastal region continued to expand. Any substantial increase in the value of the coast's products depended, however, on discovering some means to use the wasted carcasses of cattle and horses. The *estancia* had introduced some improvements, but utilization of animal fats and meat remained sporadic and inefficient. Not until the beginning of the nineteenth century did the *saladero* provide far-reaching change by facilitating a more thorough exploitation of the whole animal. It was no coincidence that the rise of the *saladero* coincided with Argentina's independence movement. The adjustment toward the coast and the subsequent predominance of the coastal towns owed much to salted meat. The *saladero* also reinforced several of the effects of the cattle hunt and the *estancia:* the development of large landholdings, the lack of crop farming, and the total neglect of livestock breeding and care.

In the eighteenth century salted meat formed a basic part of the diet on slave plantations throughout America as well as on board all sailing ships. It was in the spirit of the economic reforms of Charles III and with an eye to these markets that the crown began to explore the possibility of establishing *saladeros* in the new Viceroyalty of the Río de la Plata. Such an industry required not only cattle but also salt, a monopoly controlled by the Seville merchants. Consequently, military expeditions were sent as far south as present-day Bahía Blanca in an effort to secure supplies of cheap salt from the shores of salt lagoons and lakes. With financial support from the crown the first *saladero* in the Río de la Plata was opened on the Uruguayan coast near Colonia del Sacramento in the 1780's. Other establishments were soon built along the left bank of the estuary, but for a couple of decades drought, Indian raids, and heavy slaughter of cattle for hides discouraged expansion of *saladeros* to Buenos Aires.

The *saladero* introduced a factory system into a rudimentary pastoral economy. It purchased cattle and horses to be processed for the export trade; it made investments in equipment and buildings; it utilized hired hands for specialized tasks; and it controlled commercial outlets. At the height of seasonal activity during the summer months, the meat-salting plant provided aspects of an industrial revolution amid surroundings of blood, gore, and stench.

Long stone or plank tables, large vats of brine, barrels of salt, huge caldrons, and extensive drying and storage areas were sheltered under crude sheds. Nearby corrals held the cattle which had recently been driven in from an *estancia*. Several animals at a time were forced into a small enclosure where one by one they were lassoed, dragged to a chute, and slaughtered by cutting the neck. The hide was deftly removed and taken to a separate section of the plant where it was salted, dried, and treated with arsenic to preserve it from moths and grubs. The lean, stringy meat was peeled off in long strips an inch or two thick. By one process these strips were soaked in brine for a month and then packed in barrels between layers of salt to be used on sailing ships. More common in the Río de la Plata was the preparation of dried salted meat for the slave plantations in Brazil and Cuba. The strips were briefly dipped in brine, spread on a hide, covered lightly with salt and another hide, and the process repeated until the pile reached the height of several feet. When the resultant pressure had removed some of the liquid, the strips were taken outside to dry in the sun on racks. Almost two months of repeated salting, stacking, and drying produced a hard, greyish substance that was easily transported and could last a year without serious deterioration. The remains of the carcass ended up in caldrons of boiling water where the fats were extracted and packed in tubes as grease and tallow. Into this portion of the *saladero* also disappeared sheep and horses whose hides and fats were, at that time, their only commercial assets. Little was wasted. Bones and refuse fed the fires and reappeared to be exported as bone ash. Hoofs yielded gelatin and oils. Even items such as horns and horsehair contributed as much as 5 per cent of the total value of exports.

Although the *saladero* did not appear at Buenos Aires until 1810, its development along the Uruguayan shore intensified the economic shift toward the coastal region. The *estancia,* complemented by the *saladero,* strengthened those groups which demanded access to world markets and expected to exchange the products of the pampas for European manufactures.

The economic expansion of the Río de la Plata placed new strains on the structure of the Spanish Empire at the end of the eighteenth century. Trade with the interior and with Potosí, which now passed through Buenos Aires, remained subject to the crown's mercantilist policies. Spain produced only one-fourth of the goods exported to Buenos Aires. Furthermore, it lacked the shipping necessary to carry this trade or the industries to absorb the coast's production of hides and tallow. But Spain insisted on maintaining its position as middleman between the Río de la Plata and industrial centers of England and the

Continent. Certain merchants at Buenos Aires, mostly Spanish, favored restrictions which enabled them to monopolize this highly lucrative trade. At the same time a new and rapidly growing group of merchants, largely creole in origin, sought some means to liberalize and expand porteño trade. Their efforts were supported by the *estanciero* class, which was also creole.

The breakdown of Spanish control over the various subdivisions of the empire occurred at different times, with different emphases, and for different reasons. In the Río de la Plata, creole irritation at the ineffectiveness of the Spanish commercial and political structure, combined with the desire to exchange local products directly for manufactured goods from England and the Continent, led first to petitions for greater freedom in international trade, then to establishment of local autonomy, and finally to a major struggle for independence.

Renewed dynastic struggles in Europe sharpened the demands for local autonomy and free access to world markets. Conflicts with France (1793-95) and England (1796-1802, 1804-07), culminating in the Napoleonic invasion and occupation of most of Spain (1808-13), made a mockery of royal control and protection in the Río de la Plata. Hides and fats began to pile up in warehouses, while the pastoral industries stagnated. By 1798 the British Navy had reduced imports and exports at Buenos Aires to one-fourth of the annual average in the early 1790's. A respite from European wars in 1803 brought a sudden spurt in commercial activity, but the benefits were only momentary. The British Navy once more cut communications with Spain and in 1806 and again in 1807 brought veteran regiments to the Río de la Plata to claim Buenos Aires and Montevideo as British entrepôts and possibly as British colonies. Spain's tutelage failed in this moment of crisis. The viceroy fled inland toward Córdoba leaving a French officer serving under Spanish colors to organize the scattered regular troops and creole militia which finally expelled the invaders. Aside from the new-found pride and self-reliance which the creoles acquired from their brief struggle with some of the finest redcoat regulars, the British invasions also had an immediate commercial result. Textiles and hardware flooded Buenos

Aires and Montevideo during the few months of British occupation. Woolen ponchos from the mills of Manchester cost a third of the home-spun Tucumán product; Sheffield knives outsold blades from Toledo; and British merchants paid double the accustomed price for hides and tallow. The suspected advantages of world trade momentarily became reality.

When Napoleon moved his armies into the Iberian peninsula in 1807-08 and occupied Portugal and most of Spain, England suddenly became Spain's ally. British merchants, already in the good graces of the Portuguese government-in-exile at Rio de Janeiro, now embarked on a more subtle and effective conquest of the Río de la Plata, using woolens, cottons, ironware, and china rather than warships and can-nons. The *estancieros* promptly responded. In a famous memorandum in 1809 they set forth their demands for the right to trade with British and Portuguese merchants: "There are truths so self-evident that it in-sults human intelligence to call attention to them. Such is the proposi-tion that this country should freely import the goods which it does not have and cannot produce and export its abundant resources that are be-ing lost for lack of outlets." Confronted with the absolute need for some trade, Spanish authorities began to permit limited commercial exchange while maintaining monopolistic controls and high export duties. In 1810 the dissolution of the interim government in southern Spain temporarily left the overseas empire without a link to the crown. This event provided the creoles at Buenos Aires with an opportunity to break with Spain's commercial monopoly and to assume local direction of their affairs. During four agitated days in May 1810, while merchants, *estancieros*, dignitaries, officers, clerks, gauchos, servants, and soldiers mingled in the muddy streets of Buenos Aires, the viceroy and a con-servative *cabildo* struggled to maintain the viceregal structure. Then on May 25, threatened by creole militiamen assembled in the town's main plaza (now the Plaza de Mayo) and pressured by the leading creole citizenry, they surrendered their authority to a creole junta—to rule in the name of the Spanish crown. As yet this was not openly an inde-pendence movement. The creoles had proclaimed allegiance to the crown and still considered themselves members of the Spanish family. Subsequent acts by the junta demonstrated, however, that the creoles intended to control local government and economic development. May 25, therefore, symbolized separation from the empire, although Argentines also celebrate a second independence day, the date of the official declaration of independence by a congress meeting at Tucumán on July 9, 1816.

The opening of Buenos Aires to world trade climaxed the creole seizure of power in 1810. This logical development accentuated Argentine orientation toward markets that could absorb the products of the pampas in return for manufactured goods and food supplies. It also meant the economic eclipse of crop farming and local industries in the interior, thus laying the basis for a century-long struggle between the littoral, centered on Buenos Aires, and the provinces of the interior. The coast's prosperity depended on production of raw materials. With its rudimentary grazing economy, the coast could offer nothing to the interior. And the interior, shorn of the empire's artificial supports and the markets of Upper Peru and isolated by distance and technological backwardness, had little to offer the coast. The Industrial Revolution gave England, Europe, and the United States a head start in products, standards, transportation, and prices. In the coastal zones not only British textiles and ironware but also North American lumber and flour, French brandy and carpets, and Brazilian sugar and tobacco soon displaced the inferior and high-priced products from Córdoba, Tucumán, Salta, and Mendoza. The oxcart proved unable to compete with the sailing ship or, subsequently, with the steamship. Indeed, at times it seemed largely accidental that two such disparate halves remained linked together as one country.

It was the establishment of the *saladero* at Buenos Aires and at river ports along the Uruguay and Paraná that insured the supremacy of the coast. As mentioned above, the first Uruguayan meat-salting plants were built in the 1780's. In 1810 two Englishmen founded the first one in Argentina at Buenos Aires. Other establishments along the Riachuelo at the southern edge of the city of Buenos Aires and along the Uruguay's right bank in Entre Ríos soon followed. The 1820's saw still larger investments of local capital in the *saladeros* and an increase in political and financial favors to these highly profitable enterprises.

The *saladero*'s predominant role in Argentina's early formation can best be appreciated through the figure of Juan Manuel de Rosas, for nearly two decades the country's absolute ruler. Although, like the gaucho, the reality of Rosas has been obscured by violent debates between panegyrists and detractors, he symbolized the rise to power of the coastal cattle interests. He took no part in the creole seizure of local government at Buenos Aires in 1810 or in the subsequent struggle for independence, but he, and the *estanciero* group in general, used independence and international trade to build up their wealth and influence. In 1815, as a young man in his twenties, he formed a partnership with two colleagues to establish a *saladero* several miles south of the city of Buenos Aires. In two years he tripled his investment. Within another decade this partnership captured the balance of economic power at Buenos Aires. Control of cattle and of ports led to political control. By such means Rosas achieved the governorship of Buenos Aires and by 1835 became *de facto* ruler of Argentina.

What happened to Argentina during this man's rise to power? The creole seizure of political power at Buenos Aires in 1810 created many strange bedfellows. Gone was royal supervision of the increasingly complex forces at work throughout the Argentine area. The creoles were now on their own. The coast demanded free trade; the interior desired protection. The porteños wanted to maintain Buenos Aires' domination over the viceregal area; the interior towns insisted on local autonomy. Conservative elements at Buenos Aires accepted the coast's rude pastoral economy as it was and sought increased profits merely by an expansion of the *estancia* and *saladero*. Liberal statesmen, meanwhile, looked to crop farming, immigration, and technology to transform and modernize the country. During the 1810's a bewildering succession of juntas, triumvirates, congresses, and directories reflected this conflict of ideas and interests at Buenos Aires. Farther afield, Paraguay, Uruguay, and Upper Peru escaped from the porteño orbit. But Argentina's interior towns, after winning their freedom from Spain, possessed no outlet to the world except through Buenos Aires. At first they tried to control the authority emerging in Buenos Aires. Failing in that, they struggled unsuccessfully to liberate themselves from porteño domination.

In this chaotic situation the landowning and cattle interests of the coast constituted the one powerful group which had consolidated its wealth and position by means of independence and world trade. The introduction of the *saladero* increased the yearly slaughter of cattle for salted meat from 7,000 head in the 1790's, to 60,000 in 1822, and to 350,000 by 1827. In the decade following 1810 the revenues from the annual export of a million-odd hides had tripled. Therefore, rather than propose reform, this group favored stability and continuation of those traditions that reinforced its prestige and power: further expansion of large landholdings; rejection of immigrants, crops, livestock, or any variation from the formula of animals and land; access to and control of ports and commerce; creation of rural peons from the vagabond gaucho element; and subordination of government to its control.

This cattle civilization, of which Rosas was the outstanding proponent, soon received the support of creole governments at Buenos Aires. Restrictions limited shipping to the ports of Buenos Aires and Ensenada (twenty-five miles south of Buenos Aires on the estuary). An official expedition established a port at the mouth of the Río Negro to secure cheap, high quality salt from Patagonia—a monopoly immediately taken over by Rosas. Since drifting rural squatters could no longer be tolerated in an economy where the value of cattle was increasing, any gaucho who did not have legitimate employment on some *estancia* was subject to imprisonment for vagrancy and to a five-year sentence with a frontier detachment. Rosas went one step further than this in subjecting the gaucho to the status of a peon by deliberately cultivating the loyalty of the rural lower class. In his own words: "You well know the attitude of the have-nots against the wealthy and powerful. I have always considered it very important to acquire an influence over the poor in order to control and direct them; and at great cost in effort, comfort, and money, I have made myself into a gaucho like them, to speak as they do, to protect them, to become their advocate, and to support their interests." Such efforts won followers, and from his own peons, uni-

formed in scarlet ponchos and intensely loyal to their master, Rosas provided one of Buenos Aires' two cavalry regiments.

The influence of the cattlemen appeared most clearly in the matter
of landownership, where there existed fundamental conflict between
the interests of a grazing economy and those of crop farming. Certain
leaders in the movement of 1810 had proclaimed: "Either we create a
sound basis for settlement and cultivation of the land or we face disintegration." Far-sighted projects repeatedly provided for the survey and
subdivision of lands surrounding Buenos Aires, the grant of small lots
to immigrants, and the duty-free import of seeds and agricultural implements. One of the principal instigators of such measures was Bernardino
Rivadavia, for a brief moment in the 1820's president of Argentina.
Rather than adapt to the existing conditions, he hoped to submerge the
gaucho with industrious European peasants, to cover the grasslands
with crops, and to create a democracy of small landholders. In triumvirates, congresses, ministries, and finally during his presidency of an
Argentine confederation in 1826-27, he fought a losing battle with the
estancia-saladero interests. His basic program sought to encourage small
farms on the pampas by means of long-term leases of public lands to
colonists. Lower rents favored crop farming over grazing. But colonists
and crop farmers were not forthcoming. The public lands continued to
be used for grazing and the leases accumulated in the hands of a few
cattlemen. With the overthrow of Rivadavia, title to these public lands
passed from the state to private owners: the balance sheet of the 1820's
transferred twenty-one million acres of public domain to five hundred
individuals. Once firmly in control of the porteño political structure,
Rosas further accentuated this concentration of landownership by sales
and outright donations, by expanding the western and southern frontier
against the Indians (1833), and by confiscating holdings of political
opponents. He himself magnanimously turned down the huge island of
Choele-Choel in the Río Negro valley, which was offered to him by the
Buenos Aires legislature after his Indian campaign, and accepted instead four hundred thousand acres situated within sixty miles of
Buenos Aires.

For several years in the 1820's and 1830's the *estancia* and *saladero*

reigned supreme. The few immigrant colonies established by Rivadavia
soon disappeared, and further agrarian immigration ceased. Because
grazing lands extended to the very doors of Buenos Aires, Argentina
began to import flour from the United States and Chile. The colonial
estancia grew ever larger since land was cheap for those in political
favor and the system of exploitation rewarded volume alone and provided no incentive for improving pasturage, care, or breeding. Profits
were high, for the fiscal structure levied the same tax on the owner of
thirty thousand cattle as on a rural storekeeper. At the same time Rosas,
representative of these cattle interests, gradually enlarged his political
realm beyond Buenos Aires and became the spokesman for other
provinces. Through the customhouse at Buenos Aires flowed the bulk
of the country's imports and exports, leaving in Rosas' hands the revenues secured from customs duties. Along with the purse strings came
direction of fiscal policy. Exports of hides and salted meat and imports
of consumer goods paid minimal duties, thus favoring the coast and
contributing to the ruin of the interior's industries and agriculture. As
one Córdoba politician concluded: "Buenos Aires leaves us no alternative but to become cattlemen and shepherds." Personal alliances with
provincial governors supplemented Rosas' control of the port and enabled him to prevent the formation of any congress or constitution
which might give other areas or groups a voice in their economic and
political destinies.

The landowners' principal concerns continued to be order and stability. The conservative elements relied on Rosas to maintain their way
of life, and the lower class worshiped him. In 1835 the legislature of
Buenos Aires, seconded by a plebiscite, begged Rosas to resume the
governorship and entrusted him with "supreme and absolute powers."
Rosas maintained order, but at the cost of periodic terror and constant
repression. Two secret societies bolstered his rule. One, the *Mazorca*,
drawn from the city mob, terrorized his enemies by murder and van-
dalism. The other represented the porteño elite—merchants, *estancieros*,
military officers, and churchmen—who saw in Rosas the guarantees for
their own wealth and security. But systematic persecution of political
enemies, serious internal revolts in the early 1840's, a twelve-year cam-

paign to crush opposition at Montevideo (1839-51), and French and English blockades of Buenos Aires (1838-40, 1845-48), placed economic as well as political strains on the Rosas regime.

Although able to destroy or exile his opposition and to withstand Brazilian, Uruguayan, French, and English threats or reprisals, Rosas could not simultaneously guarantee the continued expansion of a rudimentary cattle economy. The *estancia* and *saladero* threatened Argentina with economic stagnation. Despite apparent prosperity, they limited the coast to a land of ports, *estancias*, and animals, while economically destroying the interior. The export of hides to Europe and salted meat to Brazil and Cuba could not be expanded indefinitely, yet as a group these cattlemen resisted innovation and change. Symbolic of the times was the fate of Argentina's first flock of rare Angora sheep: they were made into saddle blankets by a passing contingent of troops. The sporadic imports of Shorthorn and Hereford bulls served no purpose when *saladeros* demanded lean, sinewy meat. Wire fencing made its appearance in the 1840's, but only to protect *estancia* headquarters against wandering herds of cattle. The havoc wrought on the countryside and on export trade by civil wars and blockades was reflected in the financial crises of 1838-40 and 1846-48. Further damage ensued as many of Argentina's most progressive leaders sought refuge abroad, across the estuary in Montevideo or across the Andes in Santiago.

Although Buenos Aires attempted to impose its economic domination on all of Argentina, the reaction against Rosas in 1851-52 came not from the declining interior but rather from the spread of the *estancia* and *saladero* to Entre Ríos and to other areas of the coastal region. In the 1840's Anglo-French blockades of Buenos Aires brought merchant ships to river ports along the Uruguay and introduced Entre Ríos to the advantages of direct trade with Europe. With the termination of the blockades, the Río de la Plata system reverted to its status as an interior waterway, and Buenos Aires resumed its position as Argentina's only port. The impact on Entre Ríos encouraged that province to attack the porteño monopoly. Justo José de Urquiza, governor of Entre Ríos as well as the province's leading *estanciero* and for a decade Rosas' principal field commander, united with the besieged forces in Monte-

video, the Brazilian Navy, and the porteño exiles. Within a year Rosas
was defeated and forced to flee to asylum in England.

Since the men who overthrew Rosas, especially the exiles, also wrote
the history of his regime, Rosas has emerged in the lurid colors of a
tyrant and the period is pictured as Argentina's Dark Ages. At the distance of more than a century, an impartial version might judge Rosas
and his conservative *estanciero* supporters as men of their times, lacking Rivadavia's vision and foresight but nevertheless imposing a degree
of order and unity on the scattered Spanish towns of the Argentine
area. Buenos Aires' rural economy failed to foster immigration, diversified agriculture, industry, or any of the progressive measures deemed
unnecessary to its system of land and animals. But with its resources it
held together the core of the viceregal area and created the basis for
Argentine nationhood. Perhaps the fundamental accusation against the
Rosas era was that it provided and permitted little imagination or innovation. The remaining twenty-five years of Rosas' life in exile on a
farm near Southampton, England, best characterized the mentality of
this era. Surrounded by the most advanced techniques of intensive
agriculture in the world, Rosas wasted a fortune trying to reproduce
on one hundred and fifty acres the environment and conditions he had
known on his estates of half a million acres. Argentina might owe its
existence as a national unit to Rosas and to the Buenos Aires cattle
economy, but this heritage also prolonged large landholdings and authoritarian measures.

The fall of Rosas coincided with the first significant adjustment of
the coast's economy away from the cattle hunt, *estancia,* and *saladero.*
The *saladero* did not disappear, but its period of expansion had ended.
Sheep raising, having acquired its initial impetus during the Rosas
period, now became one of the coast's principal activities. Sheep raising
also stimulated important changes: increased immigration and rural
population, further expansion into the pampas, and introduction of
rudimentary techniques of livestock care.

During the colonial period, sheep raising had centered on the Andean region and Córdoba. But Spain's pre-eminence in sheep raising

and its monopoly of the famous Merino breed limited Argentine flocks to inferior Syrian or Pyrenean strains, and crown restrictions on the export of wool prevented expansion beyond the satisfaction of local needs. Greater commercial freedom in the late eighteenth century did little to counteract lack of capital and technology, and the numerous civil wars in the interior during the early nineteenth century further hampered sheep raising.

Around Buenos Aires the *estancia-saladero* economy at first had little use for sheep. In the decades following 1810 small flocks of Merinos from Germany, Spain, and France as well as Southdowns from England appeared in the coastal region. After the Anglo–Buenos Aires commercial treaty of 1825, Irish, Scottish, and English immigrants began to introduce new techniques, experienced labor, and capital. These developments only slightly improved native breeds, for, as one English traveler in the 1840's concluded, Argentine sheep were "very inferior; the quality and quantity of their wool, which is of all colours, being very coarse; they are also ill-shaped, long-legged, lank-bodied, and very difficult to fatten; in a word, they are a degenerate race, the consequence of total neglect." Yet wool exports increased significantly in the 1830's until they registered 7 per cent of the value of total exports. The number of sheep in the coastal zone rose from a quarter of a million in 1810 to five million by 1850, of which four million were in the province of Buenos Aires.

In the decades after 1850 sheep raising dominated the porteño economy in the same fashion that the *saladero* had after 1810. Wool exports rose sharply from an average of 6,000 tons annually in the 1840's to 11,000 in the 1850's, 50,000 in the 1860's, 80,000 in the 1870's, and 120,000 in the 1880's. By the latter decade wool contributed 50 to 60 per cent of the value of Argentina's exports. The province of Buenos Aires, which in 1810 had only a quarter of a million of the three million sheep in Argentina, by 1875 had forty-six million of the country's fifty-eight million animals. The despised animal, whose price even in the 1840's was hardly equivalent to that of an egg, had finally become valuable.

The spread of the Industrial Revolution to the Continent and the increased numbers of carpet and weaving factories in Belgium and

France created apparently inexhaustible demands for sheep's tallow and coarse wool. In Buenos Aires, as far west as the Río Salado, cattle had grazed or trampled down tough native perennials. In their place sprang up annuals—clovers, thistles, Indian barley, foxtail, and mustard, often accidentally imported by the Spanish. This refinement of the grasslands by cattle enabled sheep to graze on the pampas and turned the area around the port of Buenos Aires into a vast sheepwalk. Twenty thousand acres, which before had carried ten thousand cattle and ten gauchos, now supported forty-five thousand sheep and thirty shepherds. The more intensive use of the land and its consequent rise in value soon pushed cattle west and south toward the frontier, where they repeated their refining process on new and cheaper grasslands. Many landowners whose cattle were becoming less profitable turned their vast *estancias* over to Irish, Basque, and Scottish herders. These shepherds, operating on a shares system which rewarded them with one-third to one-half of the flock's increase and fleece, not only rapidly multiplied numbers but also improved the quality of native stock. Imports of French Merinos (Rambouillets) led to longer fibers, heavier fleeces, and better yields of tallow. Expansion directly reflected the effects of breeding, dipping for scab, shelter for animals during storms, and experienced care by laborers who shared in the profits.

The pampas began to attract a population different from that of the nomadic gaucho or *estancia* peon. Sheep moved about far less than cattle. A normal flock of fifteen hundred sheep pastured on six hundred acres in the well-watered area between the Paraná and Salado rivers. Consequently, the shepherd could settle on the land, build his mud hut, and raise a family. Those with ability, strong backs, and a certain amount of luck used the shares system to become independent sheep farmers within three to four years, thus laying the foundations for some of modern Argentina's largest fortunes and most aristocratic families. Few of mestizo or Latin origins entered this occupation, which so totally lacked the color and excitement running through the gaucho's daily existence. But Irish and Basque immigrants, hard workers inured to privation, readily accepted the heavy seasonal labors of lambing, shearing, and dipping. For the rest of the year monotony dominated their lives. Yet mutton cooked over a smoldering fire of dried sheep dung was preferable to starving in Ireland. The hope, and frequently the realization, of landownership provided stimulus for continued immigration and further expansion of sheep raising. An estimated four thousand Irish shepherds in the province of Buenos Aires at the time of the fall of Rosas increased to thirty-five thousand by the 1870's, and their labors contributed more than half of Argentina's wool exports.

The flow of immigrants and capital into sheep raising had other farreaching effects on the Buenos Aires rural economy. During the 1850's and 1860's civil strife and Argentine involvement in the costly Paraguayan War (1865-70) resulted in the breakdown of frontier defenses against the Indians. But the pressure of sheep continued to force cattle westward and southward, requiring some protection of frontier lands. Araucanian plunderers repeatedly swept through *estancias* in the region of Azul and Tandil in southern Buenos Aires and drove off the cattle to Chilean markets. During the 1870's the minister of war attempted to consolidate a permanent line of small outposts running along Buenos Aires' present western boundary. The anchor for this defensive system was a ditch, ten feet wide, six feet deep, and two hundred and forty miles long. But still the Indians came. Not until a military campaign (1879-80) destroyed the Araucanian menace at its roots in Patagonia was rural life secure. Then, at one stroke, one hundred and fifty thousand square miles—a hundred million acres—were added to the grazing kingdom.

Sheep raising encouraged not only conquest of new lands but also better use of the old. Remote *estancias* on the frontier depended more and more on middlemen near the coast who took semi-tamed cattle and fattened them for the *saladero* or for local consumption. In order to survive economically, cattle *estancias* located within the sheep zone began to experiment with wells to provide a constant water supply and with fencing for better utilization of grasslands. Although the open range died only when cattle acquired new value from the frozen meat trade at the end of the nineteenth century, cattlemen and sheepmen began to use brittle iron strands and then flexible steel wire to enclose animals rather than merely to keep them away from *estancia* headquarters. In 1854 an entire *estancia* was for the first time enclosed by wire fencing. By the 1880's fences were commonplace on large holdings as well as on small farms. Fencing and more intensive use of land also permitted crop farming to regain a foothold around Buenos Aires and in zones as far west as Chivilcoy and north toward Pergamino. Gradually cultivation of the soil began to supplement grazing in Buenos Aires and to provide the alfalfa pastures on which the pampas' agricultural prosperity would be built.

Sheep similarly played a vital role in attracting foreign capital, especially British, to the pampas, for investment not only in land but also in railroads and packing plants. The first major line, the Central Argentine (today the Mitre), was completed in 1870 from Rosario to Córdoba. Modern technology thus replaced the oxcart along the traditional trade route to the interior. By 1876 this railroad (the northern section today known as the Belgrano) was extended to Tucumán, by 1900 to Jujuy. But the most significant railroad expansion occurred during the 1880's in the sheep zones of Buenos Aires, where British investors built and managed three major systems centered on the port— the Great Southern (today the Roca), the Western (or Sarmiento), and the Pacific (or San Martín). The introduction and development of meat packing was also influenced by sheep raising. British packing interests, already at work on the transport of mutton from Australia, moved onto the Argentine scene in the 1880's. Due to serious mechanical limitations, plants at Buenos Aires soon discovered they could handle mutton better than the larger beef carcasses, and for almost two decades frozen meat shipments to Europe expanded primarily on the basis of mutton consumption.

The porteño sheep economy, therefore, marked the transition from the colonial *estancia* and *saladero* to the modern *estancia* that emerged on the coast in the late nineteenth century. Sheep attracted immigrants and capital, encouraged the conquest and settlement of the pampas, and provided a favorable environment for breeding, crops, railroads, and packing plants—in a word, conditions necessary for Argentine beef and wheat supremacy in the twentieth century. In this period of transition much of old Argentina faded and disappeared. The influx of Irish and Basques was swelled by British engineers and managers, French shopkeepers, Italian and Swiss peasants, German laborers, and Jewish refugees—totally transforming the Spanish-mestizo origins of the population. The Indian, pushed off the pampas, ceased to figure in coastal Argentina. The gaucho, hemmed in by fences, troops, and immigrants, continued to evolve into a rural peon, leaving only a legend behind him.

But certain fundamental factors persisted. A grazing economy continued to dominate Buenos Aires. Argentina produced wool, hides, and tallow for Europe and salted meat for Brazil and in return imported almost all manufactured items and much of its food supply. Immigrants concentrated in the towns and contributed to urban growth, particularly of Buenos Aires. Large landholdings remained the rule. New owners might appear, aided by profits or political advantage, but the extensive system of exploitation endured. Thus the Spanish towns became the provincial capitals of nineteenth-century Argentina, and merchants and landowners continued to dominate the economy, politics, and society.

Chapter 4 • From Colony to Nation

It took seventy years for Argentina to coalesce as a political unit. Depending on political philosophies, Argentines can date their nationhood anywhere from the assertion of autonomy in 1810 and the declaration of independence in 1816, through the abortive constitutions of 1819 and 1826, the federal pact between the coastal provinces of 1831, the first and still ruling national Constitution of 1853, the first constitutional government of all the provinces in 1862, up to the federalization of Buenos Aires in 1880. The political formation of Argentina reflected the increasing importance of the coast, dramatized in the late eighteenth century by the creation of the Viceroyalty at Buenos Aires and in the early nineteenth century by the porteño movement toward independence. The similar origins of the scattered Spanish towns, the acceptance of Spanish institutions, and the sense of belonging to a Spanish world obscured conflicts of interest. Once this Spanish structure had cracked, the coast and the interior, the towns and the countryside steadily drew apart from each other, not only in economic interests but also in way of life, customs, and culture. In political terms the principal schism of the early national period was between centralists (*unitarios*) and autonomists (*federales*), or between the advocates of strong central government and the supporters of a loose confederation of provinces. Often the centralists were porteños, while the autonomists tended to have rural interests and to come from the provinces. But political loyalties did not always follow such regional divisions, and political mantles were frequently assumed for convenience or strength. To cite a striking example, Rosas as governor of Buenos Aires sought and secured porteño hegemony of Argentina, but under the guise of autonomist colors. Ultimately, however, Buenos Aires and the urban centers formed the basis for a strong national authority, while both the interior and the countryside struggled unsuccessfully to maintain their local freedoms.

Frictions between creole and Spaniard, between landowner and royal official, between advocates of international trade and supporters of Spanish mercantilism concentrated the principal pressure for independence in the Río de la Plata at Buenos Aires. Here Spanish political and commercial control had appeared most clearly. As a result, the creoles who seized control of local government while proclaiming loyalty to the deposed Spanish monarch did so with the determination to prevent any renewal of absolute and autocratic peninsular rule. Their ambition was to perpetuate the Viceroyalty of the Río de la Plata as a unit under their own control. They sought to secure the allegiance of the vaguely defined frontier zone which would later become the Republic of Uruguay even though it meant attacking royal officers across the estuary at Montevideo. They ordered a column of troops northward toward Asunción to win that area for Buenos Aires. Another force took the inland route of Córdoba, Tucumán, and Salta to confront royalist armies sent from the Viceroyalty of Peru.

These porteño ambitions soon met resistance from the outlying areas of the Viceroyalty. The towns in this southern portion of the Spanish Empire had, by necessity, developed considerable self-reliance and independence. For two centuries they remained stepchildren of the crown, largely unnoticed and certainly unprotected. Although there was considerable trade between urban centers, and although, in political, religious, and legal matters, the citizens looked to some higher crown representative in Tucumán, Asunción, Córdoba, or Buenos Aires, they had to rely on themselves for the bulk of their foodstuffs, for defense against Indian attacks, or for immediate municipal decisions. As a result each town and surrounding rural district had its influential creole families who provided continuity and leadership and supplemented the royal governor or judge temporarily assigned to the area. These local leaders accepted allegiance to the remote and frequently ineffectual Spanish crown, but they were much less willing to transfer such allegiance to upstart creoles in Buenos Aires.

At Montevideo and Asunción porteño hopes were completely frustrated. Shortly after winning independence from Spain, the left bank of the estuary passed under Brazilian control. A renewed campaign of liberation launched from Buenos Aires involved the porteños in a war with Brazil (1825-28). In 1828, under British pressure, Uruguay was established as a buffer state between Argentina and Brazil, but civil wars and international rivalries continued to dominate much of its nineteenth-century development. Farther to the north, Paraguay declared its independence of both porteño and Spanish control in 1811 and for half a century successfully isolated itself from the turmoil of Río de la Plata politics.

The desire for local autonomy was as strong in the inland towns as in Paraguay or Uruguay. Following Buenos Aires' example and occasionally with porteño assistance, creoles from Santa Fe to Mendoza and from Córdoba to Jujuy assumed control over local municipal governments during 1810. Proximity to the centers of Spanish power at Lima and Potosí, however, soon placed Argentina's Andean region in the forefront of the independence struggle. Royal officials at Lima, unshaken by rebellion, viewed the several outbreaks around the continent as mutinies to be summarily and drastically quelled. The end of the Napoleonic ventures in Europe and the return in 1814 of the deposed Ferdinand VII to the Spanish throne reinforced this attitude. The demand for autonomy prompted no ideas of reform in royal administration but rather ruthless repression. For the moment, therefore, royalist columns from Upper Peru presented a far greater threat to local autonomy than any amount of porteño ambition, and the common struggle against Spain imposed a degree of unity on the scattered towns. After extensive fighting, porteño troops aided by local citizenry halted the royal reconquest in the northwest. In 1816 at Tucumán a congress of provincial representatives signed a declaration of independence. At Mendoza, José de San Martín, recently placed in command of porteño forces in the west, labored desperately to organize the army that would strike at the core of Spanish power—first across the Andes to Santiago and then by sea to Lima itself.

The outline, if not the reality, of Argentina thus took shape during a decade of struggles for independence from Spain. Eastward the areas surrounding Asunción and Montevideo went their separate ways, while prolonged Spanish occupation of Upper Peru provided the basis of a separate Bolivia. The threat of Spanish reconquest, however, forced the remaining towns of the Viceroyalty to co-operate for their common defense. The first faltering step toward nationhood had been taken.

During the first half of the nineteenth century the figure of the local strong man, or *caudillo*,* dominated the Argentine political scene. The elimination of royal control and the failure, despite porteño ambitions, to create any central authority resulted in fourteen autonomous provinces based largely on colonial municipalities. In this situation, the caudillo emerged as the principal element of local order and stability. Although he postponed political unification, he saved Argentina from total anarchy.

He was usually a landowner and a descendant of some powerful creole family. In the interior and on the coast, he gathered his gauchos and peons into irregular but effective cavalry forces. With this military power and through his economic and social influence, he became the government, ruling either directly or through puppets. Those with land and capital sought security in his shadow. The rapidly growing lower classes looked to him for protection. His word was law; his power absolute. The caudillo was also an eminently practical man. He recog-

* The *caudillo* originated in the turmoil of the independence period, although subsequently the meaning was extended to include any leader who captures the imagination and support of the masses.

nized or sensed the limitations of the moment: the small number of educated, wealthy landowners and merchants in proportion to the mass
of the rural and urban lower classes; the distances separating towns and
the sparseness of the population itself; the absence of capital or immigrants; the decline of crop raising and small industries in favor of the
livestock exports of the coast. He succeeded, therefore, where famous
but less realistic leaders failed. San Martín, the architect of Argentine
independence, chose self-imposed exile in France. Rivadavia saw his
schemes crumble before the practical designs of Rosas. The brilliant
military strategist José María Paz carried the torch of centralism
through the interior during the 1830's and 1840's without once achieving the reform or overthrow of the caudillos.

Yet, despite their insistence on local autonomy, the caudillos kept
alive the vague idea of an Argentine area. Ever resistant to the imposi-
tion of a central government, they nevertheless recognized the desirability of co-operation on matters of foreign relations and defense. The
danger, from the provincial and caudillo viewpoint, was that such joint
efforts might be dominated by porteños and be used to implement a
centralist regime controlled from the city of Buenos Aires. The delegates who came from the interior towns to join the 1810 junta and the
representatives to the Assembly of 1813 gave reality to these fears by
supporting porteño supremacy. The Tucumán congress which drafted
the 1816 declaration of independence subsequently moved to Buenos
Aires, only to produce the centralist Constitution of 1819 and to earn
the unanimous repudiation of the provinces. A similar congress at
Buenos Aires drafted the Constitution of 1826 and elevated Rivadavia
to the presidency of the United Provinces of the Río de la Plata, once
more causing violent caudillo reaction. It was little wonder that the
caudillos preferred alliance systems and personal contacts to any organized government. Under the influence of Rosas this autonomist sentiment led to the Federal Pact of 1831 between the coastal provinces—
Buenos Aires, Entre Ríos, Santa Fe, and, later, Corrientes. In addition
to an alliance, its articles provided for periodic meetings of the four
governors or their representatives and vested in the governor of Buenos

Aires the power to represent the provinces in international and financial matters.

These political adjustments resulted from the steady shift of prosperity, population, and resources toward the coast. Supplementing the rise of the pastoral economy of Buenos Aires was the concentration of capital, immigrants, and shipping at Argentina's one point of contact with the nineteenth-century world, and the parallel isolation and decline of the interior.

The interior's economy and society rested on a structure of the past: on the mining wealth of Upper Peru which had started to decline in the eighteenth century; on the closed mercantilist system which even the crown had begun to abandon; on artisan, crop-farming, and livestock industries that depended on internal markets; on servile, obedient masses supervised and ruled by a creole aristocracy. Independence only aggravated the problems of the interior. The disruption of trade with Upper Peru closed the major market for textiles, foodstuffs, and mules and reduced the flow of silver bullion, thus disorganizing the interior's commercial and monetary system. At the same time, requisitions of animals, levies of men, and seizures of property wreaked havoc with crops, livestock, and crafts. More than a decade of struggles with royalist forces, followed by several decades of intermittent civil war, destroyed much of the old social order. Capital gradually abandoned industry and commerce for more secure investments in land, thereby contributing to the growth of large holdings. Among the lower classes, the constant insecurity and lack of employment resulted in the disintegration of the family unit and the disappearance of trained, disciplined laborers. Landless, nomadic masses increasingly replaced the industrious peons and skilled artisans. Many formerly prosperous areas now fell back on the rudimentary economy which had existed in seventeenth-century Buenos Aires. The gaucho and the colonial *estancia* invaded the Andean region, reinforcing the conditions for caudillo rule.

As previously indicated, independence also accentuated the isolation of the interior's economy. Once the unity of Spain's mercantilist struc-

ture broke down, freight costs by oxcart and the taxes levied by autonomous provinces became expensive in comparison with ocean
freight from European factories or North American forests and farms.
The centers of the interior found themselves at the end of an extended
and costly trade route rather than in the middle of an active commerce.
In the absence of inland waterways and until the large-scale expansion
of railroads in the 1880's, the oxcart transported the bulky raw materials demanded by European industry. Mounted on two enormous
wheels and drawn by a team of six bullocks, this vehicle carried two
tons of merchandise but took three or four months for the trip between
Buenos Aires and Salta. The costs were astronomical when compared
with charges for ocean freight. By the 1830's it cost thirteen times as
much to move a ton of goods from Salta to Buenos Aires as to move
it from Liverpool to Buenos Aires. Thus freight costs alone prevented
most of the interior's products from reaching the coast on competitive
terms with overseas imports. Transport costs, for example, ate up more
than half of the selling price of Mendoza's wines in Buenos Aires. As
for exports, only dry hides, wool, and horsehair could reach the coast
at a competitive cost.

Charges by destitute provincial governments added to the burden
of transport costs and completed the interior's isolation. Commercial
exchange provided virtually the only source of revenue, since taxes on
land were negligible and income taxes were unknown. In the absence
of a central authority, each autonomous caudillo or governor levied
import, export, transit, stamp, and license taxes. Since most trade flowed
through Buenos Aires, that province collected the largest revenues. As
one moved away from the port, the number of tax barriers increased,
with resultant higher costs to consumers and lower profits for producers. Hides from Salta, ponchos from Tucumán, or wines from
Mendoza had to pass through several separate provincial customhouses
before reaching Buenos Aires, and European goods destined for the interior had to pass the same barriers. Yet in remote provinces these
charges provided only meager revenues. The provincial income of
Tucumán was less than a thousandth part of that of Buenos Aires, and
Jujuy's was almost nonexistent.

If the breakup of the Spanish Empire accentuated the interior's decline and isolation, it encouraged the continued expansion of Argentina's coastal region. Under the empire the port of Buenos Aires fulfilled limited though important functions as trade terminus, bastion against the Portuguese, and administrative capital. With independence it became the center of commercial exchange between the pampas and European industries. It absorbed almost all investment, talents, technology, and immigrants that reached Argentine shores. It was the interior's only point of contact with the outside world. From Buenos Aires emanated not only the initiative for independence but also most of the subsequent leadership, whether of San Martín's liberating expeditions, Rivadavia's centralist dreams, or Rosas' practical methods of control.

Port though it was, Buenos Aires labored under the handicap of its location until the very end of the nineteenth century. Ironically, the sixteenth-century Spaniards, searching for an anchorage for their tiny ships, elected one of the poorest sites imaginable in terms of nineteenth-century sailing vessels and steamships. The numerous branches, channels, and islands of the lower Paraná and the shallow, muddy shores of the estuary bore witness to the tremendous volume of silt deposited by this river system. The protecting sand bar which attracted Mendoza's expedition in 1536 indicated the river's tendency to obstruct shipping. The absence of a sheltered basin near the shore was further aggravated by the violent pamperos, which swept off the estuary's low right bank. Garay, nevertheless, also established his settlement here, for the volume of cargoes and the size of ships hardly demanded better facilities. Just as mules carried colonial trade along trails whose precipitousness staggers the modern imagination, so colonial expeditions and shipping had no need to search out good harbor facilities The deep basin across the estuary at Montevideo only subsequently achieved importance as a defense against Portuguese ambitions, while utilization of the desirable harbor at Bahía Blanca far down the Atlantic coast had to await the late-nineteenth-century agricultural development of the pampas.

By the time ships acquired deeper draft and a substantial trade

flowed through the Río de la Plata, population growth and royal administration had reinforced the choice made in the sixteenth century.
Buenos Aires thus became Spain's principal outlet in the South Atlantic. Although Ensenada, twenty-five miles south of Buenos Aires, had
better anchorage, it served only as a supplementary port and never
challenged the predominance of Buenos Aires. Shipping had no choice
but to adapt itself to the difficult conditions at this center of consumption and administration. The transfer of cargo and passengers was accomplished in stages. Ocean vessels anchored in the open roadstead
four to eight miles from the town. Lighters and launches plied between
ships and shallow water, still more than a mile from shore. From there,
high-wheeled carts drawn by horses or oxen brought the frequently
soaked freight and chilled travelers to piers extending from the water's
edge. Despite viceregal projects, ambitious Rivadavian port surveys,
and the construction of two long wharves during the Rosas period, significant improvements were not made until the 1890's when concrete
basins, docks, and dredged channels finally created a modern port out
of the mud banks of Buenos Aires.

Poor harbor facilities, however, never discouraged Buenos Aires' pretensions to commercial supremacy—a supremacy strongly defended by
porteños of all political shades. Throughout the independence struggles and the ensuing caudillo era, Buenos Aires consistently sought to
maintain its control of the Río de la Plata's commerce. Conflict with
Montevideo led to the expulsion of the Spanish, to friction with Uruguayan independence leaders, to war with Brazil, and finally, under
Rosas, to renewed efforts to capture that port (1838-51). Rivadavia
refused to permit free transshipment of goods through Buenos Aires
and insisted that river shipping pay duties to the porteño authorities.
Rosas reinforced this control by occupying and fortifying the island of
Martín García, thus establishing a virtual blockade of river ports along
the Paraná and Uruguay. Such measures found effective support in
economic realities. The volume of Río de la Plata trade warranted only
one sea outlet. Foreign shipping inevitably tended to unload at the
area's major city and to secure return cargoes there. The river ports
which developed with the spread of *saladeros* never absorbed substan-

tial imports. They remained small export centers that sent products to Buenos Aires, or occasionally to Montevideo, for shipment to Brazil and Europe. Only unusual circumstances, such as the blockade of Buenos Aires, brought direct shipments from Europe to these river outposts.

Despite civil wars and Anglo-French blockades, the demand of European and United States factories for hides, tallow, and wool led to an increasing volume of trade through Buenos Aires. Instead of a mere handful of ships anchored in the estuary, it was common by mid-century to see several dozen large schooners. The number of foreign merchantmen arriving at Buenos Aires tripled between the early 1820's and the late 1840's. Sketchy figures on exports suggest that the volume of hides and salted meat tripled between 1837 and 1851, while wool exports increased five times and tallow six times.

Europe's economic expansion in the early nineteenth century not only provided markets and products for Argentina but also brought new influences to Buenos Aires. Immigrants, capital, ideas, and techniques stimulated Buenos Aires while leaving the other provinces virtually untouched.

Only a few Hispanicized foreigners had penetrated the barriers of the Spanish Empire. In the Río de la Plata they entered as traders and merchants and settled at the center of commercial activity, the port. By 1810, aside from the Spanish-born element, there were less than a thousand foreigners among the city's fifty thousand inhabitants. Yet the long-established Portuguese, the newly arrived British, and the scattered Italians and French already possessed a wealth and influence far out of proportion to their numbers. During the ensuing half-century both numbers and influence grew enormously. By the 1850's foreigners comprised 45 per cent of the city's total population of some ninety thousand inhabitants. They supplied the merchants, bankers, and artisans. Cultivation of town garden plots was in their hands. Beyond the city limits, Irish, Scots, and Basques controlled sheep raising. The Italians dominated the river trade, and in towns along the Paraná and Uruguay, Basques, Italians, and French contributed as much as 20 per cent of the population. But the hinterland beyond the coast neither welcomed nor attracted the foreigner, and, save for the shepherd in Buenos Aires, he never left the towns or cities.

Various creole governments after 1810 professed support of European immigration. Obviously the sparsely settled land needed all the talent and muscle that it could secure. Yet decrees could not overcome economic facts, and immigration responded more to realities than to the needs of the country. Despite the absence of statistics, certain observations concerning early immigration can be made. To reach this remote portion of the southern hemisphere, Europeans had to travel twice as far as to the United States, with a consequent increase in expense, inconvenience, and risk. They ventured into an unknown area, for Rio de Janeiro, Montevideo, and Buenos Aires blurred together in Europe's ignorance about these ports so recently liberated from colonial status. The immigrants had only their own courage, capital, and initiative to support them. Beyond hollow words, porteño governments offered them little assistance. The first junta satisfied itself with a decree: "That English, Portuguese, and other foreigners who are not at war with us can freely enter this country; they will enjoy all the rights of citizens and their productive labors will be protected by the government." The chaos of the independence struggles and the rise of caudillos as the area's only element of stability eloquently emphasized the limitations of such guarantees. For a brief period in the 1820's the programs of Rivadavia supported immigration of European peasant families and sought to establish agricultural colonies, to provide land, implements, and food for new arrivals, and to encourage crop farming with long-term leases of public lands. But Rosas, as caudillo and *estanciero,* took the realistic, though shortsighted, view that such projects were beyond the needs and capabilities of the porteño economy. His regime consequently abolished the Immigration Commission and turned over public lands to grazing rather than to farming. Even the rhetoric in favor of immigration ceased—earning for this era an unjust reputation as antiforeign.

A sizable number of Europeans nevertheless reached Buenos Aires during the first half of the nineteenth century, most of them motivated by a thirst for adventure and fortune. Except for the several hundred families who arrived under colonization contracts in the 1820's, almost all possessed resources of their own. Many were younger sons of middle-class or wealthy families. Others were shopkeepers and tradesmen anxious for a new start or herdsmen and farmers who had heard of the opportunities in sheep raising. The great majority of the new arrivals were young men. Wives or sweethearts were occasionally sent for after the man had made good, but until the 1850's few families immigrated. Hardly any immigrants came with the intention of staying: to make a fortune and to return to their homeland was the common dream. Consequently emigration often exceeded immigration, and the ebb and flow of Europeans responded closely to depression or expansion, civil wars or peace, drought or plenty. Manual labor frequently provided the key to success. In the coastal region where the natives, wealthy or poor, considered the use of a shovel, plow, hammer, or trowel beneath their dignity, such work brought handsome wages. One traveler in the 1840's noted that Irishmen digging ditches on *estancias* in southern Buenos Aires received ten to twelve shillings per day—enough to buy a flock of fifteen hundred sheep with three weeks' labor. Wages for servants and construction workers, prices for dairy products and vegetables, profits from making shoes or repairing carriages followed a similar scale.

The Irish sheepherder, the English merchant, the French shopkeeper, the Italian river captain profited enormously. Thousands of their countrymen swelled the porteño population, added talents and labor to increase livestock production, and provided the services and products needed in the major urban center. Hundreds remained, married into creole families, and added their blood and culture to a nation in formation. Although their influence did not revolutionize Argentina, they provided Buenos Aires with a strength far beyond their numbers. The Irish and Basques, who laid the foundations for sheep raising, introduced more intensive use of the land, brought families and settlement to rural areas, and added an important export to porteño trade. At the northern and western edges of the city of Buenos Aires the first extensive use of the pampas' crop potential flourished under the care of foreigners—garden produce of fruits and vegetables and harvests of corn and wheat. The Genoese captains and their immigrant crews who built their own ships and carried most of the trade between river ports facilitated Buenos Aires' role as commercial emporium for the Río de la Plata. As for technical skills, Argentina in the nineteenth century still depended on foreigners as much as in 1607 when several Flemish millers were forcibly detained in Buenos Aires since only they could operate the town's one flour mill. Improvements in the packing of salted meat, processing of leather, and extraction of tallow came from French and English experts. And foreigners owned and operated al- most all machinery and engines, which were usually located in the city of Buenos Aires.

Investments and commerce were also concentrated at the port of Buenos Aires. Argentina had exchanged the tutelage of Spain's admin- istration for that of England's trade. Capital and credit provided the sinews for commercial expansion, and these came largely from London, the investment center of the nineteenth-century world. British com- merce and shipping now succeeded where redcoats had failed. The in- vasions had revealed potential markets and raw materials, and special licenses to English merchants in 1809-10 stimulated trade. Although the British Foreign Office could not, because of England's alliance with Spain, grant official recognition to a rebellious Spanish colony, commercial houses at Liverpool and London were not hindered by such scruples. Even before San Martín was well launched across the Andes, the British community at Buenos Aires was the city's largest and most influential foreign group. Instability momentarily checked further growth, but Rivadavia's plans for progress in the 1820's revived British interest.

Regardless of wrangles over political control or of autonomy versus strong central government, Argentina had to meet the European world in Buenos Aires. Financially the independence struggle was expensive. The Buenos Aires, or Argentine, war debt, largely underwritten by the British community, threatened to destroy the already poor porteño credit. Thus Rivadavia had to deal with British commercial interests on terms that reinforced both British and porteño influence. A private bank at Buenos Aires, created and controlled by local British mer- chants, acquired a monopoly of all banking activities. Baring Brothers, one of London's principal credit houses, made arrangements to loan one million pounds sterling for the consolidation of the public debt and the construction of port works, municipal waterworks, and frontier settlements. (The funds ultimately disappeared into costs of administration and prosecuting the war with Brazil.) As security Rivadavia pledged Argentina's apparently limitless public lands. On the rising wave of optimism other investments were made in mining, immigration, and cattle-raising ventures. Diplomatic recognition went hand in hand with the financial measures. In 1823, following the earlier recognition of the area's independence by Portugal and the United States, England broke away from its colleagues of the Quadruple, or Holy, Alliance by appointing a consul-general at Buenos Aires. Two years later England concluded an important treaty with Buenos Aires that insured British dominance in Argentina for more than a century. The terms not only reinforced England's commercial priority in the Río de la Plata, but they also guaranteed exemption from military service and freedom of religion to all British subjects in Argentina—important advantages in that chaotic and Catholic society.

The results, however, benefited Buenos Aires as well as England. The prosperity of the porteño economy was now linked to the world's major financial power. Despite international repercussions and conflicts among caudillos, the coast continued to develop in close alliance with British capital. Although Rosas might not share Rivadavia's anglomania, he never forgot the alliance. He did little to satisfy British claims for damages suffered during the war with Brazil or in the intermittent civil conflicts, and he repeatedly defaulted on the Baring Loan, but he never refused to recognize these debts. When a United States naval captain forcibly intervened at the Malvinas, or Falkland Islands, in 1831 to support North American sealing and whaling interests, Rosas broke off relations with the United States. But when the British took advantage of the disturbances to seize the islands, Rosas contented himself with vociferous diplomatic notes to the Foreign Office in London.

Later in the same decade the good relations with England brought valuable returns. French irritation at porteño refusals to extend the

privileges of the Anglo-Argentine Treaty of 1825 to the subjects of
Louis Philippe resulted in a French blockade of Buenos Aires and deliberate intervention along both banks of the Río de la Plata to unseat
Rosas (1838-40). Initially, uprisings against Rosas within his own party
at Buenos Aires, campaigns by his centralist enemies at Montevideo
and in the Argentine provinces, and the seizure of Martín García by
French marines forecast success for his opposition. Yet Rosas divided
his enemies and weathered the storm. England refused to accompany
the French in the blockade, and British trade with Argentina hardly
suffered. By 1840 England was able to mediate the difficulties, and
Rosas could assume the mantle of defender of "American independence." Rosas' subsequent efforts to capture Montevideo brought active
British intervention to the Río de la Plata (1845-48), this time reluc-
tantly accompanied by the French. But the effort to guarantee Uruguayan independence and to secure free navigation of the interior
waterways proved far more costly to British commerce than to Rosas,
and British merchants finally forced the Foreign Office to abandon
that venture. Once more Rosas emerged with the laurels of a patriot.

British commerce and investment, therefore, encouraged porteño
ambitions. Foreign interests, citizens, and property—especially British—
benefited from a privileged position at Buenos Aires. While civil wars,
declining markets, and lack of investments and immigrants wracked
the other provinces, Buenos Aires reaped profits from its contacts with
Europe.

Other changes resulted from the increased trade and contact with
Europe. During the eighteenth century, Córdoba far surpassed the viceregal capital in art, education, and religious fervor, and Salta and Tucumán possessed as much of the trappings of an educated society as
Buenos Aires. But the adjustment toward the coast isolated the interior in the past. Scholastic tradition and conservatism dominated the
University of Córdoba. The Church continued to control education
and maintained its influence over society in all the interior towns, for
even the bitter independence struggles could not destroy the customs
and heritage of two and a half centuries. The class structure, tradition,
and obedience instilled by the creole elite remained largely unshaken,

at least until prolonged disorganization and economic decline in the nineteenth century began to take their toll.

Buenos Aires, on the other hand, had always been less conservative. As a prosperous and growing port it now provided an active center for any new ideas reaching Argentina. The philosophy of the Enlightenment, the writings of Locke, Smith, Bentham, Montesquieu, Voltaire, and Rousseau, and the ideals of the American and French revolutions had an indeterminate, but vital, impact on the porteños of 1810. From such inspiration sprang many of the Rivadavian projects: the creation of the University of Buenos Aires in 1821, dedicated to scientific studies and free of Church controls; the formation of a public library, a museum, and various literary, scientific, and charitable societies; the efforts to separate Church and State and to reduce the Church's influence by the suppression of monasteries and convents; and many economic measures which aspired to create a "modern" Argentina. Even after the defeat of Rivadavia's reforms, these ideas continued to flourish at Buenos Aires. In the literary *salons* and among the educated classes, strains of Utopian Socialism, the works of Saint-Simon and Fourier, the latest waltzes or styles from Paris, even momentary excitement over phrenology, reflected an acute awareness of French intellectual currents. The talented and the intelligent from the provinces joined the young intellectuals of the city. These future writers and statesmen of Argentina rallied around the figure of Esteban Echeverría, poet and social reformer recently returned from France, to form the so-called Generation of 1837.

To the Rosas regime, however, these thinkers represented yet another element of unneeded reform and agitation, and gradually this generation slipped abroad or was driven into exile by the restrictions and intimidations of a dictatorship. Financial support was withdrawn from the university and from the elementary school system. Skepticism, scientific inquiry, and criticism languished under threats and censorship. Church influence revived. Rosas, observing the violent reaction of the provinces against Rivadavia's anticlerical measures, established a close union of Church and State, temporarily readmitted the Jesuits expelled under Charles III, and returned to the Church all supervision and support of educational and social services. But even under Rosas, the traditionalist and the man of order, Buenos Aires continued to receive and to mimic French, British, and Italian models in the opera, in clothes, in literary styles, in newspapers, and in painting.

Buenos Aires thus maintained its position as the unique point of contact with Europe. To an aspiring but somewhat retarded Spanish colony, Europe represented the source of goods, capital, immigrants, techniques, and ideas—in a word, the possibility for prosperity. As a port, Buenos Aires, whether under centralists or autonomists, progressed, while the interior stood still. By mid-century the porteños had begun to represent Argentina to the world.

Rebellion by another coastal province against porteño control finally overthrew Rosas in 1852. But Urquiza and the province of Entre Ríos could neither destroy the porteño monopoly nor subject Buenos Aires to a higher authority. Urquiza replaced Rosas' *de facto* rule with the Constitution of 1853, drafted by representatives from the provinces, and created a confederation modeled on the United States federal system. Buenos Aires refused to join this government, and during the ensuing decade of intermittent economic and political struggle, the loose confederation of thirteen provinces proved no match for the porteños. Finally when another governor of Buenos Aires, Bartolomé Mitre, achieved the Argentine presidency in 1862, that recalcitrant and powerful province joined a central government. Yet, since the controls which Buenos Aires could exert over this constitutional government were not those it had enjoyed under Rosas' rule of Argentina, the city refused to surrender itself as the permanent seat of the national government. During two more administrations, presidents and congresses ruled from Buenos Aires, but as guests of the provincial government. Only in 1880 did the ultimate step to nationhood occur: the national authorities, after several days of fighting, seized the city and forced the provincial government to abandon Buenos Aires and to build its own capital at La Plata.

The events from 1852 to 1880 reinforced porteño influence and power, albeit on different political terms from those advanced by either Rivadavia or Rosas. During half a century of political evolution, geographical distinctions between centralists and autonomists had grown ever fainter. The Constitution of 1853, written under the auspices of a revolt against porteño *de facto* rule, created a strong authority with extensive presidential and federal powers—largely aimed at dominating Buenos Aires. This structure remained oriented toward centralism, even though Buenos Aires, upon joining the government, secured guarantees of certain provincial rights. The interior provinces continued to press for the federalization of the city of Buenos Aires in the hopes of securing porteño wealth, power, and prestige for the benefit of the whole country. Porteños, on the other hand, found themselves increasingly supporting the autonomy of the province of Buenos Aires against a centralized authority represented by presidents, ministers, and congressmen from the interior provinces. But the Pyrrhic victory of 1880 merely confirmed that Buenos Aires was to control the nation. Symbolically, the provinces gained a capital. In reality, Buenos Aires, seconded by other urban centers, continued to draw upon the resources, talents, and ambitions of the country and left the other provinces and rural areas drained and depressed. Politicians might come from the interior or the countryside, but in Buenos Aires they quickly forgot their origins and adopted the life and attitudes of the porteño city. Though the porteño customhouse had long since been nationalized, the major portion of government funds were still expended in the city and province of Buenos Aires.

The development of central authority in the 1860's and 1870's ended toleration for the caudillo who had emerged from the turmoil of the independence period. Political initiative no longer rested with the local strong man and his irregular cavalry forces, but with the successful general, writer, orator, or lawyer who mobilized votes and manipulated political parties. Even the name "caudillo" passed from the leader of gauchos to the politician who stirred the urban masses. Now the caudillo traveled by carriage rather than by horseback; he commanded infantry and artillery rather than cavalry; he wore a frock coat; and he was a man of broad culture, wholly a man of the city.

The overthrow of the Rosas regime accelerated adjustments which

had already built Buenos Aires into the most populous and powerful
of the Argentine provinces. Argentina's estimated 500,000 inhabitants
in 1810 increased to 1,800,000 by 1869, date of the first national census. The last seventeen years of that period saw the most rapid growth,
with an annual increase nearly four times that of the earlier period.
The coast received the major share of this additional population. An
estimate of 1825 allotted only 17 per cent of Argentina's population to
the province of Buenos Aires as contrasted with 28 per cent in 1869.
Including Santa Fe and Entre Ríos, the coast's share of 25 per cent
increased to 41 per cent by 1869, while that of the northwestern provinces declined from 27 to 21 per cent in the same period. As in the
colonial period, the greater portion of the population lived in the countryside—three-fourths, according to the first census. But the influence
of the large numbers of rural peons, gauchos, mestizos, and Indians
was dwarfed by the wealth and power of landowners, merchants, politicians, and foreigners who lived in the major towns. The city of
Buenos Aires naturally attracted the largest population, increasing from
50,000 inhabitants in 1810, to 90,000 in 1850, to 180,000 by 1869.
Other coastal towns also expanded: the most striking case was that of
Rosario, which increased from 800 inhabitants in 1810 to 23,000 by
1869.

Immigration provided an essential ingredient in this development.
Rosas had done nothing to encourage immigration. But since Buenos
Aires was the natural port of entry for new arrivals, there had been
little need for artificial stimulation. Porteño governments after 1852
could afford to continue this laissez faire policy. The re-established
Immigration Commission languished for lack of funds, and projects
for colonization contracts or distribution of lands never progressed beyond the planning stages.

Urquiza's Confederation, on the other hand, had to make special
efforts to attract immigrants and capital from Europe. The Confederation authorities at Paraná and the provincial governments of Santa Fe
and Entre Ríos deliberately promoted immigration. The Confederation's foremost publicist and diplomat, Juan B. Alberdi, condensed the
reform philosophy of the Generation of 1837 into the underlying spirit

of the Constitution of 1853: "To foment settlement is the essence of government" (*gobernar es poblar*). Foreigners were given virtually all the rights of Argentines but without incurring the obligations of citizenship. In an effort to encourage settlement on the land, Confederation and provincial authorities brought several thousand families from Europe and established them in farm colonies near the city of Santa Fe. These immigrants provided a significant departure from the previous orientation of the coastal economy and foreshadowed one aspect of the subsequent development of the pampas—the rise of agricultural colonies dedicated to cereal production. Likewise, the Confederation took the leadership in publicizing Argentina's potentialities in Europe and, during the 1850's, commissioned several scientists to survey and report on existing resources and conditions.

After Buenos Aires joined the nation further inducements were added, such as the establishment of immigration offices in Europe and the provision of several days of free food and shelter for new arrivals at Buenos Aires. Except for a short period in the late 1880's, however, when immigrants received free passage from Europe, the government stopped direct subsidy of immigration. Despite high-flown phrases and lofty principles, neither national nor provincial authorities provided the immigrant with free homesteads, financial credit, personal security, or any of the other incentives "to foment settlement."

Economic factors rather than government policy, therefore, guided immigrants to Argentina. The first immigration statistics, covering the late 1850's, indicated the arrival of some 15,000 Europeans each year against an annual departure of 5,000 to 8,000 emigrants. By the 1860's the difference between immigrants and emigrants had widened to leave an average annual addition of 15,000 to the population, a figure that doubled in the 1870's. But financial crises in the mid-1860's and mid-1870's and the outbreak of the Paraguayan War in 1865 still caused sharp fluctuations in the number of immigrants.

Economic expansion after 1852 contrasted with Argentina's previous slow rate of growth. Steamships and regular schedules did much to alleviate remoteness from Europe. In 1832 the British established the first regular packet service to Buenos Aires, from Southampton by way of Rio de Janeiro—a two-month trip by sailing ship. Steamships took over the run in 1851, cutting the trip to the Río de la Plata to thirty-five days, and by 1860 the French also had a regular service operating between Bordeaux and Buenos Aires. In 1866 the Liverpool-Rio passenger line extended its operations to Buenos Aires. Merchant ships of many flags now entered the Río de la Plata. Some even reached Rosario on the Paraná and Concepción and Concordia on the Uruguay—encouraged by the free navigation of the interior waterways which Urquiza hastily consigned to international treaty in 1853 to prevent a repetition of the porteño blockade of up-river ports. British, United States, Spanish, and French vessels predominated, but sizable numbers also came from German and Italian ports and from Denmark, Holland, and Sweden. During the mid-1850's five hundred ships a year cleared Buenos Aires for overseas ports. By 1880 the number increased to more than four thousand.

This shipping reflected Argentine demands for European goods as well as the increasing volume of exports. Before 1850 Argentina imported an average of 500 barrels of French wine a year. Two decades later, with an estimated fifty thousand Frenchmen in Argentina to increase consumption, France sent 28,000 barrels a month to Buenos Aires. Between 1860 and 1880 the total value of imports from Europe doubled. French luxury goods, sugar, and wines registered significant gains alongside British leadership in textiles, hardware, machinery, and coal. On the other side of the ledger, wool exports rose from an average of 7,000 tons annually in the 1840's to over 100,000 tons per year by the 1880's, by the latter decade contributing more than half the value of Argentine exports. Cereals, frozen mutton and beef, and on-the-hoof shipments of cattle would soon swell this trade, but until 1880 the traditional products of wool, hides, and salted meat constituted more than 90 per cent of the value of exports.

Along with immigrants and manufactured goods came substantial European investment. Argentina lacked the money, technical knowledge, and entrepreneurial skills to develop transport facilities, public utilities, and manufacturing industries by itself. Argentines, furthermore, preferred to invest in land and cattle—enterprises which promised social prestige and fabulous appreciation, sometimes amounting to a thousand per cent in a few decades. But the country possessed great potential, and Europe's middle-class investors and major financial houses hastened to underwrite the future. The refunding of accumulated public debts in the 1870's enabled Argentina to secure credit on increasingly favorable terms. The absence of effective banking controls and the easy inflation of paper currency used in the province of Buenos Aires further encouraged speculation. The stimulation of a railroad boom was intensified by investments in banks, factories, tramways, gas works, and telegraph companies. By 1880 many of the trappings of a "modern" nation were thus being acquired, and Argentina was becoming increasingly dependent on foreign, largely British, capital.

One phase of foreign investment, the railroads, encouraged expansion while further subjugating the interior to Buenos Aires. The first stretch of track was completed in 1857, extending six miles due west from the center of Buenos Aires. During the 1860's the Northern and Southern Railroads pushed out from Buenos Aires. The end of that decade saw the completion of the Central Argentine's link between Rosario and Córdoba. By cutting freight costs to one-twelfth of that charged by oxcarts, these railroads widened the horizons of agricultural exploitation and facilitated the conquest of the pampas. They also accentuated dependence on the trade centers, particularly on the port of Buenos Aires and to a lesser degree on the port of Rosario. In essence, the railroads radiating from Buenos Aires and Rosario drained products, talents, and ambitions toward the coast. In a later decade the extensions to Mendoza and Tucumán revived Argentine wine and sugar production. But for most of Argentina, railroads merely widened the market for European consumer goods and committed the economy to continued production of raw materials for industrial Europe.

The consolidation of porteño power in the decades after 1850 contributed to a continued monopoly by Buenos Aires of the country's intellectual talents. The exiled Generation of 1837 flowed back to Argentina in 1852, only to concentrate in this city. For the next three decades the eclecticism of this group inspired statesmen, politicians, and writers to modernize the country by means of immigration, public education, constitutionalism, and material progress. Intellectuals served as national leaders. Alberdi, the spiritual father of the Constitution of 1853, became the Confederation's minister to the principal European courts. Mitre, the brilliant historian of Argentina's independence movement, was elected governor of Buenos Aires and then president. Sarmiento, probably Argentina's greatest man of letters, served as minister to the United States and president. The tide of progress and prosperity of the 1880's and the overwhelming urge to mimic European models had not yet swept over Buenos Aires. These were creative decades when two great journalistic traditions emerged in *La Nación* and *La Prensa*, the epic poem of the gaucho *Martín Fierro* appeared, and the University of Buenos Aires was revived.

A city with a quarter of a million inhabitants in the 1870's, Buenos Aires still conserved many of its traditional aspects. Only a few Italian villas departed from the predominant colonial architecture of low, mud-brick buildings constructed around interior patios. Unpaved streets, outrageous harbor facilities, and the ever-present Indian frontier had changed little since 1810. In many ways Buenos Aires was, as the affectionate title of *la gran aldea* indicated, a large village. There was strong attachment to native values. Many of the old habits remained unchallenged: the Church's importance in daily life; the long midday siesta; the constant use of the refreshing Paraguayan tea; the fondness for Spanish styles of furniture; the heavy reliance on roasted meat, stews, and corn in the diet; the abstinence of all except the lowest classes from hard liquor and only the most modest use of wines; the abundance of servants in all households; the apparent lack of concern with physical comforts in the furnishing or heating of houses; the importance of the family group, closely guarded and almost isolated from the world.

Yet, despite the aura of Spanish customs which lingered over Buenos Aires, the gulf between that city and the other Argentine towns grew steadily wider. In most of the provincial centers, the traditional values dominated society. Mass, the evening stroll in the plaza, and the gathering of men for billiards, a cockfight, or cards had not changed since colonial days. The populations had expanded, but the same small groups of creole families controlled all activities. A political revolt occasionally required some adjustments, but otherwise few innovations ruffled the steady flow of daily life. Only rarely did immigrants or foreign ideas reach such remote settlements, and even then they altered nothing.

Buenos Aires, on the other hand, attracted—as it always had—the new, the exciting, and the different. Immigrant families began to arrive in greater numbers, and the proportion of females now almost equaled that of males. Many of these newcomers clung to their cultural origins and maintained separate communities, schools, and ways of life. But their very numbers had an influence on the city. Restaurants, cafes, hotels, brothels, hospitals, Protestant churches, and foreign-language newspapers catered to their needs. They learned Spanish, if sometimes badly, and reached into all levels of society. Some married into the oldest and most select families and added names like Maguire, Sansinena, Tornquist, and Pellegrini to the rolls of porteño aristocracy. The interior as well as Europe contributed to porteño growth. Those with talents, cunning, or ambition had no desire to vegetate in the hinterland when there was fame, fortune, sociability, movement, and progress to be had at Buenos Aires. The flow of internal migration to the town, to the coast, and to Buenos Aires carried not only politicians and merchants but also servants and laborers toward the port.

Buenos Aires in the 1870's was on the brink of even more significant change. Still a large village in many ways, its rapidly growing population and wealth presaged a metropolis. Unlike the withdrawn and isolated provincial towns, the constant exposure to foreign customs and ideas as well as the increasing ease of travel to Europe encouraged porteños to question the traditional values and to search for European models. Porteño predominance had guided the emergence of a nation. Now Buenos Aires prepared to assume the leading role in the agricultural conquest of the pampas—a process that would create one of the world's great cities and build Argentina into a major exporter of beef, mutton, wheat, and corn.

Chapter 5 • An Agricultural Revolution on the Pampas

The agricultural expansion of the late nineteenth century created a new land and a new people, much as the earlier Industrial Revolution transformed the face of England and of Europe. The Spanish towns, the rise of the porteño economy, and the achievement of nationhood were important steps in Argentine evolution, but it was cereal and meat production for European markets that molded the emerging nation. The manner in which capital, immigrants, and technology reached the pampas laid the foundations for many present-day characteristics in both rural and urban Argentina. Crop farming provided the first and fundamental change. Closely connected with crops were developments in the livestock industries and in the urban expansion of Buenos Aires.

The land of Rivadavia and Rosas did not attract small independent farmers or dedicate any significant expanse of the pampas to crops. Despite isolated efforts to establish European immigrant families in agricultural colonies in rural Buenos Aires and Santa Fe, crop farming was largely limited to plots surrounding the major towns. Outside the cities, few knew even the taste of bread. The difficulty for the small holder to secure a clear title to his land, the overwhelming dedication of the export and domestic economy to cattle and sheep, the ever-present Indian menace, and the lack of transportation, laborers, and fences militated against tilling the soil.

In the 1850's the expansion of sheep raising in Buenos Aires and the establishment of several agricultural colonies in Santa Fe provided limited encouragement to crop farming. Sheep raising introduced some elements needed for an agricultural revolution by intensifying land use, raising land values, attracting immigrants, and stimulating railroad construction and commerce. But the plow did not immediately follow the shepherd. Meanwhile, the several hundred Swiss, German, and French families who had settled near the city of Santa Fe faced enormous obstacles. The first colonies were located in marginal areas exposed to raids by Chaco Indians and of little value to cattle interests. The expectation of entrepreneurs who delivered these families to Argentina and promised to provide them with land, implements, food, and seed, was that, in a few years, the penniless newcomers would repay all advances with interest. To the disillusionment of governments, promoters, and not a few colonists, farming on a remote and unknown frontier yielded no such immediate gains. Often not even the promises to colonists were honored. The experience reported at Esperanza, Santa Fe, was only too frequently repeated: "There had been no thought taken of measures of the first importance for the colonists; no houses built, no wells dug, no corrals ready for the cattle which were to be delivered by the government. No arrangements made for public order, no system of overseering [sic] to teach the colonists what they ought to do; no church and no hospitals." But in spite of hardships and misery, Indians and locusts, droughts and floods, these colonies survived. By 1870 they significantly added to wheat production and by the end of that decade contributed to the first trickle of cereal exports to Europe.

Railroads soon extended the opportunities for crop farming. At the end of the 1860's the Central Argentine Railroad from Rosario to Córdoba was nearing completion. As part of the concession to the English company that built the line, a strip three miles wide on each side of the track was reserved for colonization. Active recruiting of immigrants commenced in Switzerland and soon expanded to Italy, and in

March 1870 the first colony was established thirteen miles west of Rosario. The company offered lots ranging in size from eighty to one hundred and sixty acres for direct sale to colonists. For those without capital, the land could be rented at a small fixed charge per year with an option for future purchase. Advances in animals, equipment, food, and housing could also be secured from the company to be repaid from subsequent harvests. Within a year three more colonies appeared along the Central's tracks in Sante Fe—a total of three thousand inhabitants who promised agricultural prosperity for their communities and freight revenues for the railroad. Private land companies followed the Central's example and offered individual farm lots, with installment payments extending over periods from three to ten years. Some landowners also recognized that settlement and crop farming might increase the value of their vast and frequently unexploited holdings. Typical of the 1870's was a notice appearing in *La Nación* in Buenos Aires: "Messrs. Videla and Latorre, residents of the province of Santa Fe, are thinking of establishing a colony on their property. The total area of the colony will be two square leagues divided into 160 concessions, each measuring four squares on the front by five deep [i.e., eighty acres]. The most advantageous conditions will be made available to settlers, such as lumber for construction, oxen, tools, etc. In addition, no charge will be made for surveying and for the registration of deeds."

The dream of owning land was a principal motivation for the rising tide of European immigration to the Río de la Plata after 1870. Land companies no longer had to enlist families in Europe but could secure recruits at the port of Buenos Aires from those who had already paid their own way across the Atlantic. In the province of Buenos Aires the high value of land and the controlling sheep and cattle interests afforded little opportunity for the immigrant to achieve ownership of land. But in Santa Fe and Entre Ríos where cheap lands were still available the industrious peasant could become an owner of forty, eighty, or one hundred acres after four or five years.

The 1880's saw the solution of many thorny problems which had held back national progress. In 1879-80 Julio Roca, professional soldier, politician, and minister of war, led a military expedition to the Río Negro valley. Gone were the policies of treaties and defensive forts. Telegraph lines and Remington rifles soon overcame the lances of the Araucanians. National troops destroyed the Indian settlements and dispersed their inhabitants, many being sent as captive servants to households in Buenos Aires. This "Conquest of the Desert" opened a vast new area to exploitation and removed the Indian menace that had so effectively checked the westward and southward expansion of *estancias*, railroads, and settlements.

Hand in hand with this territorial expansion came political stability. In 1880, following a brief revolution by the porteños themselves, Roca assumed the presidency of a national government residing in the now federalized city of Buenos Aires. After the violent struggles between centralists and autonomists, between porteños and provincials, a degree of order and tranquillity descended on Argentina. The independent local caudillo had disappeared, and mass agitation for democracy, free elections, or social benefits had not yet made itself felt. In this interval the country was governed by the so-called oligarchy, a dignified, educated, progressive, and haughty elite composed of nineteenth-century liberals anxious to advance Argentine prosperity, Catholics who supported anticlerical measures designed to reduce the Church's economic and political powers, men strongly imbued with European and particularly French culture, writers and thinkers dominated by the scientific and materialistic values of positivism, politicians closely associated with landholding interests and with British capital, and statesmen ambitious not only to transform Buenos Aires into the Paris of South America but also to make Argentina a leading nation of the western hemisphere.

Economic prosperity accompanied territorial and political fulfillment. Meat lay at the core of these developments. In the Argentine littoral, beef constituted the cheapest item in the diet. During the 1860's the carcasses of 60 per cent of the cattle killed were never utilized for their meat. For Europe's rapidly expanding urban population, where meat

was a luxury far beyond the grasp of the poor, such waste was shocking. But how could the Atlantic be bridged to bring about the meeting
of supply and demand? Several entrepreneurs became bankrupt trying
to develop Europe's taste for salted beef; the strips of dry meat eaten by
Brazilian slaves were rejected by even the slum-dwellers of Paris and
London. More successful were efforts to reduce the meat's juices to
paste form. Liebig's Meat Extract, manufactured in Entre Ríos and in
Uruguay, was widely used in the hospitals and poor houses of Europe
in the 1860's and soon became a popular household item on the Continent. Inventive minds, meanwhile, tried to dehydrate meat, pack it
in vacuum tins, or inject it with preservatives, but without commercial
success. The method of getting unspoiled meat to Europe, however,
was only one side of the problem. Several farsighted landowners who
organized the Sociedad Rural Argentina in 1866 understood what the
majority of cattlemen would take three decades to comprehend: that
the stringy beef produced by native stock would never appeal to European palates regardless of its preparation. Thus began a persistent campaign to teach cattle growers that pedigreed bulls, fences, and alfalfa
were essential in a new era. But, until a European market was assured,
the *saladero* continued to reign supreme, and few could see the value of
costly blooded stock, wire fences, or alfalfa pastures.

The problem of securing the much needed market was solved in the
1880's by two methods: frozen meat and on-the-hoof shipments. In
1876 an experimental shipload of chilled carcasses arrived in Buenos
Aires from Rouen, France. Although at a banquet the leaders of porteño commerce and society were barely able to choke down cuts which
had aged for three months under less than perfect refrigeration, they
were enthusiastic about the idea. Subsequently, frozen meat (−22° F.)
won out over chilled (32° F.) as more suited to the long voyage and
the rudimentary level of technology.

Sheep rather than cattle received the initial stimulus from this new
commerce, for the smaller carcasses could be more easily handled and
preserved. British investors, simultaneously at work on the longer and
more costly transport of mutton from Australia, built the first of several
packing plants at Buenos Aires in 1882. The fact that these plants paid

50 per cent more than did the tallow factories for sheep carcasses encouraged production of an animal which could be used for its meat. As a result the Lincoln breed gradually modified the previously dominant Merino strain, and sheep growers became increasingly interested in selective breeding and superior pasturage.

On-the-hoof shipments brought similar influences to bear on cattle production. Although thoroughbred animals had long been sent across the Atlantic to Argentina, only the increased size of ships and the spread of steam navigation made the return shipment of ordinary beef cattle profitable. The first exports of live cattle in the 1870's failed commercially because of the poor quality of native stock. But by the mid-eighties the same economic incentives that were transforming sheep production began to operate on the cattlemen. The preachings of the Sociedad Rural now received impressive support in the substantially higher prices offered by cattle exporters over those paid by the *saladeros*. As a result, the British consumer gradually imposed the Shorthorn, producer of the famous marbleized roast beef, on Argentina. With the Shorthorn bulls came the demand for more fences to enclose herds and to prevent mixing or degeneration of stock. Since pampas grass put little fat on cattle, special feed pastures near the ports were developed to prepare the animals for the long ocean voyage.

The cattle and sheep interests which had consistently scorned immigration and crop farming now needed laborers. In Buenos Aires, however, the immigrant did not encounter the peculiar situation found in Santa Fe, where owners had been willing to sell a part of their holdings. In 1888 land in Buenos Aires was worth four times that of similar holdings in Santa Fe. As a result the porteño landowner had no desire to subdivide and sell his property, at least not at prices which the penniless newcomer could hope to amortize. Accustomed to the large expanses necessary for a rudimentary cattle economy, the *estanciero* had also become used to rapid increases in the value of his lands. The expulsion of the Indians and the construction of railroads had not disappointed these expectations, and the new era of meat production for Europe inflated hopes still further.

In Buenos Aires therefore the immigrant became a tenant farmer.

Such a system of exploitation benefited the *estancieros* enormously. It provided a welcome income from new or unused lands. It added a valuable hedge against fluctuations in the demand for cattle or sheep. It required little or no capital, investment, or risk on the part of the landowner, yet safeguarded for him any appreciation in land value. Most important, it provided the means to break up the soil, destroy the pampas grass, and replace it with forage for refined stock. The cattle needed alfalfa pasturage, but the landowner could not afford to plant it himself. Some tried and declared the cost for labor and equipment prohibitive. Tenant farming solved these problems—in the manner spelled out by the journal of the Sociedad Rural: "The land is first divided into fenced grazing pastures of four to five thousand acres and then subdivided into surveyed numbered lots of five hundred acres each without any intervening wire. These lots are rented on a three-year contract . . . to Italian farmers who bring their own equipment and supplies and agree at the end of the period to leave the land sown with alfalfa, the seed being supplied by the owner."

For the immigrant himself such a system of tenant farming held certain attractions. The peasant from northern Italy (for these formed the bulk of Argentina's new farming class) who arrived in Buenos Aires with his family could readily secure a position as a sharecropper. In this case, he received implements, seed, and advances of food from the landowner and turned over half his harvest in payment. Cultivation of his farm was limited to a year or two; then he had to move to a new location. His advantage, however, was that he had little to lose. He had no capital and no equipment. If the harvest were poor, he had no rent or mortgage to pay. Though insecurity and poverty might dog his footsteps, his fate was no worse than in his homeland. And if the crops were good for several successive years, the sharecropper might raise himself into the tenant farmer category or perhaps return to the city with his small hoard of capital.

As a tenant farmer, the immigrant added plows, harrows, reapers, oxen, and horses to the capital represented by his strong back. Consequently landowners sought his services even more than those of the sharecropper, for the tenant farmer assumed the whole risk and investment. The owner contributed only the use of land which probably had paid no income before and stood to be improved by cultivation. Through a contract, usually verbal, an area of two hundred to five hundred acres was turned over to the tenant for a term of three to six years. He had to build his own home, and if he chose, shelters for implements, animals, or grain. If there were no stream or waterhole nearby, he had to dig a well for his own use and that of his animals. Yet he received no allowance for improvements when he left, since, for the sheep or cattleman, a house or a shed were obstructions rather than improvements. The tenant was hardly master of his rented land. The contract sometimes allowed him a small portion for pasturage but only enough for necessary work animals. The rest he was obliged to cultivate, usually with the crop designated by the landowner.

It was this agricultural development of the pampas which underwrote Argentina's rapid economic growth at the end of the nineteenth century. Between 1872 and 1895 cultivated acreage on the pampas increased fifteen times—to almost ten million acres. Exports climbed from a value of 30 million gold pesos in 1870 to 60 million in 1880, 100 million in 1890, and over 150 million by the end of the century. Cereals rose from a negligible share of these exports in 1870 until they totaled 50 per cent of export values by 1900. Argentina now became a major producer of wheat, with annual exports from several harvests in the 1890's topping one million tons. Concern began to be voiced in the United States, where *Harpers Weekly* forecast: "The Argentine Republic promises soon to become the greatest wheat-producing country in the world." The Central Argentine line from Rosario to Córdoba, which had constituted most of Argentina's 460 miles of track in 1870, found itself by 1900 complemented by at least thirty other companies and 10,000 miles of track. Population increased from 1,800,000 inhabitants in 1869 to 4,000,000 by 1895, and the last two decades of the century left a net balance of nearly 1,500,000 Europeans in Argentina. By the 1890's Argentina was attracting each year at least 50,000 Italian and Spanish migrants (nicknamed *golondrinas,* or swallows), who crossed the Atlantic in search of high wages during the wheat and corn harvests. Even the financial crash in 1890—due to speculation and overextended credit during the booming eighties—hardly slowed the pace of agricultural exploitation.

Two events in 1900 further accentuated both the beef-cattle and tenant-farming aspects of this agricultural development. England finally closed its ports to live animals from Argentina because of the ravages of hoof-and-mouth disease. Overnight, the packing plant became the major purchaser and outlet for Argentine cattle. Statistics reflect the extent of this change. Salted beef, which accounted for 48 per cent of all meat exports in 1887, dropped to 22 per cent a decade later and to 4 per cent by 1907. Live cattle exports rose from 28 per cent in 1887 to 43 per cent in 1897, only to fall back to 8 per cent in 1907. Meanwhile, within a decade frozen beef increased from a mere 0.2 per cent in 1897 to 51 per cent of all meat exports. After 1908 improved refrigeration permitted the shipment of chilled as well as frozen beef, thus enormously improving the taste and presentation of Argentine meats to the British consumer and preparing the way for further expansion during and after World War I. In 1900 crippling blows struck the important sheep-raising industry. A serious and prolonged depression in the wool markets of France and Belgium coincided with extensive floods in southern Buenos Aires and the loss of fourteen million head of sheep. The effect was to loosen the tight hold which sheep raising had maintained since 1850 on land around the city of Buenos Aires and to turn much of this area over to crops and cattle.

A second economic boom from 1904 to 1912 provided an even greater impetus for the exploitation of the pampas resources than that of the 1880's. By 1910 the value of exports reached 390 million gold pesos, thirteen times the export trade of 1870. A veritable spiderweb of railroads covered the pampas—location for most of Argentina's seventeen thousand miles of track. Another million Europeans joined a population which by 1914 reached the eight-million mark, while the annual migration of harvest laborers from Europe now numbered one hundred thousand. Tenant farming kept pace with these developments. In 1900 only 39 per cent of the farmers in Santa Fe and Buenos Aires owned land. Six years later, as crop farming spread south and west in the pampas, ownership actually declined to 37 per cent in Santa Fe and to 26 per cent in Buenos Aires—this despite a tripling in the number of farms.

In the late nineteenth century Argentina reaped the results of a land tenure system developed during the colonial period and carried forward by Rosas and all ensuing governments. Despite the efforts of some statesmen to reverse traditional land policies, few among the elite wanted to change practices which had brought them wealth and power and which promised even greater returns in the future. Indicative of this attitude had been the initial, unenthusiastic reception of the agricultural colonies and their relegation to marginal or frontier zones. Although journalists and politicians vied with each other in attributing United States prosperity and development to homestead legislation, application of such measures to Argentina proved quite another matter. When the national congress finally passed a Homestead Act in 1884, its provisions were limited to grazing lands south of the recently conquered Río Negro frontier. In an effort to transform the vanishing gaucho into a landowner, it enabled citizens to secure fifteen hundred acres if they occupied and made improvements on the land for five years. But fifteen hundred acres was too small a unit to support sheep grazing on the barren Patagonian coast, and, although the law was not repealed until the turn of the century, few applied for homestead concessions.

Even more unfortunate was the fate of Argentina's first comprehensive land law of 1876, drafted under the supervision of President Nicolás Avellaneda, a man who had written his law thesis on the subject of public domain legislation and who had constantly demonstrated his concern for immigration and agricultural matters. On paper the law appeared as a model of wisdom. National lands were divided into sections of one hundred thousand acres and further subdivided into lots of two hundred and fifty acres. Eight lots in each section were reserved for a town and town lands. The first one hundred lots in each section were to be distributed free to immigrants, while the remainder were to be sold (a maximum of four lots per person) at a flat rate payable in installments over ten years. Special provisions, however, permitted private colonizing companies to select, survey, subdivide, and colonize lands on their own account, and speculators used these terms to make a mockery of the 1876 law. During its twenty-five years of existence, only 14 out of 225 colonizing companies which received land grants complied with the requirements for subdivision and settlement. Typical was the attitude of one concessionaire who petitioned congress that, in place of the two hundred and fifty families he was supposed to have settled on his lands, he be permitted to substitute some cattle.

In much the same fashion the territories secured by Roca's Conquest of the Desert disappeared into the hands of speculators and large land-holders. Bonds redeemable in public lands underwrote some of the cost of the military expedition. As surveying advanced with the frontier, the holders of these bonds chose their lots, each bond worth a square league (more than six thousand acres). An important auction of public lands in 1882 witnessed similar squanderings of Argentina's major source of national wealth, and, although each buyer was theoretically limited to one hundred thousand acres currently worth only a few cents an acre, speculators used agents or fictitious names to circumvent the limit. Thus, even before the financial crash of 1890 temporarily slowed this orgy of waste, the whole area of the pampas had passed into private hands, to be held for speculation, investment, or prestige, but not to be owned by those who cultivated the land.

This concentration of landownership in the hands of a few was fur-ther aggravated by an intoxicating inflation of land values: between 1881 and 1911 the value increased an average of 218 per cent in the coastal provinces, with the sharpest increases occurring in southern and western Buenos Aires. Immigrants who had aspired to own their land faced not only prohibitive prices but also increasingly unreasonable rents. An investigation by the Santa Fe government in 1902 concluded: "The landowner has believed that if in less than ten years a league worth 10,000 pesos can reach the exaggerated price of 100,000, there is no reason for the rents not to continue to increase yearly in that same proportion. In this belief, he does not rent his land in long term con-tracts because with each new contract he expects to raise the rent. The result is that as the yield declines with the exhaustion of the soil's nutrients, the rent climbs sharply, rising within six years from 12 per cent of the crop to 18, 20, 22 and even 25 per cent."

The three decades following 1880 saw the grasslands that had supported cattle, horses, sheep, and a few nomadic Indians and gauchos transformed into an agricultural kingdom. The present exploitation of the pampas began to take form. In southern Santa Fe and northern Buenos Aires corn and dairy cattle gradually took over the land, and enormous feed pastures for beef cattle developed in southeastern Buenos Aires. Wheat and sheep led the westward and southward expansion: wheat finally met its western limit at the line of minimum rainfall for crop farming, while sheep raising expanded to the barren coast and plateaus of Patagonia. This agricultural conquest created prosperity for many, provided the basis for commercial, industrial, and urban growth, and built Argentina into a leading power of South America. By 1910, when Argentina celebrated the centennial of its independence, porteños complacently accepted the idea that their nation's golden future was guaranteed by the export of meat, grains, wool, and hides. The colonists, sharecroppers, tenant farmers, harvest laborers, and peons who grew the record grain crops, planted the alfalfa pastures, and tended the blooded stock produced with their labors the basis for change in the coastal cities. But on Argentina's farmland and frontiers little had been altered except the method of exploiting these grasslands.

Isolation continued to be a predominant characteristic of the Argentine rural scene. This had been only natural in a grazing economy where few humans were needed in the countryside. But it remained true even after beef and cereals ruled the land. Roads had been unnecessary for the production of hides, salted meat, and wool. Products moved on the hoof or, as with goods to and from the interior provinces, by oxcart. For this mere trails across the plains sufficed. When railroads spread across the pampas in the 1880's, the intermediate stage of road building was bypassed. British companies built the railroads as investments. They provided cheap, rapid transportation, at least when compared with the oxcart. Isolation was apparently broken down. Farm and seaport were linked by the railroads, but links did not develop among the farms themselves or with rural communities or villages. The railroads merely served as feelers which probed into the cattle, cereal, and

sheep zones to gather in freight for the ports. They fulfilled the immediate transport needs of the countryside and thus inhibited construction
of roads. Railroad companies did not want competition, so for decades
the only roads built in Argentina were the mud ruts which radiated
from the railroad stations.

The farmer was submerged in this isolation. The transportation system did nothing to break down the remoteness between him and his
fellow men. The few existing roads remained as they had been for
three centuries, dusty shallow troughs or long canals according to the
season. Only the high-wheeled oxcart could negotiate such tracks. The
buggy, the phaeton, the sulky, and the carriage had no place on the
pampas. The gaucho and the Indian had molded themselves to their
horses. The agricultural immigrant, however, never did become a horseman; restricted to plodding oxen or to walking, he soon resigned himself to the limited horizon of his farm or colony.

Churches, schools, and clubs did not develop in rural Argentina for
the simple reason that settlement was dispersed and often temporary.
The colonies of Russian Jews in Entre Ríos and Santa Fe and, to a
lesser degree, some of the older Swiss colonies of Santa Fe possessed
some religious and cultural unity. But these were rare exceptions. Farmers in Argentina did not usually live in villages and go out each day to
cultivate the surrounding fields. Because of extensive agriculture where
a great deal of land was tilled superficially, farm homes were spread
out at considerable distances from each other. When eighty acres served
as the basic unit for crop farming, much walking or riding was required
to reach a neighbor. With five hundred acres the distance almost tripled, and the possibility of social institutions reaching the farm decreased in proportion. Weddings, funerals, and special church holidays
might warrant a long trip to town. But the priest, clergyman, or rabbi
could not minister to widely scattered families who lacked the resources
or interest to form a congregation. Education likewise faced insur-
mountable problems. Children were needed to work. Even if they could
be spared, where could schools be built that this dispersed population
could reach? As soon as one left Buenos Aires and the coastal cities,
educational facilities declined sharply in quality and number. In large

areas of the pampas they were nonexistent. The singing clubs, shooting clubs, or mutual aid societies of the Germans, Swiss, and Italians were urban institutions. They throve in the towns but not in the countryside. The average farmer lived five to fifteen miles from the nearest railroad station. He probably was forty or fifty miles from the closest town. Isolation was of a different kind from that of the eighteenth century. Rather than a horizon broken only by thistles, one could see the huts of farmers and perhaps the estate of some cattleman. But occupation of the pampas had not linked its inhabitants together.

The country store was rural Argentina's principal social institution. It provided merchandise, purchased products, and was the sole dispenser of credit. In the isolation of a lonely countryside, its role as a place of conviviality and a source of information and news was perhaps as vital as its economic functions. In many ways it took the place of the church, the school, the club, and the plaza. Its origins were colonial, for it had emerged from the grazing economy. The *pulpería* was its original expression—a bar, store, and social club for gauchos. With the development of livestock and crops, the railroad station became its preferred location, and its commercial and merchandising interests increased. Rather than glasses of raw cane alcohol, it now dispensed cheap red wine to Italian farmers, and rather than salt and the dried leaves of *yerba mate,* it sold meat, beans, and biscuits. Here, on a Sunday or in the idle season between harvest and planting, the farmer could assuage his loneliness, learn the latest crop prices and harvest rumors, and exchange news with neighbors he never visited. Yet many a farmer was not within reach of a country store; and even when he was, it did not adequately answer his social needs.

If the farmer's hut seemed remote from the rural town, it must be realized that the town itself was just as remote from the metropolis of Buenos Aires, the bustling ports of Rosario and Bahía Blanca, or the colonial city of Córdoba. By 1914, besides the ports and centers adjacent to Greater Buenos Aires, the pampas boasted only three cities of twenty to thirty thousand inhabitants: Chivilcoy, Junín, and Pergamino, all in the province of Buenos Aires. The largest nuclei of population in the province of Santa Fe, after Rosario and the city of Santa

Fe, were Casilda, Cañada de Gómez, and Rafaela, numbering just under ten thousand each. The average rural town—still typical today— had a population between two and six thousand, an unpaved main street, a bare plaza, a few stores, several squares of adobe or mud brick houses, the more pretentious of which were plastered or whitewashed on the outside. Occasionally there were a church, a school, some storage sheds, and a railroad station. If it were the seat of a political subdivision there was probably a town hall on the plaza. The inhabitants were people of modest means and education. The priest, the police chief, the justice of the peace, and the school teacher represented the town's aristocracy and authority. There was no doctor; the pharmacist attended to any serious ills. No cattlemen, no lawyers, no politicians, no bankers resided in it. In short, the average town had little to recommend it. After a visit to Rafaela in 1891, an understanding and usually sympathetic observer of the Argentine scene wrote: "All I can say, however, is that, if ever a man wishes to know what it is to have an inclination to commit suicide, let him spend a week in a camp town in the Argentine." In essence the town existed only to handle the barest needs of rural Argentina and to carry the wealth of the soil as quickly as possible to the coast.

A few of the rural population—the wealthy landowner or cattleman —enjoyed the amenities of a civilized existence. By the end of the nineteenth century the *estancia* headquarters had changed from a bare frontier outpost into a Mediterranean villa, a French chateau, or a gabled English country house, surrounded by eucalyptus groves, cropped lawns, rose gardens, and tennis courts. But for these people, country residence was limited to summer or weekend visits, and they were far better acquainted with the streets of Buenos Aires or Paris and the beaches of Mar del Plata than with the land which provided their wealth. Those who actually lived on the pampas led quite another existence. One could find neat brick homes, sheds, milch cows, poultry, garden plots, small orchards of plum and peach trees, and varied crops of some Swiss colony of which propagandists loved to boast to European immigrants. Unfortunately, such scenes were the exception. It is also well to remember that the realities which served as the basis of these lures had been developed on land which was of little value, by people who had the opportunity to buy that land, and who in all likelihood had put in thirty years of hard labor to achieve such an idyllic life.

Transiency along with isolation dominated life on the pampas. Most immigrants were already predisposed to look upon farming as an interval in which to amass a reserve that could be enjoyed in their homeland. The difficulty, at least by the 1890's, for the small cultivator to secure title to land and the livestock economy's demand for tenant farmers strengthened this sense of the temporary.

The farmer's house held little significance for him. His culture placed no value on physical conveniences, and his poverty inured him to discomfort. Home for the colonist or tenant farmer recalled few of the overtones which the word had in its Anglo-Saxon use. It was merely a cheap, temporary shelter from the elements. Most common on the pampas was the mud and straw rancho. The soil was tamped down within a rectangle measured out on the ground. At the four corners, posts were sunk. Saplings tied or wired to these posts provided a framework. To this was added a roof of straw thatch or, in later times, galvanized iron. Bundles of straw were woven into the framework and then plastered with a mixture of dirt, water, and manure to form walls. This dwelling, which could be completed in two days, was ten to twelve feet square and had a door closed by a sheepskin or piece of canvas and perhaps one or two openings or "windows" in the walls. Occasionally the interior might be divided into two rooms. If cooking were done inside there was a hole near the ridgepole to let out smoke. Usually a lean-to, attached to one side of the rancho, sheltered a small adobe baking oven as well as the open fire for cooking. Naturally there were variations in the style and comfort of this type of building. To enlarge the house one merely extended its length or added units around a patio. More substantial dwellings were built with crude adobes shaped from clay and grass.

The interior of the home further reflected the transient life and lack of concern with physical comforts. Early travelers in Argentina used to express their astonishment at the furnishings of the gaucho's abode, limited to a few ox skulls on the dirt floor. The farmer's furniture, not as picturesque, was hardly any more plentiful. It is true that, as with the pastoral society, much everyday living was carried on outdoors or under the kitchen lean-to and that during the summer the family ate, relaxed, and slept outside. A few handmade chairs or benches served as seats, and usually the house boasted a table. Bedding was a pile of sheepskins and ponchos rolled in a corner and sometimes, as a luxury, a bed for the farmer and his wife. Despite the cold and humidity of the winter season, fireplaces or heating were unknown. Fuel, often sun-dried dung, was scarce enough just for cooking. Lighting was almost as rare. Daylight governed rural hours, candles and kerosene were expensive, and few had the knowledge or desire to read. Clothing, likewise, was limited to the bare essentials. Cheap cotton fabrics predominated, despite winter temperatures which frequently dipped below freezing. One suit and a pair of shoes, or a dress and stockings for the women, were reserved for the special occasion of a visit to town. Everyday trousers and shirts, skirts and blouses, were worn and mended and remended until they were in shreds.

It can easily be imagined that these farmers were oblivious to the habits or even the possibility of cleanliness and hygiene. Sanitary facilities were unknown. Surrounded by the broad expanse of the pampas, an Italian peasant saw no need for an outhouse. Modesty or sanitation were hardly his concern. To his mind, bathing was equally unnecessary. Neither his culture nor his surroundings made personal cleanliness essential. In contrast with tropical northeastern Brazil, where disease quickly wiped out unwashed German settlers, dirt in temperate coastal Argentina imposed no serious penalties.

Their background, transient existence, and ignorance robbed these farmers of the most elementary conveniences. An eighteen-hour day of back-breaking labor was routine during the planting and harvest seasons. But almost as a reaction to this, they lapsed into total lethargy during the other seven months of the year. It is true that often there was little else to do, especially when a tenant farmer's contract dictated a single crop, prevented him from keeping hogs or cattle, and forced him to move on after a few years. Certainly the lack of ownership discouraged any attempt to plant trees to shelter his rancho from the burning sun or to provide fruit for his diet. But vegetable plots, chickens, even a few humble pumpkins or squash, were equally rare around farm houses. The universal diet was beans and corn flavored with grease. Even that staple of rural Argentina, beef, appeared on farm tables only during the harvest season to give strength for the hot, dusty labors. Then it was bought, already slaughtered, from the butcher's cart or shop. Modest in food, immigrant families were equally temperate in drink. Red wine was the sign of a special social event, a feast day, a visit to town, or the arrival of an honored guest. Cane alcohol made its appearance, as with beef, at harvest time for stimulation rather than for sociability.

Transiency on the pampas was closely related to the economic drive toward extensive rather than intensive agriculture. Landowners and cattlemen accepted European peasants with the expectation that they would continue as laborers. But Argentina had land in abundance, even if not available for ownership by poor immigrants, and much of it was virgin soil which needed to be refined by plowing. Since the labor force was small in comparison with available land, colonist and tenant contracts encouraged cultivation of the greatest possible area. Cattle, hogs, or sheep, which reduced the area under cultivation and distracted the tenant from his primary function, were forbidden. Fruit trees, decent housing, and garden plots were likewise discouraged. Inevitably in the effort to wring fortune from nature, immigrant farmers took on too much land. If a profit could be made from eighty or one hundred acres, then surely it could be tripled or quadrupled on two hundred and fifty or even five hundred acres. But the investment of effort and capital which might be sufficient to carry the risk on eighty acres obviously could not be stretched over a vastly larger area. Such evils of extensive farming were compounded by the tendency to raise a single, easily marketed crop, such as corn, wheat, or flax. Too often the single-crop gamble went against the tenant or colonist; for, if the myriad dangers of nature—untimely frosts, droughts, locusts, or rains during the short harvest season—did not overtake him and he reaped a bumper crop, the market would reward him with lowered prices, higher railroad freights, or increased equipment costs. From his limited viewpoint, there was nothing left to do but to start over again the next year in the same cycle and hope that by some miracle a profit would emerge.

Revolution on the pampas, therefore, changed the exploitation of the land. Tenant farmers, railroads, cereals, and livestock took over from the Indian, gaucho, and native cattle. These economic developments worked against small farm ownership, improved roads, rural social institutions, and better housing. The first immigrants into each new frontier, it is true, prospered and sometimes became landowners. The *golondrinas,* those migrant laborers from Europe, carried back to their homelands a substantial hoard of wages. The tenant farmer probably endured no worse conditions than in Italy, Spain, or France and often substantially improved his financial and social position. A very few even made their fortunes by starting at the bottom as farmers. But, although the cultivated acreage increased each year, men did not sink roots in the pampas. The new Argentina hardly gave the rural inhabitant the opportunity for advancement or economic gain offered him in the city. There was little to hold the ambitious or the capable in the countryside, and the story of success was most frequently told by those who left the soil after a few lucky harvests and invested their savings in a shop or piece of land in some town or city. Talent and wealth tended to concentrate in the urban centers. Thus the impact of agricultural revolution reached beyond the pampas to forge a new nation in the coastal cities and, above all, in the city of Buenos Aires. Rather than a frontier, Argentina had a city.

The growth of cities, which would eventually make the Argentines Latin America's most urbanized people, started with the Spanish towns, but the real impetus came from agricultural exploitation of the pampas. The immigrants who were drawn to Argentina in the late nineteenth century found the land already controlled by *estancieros* and speculators. With the ownership of land largely beyond their reach, the newcomers accumulated in Argentina's port cities, especially in Buenos Aires. Relatives or friends, who had arrived first and established themselves in urban occupations, drew the later arrivals into the same environment. Here were the opportunities, institutions, sociability, and wealth generally absent in the countryside.

For a moment let us imagine the position of the immigrant. He might be illiterate and in all probability poor, but he either had faith in his two strong arms or recognized that nothing could be worse than the overcrowding of land and industries at home. The thought that this was only a temporary move sustained his courage for the leap across the Atlantic. Even when he brought his family, he came as a migrant. *Hacer América* was his dream—to conquer the riches of the new world and return to his village or city to enjoy them. Save for the few brought over by colonizing companies or by the Argentine government's experiment with free passages in 1888-89, he paid his own way across the Atlantic. The increasing number of steamships plying the Río de la Plata route and the resultant competition between lines sharply reduced the cost of third-class passage. Although Argentina was twice as far as the United States from European ports, by the 1890's the *golondrina* needed to work only two weeks in Argentina to pay for his round-trip passage. The two to four weeks below decks with inadequate toilets, poor food, monotony, and seasickness constituted an unpleasant but bearable interlude. On arrival in Argentina, those who wished could secure five days' free room and board in the Immigrants' Hotel—at first a filthy, unventilated horsebarn in the center of Buenos Aires and after the turn of the century a gloomy, concrete edifice near the northern port area. Others found their way into shabby hotels, joined the households of already established friends or relatives, or lived as vagabonds along the waterfront or in the parks. After 1900, with the *golondrinas'* increasing importance to the harvest, the Argentine government took measures to insure the rapid transportation of agricultural laborers to the fields. A processing area, established between the new docks and the principal railroad station of Retiro, rushed farm workers off the ships and onto trains in record time.

In the coastal cities of the 1880's—whether among Buenos Aires' 300,000 inhabitants, the 40,000 of rapidly growing Rosario, the 15,000 located in those two provincial capitals of Santa Fe and Paraná, or San Nicolás' 10,000—immigrants formed the basis for a far greater metamorphosis than that occurring on the pampas. These cities had already absorbed the bulk of European immigrants to Argentina. The percentage of European-born ranged from a moderate 10 per cent in Santa Fe and Paraná to 50 per cent in Buenos Aires. Since Buenos Aires was virtually the only port of entry for Europeans, this city drained off a large proportion of the labor force to meet its rapidly rising need for services, construction, and production. With the exception of depression years in the mid-1870's, in the early 1890's, and just preceding World War I, there was a constant demand for workers, especially for manual laborers.

The new arrival at Buenos Aires thus faced few problems in the first part of his campaign for wealth, that is, in getting work. If he reached Argentina during the summer he could be whisked off to the wheat or corn fields merely by saying that he was an agricultural laborer. His clothes were on his back, his employer fed him, he could sleep in the open, and at the end of four months of back-breaking labor he could pocket the equivalent of thirty to forty pounds sterling. Railroad construction absorbed large numbers of workers at only slightly less impressive wages. The volume and type of agricultural products required more extensive processing and handling than the salted meat, dried hides, or greasy wool of previous years. Tanneries, flour mills, and wool-cleaning plants became necessary steps in the preparation of raw materials. The packing plants which froze the carcasses of sheep and cattle employed thousands of skilled and unskilled laborers. Two new cities emerged in the province of Buenos Aires. La Plata, established in 1882 as the provincial capital after the federalization of the city of Buenos Aires, soon became a significant administrative and port city. Farther to the south Bahía Blanca developed from a frontier village into a wool and wheat port and terminus of a major railroad system. Port construction also boomed as dredged canals, concrete ship basins, piers, warehouses, grain elevators, and railroad sidings were built at Buenos Aires and La Plata in the 1890's and at Rosario and Bahía Blanca after 1900.

Finally the needs of the growing numbers of inhabitants in the coastal cities provided limitless opportunities for immigrants. Buenos

Aires expanded to 1,500,000 inhabitants by 1914, Rosario to 220,000, Santa Fe to 60,000 and the two cities of La Plata and Bahía Blanca reached 90,000 and 60,000 respectively. With population growth, these ports sprawled back from the waterfront and created extended cities comprised of many small, almost self-sufficient neighborhoods. Masons, plumbers, carpenters, laborers, and foremen were needed to build the one- and two-story edifices, and each neighborhood required its own grocers, milkmen, tailors, bakers, cartmen, butchers, servants, and peddlers. A craze for modernization, especially in Buenos Aires, accompanied the urban growth brought on by the agricultural revolution. The narrow colonial streets and Spanish styles of architecture had to be erased. The fever to pave streets, lay out broad avenues and parks, and construct impressive public buildings and palatial private residences contributed still further employment opportunities for the thousands of Europeans who arrived in Buenos Aires each month. The immigrants themselves created new industries. Along with the imports demanded by these newcomers, local factories making macaroni, beer, textiles, and shoes began to flourish.

The opportunities in the coastal cities reinforced the effects of Argentina's land tenure system by draining off the majority of immigrants to urban occupations, often to services rather than to industries. Even those who initially made their way to the pampas as harvest laborers, sharecroppers, or tenant farmers frequently found their way back to the city. Urban life was crowded and expensive, but it provided social contacts, education, color, and activity lacking on the pampas. The poorest might cluster in the *conventillos*—slums composed of entire blocks in the downtown area burrowed by long corridors and honeycombed with tiny rooms—which developed in Buenos Aires and Rosario in the 1880's. But here their children attended school for a few years at least, and the church, the plaza, and the cafe were just around the corner.

Along with his ambition, *hacer la América*, the immigrant brought the dream to return to his homeland. Yet, just as his labors on the pampas and in the coastal ports created a new Argentina economically, so his blood formed the amalgam of a new Argentina in the social and

political sense. As a rule European nationalities did not isolate themselves by groups in the coastal cities, although La Boca, the port area
on the south side of Buenos Aires, became an Italian district, and the
suburbs of Hurlingham to the west and Belgrano to the north became
English villages. But national associations did seek to soften the adjustment to the Argentine environment for the newcomer. In this they frequently assisted the process of adaptation. The Basques, Catalans, Italians, and French united in mutual aid societies. The Germans, Italians,
British, Spanish, and French each had their own hospitals. The Germans and British maintained their own school systems, albeit under
the remote control of the Ministry of Education. Swiss shooting clubs,
Basque *pelota* or handball courts, German singing clubs, and Garibaldi
Associations existed in all the port cities. By 1900 each major immigrant group published at least one daily newspaper in Buenos Aires.
Naturally the two largest groups, the Italian and Spanish, contributing
respectively 55 and 26 per cent of all immigrants prior to World War I,
had little adjustment to make in terms of religion, language, or food.
In fact the Italians changed Argentine habits: they added macaroni,
spaghetti, and vermicelli to the national diet; they brought Italian ex-
pressions and words into the spoken language; they created *lunfardo*, a
dialect of the slums and underworld of Buenos Aires; and they revolutionized urban architecture. The great majority of immigrants quickly
learned and corrupted the Spanish language. They intermingled and
intermarried readily with Argentines or other immigrant groups. And,
as the years passed and their local obligations and attachments grew,
the dream of returning to their homeland gradually faded—never to disappear completely, but to become an impractical wish.

A country of 1,800,000 inhabitants in 1869 received an injection of
2,500,000 Europeans in less than fifty years. By 1910 three out of every
four adults in the city of Buenos Aires were European-born and the
proportion was only slightly lower in Rosario and Bahía Blanca. Ironically, however, the children of these immigrants, who dreamed so
longingly of Europe, violently rejected the European connections. Although citizens by the fact of their birth in Argentina, psychologically
they needed to assert their "Argentinism." They consequently sought

to shed all traits which could link them to the foreign land. Sometimes they even refused to speak their parents' tongue. The schools, numerous and effective at least in the coastal cities, reinforced this assimilation to Argentine values and nationalism. Only a few groups such as English and German technicians, managers, or merchants maintained isolation through ensuing generations and created separate communities like that of the Anglo-Argentines—Argentines who frequently could not speak Spanish and knew little of the country outside a British school, a British club, and a British firm.

The nation which emerged from the late nineteenth century was, nevertheless, a divided and uncertain people. On the one hand the ports, immigrants, and agricultural products provided Argentina with the trappings of a prosperous and expanding economy. Yet to step from cosmopolitan Buenos Aires into remote Salta or Jujuy was to move backward a hundred years. What was Argentina? Was it the educated, progressive elite who administered the nation, as their patrimony, from the floor of congress or the stock exchange or over an after-dinner brandy at the Jockey Club, the Club del Progreso, or the Círculo de Armas? Or was it the burgeoning middle class so evident as grocers, clerks, office managers, and foremen in the coastal cities? Or was it the Indian working in the cane fields of Tucumán or the quebracho forests of the Chaco, the Italian sharecropper in his hovel on the pampas, the Irish sheepherder in Patagonia, or the native peon in the province of Buenos Aires? Or was it the rapidly expanding urban proletariat in the ports—the mestizo cook from Santiago del Estero, the Basque laborer in the slaughter house or packing plant, the porter from Galicia, or the Italian peddler? Little wonder was it that, after a century of independence, Argentines were still searching for identity and that the nation presented simultaneously all shades of prosperity and poverty, progress and reaction, learning and illiteracy.

Chapter 6 • Two Worlds

Argentine history provides an excellent illustration of how the life of a people can be completely changed through a shift in economic focus. The area of the Río de la Plata, which had thrived from trade with the Potosí mines for much of the colonial period, turned toward the Atlantic in the nineteenth century. Spanish towns and oxcarts yielded to ports and railroads. The old Argentina did not die, but in comparison with the new it stood still. Gradually two worlds emerged, for many differences split the nation: the traditional antagonism between porteño and provincial; the free-trade interests of an agricultural economy versus the protection sought by home industries; the immigrant-saturated coast versus a Hispanic interior; the bustling activity in the ports versus the placid routine in provincial capitals; the liberal's rejection of Church temporal powers versus the conservative's acceptance of Church authority over all aspects of life; the search for new cultural and spiritual values abroad versus a reaffirmation of creole,* or native,

* Although the sense of creole applies to the distinction between Spaniard and creole of the colonial period, the popular meaning of *criollo* today is anything which is truly Argentine or native.

136

values. These rifts did not always occur along geographical boundaries; many of the outstanding leaders of the liberal, porteño elite came from Córdoba or the northwestern provinces. But, in general, Buenos Aires was the hub of progress and change, while respect for traditional values grew stronger as one moved inland.

Railroads provided the single most effective force in focusing the Argentine economy on the production of raw materials and in drawing the whole country toward the coast and the city of Buenos Aires. The basic structure of the railroad system emerged during the period 1880 to 1910 and subsequent additions and modifications, even the nationalization of the lines in 1947, failed to change the orientation of those formative decades. Foreign capital, mostly British, built the pampas system as a commercial venture and left to the Argentine government the task of establishing and managing the unprofitable lines north of Tucumán and south of Bahía Blanca needed for national unity and defense. Expectations of an agricultural export trade resulted in a system that radiated from three ports, Rosario, Bahía Blanca, and Buenos Aires. But while all three served as outlets, Buenos Aires maintained its monopoly of the import market and eventually became the terminus for all major railroad lines. Córdoba, at the northwest corner of the pampas, thus was closely linked to Buenos Aires, and the only interior centers to thrive in the late nineteenth century—Tucumán and Mendoza—did so on the basis of the production of sugar and wines for the coastal cities.

The railroads had other effects as well. In contrast with European and United States lines, the Argentine system developed without feeder lines or connecting links. Frequently the only way to move cross-country was—and sometimes still is—to take the train into the nearest port and then come out again on another of the system's spokes. Yet, since this method of transportation met the basic needs of an export economy, few roads, buses, or trucks penetrated beyond the urban radius until after 1930. Thus the isolation of the interior was prolonged. The railroads also helped to crush many of the remaining home industries by making available better, cheaper products from Europe and the United States. This competition forced local economies either to produce raw materials or to face gradual stagnation, with the accompanying drift of population toward the coast.

The initial railroad projects were not conceived as measures to tie the country more closely to the port of Buenos Aires but rather in the spirit of westward expansion. Shouts of "On to Chile" greeted the opening of those first six miles of the Western Railroad in 1857, for dreams of a trans-Andean line dominated the minds of many *émigrés* recently returned from exile in Santiago and Valparaiso. Plans for the Central Argentine line from Rosario to Córdoba, made in the 1850's during the separation of Buenos Aires and the Confederation, became a reality in the next decade—with the same vision of a western link to Chile. Appropriately, the principal organizer and builder of the Central, William Wheelright, had previously constructed the first rail lines in both Peru and Chile. In the 1870's the Argentine government commenced the Andean Railroad with a section extending from Mercedes in the province of Buenos Aires through southern Córdoba toward San Luis and the eventual goal of the Chilean border.

These first railroad ventures in Argentina encountered serious problems, not the least of which was that of securing capital. The initial section of the Western was financed with difficulty by the provincial government of Buenos Aires. In the early 1860's the national government offered unusual inducements to private capital for building the Central, including a guaranteed 7 per cent return in pounds sterling on investment, land for railroad construction as well as three miles on each side of the track for colonization purposes, liberal tax exemptions, and duty-free import of all materials needed for the building and operation of the line. Despite such concessions, Wheelright encountered much reluctance in the London money market to invest in a remote and strife-torn land. Similarly attractive terms—without the colonization land grant—were extended to the Southern Railroad which opened its first line to Chascomus in 1865 and to the Northern which began to serve the suburbs and farms along the estuary in the 1860's. Unfortunately, Argentine efforts to attract capital continued to rely on guaranteed returns of investment rather than on land grants. Had the latter method been more widely used, Argentina's landholding system might have developed quite differently, for economic self-interest, as shown in the case of the Central, dictated that railroads encourage the small independent crop farmers who would ship more freight, consume more products, and travel more than would the owners of herds of beef cattle or flocks of sheep.

By one of those quirks of history, early railroad development faced another lasting difficulty in the type and variety of gauges used. Representatives for the Western secured Argentina's first locomotives in England at a bargain price. The engines had been constructed for use on India's wide-gauge track, had been detoured to haul troops and supplies at the siege of Sevastopol during the Crimean War, and then returned to England as unserviceable. The purchase by the Buenos Aires authorities imposed the wide gauge (5′ 6″) on most of the pampas. The contract for the Central specified wide gauge, and the subsequent lines around Buenos Aires followed suit. Although able to carry heavier loads, the wide gauge also required more ties and a broader, deeper bed of rock ballast—not exactly the ideal system in an area which lacked both rocks and trees. A more serious handicap resulted from the introduction of other gauges which destroyed unity in the railroad system and imposed a costly toll in transshipping, inconveniences, and delays. The first Entre Ríos line, completed in 1872, used standard gauge (4′ 8½″), establishing the pattern for the mesopotamian provinces. The railroad northward from Córdoba to Tucumán, opened in 1876, adopted narrow gauge (3′ 3″) which would predominate in the Andean region, the Chaco, and Patagonia.

Within a few decades the hesitancy and doubts that had accompanied the birth of the Argentine rail system disappeared in an orgy of expansion and speculation. The 1880's witnessed major advances, both in the pampas and in the interior. The Southern completed its line through Olavarría to Bahía Blanca in 1884, while another more southerly route through Juárez reached Tres Arroyos in 1886, and in the same year a branch line was built to the now famous beach resort of Mar del Plata. Other lines, built or controlled mostly by the government, reached Santiago del Estero in 1884, Mendoza and San Juan in 1885, and Trenque Lauquen at Buenos Aires' western border in 1890.

But along with these accomplishments, the sudden agricultural development of the pampas introduced a competition for the power and money to be gained from railroad construction not unlike experiences in the United States and Canada. This cheap, rapid system of communication promised fortunes to anyone armed with a railroad concession. The greed of British entrepreneurs and investors soon paled in comparison with that of Argentine landowners and politicians. By the time the depression of 1890 restricted credit and speculation, the country had reaped a harvest of uneconomical lines, competing concessions, and high freight charges. Most of the twenty-two companies which operated Argentina's 5,900 miles of railroad in 1890 controlled less than a hundred miles of track apiece. At the other extreme were several large British companies which were locked in costly competition to extend their spheres of influence.

During the 1890's the national government sought to extend the railroad system to the remoter regions of Argentina. Boundary conflicts and the threat of war with Chile emphasized the need for communication with the interior of Patagonia. Under a special contract the Southern extended a line from Bahía Blanca to the Río Colorado in 1897 and to Neuquén in 1899. By 1900 a government-financed railroad also reached into the northwest to Jujuy and finally in 1908 to the Bolivian border (the Bolivian section to La Paz was completed in 1924). The dream of a trans-Andean line between Mendoza and Santiago was at last achieved in 1910 when a tunnel at 10,500 feet climaxed the engineering feat of laying a narrow-gauge track across the Andes.*

By the time another economic boom renewed private investment in railroad expansion, the Argentine government had taken steps to prevent a repetition of the wasteful speculation of the 1880's. Legislation in 1907 regulated the concessions and relations of all private railroads (now numbering thirty) with the national government. A forty-year extension was made to previous provisos for duty-free import of con-

* This line soon proved to be a financial disaster because of the lack of traffic between Argentina and Chile. Service was suspended for several years after a section was washed out in 1934. In the 1940's the tunnel was temporarily used for motor vehicles and returned to normal train service only in 1948.

struction and operational materials. Railroads were to be freed of all
taxation during this same period in return for a contribution of 3 per
cent of their net income paid to the government for the purpose of
building and maintaining rural roads around railroad stations. In addition, the government secured the right to fix rates when receipts rose
above a certain percentage of declared capital. Two years later, state-
owned lines—mostly in the extreme north and in Patagonia and comprising 14 per cent of the railroad mileage—were placed under a central
authority. Somewhat more controlled expansion, therefore, contributed
another nine thousand miles of track in the decade preceding World
War I and virtually completed the pampas system. The consolidation
of the major British companies, or the "Big Four," provided added
stability: the Southern, dominating the southern and western pampas;
the Western, largely controlled by Southern interests; the Pacific, a
hybrid composed of sections of the Andean and also subordinate to the
Southern; and the Central, which monopolized the zones north of
Buenos Aires.

At first, new ports stimulated by railroad construction actually
posed a threat to the porteño commercial monopoly. In 1854 the Central Railroad had been conceived as a means of strengthening the
position of the Confederation's outlet at Rosario. Once the line was
completed, produce from the interior provinces and cereals from the
Santa Fe colonies were exported from Rosario. The Paraná River had
cut a main channel close to the high bank at Rosario, and these natural
loading advantages were improved upon in the late 1870's by construction of railroad sidings, chutes, and grain elevators. By the 1890's Rosario handled 15 per cent of Argentine exports and nearly 10 per cent of
the imports. The renovation of the colonial port at Ensenada as an
outlet for the new provincial capital of La Plata created another challenge to Buenos Aires' commercial leadership. Dock works and railroad connections were built, and by the early 1890's La Plata controlled
5 per cent of Argentina's total trade. Following the Conquest of the
Desert and the building of the Southern's line, Bahía Blanca emerged
as a wool and wheat port, and its share of national exports rose from
4 per cent in 1889 to 7 per cent by the end of the century. The increas-

ing importance of grain exports also encouraged the development of small outlets at Santa Fe, Villa Constitución, and San Nicolás.

The port of Buenos Aires reacted slowly to these threats to its trade monopoly. As late as the 1880's, ships still had to anchor several miles from shore in the open roads—an impossible system for a port which handled several thousand vessels each year and for a land that promised soon to become one of the world's major agricultural producers. Finally, in 1887, along the estuary's shoreline in front of the city, work commenced on the Madero docks, two concrete ship basins that took ten years to build. By the turn of the century another separate harbor complex just south of the Madero docks was also nearing completion.

This modernization staved off competition. Although La Plata finished its port works before Buenos Aires, it was able to hold the advantage for only a few years. The harbor at Ensenada was too close to Buenos Aires to gain any important share of either the import or export trade. Overseas shipping preferred to make a single stop at Buenos Aires, both to discharge and to load cargo, and the railroads, particularly the Southern, co-operated by giving rebates on freight shipments to Buenos Aires. Bahía Blanca, favored with an excellent natural harbor, agricultural production of the pampas, and docks and warehouses built by the Southern Railroad, continued to expand, but only as an export center. Rosario, with French capital, made a brave effort during the first years of the twentieth century to capture import trade with a complete renovation of harbor facilities, but it had difficulty keeping even its grain export trade. The other small river ports along the Paraná and Uruguay loaded some vessels for overseas trade but transshipped the bulk of their produce by either rail or water to Buenos Aires and received all their imports through Buenos Aires.

Besides influencing the development of the pampas, the railroad facilitated the spread of an agricultural economy throughout Argentina. Relatively cheap rail transportation encouraged expansion of much of the interior's production, such as of citrus fruits, olives, tobacco, cotton, lumber, and pulpwood. The most dramatic impact occurred, however, in Tucumán and Mendoza where sugar and grape production permitted those provinces to prosper in a porteño-dominated economy.

As early as the mid-eighteenth century, sugar cane was grown in sheltered valleys of the northwest and processed by cane mills in Tucumán. Cultivation and milling gained some ground in the early nineteenth century, but the interior's sugar remained an unimportant local product overshadowed by the output of sugar plantations and mills on Brazil's northeastern coast. It was the arrival of the railroad at Tucumán in 1876 that totally changed this situation and placed the coastal cities within reach of the Argentine product.

The late nineteenth century witnessed the development of an industry whose characteristics have persisted to the present day. Tucumán, because of its climate, became the center of sugar production. Within two decades the 5,000 acres of sugar cane harvested in 1875 swelled to 135,000 acres. The substantial investments which cane mills and cane fields represented tended to concentrate control of the industry in the hands of a few wealthy landowners and capitalists. The need for modern, imported machinery merely accentuated this trend. By 1910 the nation's sugar production was the monopoly of several families who owned the thirty-four cane mills of Tucumán and the one major refinery at Rosario. Political influence guaranteed increasing prosperity. When, in the 1890's, sugar interests encountered serious competition from Brazilian and Cuban imports, a complicated tariff system of rebates and subsidies raised prices and encouraged production. As a result, considerable fortunes were built at the expense of Argentine consumers. But, at the same time, the concentration of economic and political power in a few hands, the seasonal aspects of sugar growing, and the masses of transient Indian laborers turned Tucumán into a backwash of poverty and a source of future political discontent.

Urban growth and commerce attracted some European immigrants to Tucumán—by 1914 they constituted 5 per cent of the population in the northwestern provinces—but their influence was far smaller than in the rest of the country. Modern equipment and foreign technicians often increased the mill owners' profits, but little was done to improve the lot of Indian and mestizo laborers. Since investment and ownership were Argentine, not even the cry of "foreign exploitation" could be used to arouse sympathy for those caught up in the factory system. The cane mills raised part of the sugar themselves through the employment of either wage laborers or sharecroppers. The rest they bought from small growers, who had no choice but to sell to the nearest mill at the price offered. From mid-May through August the harvest required thousands of additional hands, and from rural Santiago del Estero, from the *puna* of Salta and Jujuy, from Indian villages in the Chaco, and from across the Bolivian frontier came entire families who camped out for a hundred days and then returned home with a few bits of clothing, a colossal "hang-over," or a little cash. Working conditions grew out of colonial labor practices and frequently resembled outright slavery. The owner and investor, who reaped profits from inefficient, ignorant Indian laborers, had no interest in educating or feeding them. It was not surprising, therefore, that the northwest—Jujuy, Salta, and Tucumán in particular—led the nation in illiteracy, illegitimate births, infant mortality, and alcoholism.

The railroad brought expansion of a different sort to Mendoza. The production of grapes also had colonial origins. By the middle of the seventeenth century the irrigated oases of Cuyo shipped wines, brandies, and dried fruits to places as remote as Buenos Aires. During the nineteenth century these products continued to be the principal exports of Mendoza and San Juan, although the coast now secured much of its wine and fruit by import from France, Italy, Spain, and the United States. But after 1885 the same combination of railroad transportation and tariff protection which stimulated the sugar economy of Tucumán rapidly developed the vineyards. Mendoza's acreage rose from 250 in 1876, to 16,000 in 1890, and to 112,000 by 1910. Until 1890 San Juan possessed the larger extension of vineyards, but, with the widespread introduction of French vines to Mendoza, San Juan fell behind in acreage and wine production and maintained its supremacy only in table grapes and raisins.

With the coming of railroads, the number of foreigners in Mendoza and San Juan increased sharply. From 0.5 per cent of the population in 1869, the European element in these two provinces rose to 23 per cent, or 90,000 inhabitants, by 1914—in a period when population tripled. More significant was the fact that these newcomers, largely Italians, often became owners of small, irrigated vineyards. Technology and machinery encouraged concentration of power in the hands of major wineries, but the relatively large number of establishments—over four thousand by 1914—provided for a certain amount of competition. The process of growing grapes, demanding intensive cultivation and year-around labor, also obviated the peculiar conditions of the sugar harvest. Family labor on small units could meet most of the needs of the harvest, and, though many migrant Chilean laborers entered the Cuyo area each year, they were far better off than the Indians who came to Tucumán from Bolivia, the northwestern *puna*, or the Chaco. Benefits could be more widely distributed because of intensive exploitation of irrigated vineyards and orchards, relative proximity of agricultural zones to urban centers, rapid expansion of this protected industry during the early decades of the twentieth century, and the opportunity for farmers to become landowners. Roads, schools, hospitals, even politics were better attended to here than in any other province of the interior.

Railroads, however, also insured the subservience of interior provinces to the coastal economy. Throughout the nineteenth century, the interior's home industries struggled against porteño predominance— aided by the isolation imposed by cumbersome oxcarts. But the arrival of rails ended independence. Railroads not only took agricultural products to the coast for export or consumption, but they also brought to the interior the manufactured goods which formerly had been unattainable because of costly transportation, internal tariffs, or civil wars. Along with goods imported from Europe and the United States came an increasing volume of items manufactured, assembled, or processed in the coastal cities. The Argentine consumer continued to secure better and cheaper tools, shoes, perfumes, and engines abroad, but his everyday needs were largely met by the output of factories in Buenos Aires or Rosario. Such competition ruined many of the interior's local industries which lacked capital, equipment, or entrepreneurs. The resultant stagnation held down living standards and consumption levels throughout large areas of the interior and accentuated the disproportionate advance of the pampas region—a head which was rapidly outgrowing its body.

The rise of processing industries on the coast was reflected even in the special cases of flour, sugar, and wines. Tariff rates helped the flour mills capture the internal market during the 1870's, and in the next decade sugar and wines gained similar protection. By 1910, however, another trend was becoming noticeable. Not only had modern flour mills, located in the coastal cities and controlled by European capital, put most of the small mills of the interior out of business, but mills in the city of Buenos Aires were conquering the markets of Santa Fe, Córdoba, and Entre Ríos—all major wheat-producing provinces. In the sugar industry, although cane mills producing raw sugar remained clustered around the cane fields, the only major refinery was located at Rosario. Even the final processing of wines from Mendoza and San Juan was centered at Buenos Aires.

The agricultural revolution on the pampas, the extraordinary growth of the city of Buenos Aires, the definitive location of the national capital in this commercial center, and the establishment of a railroad net that drew the whole country toward the port strongly influenced Argentine political evolution after 1880. The president not only had constitutional authority for intervention; with the railroad system, the telegraph, and an army strengthened after the turn of the century by conscription, he also had the power to assert national authority throughout the republic. Politics now centered directly on control of national administration. Rivalry occurred along lines of social classes and economic groups, but it was conflict in which the coast's supremacy was accepted as axiomatic. An emerging middle class first raised its voice in 1890 for a share in political control and spoils, but it remained a class of the cities and towns of the pampas. Working-class sentiment and organization likewise developed in Buenos Aires and Rosario after 1890. Even the oligarchs, those wealthy landowners and capitalists from every corner of Argentina, established their center of operations, and often their homes, in Buenos Aires and soon lost touch with their provincial origins. In congress, on the floor of the stock and grain exchanges, in import and export firms, and in commercial and investment houses, the only Argentina considered or even seen was the bustling city of Buenos Aires situated at the edge of the fertile plain.

But in 1910 at least one-third of the people still lived beyond the pampas and the coastal cities—in another world which lacked the luster of Buenos Aires or the vitality of *estancias,* alfalfa fields, flour mills, and packing plants. This aspect of Argentina appeared very seldom in contemporary accounts or in subsequent historical works. Yet this other Argentina also formed a part of the nation.

These two areas defied precise definition. The convenient separation into coast and interior still presented the most valid division but with evident limitations. Tucumán and Mendoza necessarily constituted special cases closely linked to the rising urban centers of the coast. The city of Córdoba, along with the southeastern portion of that province, was also drawn into the coastal sphere, although retaining some of the colonial atmosphere. On the other hand, much of the province of Corrientes and the northern section of Santa Fe were far closer to the heritage of the Guaraní and the conquistador than to the agricultural revolution on the pampas. Thus, classification of the provinces of Buenos Aires, Entre Ríos, Corrientes, Santa Fe, and Córdoba as "the coast" and the rest of Argentina as "the interior" only approximates the realities of 1910.

Census figures documented a population expansion throughout Argentina in the late nineteenth century. As in the early national period, the coast received the whole benefit of immigration, while the interior grew much more slowly. Between 1869 and 1914 the population of the city and province of Buenos Aires rose from 500,000 to 3,600,000, increasing the porteño share of the national total from 28 per cent to 46 per cent. In the same period the interior's share declined from 40 per cent to 19 per cent.*

* The five coastal provinces—Buenos Aires, Santa Fe, Córdoba, Entre Ríos, and Corrientes—accounted for 77 per cent of the national population in 1914, as contrasted with 60 per cent in 1869. By 1914 the territories in Patagonia and the Chaco contributed 4 per cent.

Since agriculture in most of the interior had to rely on irrigation, the already sparse population was dispersed along valleys and river banks. The trend toward urbanization which played such a fundamental role on the coast did not extend to the interior. Here few forces drew people together in cities. The provincial capitals, invariably towns established during the Spanish conquest, met the modest administrative and commercial needs of the area. Except for the special cases of Mendoza and Tucumán, they expanded no more rapidly than the surrounding countryside. The extraordinary growth of the coastal cities caused the overall proportion of rural population to fall from three-quarters in 1869 to less than one-half in 1914. But in all the interior provinces except Tucumán the rural population (classified as living in settlements of less than two thousand inhabitants) numbered between 70 and 85 per cent of the total.

The railroads did bring about an increase in commerce, mining, and agricultural production, and, as a result, a few secondary centers arose in the interior after 1900, but there was nothing to compare with the spread of towns on the coast. The 1914 census clearly illustrated the extent of the division. Outside of the federal capital, the urban population of the province of Buenos Aires had increased since the previous census (1895) from 61 towns with 316,000 inhabitants to 147 towns with 1,120,000 inhabitants. On a smaller scale, the same development occurred in Santa Fe, Entre Ríos, Corrientes, and Córdoba, and, as might be expected, in Tucumán and Mendoza. Elsewhere, the capitals —usually containing 10 to 20 per cent of the provincial population— provided almost the only exception to a rural environment dominated by farms and small villages. Besides the city of San Juan, that province boasted only two small towns. In the extreme northwest, Jujuy's urban population numbered 15,000, divided among the capital and three towns. Even Santiago del Estero possessed only three towns besides the capital, a total urban population of 35,000.

The cities and towns of the interior provided an accurate reflection of the colonial past, not only in numbers but also in composition of population, class structure, way of life, social customs, and intellectual activities. Here little had changed since the eighteenth century, when the decline of Potosí's silver wealth and the emergence of the port of Buenos Aires began to cast a shadow over the interior. While French ideas, Italian blood, and English capital inundated the coast, the impact of European influences in the interior was limited to Mendoza and Tucumán. Elsewhere, except for migrants from Chile and Bolivia, foreigners added little to the population.* As a result, the growth that occurred in the interior came largely from natural increase. In these provinces large families with an average of four to six children continued to predominate, unaffected by the contemporary trend toward smaller families in the coastal cities. San Juan, Tucumán, Jujuy, and Santiago del Estero boasted the highest birth rates in the nation—between thirty-nine and forty-one per thousand inhabitants. Yet this was balanced by high rates of infant mortality and by a life expectancy that ranged from thirty-five to thirty-nine years in most of the northwestern provinces.

In the interior towns a traditionalist type of society continued to hold sway, untouched by the radical transformations taking place in the coastal region. The majority of provincial capitals remained small cities, built in accord with the plans of their conquistador-founders. By 1914 only two had expanded significantly: Tucumán with 91,000 inhabitants and Mendoza with 59,000. The rest had grown slowly: Salta, 28,000; Santiago del Estero, 23,000; San Juan, 17,000; San Luis, 15,000; Catamarca, 13,000; and La Rioja and Jujuy with 8,000 each. Although size was not the whole story, these figures suggest severe limitations on any efforts to bring progress, change, or prosperity to provincial capitals. The smallness of the urban center placed effective checks on educational facilities, community services, local revenues, and opportunities for exchange, consumption, or advancement.

All provincial capitals were founded and continued to exist as centers of administration and trade. These cities controlled large, sparsely settled territories, as in colonial times, and provided the only markets for the exchange of goods. Yet in the interior these functions remained

* The 1914 census registered 5 per cent of the population in Salta and Jujuy as European born, 2 per cent in Catamarca, 3 per cent in Santiago del Estero, 8 per cent in San Luis—contrasted with 39 per cent in the province and city of Buenos Aires or 34 per cent in Santa Fe.

modest. The governor of Buenos Aires might almost equal the president in power and prestige, while the size of Buenos Aires' provincial budget compared favorably with that voted by the national congress. But many a governor in the interior disposed of budgets smaller than those allocated by town councils on the coast and presided over the barest of provincial assemblies, law courts, and police forces. The gradual disappearance of local autonomy turned much of provincial government into a bureaucratic extension of national authority—posts to be sought as stepping stones to higher power or, more often, as comfortable, undemanding sinecures. The possibilities for commercial expansion were likewise limited. A mass of population which lived at little more than subsistence level topped by a tiny elite class provided neither producers nor consumers to swell the flow of trade through the interior.

Perhaps most resistant to change in these interior cities was the class structure. The descendants of the conquistadors still constituted the elite. For three centuries they had maintained a pure lineage, marrying only within their class and rejecting any introduction of new blood within their society. Here the immigrant or middle-class person found himself excluded from upper-class homes even more effectively than on the coast. The very smallness of this elite in the capitals, rarely numbering more than a few hundred persons, led to considerable inbreeding, further aggravated by the fact that the most ambitious and talented were almost invariably drawn away to the coast by opportunities in government service, the professions, or business. Symptomatic of the social cleavages in interior cities was the arrangement found at La Rioja for the biweekly evening band concerts in the plaza: the town's aristocracy enjoyed an enclosure with garden, reclining seats, and promenade in the center of the plaza from which the police barred all others. Throughout the interior the arrangements for any ball or celebration always included a place from which the common people could watch without being admitted to the festivities.

The elite of the interior supported itself from large landholdings, supplemented by occupations in government, Church, law, medicine, and commerce. Compared with the *estancieros* and landowners of the pampas, those of the interior were poor. Rarely did they expend either capital or effort on their holdings, and since land was valued for social prestige and political influence at least as much as for economic gain, owners contented themselves with paltry returns from grazing and tenant farming. This elite also monopolized political power and, by the end of the nineteenth century, was satisfied to divide, rather than to fight over, political spoils. The Church likewise continued to be a bulwark of the aristocracy, for religion played a more vital role in the interior than on the "liberal" coast. The position of the cathedral on the main plaza facing the cabildo represented a very real share of temporal power carried over from the days of the Spanish Empire. The membership and control of convents, monasteries, private schools, the priesthood, and all high Church offices belonged to the aristocracy, and, as such, represented an important part of its economic and political dominance. The favored profession of law, necessitating university training in Buenos Aires, Córdoba, or, after the turn of the century, in La Plata or Santa Fe, tended to draw off the talented toward the coast. After a few years in these urban centers many preferred to escape the provincial atmosphere permanently or at least to seek a career in politics that might soon return them to the coast. Commerce still enriched many an aristocratic creole family, although care was exercised not to dirty one's hands with the actual dispensing of merchandise. The elite dominated the wholesale trade: the import of fine European consumer goods; the sale of mules for work in the Bolivian mines; the export of boots and sandals for the Indian miners; the shipment of agricultural and mineral raw materials to the coast; and the handling of carriages, woolen homespun, and such native manufactures which had not succumbed to outside competition.

The middle class in the interior had to be considered as a social rather than as an economic group, since many of its members were as well off as the sometimes impecunious but proud descendants of the conquistadors. As on the coast, this was a wholly urban class comprised mostly of foreigners. In size it was, if anything, smaller than the elite, and its position hardly justified the description "middle." Isolation, division, and transiency were its predominant characteristics. Rejected by the upper class, its members in turn held themselves aloof from the masses. Yet, unlike the elite which did form a powerful, well-integrated class closely linked by family ties, the middle-class inhabitants possessed no common bond beyond occasional national loyalties—an Italian mutual aid society, a Basque association, or a Syrian social center. Furthermore, few of the middle class developed any attachment to the particular capital or town in which they found themselves. Whether descendants of creoles or immigrants, or recent arrivals from Europe, their principal motivation was economic advance. For the moment they had no political power, and socially they had not arrived. Consequently, the drive was to gain acceptance and position through wealth wherever opportunity arose.

Retail commerce, technical services, and certain management functions provided occupations for the middle class. Every interior capital and town had its pharmacist, barber, and baker. The Andean cities usually boasted a handful of mining engineers and office managers of British companies. After the arrival of the railroad, most towns needed station managers, telegraphers, and dispatchers. Rare was the urban center that could not claim a French hotel keeper or a German merchant. The school systems, provincial courts, and administration added a corps of poorly paid teachers and clerks to this amorphous middle group. Most of the middle class were immigrant Spaniards and Italians, while after 1900 increasing numbers came from the Levant.

The urban lower class, as in colonial times, numbered 80 to 90 per cent of the city population and was composed of all those who labored with their hands, performed menial services, or otherwise did not qualify for the elite or middle classes. The amalgam of several centuries produced a dark-skinned yet thoroughly Europeanized individual who spoke—but rarely read—Spanish and bore little cultural or even racial resemblance to his Indian or Negro ancestry. These were not a downtrodden people, but they sorely lacked the education, sanitation, and nutrition to improve their situation. Disease, unhealthy diets, economic stagnation, and a rigid caste system bred a quiet, resigned, and indolent lower class. Malaria and tapeworm were endemic in most of the northern provinces; goiter afflicted the inhabitants of Mendoza and Santiago del Estero; and tuberculosis and influenza flourished, due to the inade-

quate housing and malnutrition. This class contributed in large measure to the high infant mortality rates and the short life expectancy of
the interior provinces. Here also starvation was far more prevalent than
on the meat- and grain-producing coast. Even in the mountain valleys,
Nature was a hard master, and the verdure of irrigated farms and orchards only emphasized man's dependence on water. More injurious
than starvation was the constant malnutrition. Boiled corn or boiled
rice constituted the universal diet of the interior—not always in the
tasty regional dishes now served in porteño restaurants. Vegetables,
fresh meat, and milk remained beyond the reach of urban masses. The
chewing of fresh sugar-cane stalks and the excessive consumption of
caña, or alcohol, frequently indicated the shocking lack of any other
nourishment. In the puna of the northwest, as in Bolivia, the chewing
of coca leaves was frequently all that made life endurable.

Urban residence provided access to more social services than could
be obtained in the country, but in the interior this advantage was hardly
significant. By the first decades of the twentieth century the interior
capitals had no more than a handful of doctors, and these were more
than occupied with the 10 per cent of the population who were well
enough clothed, fed, and sheltered to have a chance for recovery, and
who could also afford to pay. Municipal and Church hospitals, as a
general rule, provided little more than a place to die, and no one entered them until all hope was lost. The middle and upper classes had
their own wells, collected rainwater from their roofs, or in some capitals
connected into municipal water systems, but the poor relied on public
wells or irrigation ditches. Since few towns had any adequate means for
disposing of sewage, the incidence of typhoid fever and dysentery
within the lower class was high.

The Church was omnipresent in these provincial capitals, and, even
in a city as closely linked to the coastal economy as Córdoba, its influence remained paramount. Yet its responsibility for the well-being of
the community had been reduced by national legislation in the 1880's,
and reform elements which emerged in the 1890's were unable to revive
the Church's social mission until after World War I. Eliminated from
the public school system in 1884, supplemented by the state in matters

of civil registers, marriages, and burials, and removed from overt political control, the Church became a conservative body struggling to preserve vestiges of its former glory. The wealth remained: in Córdoba the Church owned at least one-quarter of the city's real estate; in Catamarca its magnificent and imposing cathedral, built over a span of several decades beginning in the 1850's, contrasted strangely with the poor and backward urban center; in all the capitals it maintained large and frequently luxurious convents and monasteries. The masses and, above all, the women, supported the Church, but only in an occasional hospital or orphanage or among a few parish priests did one find the zeal and abnegation which had once spread the Catholic faith into the remotest regions of the continent.

The interior suffered from poor educational facilities, at least in comparison with the coast. Diligent efforts by Argentina's statesmen, led by Sarmiento himself, reduced the illiteracy rate from more than two-thirds in 1869 to a little over one-third by 1914, encouraged the building of primary schools by the provinces, established a secondary school system under the supervision of the national government, and created a university structure second to none in Latin America. But as with immigration, foreign investments, and living standards, the effect of these measures was overwhelmingly concentrated on the coast and in the cities of Buenos Aires, La Plata, Rosario, Santa Fe, and Córdoba. Decades of anarchy and civil strife, the poverty of provincial treasuries (aggravated by an inevitable tendency to consider education as the part most easily sacrificed in any budget), and the logical tendency of national authorities to place funds, teachers, and efforts in areas where obstacles seemed less staggering, robbed the interior of any fair share in Argentina's educational campaign. By 1914 only 48 per cent of school-age children attended school in Salta and Jujuy and 44 per cent in Santiago del Estero, as contrasted with 61 per cent in the city and province of Buenos Aires. Despite the legal requirement of school attendance through the age of fourteen, it was well into the twentieth century before many children of the lower class in the interior cities and towns completed more than a couple of years of instruction. Elementary education thus became largely the privilege of the middle class and the elite.

Although education was tuition-free, access to the secondary level in the interior was even more restricted than to the primary grades. By the last decades of the nineteenth century, *colegios* and normal schools* had been established in each of the provincial capitals, but they were poorly attended in comparison to similar institutions on the coast. At least the normal school served the educational process by providing slightly trained men and women for the elementary school system. But the *colegio's* emphasis on university preparation tended to limit attendance to the sons of the wealthy who had the time and opportunity to pursue the university studies of law and medicine. To fill the gap, the national government opened several secondary institutes in agronomy, animal husbandry and viniculture. Lower-class parents, however, lacked the resources to send their children through even these courses of study, while the middle classes aspired to the professions as the only path to success and status.

Investments, government expenditures, and intellectual opportunities similarly distinguished between two Argentinas: one of progress and development, the other of conservatism and stagnation. In Mendoza and Tucumán, French and Italian capital built several of the important wineries and sugar mills. But beyond that, the interior provinces had only unproven mineral resources to attract foreign investors. Silver, gold, and copper were exploited on a small scale in Catamarca and La Rioja. In Mendoza and Salta surface seepage indicated the presence of oil. Antimony, manganese, iron, lead, tungsten, and coal, along with marble and slate, were known to exist in varying quantities and qualities along most of the Andean chain and eastward as far as the Córdoba

* The Argentine *colegio,* which is patterned on the French *lycée,* is not the same as high school in the United States. The *colegio* usually offers five years of rigorous classical training following seven years of elementary schooling. Graduation with the degree of *bachillerato* qualifies one to embark directly on professional training in law, medicine, engineering, or teaching and is perhaps equivalent to sophomore level in most United States colleges. The normal school consists of five years following elementary instruction and is dedicated solely to the preparation of primary school teachers.

hills. But such prospects were overshadowed by the dazzling investment opportunities on the pampas. In view of the long and costly freight hauls to the coast, the legal wrangles surrounding all mining claims, and the inadequate supply of capital, machinery, and trained workers, it seemed simpler to buy coal and metals from Europe and oil and kerosene from the United States. To attain self-sufficiency in oil (as Argentina finally did early in the 1960's), to reach the remote coal deposits, or to develop a significant extraction of metallic ores would have required major investments and probably major sacrifices. For the moment neither the ruling elite nor British entrepreneurs saw any purpose in developing the interior's rich but distant potential. Only when oil was accidently struck at Comodoro Rivadavia on the coast in 1907 did the national government reserve certain subsoil rights to itself and subsequently create a federal oil agency. Even then, exploitation languished for another half century.

The interior provinces secured equally few benefits from government expenditures. The area suffered from a lack of taxable resources. Landowners ruled provincial councils even more absolutely in the interior than on the coast, and they refused to allow themselves to be burdened with fiscal demands. Commerce and the tiny middle class provided only a trickle of revenues from license, stamp, and produce taxes. In 1910 the budget for the province of Mendoza totaled 5 million pesos, for Santiago del Estero 3 million, for San Juan 1.5 million, and for La Rioja 0.3 million, at a time when the province of Buenos Aires was spending 38 million pesos. Provincial capitals received water systems at national expense, government-built railroads reached into the remoter provinces, and irrigation projects were discussed for several of the Andean provinces. But, as with education, appropriations for public works tended to favor areas that could show immediate benefits and results. Millions were spent (ironically by presidents and congressmen from the interior) to modernize the new federal capital, Córdoba received the bulk of irrigation funds, and an army of federal experts and engineers remained concentrated in the coastal cities.

It is almost superfluous to point to the intellectual desert in the interior. Many of Argentina's great men of letters and arts were born outside the coastal fringe, but almost without exception they were drawn to the city of Buenos Aires. A veritable flowering of artistic and intellectual potential during the first decades of the twentieth century contrasted with the occasional masterpieces of Sarmiento and Hernández in the nineteenth. But this spiritual and cultural achievement of nationhood was built on the porteño monopoly of the country's talents. Provincial capitals remained oases where men of promise tried out their abilities, wrote and edited the daily or weekly newspapers, printed their verses, painted or composed while pursuing success in politics, law, or commerce. But only in Buenos Aires could these men find communion with kindred talents and the necessary contact with European ideas and models.

Life in the interior capitals moved in the leisurely pace of the colonial centuries. Hotels and restaurants were inferior and expensive. Amusements were few, limited to cockfighting and gambling, an occasional band concert in the plaza, or the gathering of upper-class men at the town's principal cafe for an evening of talk, billiards, or cards. May 25 was celebrated with fireworks, speeches, brightly lit houses, and the fresh whitewashing of buildings. A wedding or wake provided an excuse for dancing and drinking at all social levels, while many of the lower class lapsed into a drunken stupor each Sunday. Everywhere the condition of streets was abominable; they were almost always unpaved except for those near the central plaza. Electric street lights replaced the flickering tallow wicks in the main plaza and along a couple of the principal streets. But the power came from steam plants run on imported coal rather than from the energy of nearby mountain streams.

Beyond the provincial capitals and the infrequent secondary towns lived the 70 to 85 per cent of the population that provided the labor for the interior's agriculture and mining. There was no upper or middle class here save for an occasional patriarchal landowner who chose to live on his holdings, a wandering peddler, or a country storekeeper. The centuries apparently had stopped for the rural interior and for remote regions of the littoral such as Corrientes.

Even in the late nineteenth century Indians figured among the rural masses far more than porteños cared to admit. In Salta, Jujuy, Santiago del Estero, and Corrientes, pure-blooded Indian communities lived much as they had before the Spanish conquest, exposed only to occasional contacts with Argentine economy and society. The Quechua or Guaraní language, the diet of corn or potatoes, the dress, religion, and social customs had changed but little. The village economy was based on subsistence agriculture and raising goats and sheep. The Indian entered the mestizo-Hispanic environment only in the sugar fields of the northwest or in the lumber camps of the Chaco. From this brief exchange he acquired some superficial aspects of a new culture: a pair of pants or a shirt, a mirror or a hat, a fondness for cane alcohol, and an understanding of Spanish. Such limited acculturation did not immediately destroy the Indian way of life or the deep distrust of Hispanic and foreign peoples, but it facilitated eventual absorption within the formless lower class of rural Argentina.

Throughout most of the interior, however, the Indian element had blended into the mestizo lower class. From these people came the herdsmen, gauchos, miners, tenant farmers, contract laborers, peons, and squatters of the interior. After 1900 coastal Argentina also began to draw on this poorly paid, ignorant labor force to help with cereal harvests, railroad building, and construction projects. The census of 1914 registered a marked increase in migration toward the coast from La Rioja, Catamarca, and San Luis—amounting to as much as 30 per cent of the population in those provinces.

The same aspects of malnutrition, poor housing, and lack of ambition that characterized the urban workers in the interior afflicted the rural lower class. Social services of government and Church totally bypassed them. Not until well into the twentieth century would schools reach out into the remote regions and make the white smocks of school children a familiar sight along the paths and roads of rural Catamarca, Santiago del Estero, or Corrientes. As in pre-Conquest times, medical care was in the hands of healers whose art alternated between an expert use of native herbs and a mystical faith in strange concoctions of dried monkey brains, powdered snake skins, and the like. Religion frequently combined a fanatic acceptance of Catholicism with the superstitions, deities, and lore of Indian heritage. Promiscuity and loose family attachments helped to blend the racial strains but contrasted sharply with the isolation of middle- and upper-class women.

Such, therefore, were the aspects of a world which existed beyond the coastal cities, the pampas, and the railroad net of late-nineteenth-century development. In the capitals, towns, and countryside of the interior provinces and even in the remote regions of the littoral lived a people almost a century removed in tradition, culture, and way of life from the coast. Gradually the coast would absorb this other Argentina. Better communications would link the nation together. Economic opportunities or military conscription would draw individuals to the coast and open their eyes to a different existence. Other provinces would follow the lead of Córdoba, Tucumán, and Mendoza and prosper on the basis of integration with the coastal economy. Urban centers in the interior would expand. Even the countryside would finally feel the effect of roads, schools, dams, doctors, and priests. The gap, nevertheless, was not one that could be closed easily or quickly, and the dichotomy between porteño and provincial, between coast and interior, between urban and rural, remains to trouble Argentina today.

Chapter 7 • The City and the Factory

The impact of Argentina's late-nineteenth-century expansion principally affected the ports and the city of Buenos Aires. Neither the countryside nor the interior reaped a substantial share of the prosperity and progress which came as a result of the coast's agricultural revolution. At this crucial moment in the evolution of the nation, development remained focused on a city rather than on a frontier. The Conquest of the Desert, the building of railroads, and the advances in agricultural exploitation turned the Argentine people increasingly toward their capital city as the fountainhead of opportunity and success. At the same time, stimulated by this urban orientation, factories began to expand, at first into the initial processing of raw materials for export and then into the production of consumer goods. Two predominant trends of twentieth-century European and United States economic development—urbanization and industrialization—thus became fundamental factors in Argentina's modern growth.

The federalization of the city of Buenos Aires in 1880 had as its political objective the subjugation of the porteños and the appropriation of the port's wealth, prestige, and power for the national benefit. The

result, however, was that the city captured the nation. Buenos Aires
and the other coastal cities came to embody modern Argentina. Along
with the phenomenal growth from 300,000 inhabitants to 1,500,000 by
1914, there occurred the total transformation of the sprawling village,
or *gran aldea,* into one of the world's metropolises. All that could be
said for Buenos Aires in terms of population expansion, economic
growth, modernization, and social change, applied on a smaller scale
to the other pampas ports of Rosario and Bahía Blanca and to the cities
of Avellaneda, General San Martín, and Lomas de Zamora that had
begun to add their weight to the area of Greater Buenos Aires.

Physically the Buenos Aires of 1880 was a colonial city. The narrow
streets still followed the plan laid out by Garay three centuries before.
The built-up area was small, not exceeding two hundred blocks—fifteen
blocks west from the Plaza de Mayo and six or seven blocks north and
south of that same plaza. In the center of town a few streets had been
paved during the 1870's with cobblestones or granite squares from the
island of Martín García. Most, however, alternated according to season
and rainfall between dusty ruts and treacherous quagmires filled with
potholes and the refuse of animals and humans. Directly from the
streets' edge rose the mud-brick walls of the low one- and two-story
buildings. Heavy iron grillwork barred the infrequent windows, and
cumbersome paneled doors sheltered family or merchandise from the
outside world. Occasional sidewalks narrowed the streets still further,
and along some lanes that led toward the river these brick or wooden
structures raised the pedestrian a full yard above mud, offal, and rush-
ing torrents common during the rainy spells.

In the 1860's several private companies laid trolley tracks along the
central streets, and horse-drawn trams provided a welcome supplement
to the universal travel by horseback. Police were organized on a regular
basis, replacing the night watchman who since colonial times had
sounded his cry of "Two o'clock, clear, and all is well." A small number
from the police force were detailed to serve as firemen. Only a few
principal streets had lighting, however, and, though gas jets made their
appearance in the 1850's, they were still outnumbered by flickering tallow wicks. With this, municipal conveniences ended. The Western

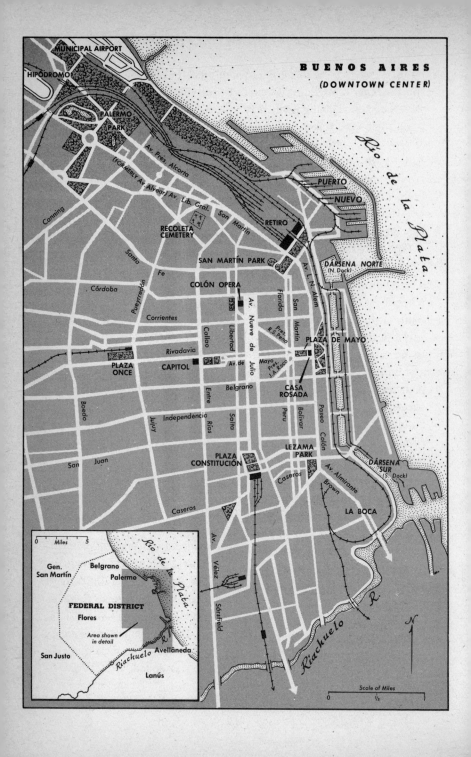

BUENOS AIRES
(DOWNTOWN CENTER)

MUNICIPAL AIRPORT

HIPÓDROMO

PALERMO PARK

Av. Pres. Alcorta

(FORMERLY Av. Alvear) Av. Lib. Gral.

San Martín

Canning

Santa

Fe

Córdoba

Puerrredón

Corrientes

Callao

Libertad

Rivadavia

RECOLETA CEMETERY

SAN MARTÍN PARK

COLÓN OPERA

PLAZA ONCE

CAPITOL

Av. de Mayo

Av. de Julio

Nueve

Florida

San

Martín

Pres. R.S. Peña

Pres. J.A. Roca

RETIRO

PUERTO NUEVO

DÁRSENA NORTE
(N. Dock)

Río de la Plata

PLAZA DE MAYO

CASA ROSADA

Av. L.N. Alem

Belgrano

Entre

Ríos

Salta

Perú

Bolívar

Paseo

Colón

LEZAMA PARK

Boedo

Independencia

Jujuy

San

Juan

PLAZA CONSTITUCIÓN

Caseros

DÁRSENA SUR
(S. Dock)

Caseros

Av. Almirante

Brown

LA BOCA

Vélez

Sarsfield

Riachuelo

R.

N

Scale of Miles

0   ½

---

0   Miles   5

Gen. San Martín

Belgrano

Palermo

Río de la Plata

FEDERAL DISTRICT

Flores

Area shown in detail

R.

San Justo

Avellaneda

Riachuelo

Lanús

Railroad extended a waterpipe some distance into the estuary in order to secure fresh water for its locomotives and in 1868 began to provide water for a few individual homes. But, despite recurrent plagues, elaborate projects for water supply were not carried through, and the city as a whole depended on water carts filled at the river's edge, on shallow wells too often located next to outhouses, or, in the houses of the well-to-do, on rainwater collected from the flat roofs. Open sewer systems took advantage of the slight slope toward the river and eventually dumped most of the city's waste into the estuary. Enough sewage also found its way into the streets and into the ground to contribute to the cholera and yellow fever plagues that decimated the porteño populace and emptied the city during several summers in the late 1860's and early 1870's.

Parks and plazas were not yet things of beauty. By the 1860's a few scraggly trees adorned the city's principal plaza facing the Cabildo, while during the next decade Sarmiento took the first steps to transform Rosas' former residence at Palermo into a porteño Bois de Boulogne by planting several avenues of stately palm trees. But the general aspect of the city was barren. The huge open plazas of Retiro, Once de Septiembre, and Constitución at the city's northern, western, and southern extremities were rutted fields to which oxcarts and then railroads brought produce from the countryside. The muddy waters of the estuary lapped at the foundations of the colonial fort, where during Sarmiento's presidency an initial section of the new government house, or Casa Rosada,* was built. The river bank extended north and south along today's avenues of Leandro Alem and Paseo Colón—a full mile inland from the present shoreline. Aside from the already noted inconveniences caused shipping and passengers, new arrivals to Argentina's principal port never ceased to be astonished by two long-established customs enacted on the sloping bank. Each morning crowds of Negro and mulatto washerwomen arrived to pound and scrub Buenos Aires' dirty linen in the stagnant pools and yellow water, while on summer

---

* Under Sarmiento, the addition to the old fort that was used as a government house was painted pink or rose, thus giving rise to this traditional name for the executive office building. The presidential residence is located in the northern suburb of Olivos.

evenings, men and women, black and white, rich and poor (although segregated by area) splashed and bathed in the tepid, knee-deep water. The Plaza de Mayo, on which the Cabildo, Cathedral, and Casa Rosada all face, was divided by an arcade of shops and a street into two separate sections. Until the 1860's the eastern half remained an open field, bordered on one side by a vacant lot that served as a garbage dump.

The city, however, showed some signs of its future extension. The Italians built up the southern port areas of La Boca and Barracas, while expansion across the Riachuelo River laid the foundations for the future city of Avellaneda and signalled the beginnings of Greater Buenos Aires. Fingers of settlement followed the railroad tracks of the Southern, Western, and Northern out of Buenos Aires. Many English and Germans and some porteños started to move northward to homes in Belgrano, San Isidro, and San Fernando. The aristocratic element shifted to the city's northern edge along the streets of Córdoba and Santa Fe and left the blocks adjoining the Plaza de Mayo to commercial and business houses. The patio style of construction further encouraged this type of sprawling city. Only a few villas raised a third or fourth story above the low skyline. Homes on the city's outskirts frequently occupied an entire block, and even in the center each house usually boasted three patios extending back from the street: the first for family use; the second for servants and household needs; and the third for garden, well, outhouse, and fruit trees.

This was the city that by 1910 even Parisians would claim as the Paris of South America after a Cinderella-like transformation from *gran aldea* into the beautiful and prosperous queen of the Río de la Plata. Much of the change was physical. Federalization itself provided administrative and financial impetus for modernization. No longer was the national government in an anomalous position as "guest" of the provincial authorities. Now the city's intendant was a presidential appointee, the police and other municipal functions were placed under federal control, and the city's budget was supported by the national treasury. Most important of all, presidents such as Roca from Tucumán or Miguel Juárez Celman from Córdoba and ministries and congresses dominated by provincials wanted to build Buenos Aires into the showplace of Argentina. Consequently, the city continued to receive at least as large a share of the greatly increased national revenues as it had under Rosas or Mitre. Diehard porteños, embittered by an apparent loss of control over Buenos Aires, established the provincial capital at La Plata in 1882, laid out broad avenues and parks, planted eucalyptus groves, erected magnificent public buildings, and endowed the city with a bureaucratic existence, all as a challenge to Buenos Aires. Their resentment, however, was short-lived. La Plata expanded rapidly as an administrative center—to 90,000 inhabitants by 1914—but the provincial capital was too close to the seat of national authority to assert its autonomy. Buenos Aires remained the home of porteños and at the same time became the mecca of all Argentines.

Under the guidance of a particularly vigorous intendant, the booming eighties endowed Buenos Aires with its first major physical improvements. The Plaza de Mayo began to assume the appearance which it has today. The north wing of the Casa Rosada was completed in 1882, and several years later the alley which separated the two sections was closed by an imposing portico. An unprecedented day-and-night wrecking operation cleared away the arcade of tawdry shops that divided the plaza in time for the May 25 celebrations of 1884. Buenos Aires' narrow colonial streets then began to receive some attention. Appropriations were made for a broad avenue to run directly west from the Plaza de Mayo—a widening that, before completion in 1894, brought down many old buildings and even chopped three arches off the historic Cabildo. More ambitious plans to open the choked downtown area had to wait until the 1930's for execution: a northern diagonal that departed from the Plaza de Mayo and cut through seven of the city's most built-up blocks before ending in a white marble obelisk; a southern diagonal that ended only a few blocks from the same plaza after removing another three arches from the Cabildo; one of the world's widest (480 feet) and most costly avenues, the Nueve de Julio, built to unite the proposed ends of the northern and southern diagonals; and widening of streets such as Callao, Entre Ríos, Corrientes, Córdoba, and Santa Fe. Fortunately for municipal indebtedness and future traffic the narrow colonial streets did not extend more than ten or fifteen blocks beyond the Plaza de Mayo. Outside that central area broader streets were laid out before buildings filled in the blocks.

Open sewers and dirt streets disappeared from downtown Buenos Aires during the 1880's. The long-projected municipal water and sewer system was completed in the central part of the city in 1886, although delays followed in connecting these facilities to houses. Efforts to remedy the impossible transit conditions also bore results with the paving of more than a third of the five thousand street blocks by the late eighties. Square granite paving stones gradually replaced the round cobblestones, but the search for smoother paving materials continued. Wood paving became popular in the early 1890's, particularly after experimental asphalt paving turned to black glue under the hot summer sun. It was soon found, however, that asphalt imported from Trinidad did not melt in the sun, and by the turn of the century porteño ladies were enjoying relatively comfortable carriage rides (aided by the first use of rubber tires) over a steadily expanding network of asphalted streets and avenues.

Along with these improvements in the aspect of streets came innovations in the city's transportation system. By 1905 electricity had largely replaced the overworked horses of the city's trolley system. All varieties of carriages and horse cabs and even a few automobiles now circulated through porteño streets—since 1889 keeping to the left in British fashion. (The formerly used right-hand drive was restored in 1945.) How rapidly the city was changing was emphasized in 1911 when work began on the Avenida de Mayo subway. Three years later, the British-built line was opened to its present extension four miles west of the Plaza de Mayo—only a decade after New York City had completed the first major subway in the hemisphere. But, like the diagonals and avenues, the completion of Buenos Aires' other important subway connections had to wait until the 1930's.

Construction thus became the city's major industry. The massive public works program that accompanied the boom in the eighties was slowed by the crash of 1890 but regained its momentum during the first decade of the twentieth century. Impressive government buildings of granite and marble appeared on every hand. By the time of the centennial celebrations in 1910 an enormous, half-finished Capitol crowned the opposite end of the Avenida de Mayo from the Casa Rosada. The Colón, the city's principal theater and opera house, moved from its original building on the Plaza de Mayo to its present magnificent structure. Office buildings, hotels, and private palaces replaced many of the one- or two-story, patio-style houses in the center of Buenos Aires. The 1887 municipal census registered 34,000 houses, but only 436 had three stories and 36 a fourth story. By 1910 the city could claim over 110,000 buildings, of which 3,252 had more than two stories and 68 reached to seven stories or higher. No longer was Buenos Aires characterized by a low, level skyline. Along streets near the Plaza de Mayo rose tall buildings housing offices, stores, and apartments of a burgeoning city. Farther out, along Córdoba, Santa Fe, and the new Avenida Alvear, the three- and four-story, Italian-style villas of the elite were a symptom of the city's changing life.

Fortunately, beautification accompanied the porteño craze for modernization. In the Plaza de Mayo palm trees and then banana trees were planted, and marble benches and paths complemented the plaza's newly acquired spaciousness. Trees spread their shade at Retiro, Once, and Constitución. The elegant Plaza San Martín now dominated the rise near Retiro, and to the northwest several small hillocks near the cemetery of the Recoleta were transformed with spreading gum trees and gardens. Rosas' former estate at Palermo became a source of porteño pride and pleasure on which the city lavished trees, fountains, lakes, statuary, and flower gardens. The broad avenues leading to this park not only attracted the high society of Buenos Aires for fashionable afternoon drives but also were the location of the aristocracy's private palaces and gardens. The mud flats along the estuary underwent even more striking alterations. The port works, begun with the Madero docks in the late 1880's, provided the city with a definite waterfront. Construction extended in the 1910's to the New Port area near Retiro and reclaimed hundreds of acres, a large portion of which was reserved for parks and promenades. The banning of washerwomen from the river banks in the late 1880's and the completion of municipal baths in the 1920's ended two long-standing porteño traditions. The passing of an era could also be seen in the spread of electric lights through the central streets and their extension to the suburbs, where in 1931 the last gas jet was extinguished.

Behind this physical metamorphosis occurred a significant change in the way of life and attitudes of the inhabitants in the coastal urban centers—a transformation more difficult to define than that of concrete and marble, parks and avenues, or waterworks and lights. Although the economy and society of these urban people were not everywhere equal, the growth of Buenos Aires was indicative of what was happening on a smaller scale in the other cities of the pampas and the coast. The quintupling of porteño population in the thirty years from the 1880's to World War I was paralleled by Rosario's rise from 40,000 inhabitants to 220,000, Santa Fe's increase from 15,000 to 60,000, the emergence of two new cities at Bahía Blanca and La Plata, and the development of thirty-two other cities in the coastal region with populations over 10,000. Unlike the provincial capitals of the interior, whose existence and progress depended solely on the administrative and commercial needs of the immediate, and frequently poor, environs, the increasing numbers in the coastal cities could draw their sustenance from a broad base of national commerce, a rich agricultural production, a growing community of processing and manufacturing industries, and an expanding bureaucracy.

Despite demographic and economic growth, the urban settlement of Buenos Aires was extraordinarily dispersed. At the end of the nineteenth century neither bureaucracy nor industry required large numbers of employees concentrated in one location. The trolleys and trains, then the subways and buses, introduced at the moment of the city's sudden development, encouraged people to spread out as in few other metropolises. Land was cheap and plentiful and no physical obstacles, except the estuary on the east, limited expansion. Buildings, although departing from the colonial limit of one or two stories, never reached skyscraper proportions (the highest today rise to slightly over forty stories). As a result Buenos Aires sprawled over an increasing proportion of the seventy-four square miles of the federal district and, particularly after 1900, into the surrounding towns and cities of Greater Buenos Aires.

Only the downtown center remained compact and small. Florida became the street of elegant shops, limited to pedestrian traffic during most of the daylight and evening hours. The area just north of the Plaza de Mayo developed into the city's financial district. Many important commercial houses lined the Avenida de Mayo. Corrientes was the street of bright lights, cabarets, and dance halls. Some waterfront streets were known for their brothels and places of low resort.

The city that stretched beyond this downtown area was made up of hundreds of local communities, or *barrios*. The physical outline of the *barrio* was vague—sometimes oriented to a Church parish or a political district, but more often depending on the sense of community developed by a store, a bar, or a particular group of friends. In the same way that the *gran aldea* found sufficiency in the family unit, so the emerging metropolis oriented itself to the *barrio*. It was here that most men worked, lived, and played. According to the 1895 and 1914 censuses, the great majority of the economically active population was occupied in commerce and services—almost 10 per cent in domestic service alone. These occupations throve on the fact that each *barrio* required its own grocers, butchers, clerks, peddlers, cartmen, and peons. Even factories were widely scattered across the city. Except for packing plants, tanneries, and flour mills located along the Riachuelo, most processing and manufacturing were carried out in household establishments employing fewer than ten workers.

The increase in the number of one- and two-story houses—from 33,000 in 1887 to 108,000 by 1910—emphasized the spread of the *barrios* along the Riachuelo in the Boca and Barracas districts, along the Western Railroad, and into the former suburbs of Flores and Belgrano. Beginning in the 1880's there was some concentration of lower classes in downtown *conventillos,* but the general tendency was to move away from the central part of the city and to seek out cheaper, undeveloped areas. Consequently, as a district filled, there was little pressure to add third and fourth stories or to do away with patios. New arrivals merely moved on to develop yet another *barrio*. Despite the in-

crease in urban land values and the spread of office and apartment
buildings, remnants of this type of growth can still be seen in Buenos
Aires. Within twenty or thirty blocks of the Plaza de Mayo exist
middle-class and lower-class neighborhoods that enjoy quiet, shaded
streets, variations on the patio style of construction, and only a few
buildings over two stories in height.

The *barrio* also provided the center for most of the social services of
the metropolis. Although the Church never possessed the predominant
influence on the coast that it had in some of the interior cities, the
great majority of porteños continued to be baptized, married, and
buried by their local parish priest. Beyond the spiritual services, the
Church's hospitals and orphanages often extended more immediate and
effective help to the *barrio* than did centralized municipal institutions.
Primary instruction, removed from Church influence in 1884, expanded
into every *barrio*. By 1914 the literacy rate in the federal capital rose to
80 per cent, and four-fifths of the school age (6-14) children in the
city were attending classes. Despite the weakness of community organization in Argentina, the common interests found in a *barrio*, especially among the immigrant element, encouraged many mutual aid
societies and prompted some of the first employee or labor associations.
As the middle and lower classes advanced into the political arena after
1890, the *barrio* also became significant as a sounding board for politicians.

For the mass of the porteño populace, entertainment revolved around
the *barrio*. Within the local community could be found the social contact and identification which had begun to vanish in the impersonal
downtown operas, theaters, restaurants, bars, and dance halls. Men
frequently gathered for an evening of conversation, cards, or billiards
at the corner bar.* Toward the end of the century the typically Argentine tango began to make its appearance at social gatherings in the
poorer districts. Of vague parentage, most probably developed from
Negro and waterfront origins, the dance was long barred from re-

* Even today most Argentine cafes, at least in the *barrios*, are only for men, with
a separate enclosure, the *salon de familias*, for families or for women and their
escorts.

spectable society for its supposed lasciviousness and sensuality. Only after gaining popularity in Paris just before World War I did it advance into fashionable porteño parties and into dance halls along Corrientes, reaching its perfection in the 1920's under the genius of the composer and singer Carlos Gardel. From similar humble origins in the *barrio* came another Argentine tradition, the present national sport of *futbol,* or soccer, introduced by the English during the 1870's and 1880's at several of their schools and athletic clubs. At first ridiculed as the sport of the "crazy English," it soon developed into the Sunday or holiday pastime for *barrio* teams and then worked its way into the national fiber to an even greater degree than football or baseball in the United States.

The *barrio* nurtured one other phenomenon at the turn of the century which had none of the lasting qualities of the tango or *futbol* but which has acquired a literary and social recognition second only to that of the gaucho. The *compadrito* escapes facile definition, for he embraced the many types and psychologies of a rapidly urbanizing and changing people. He was at once the neighborhood dandy, bully, and sport. Much of the gaucho's pride, courage, and gambling instinct reappeared under his urban veneer. Whether he came from the city's best families or from the poorest slums affected neither his appearance nor his actions: his tight-fitting black suit and highly polished shoes; his ever handy knife or pistol; his insolent stare directed toward any moderately attractive woman; his readiness to engage in any escapade or to accept any challenge. For a couple of decades he flourished in the suburbs of Buenos Aires. Then, with the increasing complexity of urban life, he melted away, leaving behind only a legend and a few of his milder traits to be copied by subsequent generations.

The class structure of Buenos Aires most clearly portrayed the fundamental change that late-nineteenth-century economic development brought to Argentina. Social mobility and complexity were its outstanding characteristics. Here we can find only traces of the rigid caste system of the interior capitals, for on the coast the blood of the conquistadors and even that of the generation of 1810 had been diluted to the vanishing point.

In the *gran aldea,* upper-class families still prided themselves on their colonial lineage. But the oligarchy—the landowners, financiers, politicians, and merchants who emerged with agricultural exploitation of the pampas—brought new blood and a dominant spirit of material progress to the elite class. Many were *nouveaux riches,* for in a rapidly growing nation wealth did much to compensate for tradition. The Irish or Basque sheepherder or the Italian peasant who made a fortune from the pampas might not be quite acceptable, but his children, educated and sophisticated, could move in the highest circles. That is not to say that the elite of porteño society lost its exclusiveness, as the membership of the venerable Club del Progreso or the Jockey Club or the Círculo de Armas, organized in the 1880's, could testify. But the French, German, English, and Italian names that dotted the society columns of *La Nación* and *La Prensa* indicated that the criteria for selection were being broadened.

In size the elite class of Buenos Aires remained small. In a city of a million and a half, this oligarchy did not include more than two hundred family names and in numbers totaled far less than one per cent of the population. Political connotations in Argentina have since tended to equate oligarchy with *estanciero.* At the end of the nineteenth century the economic base of this elite did rest on the wealth of the pampas, but, although many subsequently bought land for social prestige, not all were landowners and only a minority were cattlemen. Commerce, banking, politics, and, increasingly, the processing industries built many family fortunes, and speculations during two economic booms created more financial empires than they destroyed. In politics as well as in society, this elite was far more united than any previous or subsequent ruling group. With its wealth intimately linked to agricultural production, there was little of the struggle between protectionism and free trade or between industry and agriculture that wracked Argentina after 1930. Although distinct political tendencies existed within the oligarchy, the bitter divisions between centralists and autonomists had faded. In this "society of gentlemen" problems could almost always be solved to the members' satisfaction and interests. For more than three decades—from the 1880's through the early years of World War

I—this elite class ruled the rich inheritance of the pampas as enlightened and progressive trustees. They owned the land and controlled the means of production. They appointed presidents and congresses from their own ranks with only a pretense at elections. They encouraged foreign investments and European immigration. They modernized the cities, extended the educational system, and fostered the sense of a nation in Argentina.

Taken as a class, the oligarchy was a rich, charming, educated, and cosmopolitan group. Fortunes were enormous, contrasting sharply with the modest incomes of previous decades or with the relative poverty of the elite in the interior. A three- or four-story villa, often overfurnished and overstaffed, constituted the average town house. Depending on the source of income, there was also a pretentious residence on some *estancia,* an elegant house and garden north of Buenos Aires on the way to Tigre, or, as the custom developed to escape the porteño summer, a chalet in the Córdoba hills or at the beaches of Mar del Plata.

Among the upper class the immediate family continued to be large, and grandparents, unmarried aunts, uncles, and cousins, and married children frequently swelled households to twenty or more members. The framework of the patriarchal home subsisted, but wealth modified its structure. Family fortunes were often held together by corporate arrangements; however, the legal requirement of an equal division of estates among children weakened the economic core of the extended family. The training of boys remained oriented toward the classics and a law degree, yet in an expanding economy their careers were no longer strictly circumscribed by the traditional professions. Government and commerce needed untold numbers of administrators. Industry afforded new fields for initiative. Even the arts and letters attracted a share of talent from the elite class. Travel in Europe became an accepted standard for the new generation. Local university training was frequently completed by a course at the Sorbonne, Heidelberg, or Cambridge. Not unnaturally the rebirth of intellectual concern and vitality at Buenos Aires, as well as the era of the Argentine playboy in Paris, dated from the final decades of the nineteenth century. The life of the ladies changed more slowly, but even here the older bondage to needlework, cooking, and household management gave way to an appreciation for French, English, and German, a witty dinner conversation, or a pleasant musical repertoire.

In contrast to the upper class, middle-class society at Buenos Aires had a complexity that makes analysis more difficult. The development of this class revolutionized Argentina's social structure and introduced new and decisive factors into the twentieth-century scene. Prior to the 1880's there were only two classes: the *gente decente*, or the socially acceptable class, and the poor, or laboring, class. Immigrants with a little capital or special talents and some of the small retail merchants might foreshadow a middle class, but they were too insignificant to be one. Then, within a few decades, prosperity and numbers greatly extended the scale of economic and social groupings. Between the aristocracy and the poor lay a new and rapidly expanding element which by 1914 constituted nearly a third of the porteño population.

As in the interior cities, these coastal middle classes came largely from immigrant origins. Many of the two and a half million Europeans who remained in Argentina in the several decades prior to World War I improved on their former condition as peasants or laborers or at least saw their children rise out of the lower classes. "Decent" families who did not have the wealth or prestige to join the oligarchy also swelled the middle segment. Occupations accentuated variations among the middle classes. Between a high government official and a bank clerk, an owner of a small factory and a primary school teacher, or an army officer and a neighborhood grocer existed sizable social and economic differences. Yet in an expanding economy there was a great deal of social mobility, and at the top of the many rungs of the middle classes lay upper-class status to be attained by wealth, talent, or marriage.

The surging prosperity and activity of the coastal cities in the early twentieth century endowed Argentina with the reputation of a middle-class society. But the persons who filled the streets, cafes, theaters, apartments, and universities of Buenos Aires, La Plata, Rosario, and Córdoba represented only a part of the modern nation. Significantly these members of the middle sectors had not convinced even themselves of their existence as a class. Their eyes were still fixed on elite values, and any sense of belonging to a class was limited to holding themselves aloof from the laboring groups.

The middle classes thus possessed dignity and ambition, but they lacked unity. Individuality and personal success might be fostered by competition, but as a political group these classes remained amorphous and powerless. Their very size and the variety of origins made cooperation difficult. They had aspired to political leadership ever since the late 1880's. But from their first mandate under the popularly elected Hipólito Yrigoyen in 1916 they demonstrated the woeful division and vacillation that now appear endemic to the Argentine political scene.

The universal striving of these middle classes was upward in social terms: to secure a better education for their children; to imitate the morality, society, and amusements of those just above them on the economic scale; to be clean and well dressed; and to maintain the outward appearances of prosperity even if this meant real privation in the home. Jobs and residences in Buenos Aires became accepted goals of the middle classes. But, as a consequence, the middle groups suffered from the frustrations of urban living and the high cost of housing. The inflationary pressures of Argentina's rapid economic expansion struck hard at the size of the middle-class family, which by 1914 declined to an average of less than three children.

At the base of the city's economic and social pyramid existed the two-thirds of the porteño inhabitants who labored with their hands. Even here change was evident. By 1914 the lower classes were no longer significantly mestizo or mulatto but European. Mestizos and Indians began to trickle toward the coast from the northwestern provinces but not in sufficient numbers to stand out among the influx of Spanish and Italian laborers and peasants. Despite increasing employment opportunities, economic benefits were slow in reaching the lower classes. Bread, spaghetti, and vegetables did provide a diet that was far more nutritious if not more plentiful than that of earlier decades. But real wages climbed only slightly during the economic booms of the

1880's and 1900's and declined sharply in the ensuing depressions. Inflation and high living costs created frequent privation, particularly in housing.

European workers and influences, however, brought the desire for material improvement to the lower classes and dissipated much of the resignation, humility, and apathy that had characterized the urban poor in the *gran aldea*. The *barrio* not only assisted in the adjustment of immigrants to their new homeland but also stimulated an awareness of common problems and goals. Intellectualism invaded the workers' world with the formation of the Socialist Party in the 1890's and the creation of lending libraries and night schools for laborers. Primary education now reached most urban children, and, as a result, with each decade more and more laborers read daily newspapers. At the same time labor agitators and anarchists accompanied the rising tide of immigration from Spain and Italy. In socialist groups, street meetings, and cafe discussions the urban worker became aware for the first time of his own identity and of the possibility for joint action. By 1900 he had begun to battle bloodily in strikes and demonstrations for recognition and advancement. Intellectuals, writers, even some politicians now concerned themselves with labor's problems. For the moment the gains were largely limited to marginal areas such as mandatory Sunday rest, often accompanied by a half-Saturday, and the establishment of a ten-hour, and sometimes eight-hour, day. Upper- and middle-class reaction encouraged the government to place strikers and labor organizers beyond the law. The facility by which diligent workers could still raise themselves or their children into the middle classes also served to postpone successful labor union action until after World War I.

The development of the *barrio* and the emergence of significant middle and labor classes were accompanied by an industrial revolution that followed closely on the heels of Argentina's agricultural revolution. In Latin America the introduction of industry into economies primarily devoted to production of raw materials proceeded at various times and under widely differing conditions. The broad view has credited the two world conflicts, which temporarily diverted the production of the great industrial powers away from consumers, and the world depression, which exposed raw material producers to serious losses, with the major role in stimulating this area's industrial growth. The Argentine case, however, presented particular problems in economic growth which would subsequently hamper the country's adjustment to a world emerging from the depression of the 1930's and the conflict of the 1940's. Despite early development of processing industries, the orientation toward European markets and factories discouraged diversification of products, exploitation of mineral resources and hydroelectric potential, and expansion of highway systems.

By the beginning of the twentieth century, manufacturing industries contributed nearly 14 per cent of Argentina's gross national product, as contrasted with 37 per cent provided by agricultural activities. Although small local industries in the interior, lacking tariff protection, capital, and technology, remained at the level of artisan enterprises, the coast was building an extensive industrial plant to process the products of the pampas. Those elements which developed the agricultural export economy—railroads, European immigration, urban centers, technological and managerial skills, domestic and foreign capital—also provided essential ingredients for industrial expansion. Thus by 1913, when the second economic boom built on agricultural exploitation ended in depression, the country's manufacturing age was well prepared.

Yet this was not industrialization that necessarily promised balanced growth or economic independence. Initially, industrial expansion acquired neither the volume nor the direction commensurate with the impetus of the agricultural revolution. A quintupling of imports in the two decades preceding World War I emphasized the degree to which European factories were called upon to supply the country's rapidly rising consumption. Along with capital goods and machinery came increased imports of consumer goods and luxury items to satisfy a demand that the innumerable small factories in Buenos Aires could not meet. Industrial capital gravitated toward the processing of raw materials; half the capital and production value was concentrated in the food industries alone. By 1914 Argentine plants supplied 37 per

cent of the processed food consumed in Argentina, but only 12 per cent
of the metals and machinery and 17 per cent of the clothing were
locally produced. For the country as a whole the exchange of raw materials for finished goods meant favorable trade balances, profits from
the land, and a slowly rising standard of living. Since multilateral trade
and laissez faire still enjoyed respectability, few were concerned if
Argentina did not produce tractors, electric generators, or street cars
and imported coal, lumber, and kerosene, or if Argentina's exports were
largely restricted to meat, wheat, and wool. Economic planning neither
supported nor opposed industrialization—it was nonexistent. The first
protective tariffs had been applied to alcohol, wine, beer, hats, shoes,
clothing, flour, and some foodstuffs in the 1870's and to sugar and certain assembled items in the 1880's. But rates were determined by the
immediate need for funds and by the effectiveness of pressure groups,
rather than by principles of reciprocity or protectionism. Although tax
policies and credit institutions tended to favor landowners and agricultural interests, even here there was an absence of clear economic
objectives.

These considerations partly explain the peculiar structure of Argentine industry prior to World War I. One segment was made up of
large-scale establishments: meat-packing plants, tanning factories, flour
mills, electricity and gas plants, sugar refineries, and some breweries,
wineries, paper and lumber mills, and textile plants. These factories
employed the most modern equipment, technical skills, and accounting
procedures, used a high ratio of horsepower to laborers, and commanded outstanding entrepreneurial abilities. Their labor forces ranged
from a few hundred to a few thousand and their capital from one
million to five million dollars. Almost all were the creations of individual immigrants and remained under family rather than corporate control. Foreign subsidiaries appeared in the power and meat-packing
fields, but not until the 1920's were there major investments of foreign
capital in Argentine manufacturing or significant increases in corporate
ownership.

The other segment of industry was the myriad small factories that
numerically comprised almost the whole of Argentina's industrial es-

tablishment but represented only tiny fractions in capital, horsepower, or value produced. It was on these industries that Argentina depended for its locally produced consumer goods: shoes, bread, paints, hairbrushes, bricks, cigarettes, macaroni, glass, blouses, hardware, furniture, matches, hats, candies, liquors, butter, acids, suits, and grain sacks. Like the large-scale processing industries, these small plants sprang from the initiative of immigrants and continued under family ownership. Few employed more than ten workers, and many artisan shops depended only on family labor or at most a couple of helpers. Lack of capital or access to credit, outdated machinery and methods, and low ratios of technology and horsepower to laborers placed many of these small factories in marginal positions, where they could easily be overwhelmed by foreign competition or by the appearance of some large domestic manufacturer in their field.

Such then was the status of Argentine industry at the oubreak of World War I. Some elements favored further expansion but most of it was accommodated to an agricultural export economy. The next six years of war and ensuing depression in Europe gave a thrust to Argentine industrial development that neither expanding agricultural production nor sporadic tariff protection had previously afforded. The impact of war needs, submarines, and blockades suddenly meant that the Argentine consumer could no longer depend on Europe to supplement the output of local factories. United States merchandise partly filled the gap. Commerce with the United States increased considerably during the war years, and the United States temporarily replaced England as the principal supplier of goods for Argentina. Nevertheless, by 1918 importation of foodstuffs, hardware, paper, metals, and clothing decreased 50 per cent from prewar levels. Coal imports suffered a decline of two-thirds, and construction materials of one-third. Significantly for Argentina's industrialization, the importation of heavy machinery and factory equipment fell even more sharply—to one-seventh of 1913 levels—and did not recover until well into the 1920's. But shortages in items whose manufacture did not require complicated equipment encouraged industrial expansion. Not only the cattleman who exported chilled beef to the Allies but also the manufacturer who supplied textiles, shoes, or chemicals to local markets made enormous profits.

Admittedly the effects were spotty. World War I and the postwar depression of 1919-20 did not last long enough to alter the basic structure of the Argentine economy, and Europe quickly recovered its productive capacity and turned to the reconquest of overseas markets. At the same time Argentina lacked sufficient domestic capital, machinery, and technical and entrepreneurial skills to expand overnight from processing industries to heavy industries, or even to light industries. But the momentary interruption of European production provided the breathing spell necessary to establish several new industries on the Argentine scene. The production of vegetable oils quadrupled during the war and by 1920 met four-fifths of the national demand. By the same year Argentine plants increased the production of cement to cover one-third of the country's needs. The chemical industries acquired new importance. War shortages also stimulated efforts to manufacture paper and cellulose, although domestic production came nowhere near meeting the country's voracious appetite for newsprint or the requirements for quality paper. Less clear was the impact on textile industries. The domestic woolen industry began to demand and absorb increasing quantities of washed wool, and substantial profits came from the blankets and cloth sent to Allied forces in France. The cotton industry also expanded with the addition of numerous small spinning and weaving establishments in Buenos Aires. But, though production of underwear, stockings, and shirts doubled during the war, the industry's inefficiency and dependence on imported raw materials left it exposed to competition from the mills of Manchester, Lyons, and Lowell.

The war also emphasized serious shortages in Argentina that had long served as arguments against industrialization—for example, the absence of easily exploitable reserves of metallic ores and the lack of cheap sources of power. The war revived some interest in mining: several new lead-smelting plants were established to process ore from Jujuy and Mendoza; a little copper, manganese, and iron were mined; and high sea freights encouraged the rapid expansion of a domestic salt industry. More significant, however, was the failure to develop local sources of energy. The coal burned in Argentine locomotives, steam engines, and electric generators came almost entirely from England. A two-thirds cut in coal imports, combined with a 50 per cent price rise, merely caused railroads and industry to convert temporarily to wood, charcoal, or straw. Suspected coal deposits along the Andes appeared too remote or too poor in quality to warrant exploitation, especially since the British supply would shortly be renewed. Similar attitudes applied to petroleum resources proved far more damaging in the long run, since oil was rapidly gaining on coal as a source for industrial energy. Sporadic efforts in the 1890's to exploit oil in Mendoza and Salta had been commercial failures. In 1907, when a well-drilling crew at Comodoro Rivadavia on the Patagonian coast struck oil instead of water, the national government asserted its control over subsoil rights in the region. Some drilling concessions were extended to national companies and foreign subsidiaries, followed in 1922 by the organization of a national oil agency (Y.P.F. or Yacimientos Petrolíferos Fiscales) and in 1925 by the opening of a modern refinery at La Plata. But local production met less than half the country's needs. Meanwhile Argentina's hydroelectric potential remained totally untapped. The shift to electrification in urban transport and industry in Buenos Aires, Rosario, and other cities meant that enormous quantities of imported coal or oil were transformed into electrical energy by turbines. Although the hydroelectric potential of the Andean streams or of the upper reaches of the Paraná River was far removed from coastal industry, the more practical projects to dam and utilize the waterpower of several rivers in Córdoba received equally little attention.

The 1920's witnessed the renewal of many prewar trends. Cereals recovered from the slump imposed by the lack of wartime cargo space and once more overtook meat and hides. The economy throve on the export of wheat, corn, beef, mutton, and wool. Industrial production was less favored. Expanded internal consumption afforded a certain margin to local industries, and some factories took refuge in assembling or processing semi-finished goods imported from abroad. But the rapid re-entry of European industry into world markets slowed or halted the development of many of the country's infant industries, when it did not kill them outright. By 1924 the traditional Argentine dependence on England had reappeared. Curiously enough, the popularly elected Radical Party regimes—for the first time representing middle- and lower-class interests in government—took few steps to protect nascent industry, and tariff rates in the 1920's actually declined to their lowest levels in half a century. Particularly hard-pressed were the textile and metal industries. Studies of the cotton textile sector revealed the wide gap that separated Argentine manufacturers from their European competition: costs of production in spinning amounted to two and a half times that of European factories, low productivity and inefficiency made labor costs four times as high, horsepower cost five times as much, and credit was seventeen times as expensive.

The world depression of the 1930's counteracted some of the anti-industrial trends by introducing several factors favorable to local manufactures. In five years the trade of all major nations dropped to one-third of 1929 levels and did not recover until the end of the decade. European and United States industrial production suffered serious setbacks, frequently amounting to a 50 per cent reduction in output. Many of the forces which encouraged local Argentine industry during World War I were thus reproduced but for a longer time. Furthermore, the impact of the depression was sufficiently violent and lasting to destroy any illusions that this was only a momentary interruption or that raw material producers could profitably and securely renew their dependence on highly industrialized nations. The fact that the importation of manufactured goods in 1932 required an exportation of agricultural products 65 per cent greater than that needed four years earlier provided the country with a harsh lesson. At all levels, there developed a conviction that industrialization was the best defense against catastrophic drops in the price of cereals, hides, meat, and wool.

The depression, like World War I, stimulated certain segments of the economy but did not necessarily provide for healthy industrial development. The decline in both the value and the volume of Argentine exports and the widespread unemployment and restriction of credit at home sharply reduced Argentine imports. If pounds sterling or dollars were not available to buy goods abroad, one got along with the local product—to the gain of Argentine industry. In the years just prior to World War I, 40 per cent of Argentine consumption had come from abroad. By 1936, with a doubling of the value of goods consumed, the country depended on imports for only 24 per cent of its needs. Argentine production of vegetable oils, which had lost ground during the 1920's, supplied 90 per cent of the local demand by 1939. Argentine cement captured 98 per cent of the internal market. In many consumer fields, such as rubber and aluminum goods, candies, electric light bulbs, and perfumes, local factories now supplied national demand, importing raw materials when necessary and assembling the finished product.

Yet, while stimulating the production of certain items, this reduction in imports posed a fundamental problem for Argentine industry. If lack of foreign exchange and the high price of manufactured products curtailed the importation of consumer goods, these factors reduced importation of capital goods even more. The sharp drop in imports of machinery and factory equipment experienced in World War I repeated itself in the 1930's. At the very moment that expanding industries needed new plant material or that railroads and electric power stations required rolling stock and replacements, Argentina lacked sufficient foreign exchange and adequate import controls to insure basic industrial development.

Maintenance of Argentina's traditional markets for agricultural products constituted a second major obstacle for balanced industrialization. As European nations sought to reduce their dependence on foreign food supplies and England looked increasingly to Commonwealth production, multilateral trade systems began to collapse. By 1933 England, with the Roca-Runciman Pact, forced Argentina to "buy British" as the alternative to losing its wheat, wool, and beef outlets to Australian and Canadian competition. In a renewal of the commercial agreement three years later, England obtained further concessions for British goods in Argentina, even to the extent of eliminating the private bus lines that posed a threat to the British-owned transport system in the city of Buenos Aires. Such handicaps were repeated in other bilateral trade arrangements. Argentine efforts to protect its own industries through tariff measures and export-import controls thus faced constant harassment from the conflicting need to maintain the dwindling supply of foreign exchange earned by traditional agricultural exports.

Throughout the 1930's the country's transport, mineral, and energy needs continued to suffer from neglect. The only bright spot was the enactment of a highway construction program in 1932. During the next ten years, 32,000 miles of provincial and national roads were added to a system previously totaling a bare 5,000 miles. Elsewhere the depression discouraged activity. The British companies which still owned and controlled 70 per cent of Argentina's railroads failed to renew rolling stock or to maintain track and equipment. Government lines that served the remote Patagonian, Chaco, or Andean regions were equally inefficient and neglected. No further steps were taken to exploit copper, lead, iron, manganese, or zinc reserves, and the country had to import these metals essential to its industries. Despite some increase in oil production, Argentina still satisfied less than half its rapidly rising consumption needs. Meanwhile the potential for the production of natural gas, coal, and hydroelectric power remained virtually untouched.

The shortage of capital goods, the hesitant adoption of protectionism, and the failure to develop transport, mineral, and energy resources underlay much of the continued floundering by Argentina's light industries. Textiles posted significant advances in capital investment, technology, number of employees, and total production, and large mills in Buenos Aires increasingly replaced the numerous small marginal shops. By 1939 the bulk of cotton and woolen thread used in the country came from domestic mills, and 85 per cent of woolen cloth was locally produced. But Argentina still imported 60 per cent of its cotton cloth, and its total cotton textile output amounted to only one-third of that produced by Mexico, a country considered at that time more underdeveloped than Argentina. Similar conditions prevailed in the automotive assembly, chemical, paper, and electrical sectors, all of which depended heavily on the importation of parts, equipment, or raw materials. The 1930's saw the beginning of Argentina's long period of "demotorization"—from a country that boasted three automobiles per one hundred inhabitants in 1929 to one that had less than two per one hundred by the mid-1950's. The sharp reduction in vehicle imports and the failure to build new assembly plants reduced the benefits sought by the government's road-building program and slowed the development of rubber, gasoline, and tourist industries. In the chemical field output increased fivefold between 1914 and 1939, but Argentina still lacked adequate production of fertilizers, paints, dyes, explosives, plastics, cellulose, paper, film, and synthetics. The electrical industries provided for half the national needs by 1939, but on the basis of imported raw materials and parts. The production of electric motors, elevators, and replacement parts lagged far behind demands for both quality and quantity.

World War II encouraged development of the Argentine economy along the same lines laid out in World War I and in the depression: the reduction of imports, both consumer and capital, and the steady expansion of local industry to fill the gap. Yet the country labored under handicaps which six years of world conflict only accentuated: a run-down transportation system, lack of developed energy resources, insufficient machinery and equipment, uneven development of light industries, and the absence of a steel industry. Only the handsome profits that Argentina now reaped from its agricultural exports provided a contrast to the depression years, but even these profits did little more than feed internal inflation. The heavy industries of Europe and the United States were committed to war production rather than to the manufacture of industrial equipment. Furthermore, Argentina's equivocal neutralist or pro-Axis stand, as well as its remoteness, cut it off from the major supplies of capital goods which the United States sent to Brazil and especially to Mexico in the years from 1940 to 1945.

Nevertheless, by the end of World War II Argentina had emerged from its agricultural age and was beginning to enter an industrial phase. Despite gaps made evident by the war years—power stations which had to burn corn and straw, factories crippled by lack of replacement parts, highly inflated prices for industrial goods—the Argentine people and government were now committed to industrialization. The military dictatorship which assumed control of the country in mid-1943 supplemented the wartime stimulus to industry with subsidies and protective tariffs. The swelling urban population that, according to the 1947 census, placed 63 per cent of the 16,000,000 inhabitants in cities and towns and concentrated 4,600,000 in the metropolis of Greater Buenos Aires provided both consumers and factory workers. The industrial labor force, largely centered in the coastal cities, expanded from 500,000 in 1935 to 1,800,000 by 1947. The number of industrial establishments increased during the same period from 39,000 to 86,000. In the years immediately following the war, manufacturing industries contributed 24 per cent of the gross national product, surpassing the agricultural sector's 19 per cent.

Argentina's post-1945 economic development belongs to the contemporary scene. But before closing this discussion of the effect of two world conflicts and a world depression on Argentine industrial growth, we should mention several legacies left to modern Argentina.

Industry sharply accentuated the porteño predominance which had already emerged from the agricultural economy. Urban and industrial concentration primarily affected the area of Greater Buenos Aires and a narrow coastal strip extending north toward the city of Santa Fe and south to La Plata. Here 75 to 85 per cent of the nation's industrial manpower, capital, and establishments were located. As a result, the gap between the interior and the coast and between the countryside and the city widened in proportion to the increase in industrial output. Between the census of 1914 and the industrial census of 1935 capital investment in the coastal zone had more than doubled, while elsewhere it either declined, as in the Andean provinces, or remained constant, as in the case of Entre Ríos and Mendoza. By 1935 there were thirty industrial activities with an annual production worth at least ten million pesos in the federal capital, seventeen in the province of Buenos Aires, and seven in Santa Fe, but only two in Córdoba and two in Entre Ríos. In the rest of the country only the wineries of Mendoza, the sugar mills of Tucumán and Jujuy, the cotton gins of the Chaco, and the oil wells of Chubut reached the ten-million-peso mark. This underdevelopment of the other provinces placed its own limitations on industrial growth. Every peon who did not buy and use a bicycle, a radio, a plowshare, or a toothbrush meant one less consumer for Argentine industry.

The distinction between large factories utilizing modern equipment and small artisan shops continued to characterize Argentine industry. The first extreme created a proletariat numbering nearly one-third of the 1947 industrial labor force of 1,800,000 and located almost entirely in Greater Buenos Aires. Among such blue-collar workers the low wages of the depression and high costs, especially in urban rents, contributed to precarious living standards and discontent. These literate, skilled laborers, usually sons or grandsons of European immigrants, constituted a new and potentially powerful force in politics and society, easily unified and mobilized. The development of corporate ownership and the great increase in foreign investment in the manufacturing industries during the depression years added to this group's class consciousness and made them more susceptible to nationalistic appeals. The large factory also contributed to the wealth and importance of a new elite class, the industrialists, with traditions and interests quite different from those of the landed oligarchy. Although outnumbered by the agricultural elite, this industrial sector achieved a dominant influence in the post-1943 regimes and strongly oriented Argentina's subsequent industrialization programs. At the other extreme were numerous small shops and plants employing nearly half the industrial labor force in units of fewer than ten workers. This segment represented a drain on Argentina's productive capacity because of its minimal use of capital and technology. At the same time it postponed the spread of class consciousness and industrial organization to a large segment of workers and entrepreneurs.

Industrialization left an important though less tangible legacy in the growth of nationalism. The spirit of economic nationalism developed largely from the impact of world depression on Argentina. While the Argentine middle and lower classes suffered less than those in the highly industrialized economies of western Europe and the United States, the elite sector—agricultural, commercial, and industrial—incurred substantial losses. In great measure these losses were attributed to Argentina's dependence on foreign buyers, who took its raw materials, and on foreign sellers, who provided consumer and capital goods.

Statistics supplied the proof of steadily rising costs that Argentina had to pay for foreign manufactured goods in the face of falling prices for its agricultural commodities. With the expanded political role of the middle and lower classes in the twentieth century, resentment against Argentina's "inferior" position quickly spread through all segments of the population. The British streetcar company, the United States oil firm or packing plant, the foreign manufacturer, and the Italian immigrant were reviled in the newspapers, investigated by Senate committees, and showered with public abuse. Railroads that had been attacked only when they were unable to deliver enough freight cars at harvest time now became monsters of British imperialism. The 1936 renewal of the Roca-Runciman Pact, which disbanded the cheap, efficient system of small, private buses to protect the English monopoly of Buenos Aires' municipal transportation, brought rioting crowds into the porteño streets. The remote specter of *yanqui* aggression that had first been denounced in the Spanish-American War became an immediate reality for thousands of Argentines in the veiled references to oil interests behind the bloody Paraguayan-Bolivian conflict of the early 1930's, in the threat of private exploitation of Argentina's presumed but as yet unproven petroleum reserves, and in the privileged and frequently monopolistic positions of the Swift, Armour, Wilson, Goodyear, and International Telephone and Telegraph companies. The 1935 industrial census indicated that nearly half of the country's industrial capital came or was controlled from abroad. On all sides products of international subsidiaries—such as Cinzano, Bols, Nestlé, Crosse and Blackwell, Harrods, Arden, Lever Brothers, Colgate, Chesterfield, Ford, Phillips, General Electric, RCA Victor, Bayer, or Johnson and Johnson—permeated the daily life and language of Argentines. Finally, the two world wars and the depression brought to an end the massive immigration of Europeans. To take their place at menial tasks in the coastal cities came increasing numbers of mestizo and rural laborers from the interior. The hiatus in immigration broke attachments to the old countries. By the second or third generation, descendants of Italian, Spanish, or other European immigrants had lost any loyalty to their origins and became the most violent and vocal of Argentine nationalists.

Chapter 8 • Consolidation of a Nation

The year 1890 presaged new political formations in Argentina in much the same fashion that the economic booms of the 1880's and 1900's gave emphasis to an agricultural revolution, or the depression and World War II ushered in an industrial age. What a leading Argentine historian has called the "alluvial era" was approaching a climax, and it now became a question how hundreds of thousands of recently "deposited" immigrants would fit into the national life. Along with this process of absorption came the first signs of a break with the traditional social structure of elite and masses—in the establishment of the reformist Radical Party and in the 1890 revolution against the corruption of the oligarchy.

In political terms Argentina had barely become a nation by 1890. Eighty years had passed since the first cry for autonomy launched Buenos Aires toward independence, but hardly thirty had elapsed since a national authority emerged from the conflict between porteños and provincials, and only ten since the government was firmly anchored in the city of Buenos Aires. A declaration, a constitution, a president, and a capital only provided elements, not the reality of nationhood. Creating

189

that reality was the task of new forces which became increasingly vocal and active after 1890.

The arrival during the 1880's of one million immigrants—850,000 of whom remained in Argentina—might have been expected to cause an immediate political and social transformation. But the change that these immigrants fostered was one of gradual evolution produced mainly by their sons and daughters and by Argentina's general economic growth.

The immigrants themselves remained largely apolitical. Their life in Europe had given them no experience and little expectation of a role in government. In addition, they had come to Argentina as transients to make money, not to become embroiled in political questions for which they had no understanding or sympathy. Although by the turn of the century only two years' residence and a sworn statement before the local justice of the peace were required for naturalization, few immigrants availed themselves of the opportunity. The Constitution of 1853 gave them all the privileges and guarantees of Argentine citizens, and several provinces even permitted them to vote in municipal elections. As foreigners they could not be called upon to serve in the National Guard or be conscripted for a year's military service. Though the shadow of foreign gunboats and the threat of direct intervention no longer loomed over the Río de la Plata, immigrants still enjoyed the support of their consular and diplomatic agents.

Their own sentiments, however, provided the principal key to their nonparticipation in local politics. Immigrants never thought of themselves as Argentines. They remained Italians, Frenchmen, Germans, and Spaniards—or, more accurately, Basques, Lombards, Asturians, Bavarians, and Parisians—even when they raised families and died on Argentine soil. Each economic depression in Argentina sent immigrants scurrying back to Europe, where, in adverse times, one could have the comfort of being in one's homeland near family and friends. The entry of Italy into World War I in 1915 caused thousands of young Italian reservists to leave Argentina, with hardly a desertion to the haven of Argentine citizenship. Indeed, such loyalty to the homeland contributed to a net loss of twenty to thirty thousand Europeans yearly from

Argentina during the war years. Only rarely were immigrants drawn into the political arena in Argentina, and then it was because of immediate grievances rather than through an interest in issues or personalities. An example was the notorious incident of a body of Swiss sharpshooters who, protesting persecution of their agricultural colony by the Santa Fe governor, joined in the Radical Party revolt of 1893, much to the discomfiture of national troops sent to suppress the outbreak.

At the same time the immigrants influenced but did not seriously alter Argentine society. The influx of the 1880's was 60 per cent Italian and 18 per cent Spanish in origin. Occasionally these were peasants, but most often they came from the towns and cities of Europe. No radically different characteristics distinguished these newcomers; their south European customs readily blended with the Hispanic traditions of Argentina. Church and religion played important roles in their daily lives. Like the colonial Spaniard, they placed particular emphasis on dignity, outward appearance, and dress, and displayed a fatalistic attitude toward life along with their fondness for gambling. They sheltered their women and their homes from friends as well as from strangers. Even the extravagant and florid phrase afforded no conflict with Hispanic culture.

Further facilitating the process of absorption was the receptive and usually friendly attitude maintained by Argentina toward immigrants, at least until the world depression of the 1930's. European immigrants had always been accorded preferential treatment by Argentine constitutions, treaties, and laws. Religious freedom in this predominantly Catholic nation was guaranteed to Englishmen in 1825 and extended to all foreigners by the Constitution of 1853. Foreigners might be stereotyped, even contemptuously, as crazy Englishmen, hardworking Lombards, industrious Basques, or plodding Galicians, but rarely were they discriminated against, rejected, or isolated because of their nationality. Only occasionally did Argentina react against supposed threats to its Europeanized culture. Proposals for Chinese or Japanese colonization never received a hearing. The establishment of the Jewish Colonization Association in 1891 and its selection of Argentina as a settlement area for Russian *émigrés* aroused journalists to violent accusations that there was a plot to submerge the nation with two million

Jews. Such fears quieted when only a handful of paternalistic farm colonies emerged in Entre Ríos, Santa Fe, and Buenos Aires. Likewise, the development of several powerful Jewish firms that controlled brewing and the grain and textile trades kept strains of anti-Semitism alive in the coastal cities but never led to active or official persecution. The first restrictive measures toward foreigners sprang rather from the threat of labor agitators and anarchists at the turn of the century. The Foreigners' Residence Law permitted the arrest and deportation of any alien deemed undesirable by the authorities, and occasional abuses in its application earned it an unsavory reputation among immigrants.

Perhaps most significant was the relative lack of nationality groupings in the cities, especially among the lower classes. The Italian predominance in the Boca and Barracas districts or the middle-class English and German atmosphere of Hurlingham and Belgrano have already been noted. For many years the dwindling Negro and mulatto population tended to congregate in Barracas. A Jewish community developed north and west of the streets of Corrientes and Callao, and in the port area north of the Plaza de Mayo there were concentrations of Syrians. But in no sense were these such distinct communities as New York's Negro and Puerto Rican areas or Boston's Irish and Italian districts. In businesses, residences, and pleasures, Buenos Aires and the coastal cities presented an indiscriminate jumble of nationalities, accents, and languages. The several foreign language newspapers, the five foreign community hospitals, the innumerable mutual aid societies, and the many social and sporting clubs served distinct nationalities, but they did not divide or isolate these groups. The common ground for all lay in a tolerant Argentina that accepted most European customs or habits as its own. The result was a culture that by the early twentieth century appeared to be "Italianized Hispanic" but that increasingly asserted its "Argentinism."

In language, diet, and dress, the hand of the immigrant could be seen—not, however, in the addition of distinctive features but rather in the achievement of urban conformity. The slurred pronunciation of the Río de la Plata, the hardening of the soft Spanish tones of *ll* and *y* to an approximation of the English *j*, and the contraction, possibly with origins from medieval Spanish, of the plural "thou" (*vosotros*) to the *vos* used in familiar conversation were all assiduously copied by the immigrant. With the exception of some Anglo-Argentines, the immigrant inevitably learned Spanish. But the varieties of accents and grammatical constructions heard on the streets of Buenos Aires or Rosario gave Argentines a remarkable tolerance for the abuse of their language. Even today the porteño uses little of the haughty incomprehension of the Frenchman or the real incomprehension of the North American in responding to the stranger who essays a few stumbling phrases in his language. The overwhelming presence of Italians further corrupted pronunciation, added a new vocabulary of gestures, and contributed some of the most acceptable words in Argentine slang, such as *morfar* (to eat), *chau* (a familiar term of farewell descended from *ciao*), or *pibe* (an affectionate or patronizing equivalent of "kid"). By the end of the century there developed in the slums and waterfront districts of Buenos Aires an Italianized dialect, or *lunfardo,* totally incomprehensible to the uninitiated. But, above all the variations, the typical porteño speech survived—thanks largely to the immigrants' children, who cringed at their parents' pronunciation and sought to imitate all local customs to perfection.

Somewhat the same process affected the Argentine cuisine. Beef, especially the *bife,* or steak, continued to reign supreme as the principal item of rural and urban diets in the coastal region. White bread and fried potatoes became staples of all urban classes, while corn and *yerba mate* were increasingly limited to rural and interior Argentina. Though many a porteño still drank an early *mate* upon rising, tea and coffee were now the common beverages of the coastal cities. In Buenos Aires and Rosario the traditional corn dishes of *mazamora, locro,* and *humita* and even the tasty meat turnover, or *empanada,* appeared only at fiestas. There was now a predominant Italian influence, seen in the heavy use of olive oil, garlic, and onions, and in the introduction of macaroni, spaghetti, and many other pastes or *pastas* as cheap but varied additions to all menus.

The neighborhood bar and the downtown restaurant similarly adhered to common features. Even today a visit to a single porteño cafe

introduces one to all of them. In polyglot Buenos Aires there are virtually no international restaurants or exotic foreign dishes. The large
room with a high ceiling, the small square tables with their white coverings, the jacketed waiters, and the menu featuring grilled meats set
a universal standard for Argentine restaurants, regardless of price range.
Such standardization extended even to porteño clothing, giving the
Argentines a reputation for conservative dress. School children appeared
to be a Lilliputian army in their white smocks, a uniform that erased
many class distinctions. Smocks covered office and factory workers during the working day. A dark suit, hat, tie, and highly polished shoes for
the men and a black or conservative dress for the women were worn
by all who strolled along downtown streets. By police order, until 1954,
a man could not shed his coat even in the park—and this in the sticky
porteño summer.

Along with the superficial aspects of a national culture came definite
pressures to enforce "Argentinism"—exerted strongly on and by the
new citizens born to immigrant parents. The educational system provided the most effective means to instill conformity and patriotism. The
children naturally treated as superior the values of the society in which
they lived and looked down upon parents who spoke Spanish badly
or were not adept in Argentine surroundings. Poverty, illiteracy, and
lack of instruction made it virtually impossible for the great majority
of immigrants to counteract such rejection. Only in the middle-class
families of English and German managers and technicians were children raised somewhat outside the Argentine environment and sent
to private schools that emphasized the language and culture of their
parents.

The anticlerical legislation of 1884, which removed the Church from
a teaching role in the public schools, led to greater government control
over education. During the first years of the twentieth century the
minister of education took further steps to insure the indoctrination of
the rising tide of school children. All instruction had to be given in
Spanish, and a uniform curriculum was taught in all public and private schools—although less stringently adhered to in the latter institutions. New textbooks were commissioned for the school system. School
children actively joined in the parades and ceremonies for May 25 and

July 9, and teachers preached a cult of such national heroes as San
Martín and Belgrano. Boundary difficulties with Chile in the late
1890's and the centennial celebrations of 1910 provided additional opportunities to reinforce the children's patriotic ardor.

The Argentine government made its authority felt in other areas as
well. At the turn of the century all young men were required to regis-
ter for compulsory military service and were subject to call at the age
of twenty. The disciplined and regimented Argentine army, strongly
influenced by German military missions after 1900, did not teach democracy, but a year in the barracks provided illiterates with the rudiments
of reading and writing and gave conscripts elementary concepts of
public health and some notion of the existence of a national authority.
Official policy sought to mix conscripts from all areas and classes, and
the Indian from the *puna* or the Chaco frequently found himself
drilling alongside a clerk from a porteño bank or a son of an Italian
peasant. This might not lead to understanding, but at least it made the
extremes aware of each other's existence. In 1912 a significant measure
extended the privileges and obligations of citizens in electoral matters.
After two decades of struggle by the Radical Party, all men (and
women after 1947) over eighteen years of age received the right to vote
by secret ballot but with the added prescription that suffrage was
mandatory and failure to vote was punishable by fine. The enrollment
booklet the men received upon registration for military service served
as the voter's identification, as his record of having voted, and as a
document for all civic and legal matters. The expansion of government
bureaucracy made the individual increasingly aware of the state's authority and, consequently, of nationalism. In the late nineteenth century civil registers replaced the files of parish churches; licenses were
required for marriages; education, health, and welfare institutions, fire
brigades, waterworks, postal and police departments—in short, the
whole gamut of public services—expanded prodigiously under municipal, provincial, and federal authorities.

The significant political developments of the 1890's, however, did
not come from immigrants or nationalist pressures but rather from another new element of modern Argentina, the middle classes. This

group, which played such a vital role in the expansion of coastal cities and reaped so many benefits from the agricultural revolution, aspired to join the oligarchy in directing the political destinies of the nation.

Elections were mere pantomimes, although not all were as lopsided as the plebiscite in 1835 that gave Rosas absolute powers over the province of Buenos Aires by a vote of more than nine thousand ayes to four nays. The voice of authority inevitably determined the outcome, and the sympathies and loyalties of local caudillos decided how and for whom votes were cast. Even when the caudillo descended from his horse after mid-century and addressed himself to the urban populace as a politician, the ballot box continued to cause violence. Now bricks, swords, and revolvers controlled the results at electoral tables, where the voter had to present himself and openly attempt to deposit the distinctively colored ballot of his party. By the 1880's some of the cruder methods of influencing the outcome were modified by stuffing the ballot box and purchasing votes. But these measures merely confirmed the control over elections exercised by incumbents. The upset of a favored candidate in one of the provinces inevitably brought rapid intervention and a new election to remedy the error.

The boom of the 1880's, with its balm of prosperity, gathered all elite groups—anticlerical liberals and pro-Church conservatives, soft-money *estancieros* and hard-money bankers, francophile porteños and creole provincials, autonomists and centralists—into one national party and blotted out earlier political conflicts. Even the wounds of the porteños' revolution against federalization of their city were quickly healed. Gradually control of both party and government was centralized in the hands of the president.

But the unprecedented wealth and the undivided power of the elite class in the eighties were not wisely handled, and self-interest led to economic and political crisis in 1890. The absence of a national currency long obstructed sound fiscal planning. Paper notes, of which the most widely used and acceptable were the porteño issues originally supported by the Buenos Aires customhouse, fluctuated wildly in gold value with every revolution, war, depression, or boom. Early in his administration, Roca established a national currency freely convertible to gold—a reform which he ranked alongside the Conquest of the Desert in importance to Argentine development. Yet by 1885, inflation and a lack of gold reserves forced authorities to declare the inconvertibility of the paper peso and to revert to the daily market quotation for the peso's gold value. Such abandonment of hard money initially suited the country's principal economic interests, especially the *estanciero*, agriculturist, and exporter who paid their local costs in depreciating paper and received pounds sterling or the equivalent for their products. From this, however, followed an inflationary cycle of paper emissions to meet government expenditures and to stimulate further economic expansion. Faced with disaster, the Juárez Celman administration in 1890 even resorted to clandestine printing of banknotes. But as the peso fell from 100 to the gold ounce in 1884 to 350 in the early 1890's, the benefits even for agricultural interests began to dwindle. Much of the boom had been financed with land mortgage bonds. These bonds, widely accepted in Europe during the late 1880's, were repayable in paper currency, the depreciation of which seriously curtailed Argentine credit abroad.

But it was the emerging middle classes of the coastal cities which were most affected by the spiraling currency. Inflation cut deeply into salaries, pensions, and profit margins and magnified the gap in economic interests between the landed class on one side and the storekeeper, small merchant, clerk, army officer, school teacher, office manager, and engineer on the other. At the same time these middle-class groups were thoroughly disillusioned in regard to the processes of so-called democracy. Total apathy greeted elections. No doubts existed as to which party would win, for, barring military revolution or intervention by the national government, the incumbent invariably chose and elected his successor. In the city of Buenos Aires, where more than half the names on the election registers were fictitious or invalid, those in charge of electoral tables possessed a convenient margin to assure victory. Yet, even with the stuffing of ballot boxes, the vote in this city of half a million inhabitants rarely exceeded ten thousand during the 1880's, for the average bourgeois saw little point in endangering job, life, and limb for a lost cause. In other cities, especially those of the interior, citizens had little role in determining the outcome of elections, while in the countryside the *jefe político* (an appointed political administrator of a rural district) or military commandant delivered the votes of gauchos and peons in accord with higher orders.

The widespread corruption and peculation of the late eighties reflected still further discredit on the oligarchy and fueled middle-class discontent. Congressmen, ministers, and judges now had the opportunity to decide upon authorizations to build railroads, acceptability of public works, or permissions to colonize lands—each project involving enormous sums of money. A rapidly expanding bureaucracy with a characteristic fondness for paperwork and the long-established legalism of the Spanish mind added administrative procedures, or *trámites*, until only experts armed with ample funds and know-how could finally emerge with desperately sought authorizations. In this situation speculation and the craze for making money swept away a public morality established by earlier and poorer administrations. To the profits from railroad ventures, wine and sugar industries, public works programs, and agricultural exploitation of the pampas were added fortunes and bribes wrung from public office. Corruption infected all levels of the Juárez Celman administration, from the customs inspector who looked the other way for a ten-peso bill to the judge who gave a favorable decision to whichever party offered the most in terms of his personal gain. The public came to believe that any government official, from the president down, could be bought.

Disillusioned by corrupt government and hurt by unbridled inflation, the middle classes began to demand a voice in political matters. A protest movement, largely composed of university students and professional men, took shape in the city of Buenos Aires. Most of its members were of creole origin, for, in the beginning, it attracted few immigrants. The principal objective was enunciated at a mass meeting in late 1889: "The guarantee of public liberties, especially effective suffrage, without fraud or government intervention in elections." Around this banner rallied the most heterogeneous elements: formerly elite families who, with the rise of the oligarchy, had fallen back into the middle classes; Catholic groups angered by the anticlerical bias of the oligarchy; fragments from all the traditional political tendencies whose only common goal was the overthrow of the present regime; and reformers who sought government by will of the majority. Despite the potential divisions, the protest momentarily captured porteño imaginations. The movement, which initially incorporated the words "Civic" and "Youth" in its title, emerged in early 1890 as the Unión Cívica and was hailed by 15,000 followers in the largest political rally Buenos Aires had ever known.

At this moment Argentina received the full impact of the financial crash. With the exception of the railroads, the credit that Europe extended to Argentina during the 1880's went largely into loans to national, provincial, and municipal governments and into land mortgage bonds. Once the reliability of Argentine schemes became suspect, many of the ambitious projects dissolved overnight. Governments found themselves without funds. Public works were halted. Banks closed their doors and in mid-1890 declared a moratorium. The influx of European immigrants ended, and emigration increased. The collapse of the stock exchange ruined many who had speculated wildly, and the peso's value declined at an ever sharper rate. The urban middle classes suffered acutely, for the crash wiped out prospects and savings. Hatred welled up against the oligarchy, and by May 1890 some of the leaders of the Unión Cívica felt they had sufficient support to organize a rebellion against the Juárez Celman regime. Military elements joined with the civilians, but divided counsels and lack of co-ordination postponed plans. When disclosure of vital secrets threatened the conspiracy in late July, the revolutionaries launched their attack, and street fighting broke out in the city of Buenos Aires.

The suppression of this revolt after three days of bitter conflict revealed both the disunity of the protest movement and the flexibility of the oligarchy. The revolutionaries held an initial advantage in the city of Buenos Aires, but they failed to capture the president or the vital control centers of government. Outside of Buenos Aires and perhaps Rosario they stirred little sympathy. Uncertain division of command between civilians and military gave the national authorities the chance to bring supplies and loyal forces from garrisons in Rosario and Córdoba. At the same time the oligarchy proved more than willing to sacrifice Juárez Celman as a symbol of all the mistakes and grievances of the eighties. "The revolution has been crushed, but the government is dead," was the epitaph voiced on the floor of the Senate, and few were willing to listen to the defense: "Whatever the President's errors, every one of us has been his collaborator." Abandoned by his colleagues, Juárez Celman turned over executive powers to his more astute and acceptable vice-president.

The sacrifice was sufficient. The oligarchy maintained political supremacy and extended its control for another quarter century. Some of the elite learned from the crisis. Prosperity became tempered with stability. If the depression momentarily slowed economic development, it was followed by the even greater economic boom of 1904 to 1912. Roca, the symbol of expansion and confidence, returned to the presidency for a second term in 1898. The following year he took advantage of the peso's recovery to re-establish its convertibility to gold—but at 227 instead of 100 pesos to the gold ounce. Production and exports based on an accomplished agricultural revolution now kept pace with speculation. With meat and cereals Argentina turned its former deficits with England into favorable trade balances. The oligarchy accepted new elements and new ideas within its ranks. As long as rising opportunities for urban middle classes lessened the effectiveness of the appeal for suffrage, the elite class could continue to control the ballot box and the public till.

The reformers emerged from the 1890 revolution as divided as they had entered it. A sizable portion of the Unión Cívica followed Mitre, that venerable elder statesman of porteño nationalism, into an electoral accord with Roca and the oligarchy. The hard core of the Unión Cívica reconstituted itself in mid-1891 as the Unión Cívica Radical, or Radical Party,* pledged to a nationwide campaign to secure the uni-

---

* The party officially accepted the designation "Radical," already sanctioned by popular use, at the end of 1892. The translation is not a happy one, for the original sense was one of vindication of basic civil rights and adherence to the true purpose of the Unión Cívica rather than the advocacy of extreme change connoted by the English word. Once this middle-class party achieved the presidency, its basically conservative nature was clear, for its economic and social policies were anything but "radical."

versal secret ballot for male citizens by all available means, including revolution. Appeals to civic ardor in 1893 and 1895 temporarily captured large parts of the provinces of Buenos Aires and Santa Fe by revolution, but the Radicals proved unable to resist the oligarchy's skillful manipulation of armed force, intervention, amnesty, and conciliation. In each case the revolts flickered out after a few weeks of demonstrations and some sporadic fighting. In 1896 two principal leaders of the Radical Party died, and the following year yet another important segment of Radical opinion surrendered to Roca's blandishments.

By 1900, however, a new principle and a new caudillo had taken control of the Radical movement. "Intransigence" became the guiding force of Radicalism—the refusal to vote or to participate in public life until free elections were guaranteed. Beneath this philosophy lay the personality of Hipólito Yrigoyen. University and business associations linked him to leaders of the oligarchy, but he became the champion of political justice, and at his funeral in 1933 he was honored by sorrowing multitudes as the first Argentine president to defend the common man. He possessed few of the characteristics of Argentina's nineteenth-century leaders. Taciturn, introverted, a poor orator, he nevertheless galvanized the middle and lower classes by a certain mystical leadership. A meticulous organizer who created a disciplined and loyal party structure through countless individual interviews and small informal gatherings, he built an electoral machine which paralleled and often excelled that of the oligarchy. To Yrigoyen, revolution or the secret ballot afforded the only means by which the Radicals could capture power. But in his expert handling of both weapons he neglected all others: the Radical Party, even after gaining power, was never able to carry out effective economic and social reforms or to make more than symbolic appeals to the lower classes. The political issue of democracy was suffrage, and with that all problems presumably could be solved.

The Radicals' pretensions that they represented the disfranchised mass of citizens were challenged from both the left and the right. The Socialist Party, which emerged in the 1890's, attempted to capture leadership of the urban working classes with specific proposals for shorter working hours and better labor conditions. Yet the Socialists were divided between international, anarchist, utopian, and nationalist philosophies and torn between theoretical discussion of their principles and the practical need to organize strikes and labor unions. After 1900 an increasing influx of anarchists from Spain and Italy secured impressive support from discontented industrial workers, although the movement suffered from a similar division into intellectual and syndicalist groups. The violent aspects of anarchism eventually created fear and hatred among the middle classes as well as the oligarchy. Anarchists and some Socialists were singled out for arbitrary arrest, deportation, and police torture—repression not usually meted out to Radicals, who played politics under the established rules of revolution and amnesty. Finally, within the oligarchy itself there developed a significant movement to extend suffrage and even to guarantee the secret ballot as the best means to win public support and retain the elite's control of Argentine politics.

Despite the formidable odds of apathy and opposition, Yrigoyen spun his party network across Argentina, in provincial capitals and coastal towns, in army garrisons, and even in government offices. With tenacity and patience he repaired the holes torn in his web by police surveillance, arrests, dismissals, and transfers and steadfastly refused to compromise with regimes that did not guarantee free elections. Early in 1905 another Radical revolution broke out simultaneously in the provinces of Buenos Aires, Santa Fe, Córdoba, and Mendoza, only to face the usual process of rapid suppression and amnesty. Almost immediately Yrigoyen returned to tireless reconstruction and extension of the party. The times favored Yrigoyen's and the Radical Party's immediate objective, for a substantial number of the oligarchy recognized the growing appeal of political reform. Presidents now repeatedly consulted with Yrigoyen, not only in the hope of overcoming his intransigence but also with a view toward instituting acceptable electoral reform. Behind such proposed changes lay no romantic concept of surrender to Jacksonian democracy but rather the realistic expectation that the oligarchy might steal the mantle of reform and deprive the Radicals of their only popular appeal or unifying purpose.

In 1910 the oligarchy chose Roque Saenz Peña, the spokesman of this liberal or reform wing, as president, with the clear realization that he would seek electoral reform. Two years later, after a bitter congressional struggle, Saenz Peña secured the law of universal and secret male suffrage that thereafter carried his name. As youths of eighteen registered for military service, their names were entered on election registers, and they incurred the obligation to cast their ballot in national elections. No longer did voters have to vote orally or deposit the distinctively colored ballot of their party before the watching eyes of their fellow citizens. The law afforded the voter the secrecy of a closed booth, where he selected a list of candidates, and the security of a sealed urn, into which he deposited his vote. As a final assurance to the minority, the party that ran second in any province received one-third of the seats at stake in the national Chamber of Deputies while the majority party was limited to two-thirds of the representatives.

Free elections, however, depended on enforcement of the law, and that the oligarchy was not willing to guarantee. Yrigoyen struggled to maintain the principle of intransigency until such guarantees were forthcoming, but he struggled vainly against the enthusiasm of his own party. In the city of Buenos Aires and in the province of Santa Fe the Radicals won their first seats in congress, albeit with slim margins and amid scenes of violence and fraud. The law's principal guarantor, Saenz Peña, died in 1914, and Yrigoyen redoubled his insistence that the Radicals return to intransigency. But, despite Yrigoyen's reluctance to run for office, the 1916 election carried him to the presidency by a margin of one electoral vote.*

The Radicals won the presidency in 1916 with an electoral machine built during twenty-five years of revolution and preparation. In the coastal cities the Radical cause was strengthened by the entrance into political affairs of urban middle and lower classes, especially the native-born sons of immigrants who had settled in Argentina during the 1880's. The rejuvenated and liberalized elite still suffered from the

* The election hung in the balance until the electoral college met, because, although Yrigoyen won a majority of the popular vote, he did not secure a majority of the electors. A group of dissident Radicals from Santa Fe controlled the deciding votes. Finally, despite Conservative blandishments and their own personal opposition to Yrigoyen, they gave support to a Radical victory.

label of "oligarchy," and the intellectual Socialists and hunted anarchists showed little promise of achieving political control. In contrast, Yrigoyen surrounded himself with a mystique of democracy and political rights that turned him into the caudillo of these new voters.

The ascendancy of the Radicals from 1916 to 1930 altered Argentine politics in several aspects, but it failed to strengthen or perpetuate democratic institutions and stability. The Radicals, disclaimers notwithstanding, consecrated party organization and revolution as the principal means to gain power. The opposition, therefore, necessarily resorted to the same proven tactics. Political machines served to harden divisions into what Argentines have characterized as "political hatreds." The oligarchy, for all its exclusiveness, not only had drawn on a wide range of opinions and trained abilities within the elite but also had received constant renewal of talent from below. Party organization, on the other hand, thrived on service, seniority, and patronage which reduced flexibility in recruiting talent. Professional politicians who had risen through the ranks increasingly dominated ministries, congresses, and the country. The figures whom Yrigoyen appointed in 1916 provided a refreshing change from the families who had dominated porteño, and consequently the nation's, social and political life under the oligarchy. Yet government by unknowns brought not so much an introduction of new ability as the discarding and alienation of all those who had not served in the Radical cause.

The other avenue to power—revolution—was no Radical innovation, but its glorification as a viable political weapon brought unfortunate consequences. Now even the most pacific civilian leadership had to respect the military and rely on it for support and protection. The Argentine army had fought its last foreign war in the 1860's and faced its last border tension at the turn of the century. Rather than losing importance in the twentieth century, however, the army increased its role in national life and politics. Universal military training merely provided a mass of raw recruits to fill the ranks. But the cadre and regular army developed a sense of autonomy. German training missions, modern weapons and techniques, and *esprit de corps,* all contributed to the disdain felt by middle-class officers for politicians and political parties.

Although one sector stood for constitutionalism, the army as a whole tended to intervene more and more in politics, not only to secure larger appropriations and broader privileges but also to influence economic and foreign policy.

These potential dangers to democracy in Argentina were further accentuated by the Radicals' inability to carry out a program that would meet middle- and lower-class aspirations. Certainly a large part of the failure can be attributed to obstruction by Conservatives. Yrigoyen embarked on the presidency in 1916 with a minority in the Chamber of Deputies, only one representative in the Senate, and provincial control limited to Santa Fe, Córdoba, and Entre Ríos. Despite wide use of presidential powers of intervention, the Radical advance beyond the coastal cities was extremely slow. Political change had little chance in those interior provinces where society remained untouched by prosperity, immigration, urbanism, or a middle class, and where stability contributed to Conservative control of government. At the national level, the Senate, elected by provincial legislatures, remained a bulwark of Conservatism until 1930. The overthrow of Yrigoyen by a military coup in that year was apparently influenced by the threatened loss of such a vital Conservative veto. But Yrigoyen himself shared responsibility for the difficulties encountered by the programs of the Radicals. The caudillo's overwhelming personal domination of party and government accentuated conflicts within Radicalism. His successor in the presidency represented the conservative wing of Radicalism, which soon began to resist the caudillo's supremacy—a split that widened still further when a nearly senile Yrigoyen was re-elected president by popular acclamation in 1928.

Of the many proposals for reform advanced by the Radicals, few survived the combination of Conservative obstruction and internal party divisions. The general balance sheet, therefore, remained one of failure. In the distribution of land, in the establishment of controls over transportation and public utilities, and in government exploitation of natural resources, especially of oil, Radical projects were repeatedly defeated or postponed. While neighboring Uruguay developed one of the most advanced programs of social legislation in the world, the Radicals disillusioned the working classes by violently repressing industrial strikes. During the postwar depression Radical authorities were faced with severe outbreaks of labor violence in the city of Buenos Aires, aggravated by Conservative intrigues. The strife reached a climax in the "Tragic Week" of January 1919 when streetcars were burned, machinery destroyed, and citizens shot. Finally military intervention was required to restore order. Less dramatic but nonetheless damaging to Radical prestige in the cities were defeats imposed on social security and minimum wage laws. In economic policy the Radicals proved equally unsuccessful in implementing programs for industrial development or tariff protection. In a word, the Radicals, having achieved power on the platform of political reform, could not maintain leadership in other areas and consequently abandoned the urban populace to political drifting.

The major Radical accomplishment occurred not in the political arena but in the field of education. At the University of Córdoba in 1918 there developed a movement known as the "University Reform" that soon spread throughout Latin America. Fundamental to Latin America's present-day university structure, the "Reform" program secured autonomous university government shared equally by students, alumni, and professors. Finances and ultimate authority remained in the hands of the national government, but middle-class groups were now able to break the Conservative monopoly of university administration and teaching. Student and alumni participation in governing councils and in the selection of university officials and faculty stimulated improvements in curriculums and teaching. In the long run, however, abuses of the reform spirit brought higher education increasingly into the realm of politics and led frequently to a breakdown of standards in the universities.

The political drift experienced during the relatively prosperous twenties turned into disaster for the Radicals with the advent of the world depression. By 1930 Yrigoyen and the Radicals were thoroughly discredited on all fronts. The government took no measures to meet the impact of the depression on the cities. Graft and intervention flourished. The Conservatives conspired openly with elements of the army. Congress, newspapers, and even the people who had re-elected Yrigoyen now repudiated the aged caudillo. Chaos threatened to overwhelm the country. On September 6, when a column of troops left the military college located just outside the city of Buenos Aires, the doors to the capital and to the Casa Rosada lay open to them. The commanding general of the revolution quietly assumed control of the country with the open support of Conservatives, Communists, and many Radicals and the acquiescence of the great majority of the population.

Thus ended Argentina's first attempt at government by the middle classes. In less than two years the military turned over powers to a constitutionally elected president. The ensuing Conservative regimes that ruled the country from 1932 to 1943 renewed some of the benefits as well as many of the faults of the former oligarchy. As we have noted, the rising tide of economic nationalism and industrialization forced the government to walk a tightrope between world markets for meat and grains, secured by the Roca-Runciman Pact, and the demands for protection and support from its own industry—a dilemma temporarily resolved by the outbreak of World War II. In the political field the Conservatives regained control of the ballot box, the Saenz Peña Law notwithstanding, and sought to capture leadership of the middle sectors by the selection of anti-Yrigoyen Radicals as presidents and ministers.

Political drift, however, only worsened under the Conservatives. The sons of Argentina's second wave of immigration reached voting age in the 1930's, yet in political terms these citizens hardly existed. Politics became increasingly divorced from economic and social reality. A disillusioned citizenry found few contacts or responses on the political scene. The Conservatives provided traditionalist rule by an elite class that remained closely allied to British interests. The Radical and Socialist parties offered only the unappealing alternatives of old men and old ideas, unchanged since the once dynamic era of the 1910's. Even the Communists suffered from dissension. The Church, more concerned with prestige and pageantry than with fundamental social problems, contented itself with perfunctory support of the regime. The labor union movement, torn by various socialist and syndicalist tendencies and unable to strengthen itself during Radical administrations, found

organization even more difficult under the frankly hostile Conservatives. Finally, those sectors of the army which supported Conservative
ambitions in 1930 now added admiration for Fascist techniques to their
previous disdain for politicians. In moments of crisis these officers were
only too willing to assert autonomy and independence of any civilian
government.

Renewed prosperity built on Europe's gathering war clouds momentarily obscured this real poverty in Argentine politics, and world opinion in the late 1930's accepted Argentina as one of the most stable
and progressive democracies in Latin America. It was true that half a
century of political consolidation had gradually built a central authority and a national spirit, but little integration of the parts resulted.
Military groups, political parties, and economic classes, rather than
promising unity, represented sources of division and conflict. A military coup against the Conservatives in 1943 merely ripped off the
façade of democracy, revealing many of the present-day political problems in their stark reality.

The generations between 1870 and 1930 not only consolidated an
Argentine nation but also made Argentina the leader of the Latin
American artistic and literary world. By 1910 Buenos Aires was the
cultural mecca of South America and, in the opinion of many, of the
hemisphere. The brilliant performance of *Aïda* that reopened the
Colón in its imposing 3500-seat opera house in 1908 ushered in nearly
half a century of great music in which talent was drawn southward
during Europe's summer months, placing Buenos Aires on a par with
Milan, London, and Berlin for opera, ballet, and concerts. In the field
of journalism those bulwarks of the porteño press, *La Nación* and
La Prensa, were reinforced by *El Diario* (1881), the socialist *La Van-
guardia* (1896), *La Razón* (1904), and the more popularly oriented
Crítica (1913) and *El Mundo* (1928). During the first decades of the
twentieth century the porteño public was one of the best read in the
world, supplied with the latest European and North American publications and with an admirable selection of literature from outstanding
editorial houses such as Peuser and Kraft. In the realms of painting,

sculpture, and architecture, Argentina could boast tremendous activity and interest in the galleries along the elegant porteño thoroughfare of Florida, in commissions for statuary to adorn private gardens and public parks, and in the building of its rapidly growing cities. In a nation that had produced Sarmiento and Hernández, playwrights and authors now immersed themselves in a critique of Argentina's rapid economic rise and in the search for new values and standards.

The maturing of Argentina's artistic and intellectual endeavors was best dramatized in the ferment and talent of the literary world. Preoccupation with change underlay most themes. The spirit of progress absorbed the Generation of 1880, just as the Generation of 1910 would express concern for national and esthetic values.* Through both generations ran the dualism already seen in other aspects of Argentine life and clearly portrayed in the two masterworks of Argentine literature. *Facundo,* Sarmiento's profound sociological study of the gaucho, caudillo, and life in the interior of Argentina, had its roots in one fundamental current of Argentine culture—that of elite, educated, cosmopolitan, secular, urban, and democratic values, linked to centralist or porteño views. Hernández' *Martín Fierro,* the epic of the gaucho's struggle and defeat by "civilization," dignified alternative values—the role of the masses, intuitive or practical knowledge, the creole and Spaniard, the Church, the countryside, and the authoritarianism of the caudillo. This second tendency found its traditional political expression in the provincial or autonomist position. Such distinctions frequently overlapped or became blurred within literary schools or even within individual authors, much as in the case of Argentina's political or economic dichotomies. But from the struggle and interplay between these two sets of values emerged a truly Argentine literary heritage.

During the latter part of the nineteenth century the doctrine of positivism exerted a dominant influence throughout Latin America. While in Argentina it never became the credo of government as it did in the 1890's in Mexico under Porfirio Díaz or in republican Brazil, applica-

* These so-called generations are arbitrary and commonly accepted designations that approximately divide Argentine writing into the periods 1870 to 1900 and 1900 to 1930.

tion of its scientific and materialistic principles to government deeply permeated the thinking of the oligarchy, Radicals, and Socialists. In its Argentine form it also owed considerably less to Comte than to Darwin, Spencer, and the eclecticism of the Utilitarians and Utopian Socialists. Yet the immense strides taken by Argentina and the problems encountered in both boom and depression encouraged Argentines to accept a philosophy based on empirical reasoning and the physical sciences.

Literature reflected this emphasis on material factors, although the doctrines and messages that resulted were often quite contradictory. The generation which returned to Argentina after the overthrow of Rosas forecast one constant theme: the application of reforms to develop the nation. Alberdi, spiritual father of the Constitution of 1853, advocated European immigration as the country's great need. Sarmiento saw primary and secondary education as Argentina's salvation. Other major figures sought solutions in codification of laws, in settlement of the land, in expansion of a national authority, or in scientific curriculums for the universities. Even historians were stirred by reform. Mitre's carefully researched studies of the independence figures, San Martín and Belgrano, provided fuel for bitter polemics between those who wrote documented scientific treatises and those who preferred embellished literary creations based largely on intuition.

The country's rapid growth and the influence of positivism served to fragment this reform tendency into the many distinct schools of the Generation of 1880. Much of the printed material that issued from Buenos Aires during these years dealt with the dreams of Argentine wealth and potential but hardly qualified as literature. The nation adopted French literary styles along with boulevards, Parisian fashions, and the French language. Outstanding among the contributions of francophile porteños was the elegant but realistic reminiscence of school days, *Juvenilia,* by Miguel Cané. Gradually the realist and naturalist schools replaced the romantic inspiration that Echeverría had imported into Argentina in the 1830's. Some of the imitations of Balzac, Flaubert, and, above all, Zola were pale and uninspired. Occasionally, however, writers rose above the purely imitative. Lucio V. López in *La gran aldea* skillfully dealt with the changing customs of

Buenos Aires and the disappearance of the "large village." José M. Miró, writing under his pseudonym Julián Martel, contributed a masterfully cruel, although bitingly anti-Semitic, sketch of the stock exchange crisis of 1890 in *La Bolsa*. Perhaps most innovative of the naturalist group was Eugenio Cambaceres. Two novels, *Sin rumbo* and *En la sangre,* crudely portrayed the harsh impact respectively of the *estancia* and the *conventillo* environments on human life.

In the world of education and ideas, the emphasis on reform contin- ued to produce major figures whose activity and influence extended well into the twentieth century: Paul Groussac, a Frenchman and literary critic who presided over the golden era of the National Library (1900- 1929); Joaquín V. González, the humanist-founder of the new Univer- sity of La Plata; Alejandro Korn, a philosopher who advanced the tech- niques of German university and scientific teaching in Argentina; and José Ingenieros, a prolific scholar renowned for his provocative studies in sociology and history.

More lasting in terms of enjoyment for the casual reader was the parallel development of native themes. Almost in reaction to economic advance and to overdoses of immigration, both creative talent and the public sought relief in an older, more colorful Argentina. Although the origins of this genre sprang from romanticism and from works such as Echeverría's portrait of the Rosas era in *El matadero,* greatness was achieved only in the second half of the nineteenth century with Hilario Ascasubi's *Santos Vega,* the nostalgic reconstruction of rural life in the late colonial period centered on the figure of a lengendary gaucho ballad singer, Estanislao del Campo's *Fausto,* the amusing yet perceptive version of Gounod's opera as recounted by a gaucho to his companions, and, above all, the two parts of Hernández' epic, *Martín Fierro,* dedicated to the struggles and sufferings of a gaucho unjustly condemned to military service on the Indian frontier. The porteño public at the end of the century popularized another legendary gaucho of the Buenos Aires frontier even more than Santos Vega or Martín Fierro. The character of Juan Moreira was first captured in prose by the prolific and careless pen of Eduardo Gutiérrez and achieved still greater fame when the story was adapted to the theater in pantomime.

Concern with the gaucho led to exploration of related subjects. The

Indian frontier was treated by the master raconteur and soldier, Lucio V. Mansilla, especially in his *Excursión a los indios ranqueles*. At the turn of the century, life and manners along the Patagonian coast and in the delta of the Paraná River were immortalized in the stories and novels of José Álvarez (better known by his pseudonym of Fray Mocho), and the customs of the pampas and of that frontier port town of Bahía Blanca came to life as the "Pago Chico series" of Roberto Payró. The latter's *Divertidas aventuras del nieto de Juan Moreira* still stands as the classic tongue-in-cheek sketch of the political and social climber. Gradually the emphasis in the treatment of rural and gaucho themes shifted to the subtleties of character and emotions. In the 1920's the novels of Benito Lynch, cast in the countryside of Buenos Aires, and Ricardo Güiraldes' timeless evocation of a boy and a gaucho in *Don Segundo Sombra* provided masterpieces of mature style and content, and at the same time the short stories of the Uruguayan, Horacio Quiroga—the Poe of the Río de la Plata—brought the vivid colors and horrors of the Chaco jungles home to city dwellers.

The first decades of the twentieth century were exciting and changing times for Argentina, which were mirrored in the anger and ferment expressed by the Generation of 1910. By now Buenos Aires was an intellectual center of the hemisphere, and to it flowed not only the latest ideas from Europe but also the talents of Latin America. Fertile seeds had already been planted in the 1890's. The Nicaraguan poet Rubén Darío, that apostle of *modernismo*, or the symbolist school, in the Americas, stimulated avant-garde reviews and literary groups during his five-year residence in the porteño city. Marxism, socialism, bohemianism, and anarchism mingled in a heady brew that helped to arouse new ideas and new abilities. The Spanish-American War and the rebirth of Spanish letters led by Spain's Generation of '98 echoed and re-echoed through the porteño intellectual community, bringing a rejection of *yanqui* imperialism and admiration for the forgotten mother country. Across the estuary the Uruguayan José Enrique Rodó preached a powerful message to the youth of South America in his essay *Ariel*, in which he warned them to repudiate the materialistic Caliban personified by the United States and to develop their unique spiritual values. At the same time, however, French influences never ran stronger. Profits from cattle and grain made Paris an attainable mecca where Argentine artists and writers could immerse themselves in new modes and schools and seek inspiration for their own national culture. Verbal elegance and style became the primary goal of many an aspiring modernist author. Perhaps no one achieved more resounding success in this aspect than Enrique Larreta when, in 1910, he published his rousing historical novel, *La gloria de Don Ramiro,* set in the sixteenth-century Spain of Philip II.

From this turmoil of ideas and influences emerged the movements and writings which constituted a national literature, whereas before there had been only isolated masterpieces. Prosperity permitted Argentina the luxury of the arts, and numerous writers, painters, and musicians now devoted themselves primarily to creative efforts. Wealth enabled Argentina to indulge also in introspection and self-criticism, as the Generation of 1910 concerned itself with building a national ethos, with problems of social injustice, and with self-conscious rebellions against form.

In their efforts to discover just what constituted "Argentinism," authors helped to guide the emergent spirit of nationalism. Two tendencies predominated: the liberal, led by the essayist and literary critic Ricardo Rojas, who directed his countrymen's attention to the provinces and to the European-Indian heritage that had formed the Americas; and the authoritarian, characterized by the novelist Manuel Gálvez, who emphasized Argentina's caudillo traditions and the psychology of a mass society. Social protest provided another facet of this generation. Shades of Zola still permeated works such as Gálvez' *Nacha Regules,* built around the themes of prostitution and the porteño waterfront. From the humble origins of *Juan Moreira,* the theater after 1900 also began to give the porteño public harsh but masterful portraits of customs and life in the new Argentina, especially in the work of the Río de la Plata's greatest playwright, the Uruguayan-born Florencio Sánchez. In the few productive years before his early death in 1910, Sánchez artistically blended pathos and humor in three classic studies of the rural-urban and immigrant-native dilemma—*M'hijo el dotor, Barranca abajo,* and *La gringa.* Poets contributed the final major literary influence of the Generation of 1910 in their concern with form. Essayist, biographer, novelist, but above all poet—Leopoldo Lugones continued the impulse given by Rubén Darío in the 1890's. Although his later prose and verse ranked him alongside Rojas and Gálvez as a builder of nationalism, his principal impact was on the poetic world that produced at least a dozen outstanding figures in the 1920's. The question of form finally led to a sharp split in the literary camp. In the 1920's two groups emerged: the one, named after the workers' suburb of Boedo, maintained the conservative style of the naturalist school and the content of social protest, along with a political orientation toward communism; the other, taking its name from the fashionable street of Florida, proclaimed nationalist and liberal values but continued to receive its inspiration from avant-garde movements in Paris.

The bridge to the contemporary world of letters was fashioned in the bitterness and doubts of the 1930's. The Generation of 1910 had rebelled against form, had concerned itself with social injustices, and had struggled to build a national literary expression. Its successors turned introspective. What had happened to their country concerned them more than what Argentina was or could be. Ezequiel Martínez Estrada plumbed the depth of the Argentine soul in his *Radiografía de la pampa* and *La cabeza de Goliat,* while Raúl Scalabrini Ortiz attempted to analyze the porteño character through the man who stands at the city's center on the corner of Corrientes and Esmeralda in *El hombre que está solo y espera.* In a different and often autobiographical vein, Eduardo Mallea struggled in his lengthy and densely written *Historia de una pasión argentina* to link the "visible Argentina" with the "invisible country." Far easier to grasp were the intuitive and artistic explorations of the seamier aspects of life portrayed in two novels, *Los siete locos* and *Los lanzallamas,* and the vivid journalistic sketches, *Aguafuertes porteñas,* by that forerunner of today's "angry young men," Roberto Arlt.

As Argentina appeared to drift in the years during and following Perón, doubts continued to harass the contemporary generation of writers. Operas, concerts, lectures, exhibitions, and publishers' lists provided frequent and polished offerings, and porteños complacently prided themselves on a cultural life which they judged to be unsurpassed in the hemisphere. But the golden era marked by the Generation of 1910 seemed to have waned, and rising talents in Mexico, Brazil, and elsewhere challenged Argentine dominance of the Latin American cultural scene.

Compelling philosophical concerns have caused some writers to turn their backs on the dual heritage of *Martín Fierro* and *Facundo* in favor of exploring new perceptions of reality and the anguished alienation of contemporary man from his society. These preoccupations have won for individual Argentine talents international recognition in the literary field, just as Alberto Ginastera has gained world fame as a composer or Leopoldo Torre Nilsson as a film director. Prominent are Adolfo Bioy Casares, author of *La invención de Morel,* the existentialist Ernesto Sábato, author of *Sobre héroes y tumbas,* and Julio Cortázar, whose *Rayuela* has received particular note abroad.

But the drama and excitement of the Argentine experience still move many creative spirits. Best known among these is Jorge Luis Borges, who has secured world-wide prestige with his essays and poems and who, through his novels and short stories, ranks as the country's leading creator of prose fiction. Many of his works are available in English, French, and other translations. Significantly, his characters, even when not clothed as gaucho, compadrito, provinciano, or porteño, retain an Argentine flavor. And despite the strongly metaphysical concerns which motivate Borges and his characters, he projects the clarity of a storyteller through even the most complex issues and problems.

Equally promising for the future of Argentine letters has been the tendency to turn to the real world, including the political arena, for inspiration. Works such as *La creciente* by Silvina Bullrich, *Fin de fiesta* and *Escándalos y soledades* by Beatriz Guido, or *Se vuelven contra nosotros* by Manuel Peyrou have seized on contemporary political and social problems and have couched them in creative literary terms. In similar fashion, some of this generation's "angry young men and women," such as David Viñas in *Dar la cara* and *Los hombres de a caballo,* Iverna Codina in *La enlutada,* or Dalmiro Sáenz in *Hay hambre dentro de tu pan* have developed themes of social criticism in terms which promise to last far beyond their lifetimes. Even the bleak introspection of the 1930's seems to have given way to more creative tones in Julio Mafud's *El desarraigo argentino* or *Psicología de la viveza criolla*. The quality of such contemporary writers will have to stand the test of time, but their works clearly indicate a richness of talent and inspiration which bodes well for Argentine literature.

Chapter 9 • The Crisis of
Contemporary Argentina

Argentina in the 1970's faces continuing crisis. This endemic condition first became evident in the late 1920's and has contributed to economic inertia, political instability, and moral malaise ever since. The drift of recent decades puzzles statesmen, politicians, social scientists, and humanists. No facile analysis or ready diagnosis seems to suggest the causes or cures. Economic, political, sociological, even psychological explanations for Argentina's anemia leave much unanswered. Relatively high literacy and living standards, an apparently homogeneous population, an agricultural economy with strong trends toward urbanization and industrialization, all speak of a country which can sustain the impetus of its "take-off" and maintain the resultant prosperity. But no political leader in recent years has been able to move the nation forward. Even the Argentine people at times seem incapable of galvanizing themselves for the forward leap into development and progress. The problems and focuses differ according to the sector, class, or generation concerned. But from the significance and various meanings of words such as nationalism, militarism, industrialism, and urbanism there emerge the main themes of Argentina's present and on-going crisis.

217

The spirit of nationalism, although a major force in recent Argentine political history, came late to this area. Loyalty and patriotism were first felt for the local region or the provincial caudillo. Even in the late nineteenth century authorities in Buenos Aires still had difficulty in making nationhood meaningful beyond the limits of the coastal provinces. In international affairs considerations of nationalism were equally absent. From independence until World War I, Argentina could, with considerable justice, be considered a Spanish-speaking appendage of the British Empire. Throughout the nineteenth century the British Foreign Office acted as arbiter in the Río de la Plata between its two protégés, Brazil and Buenos Aires. By 1870 more subtle controls of investment, trade, and favors had replaced gunboats and intimidations of earlier years, but the result was the same. The oligarchy became a credit and a support to British interests rather than the defender of Argentine nationalism or hegemony in Latin America. As the nation became more European in blood and culture and Buenos Aires became more Parisian, Argentine diplomats disdained the heritage and problems of their neighbors. Beyond some scattered territorial disputes, Argentina shared few interests with any Latin American community. Nonalignment with territorial systems or alliances hardened into an Argentine belief that the country's principal bonds were with Europe, not with Latin America. When, after 1889, the United States began to advance its economic and diplomatic sphere southward by means of the Pan American Union, Argentine statesmen, faithful to pro-British sentiments, stood as a bulwark against *yanqui* attempts at hemispheric solidarity.

Nationalism, therefore, was a product of the twentieth century and of recent events in Argentine growth. Much of it sprang from the uprooting process initially connected with the era of massive immigration and continued after 1930 by internal migration. Traditional social and psychological values were being undermined. As a result, nationalism developed largely from the deliberate efforts in the schools to foster patriotism, the military service demanded of all young men, the unifying force of railroads, highways, newspapers, and radios, and the intellectual and middle-class concern with an Argentine ethos. Nationalism also had an economic basis: the rejection of what came to be viewed in the popular mind as foreign exploitation of the country's resources and wealth.

Nationalism developed primarily from the middle and lower classes. It was the son of the immigrant who rallied to patriotic fiestas and parades. It was the city dweller who hearkened to the themes of gaucho and *criollo*. It was the storekeeper, the grocer, and the clerk who responded to the denunciations of foreign-owned railroads and utilities. It was the peon and the laborer who applauded the diatribes against British pounds and *yanqui* dollars. It was the country's middle-class leaders—in government, in the universities, in the press, and in business —who set the tone of "Argentinism." But at the same time that this nationalist spirit had a broad base and formed an integral part of modern Argentina, its manifestations were largely negative. It railed at contracts that permitted foreign development of the nation's oil resources. It galvanized voters against presumed interference in internal politics by a United States ambassador.* It toppled the politician, university rector, or labor leader who became too closely associated with foreign groups. It grumbled at British possession of the Malvinas, or Falkland Islands. But nationalism has so far failed to build a broad base of consensus or community in Argentina. Its failure to develop as a constructive force reflects part of the country's contemporary crisis. Even today nationalism leads few to tighten their belts or to work harder. Patriotism has not blocked the periodic flights of domestic capital abroad, and Argentine technical and professional men still migrate in astonishing numbers to other countries where their talents are better rewarded.

More tangible than nationalism as a force in determining recent Argentine political events has been the role of the military. The tradition of military leadership and guidance in political matters has been an integral part of national development. Since independence, civilian groups have always appealed to segments of the military for assistance and support, and the army in particular has provided the country with

* Spruille Braden's "pro-democratic" statements during his brief appointment to Argentina in 1945 and his subsequent involvement in the publication of the State Department's Bluebook, an exposé of Nazi activities in Argentina, were cleverly and effectively presented to the Argentine public as evidence that the United States had intervened to influence the outcome of the 1946 elections.

many of its statesmen. The Argentine officer, like most of his Latin American colleagues, considers himself to be far more than a professional soldier. The reorganization and modernization of the armed forces at the beginning of the twentieth century aimed at placing the military beyond politics, but in reality officers only acquired a feeling of superiority over the politicians. The smattering of law, literature, history, economics, psychology, and international relations which career officers received along with their engineering and military training not only rounded out their preparation, it also encouraged their self-confidence as experts in all fields. Factors that have already been indicated—the insistence on military autonomy, the influence of German training, the growing *esprit de corps*—further contributed to military disdain of civilian competence, particularly in times of crisis.

The failure of the Radical Party and of Yrigoyen to meet the challenge of world depression gave strength to this military viewpoint and appeared to justify the Revolution of 1930. The young officers who joined that movement believed in the superior wisdom, efficiency, and altruism of military men. In their eyes, ineffectual political parties, landed oligarchy, British economic domination, and all the evil heritages handed down from the country's late-nineteenth-century development must be gradually eliminated. When civilian leadership failed, the military elite had to be ready to supply the necessary guidance.

Disdain for political parties was strengthened during the decade of the 1930's in which Fascism appeared to solve so readily the problems of Italy and Germany. Many Argentine officers completed their training in these countries. Even civilian and intellectual leaders began to share an admiration for the Fascist doctrines of racism, the corporate state, and authoritarian rule. After illness incapacitated Argentina's pro-Allies president in 1940, certain elements in the government turned increasingly toward the Axis. Democratic institutions, meanwhile, steadily lost ground because of the farcical elections held by Conservative regimes and the obvious inability of Radicals or Socialists to mobilize public support.

The attitudes of the armed forces, nevertheless, were far from monolithic and unchanging. To a significant degree the military reflected the forces and tensions of the political scene. Aside from the traditional split between army and navy, the army itself was composed of many distinct groups. Some of these complex divisions were revealed when in June 1943 the military once more intervened in a crisis and assumed political control of the nation. One sector of the army, most of the navy, and the overwhelming majority of the middle and upper classes favored the Allied cause and the constitutional apparatus of government. Their initial support thus went to a coup which promised to overturn the frankly pro-Axis regime. Other military elements, the still badly fragmented labor movement, and many vociferous nationalists were violently opposed to the Conservative candidate, a wealthy Salta landowner with pronounced British ties, who would inherit the presidency in 1944. There were also Axis groups, such as the strong-armed youth organization called the Alianza and the influential newspaper *El Pampero,* directed from the German embassy in Buenos Aires, which sought to link Argentina still more openly with the Nazi side. Other groups in the armed forces and many industrialists were primarily concerned with Argentina's loss of military and economic potential alongside Brazil, and they sought a regime to remedy that deficiency. As in 1930, therefore, the doors of Buenos Aires and the Casa Rosada lay open to the military column from the Campo de Mayo, and citizens of all political persuasions quickly accepted the military's guardianship.

Since 1943 the apparent unwillingness or inability of political parties to compromise and work together has encouraged military men to increase their political activities. The result has not been the traditional democratic process found in western Europe, in the United States, or even in Argentina during the 1920's. Many Argentines have been humiliated by the repeated interventions and coups that have dominated the political scene, particularly since 1955. Yet, for all the turmoil, the military created an apparatus for decision making which political parties were unable to provide. The interplay of various tendencies within the armed forces gave a semblance of representative government; and, although on various occasions tanks paraded through the streets of Buenos Aires, warships maneuvered off the coast, and even bombs were dropped, the military managed to resolve its differences without appeal to prolonged conflict or civil war.

The military kaleidoscope consequently has determined Argentina's recent political history. The "colonels" who rose to power in the 1943 coup distrusted democratic institutions: they dissolved congress and political parties, established press controls, and postponed elections indefinitely. The Church was courted by reinstituting religious instruction in the schools, thus temporarily overthrowing part of the anticlerical legislation of the 1880's. Tariffs and subsidies assured government support of industry, and economic controls pointed toward the shadowy goal of a corporate state. The pro-Allied guise, which had been assumed for the convenience of diplomatic recognition, soon reverted to traditional hostility toward United States influence in South America, now heavily colored by admiration for fading Nazi Germany. Yet nationalism and the protection of Argentine interests remained paramount. A break in diplomatic relations with Germany under pressure from the United States in early 1944 caused internal upheaval and only strengthened the pro-Axis group. But a year later this same government declared war on Germany and Japan in order to achieve acceptance in an "Allied world."

The upsurge of middle-class democratic sentiment at the war's end and the sympathies of numerous "constitutionalist" officers promised to return the armed forces to the side of traditional civilian government. As a first step, Juan D. Perón, a key member in the "colonels' group" and already a symbol of lower-class aspirations, was forced to resign the vice-presidency in October 1945 and was placed under arrest on the island of Martín García. But the so-called democratic forces remained divided and disorganized. In the resulting chaos, the military turned in desperation to Perón to control the lower-class agitation he had unleashed. Several months later, Perón won 56 per cent of the popular vote and thus the presidency. Even his opponents admitted the election was probably the freest and most honest (at least in the actual casting and counting of ballots) that Argentina had ever experienced.

With the inauguration of Perón, some analysts predicted the dawning of a new era in which Argentina would achieve both industrial power and popular democracy. But dramatic and costly economic policies and social programs attempted to accomplish too much too quickly. Certain sectors and classes scored momentary gains but without any overall increase in productive capacity or national purpose. Most distressing for many middle-class Argentines was the cavalier disregard for the traditional, albeit often ineffectual, forms of constitutional democracy. Perón could not tolerate opposition. Labor union leaders who challenged his wishes found themselves in prison or in exile. Impeachment proceedings removed opposition from the Supreme Court. A malleable Senate and Chamber of Deputies soon gagged the few members who dared to criticize the presidency. Intervention in the provinces removed governors or legislators opposed to Perón. The universities and schools quickly lost their independence; students and faculty either acquiesced or left Argentina. Radio stations and newspapers became government propaganda outlets. Perón's new wife, Eva Duarte, who some say masterminded his return to power following his arrest in October 1945, mounted a vast social security, public charity, and public relations effort to deify Perón as the country's savior. Secret police, concentration camps, political arrests, and repeated states of siege became accepted components of the increasing centralization of political power. By 1949 Perón could make significant revisions and amendments to the Constitution of 1853, including authority to succeed himself in the presidency, and establish the Peronist Party as an official government political party.

Perón, despite his appeals to the masses and the military, proved unable to unify the country or to resolve the difficult adjustments from an agricultural to an industrial economy. For several years he traded on the Argentine credit built up by wartime sales to the United States and England and on postwar demands for Argentine agricultural products. But costly and often wasteful policies failed to generate internal demand and capital to build the required infrastructure or to sustain steady industrial development. As increasingly serious economic problems confronted Perón after 1951, he turned to more extreme demagoguery, to heavy reliance on foreign capital, and finally to violent attacks on suspected enemies within the oligarchy, the Church, and the armed forces. His rule—some called it dictatorship—nevertheless seemed quite solid until the very year of his overthrow in 1955.

On the surface the great majority of the armed forces gave Perón its wholehearted support. But nearly ten years of Peronist rule emphasized one inherent threat to the military position—the rise of the lower classes. The strength of labor unions, the effective appeals to the masses, the threat of a worker militia, the lower-class distrust of the military, all contributed to make the armed forces and the lower classes distinct, and often rival, pillars of the Perón regime. At times the military as a caste refused to accede to Perón's directives. Thus, in 1951, the military vetoed Eva Perón's candidacy for the vice-presidency. After her death in 1952, military pressures increasingly worked against labor union power. Twice, in September 1951 and in June 1955, groups within the armed forces attempted to regain control of the situation and remove Perón from power. It was a military coup, emanating from the Córdoba garrison, which finally overthrew Perón in September 1955.

Initially the new military regime attempted to reconcile all elements within the country, including the followers of Perón. But certain embittered civilian and military groups refused to forgive or forget the Perón years. The seeds of discord bore immediate fruit in a shake-up within the military regime. The ensuing caretaker government under General Pedro Aramburu committed itself to turning the power over to civilian authorities in 1958. In its adamant refusal to reincorporate Peronists in the body politic, however, the Aramburu regime deepened the basic schism which would trouble and finally undermine all subsequent governments. Furthermore, the old divisions, personalities, and quarrels reappeared and absorbed energies that might better have been applied to the pressing economic and social problems. The presidential elections presaged instability. The Radicals, divided from their beginning into a moderate group and an intransigent or leftist group which Yrigoyen himself had epitomized, went to the polls with two candidates. Arturo Frondizi, standard bearer of the intransigents (Unión Cívica Radical Intransigente), campaigned openly for the Peronist vote by pledging his support to labor unions and to a reincorporation of Perón's followers in the country's political life. This appeal, reinforced by orders from the exiled Perón, gave Frondizi an estimated two million Peronist votes (about one-third of the electorate), which provided the margin of victory over the other Radical sector (Unión Cívica Radical del Pueblo) and the numerous splinter parties that had sprung up on the eve of elections.

The Frondizi administration remained in power for nearly four years before being overthrown by a military coup. During these years the military's constant intervention in government became still more evident. Frondizi sought support from many groups: from the Church, through a most un-Radical attempt to elevate Catholic institutions of higher learning to the privileges and prerogatives of the national university system; from labor, by periodic wage boosts when inflation cut real wages too drastically; from agriculturists, by devaluation of the peso; and from industrialists, by obtaining international loans and permitting extensive imports of capital goods and raw materials. In economic policy he supported agriculture and foreign investment as the only means by which Argentina could secure the essentials for eventual industrial growth. He confronted and solved the problems surrounding the exploitation of oil. He restored international confidence in Argentina. He maintained the appearances of democracy, even though Argentina remained under virtual martial law. But the thirty-five attempted coups against his administration, culminating with a successful one in March 1962 which removed Frondizi from office, clearly revealed the process of adjustments within the armed forces and in government. The cabinet members who represented the army, navy, and air force acted as the final arbiters in all matters, and decisions were made in response to pressures and demands within the military. In the last analysis, government did not rest on political parties, public participation, or civic responsibility, but on the support and acquiescence of the armed forces.

This pattern of military tutelage, encouraged by periodic economic crises, repeated itself with depressing regularity throughout the 1960's. Although the inauguration of the president of the national Senate as chief executive in Frondizi's place provided a semblance of constitutionality (the vice-president had resigned in 1958), control really rested in the hands of the military. Public confidence and tranquility was shaken repeatedly during 1962-63 by the unflattering spectacle of open clashes between factions within the military. Any illusions that Argentina possessed a monolithic military structure vanished as Sherman tanks on two occasions occupied strategic points around the city of Buenos Aires and subsequently overran the principal Argentine naval base and destroyed airfields. Gradually one group of officers, known by war-game colors as *azules** and possessing particular strength within the armored or cavalry branch of the army, emerged in control of the country's military high command. During this critical struggle, the *colorados*** lost command positions, retired, or otherwise were politically neutralized. The confrontation elevated a cavalry general, Juan Carlos Onganía, to commander-in-chief of the army and placed him in a role similar to Aramburu in 1955-58 as guarantor of a return to civilian rule.

The elections, which were held in mid-winter 1963, seemed to confirm the worst doubts about the ability of political parties to work within a democratic structure. At stake was every elective office in the country, and yet no lasting cooperation or coordination emerged among the thirty-nine different parties who put up presidential electors. At the last minute, the authorities even removed from the ballot the candidates of a major party which was supported by Frondizi and Perón. By election eve in early July, confusion reigned. President-elect Arturo Illia, a country doctor who represented the Radical sector opposed to Frondizi (Unión Cívica Radical del Pueblo), garnered a mere 25 per cent of the popular vote and needed substantial help in the electoral college from minority parties. The number of blank ballots, generally considered to be Peronist votes, had declined to 24 per cent from the 32 per cent recorded in favor of flesh-and-blood Peronist candidates in 1962. The decline was hardly significant, however, for hard-core Peronist sentiment still contributed more votes than those cast for any other candidate except Illia. Furthermore, many Peronists, fearful that otherwise Aramburu might win the presidency, reportedly voted for Illia.

---

* Also referred to as *legalistas,* since they favored a non-political, professional military.

** Variously known as *gorilas, continuistas,* or *golpistas,* these officers supported close supervision of the political scene by the military. Their leaders came primarily from the infantry and the navy.

Despite the lack of consensus, mandate, or majority, Illia, neverthe-less, embarked on a presidency in late 1963 in a moment of political calm, with a people exhausted by political bickering and military coups and with the armed forces controlled by officers determined to let the constitutional and political processes have another chance. In a fashion reminiscent of Hipólito Yrigoyen but without that leader's political astuteness or charisma, the doctor from Córdoba diagnosed his nation's problems as political and concluded that economic and social difficulties would correct themselves once civilian government and political parties ruled. Unfortunately his efforts to be neutral degenerated into a do-nothing policy which alienated major groups in business, agriculture, and labor and failed to stir even an apathetic response from the public at large. Meanwhile, his sincere attempts to reincorporate Peronists into political activities aroused fears among anti-Peronist elements. Like Frondizi, Illia gambled that his government had made inroads on Peronist popular appeal. But the 1965 congressional elections saw Pe-ronist candidates not only walk off with a large block of seats but also outpoll Illia's party in popular votes. As a result, Illia apparently re-adjusted his strategy in favor of polarizing the Radical and Peronist positions. Several local elections in the first half of 1966, however, dashed hopes that the electorate would reject the Peronist extreme. Those in the middle and upper classes adamantly opposed to Peronismo —and there were many who held powerful positions in business and the military—looked ahead to the 1967 congressional and gubernatorial con-tests with increasing uneasiness.

To no one's surprise, and with public acceptance if not acclamation, the military once more intervened at the end of June 1966 to remove what many saw as a well-meaning but incompetent president. The tri-umvirate of army, navy, and air force commanders dissolved congress, provincial legislatures, and political parties and called upon Onganía to assume the presidency. Ironically the man who had insisted on a return to civilian rule in the crucial 1962-63 period now advocated preparation of the necessary basis for political democracy—another way of saying that a military regime must secure the economic development and so-cial integration which had eluded political parties for the last several decades. As part of this process, the new government maintained the Constitution of 1853 but subordinated it to the newly established Estatuo de la Revolución Argentina, or Statute of the Argentine Revolution.

At first the new authorities stumbled repeatedly. Fearful that the universities harbored some Communists and desirous of more centralized control over the university structure, they intervened with a heavy hand. Lost was the autonomy as well as the tripartite rule by faculty, students, and alumni secured nearly fifty years before by the "University Reform." As a result, faculty, especially in the exact sciences, left Argentina in droves, many of them for jobs in United States, Venezuelan, and Chilean universities. Unduly concerned with public morals, various officials mounted campaigns against miniskirts, "lovers' lanes," and nightclubs. Onganía's brother-in-law appeared particularly ridiculous when, for similar reasons, he prohibited the performance of Alberto Ginastera's opera Bomarzo at the Colón. Even a sense of humor seemed lacking: Tía Vicenta, the leading satirical journal, was banned after portraying Onganía as a walrus on its front cover.*

The eventual success or failure of the new government, however, would be determined by labor, business, and the military, not by intellectuals. Here the record was slightly more promising. The labor unions eyed Onganía with some skepticism. In early 1967, after an initial waiting period and more significantly after the appointment of a new Minister of Economy and Labor, a series of scattered strikes developed momentum and presented a major challenge to the government. Energetic responses, including jail sentences for several union leaders, along with a slowing down of inflation and major divisions within union leadership, resulted in a year-long truce between labor and government. In similar fashion, Onganía demonstrated ability to control rival military factions. Argentina's pampered officers, long recipients of generous living allowances and fringe benefits, secured further pay boosts which made them the envy of the professional and upper-middle classes. At the same time, Onganía lived up to his reputation as an unsmiling dis-

---

* Insult was added to injury, since not only Onganía's mustache and features but also a play on slang terms made the analogy particularly disrespectful.

ciplinarian who brooked no threat of insubordination. He met rumors of a coup in the winter of 1968 with immediate replacement of the commanders-in-chief of all three services.

Onganía's apparent ability to deal effectively with challenges to his regime, coupled with some success in increasing productivity and curbing inflation, led many observers to conclude erroneously that his extended rebuilding program for Argentina might actually be fulfilled. Business interests, in particular, seemed receptive to the "three-stage revolution" advocated by Onganía. According to this doctrine, Argentina first needed to rebuild itself economically; the second phase would provide social restructuring; and the final political phase, perhaps a decade later, would return the country to an electoral system. Some warning signs in demonstrations against Onganía and ensuing arrests occurred in early 1969. But widespread violence unexpectedly arose in May 1969. It was apparent that the authorities and the public at large were generally unaware of the profound divisions and socio-economic problems which still made Argentina an extremely difficult country to govern.

What started innocently enough as a university student demonstration against increased cafeteria prices in the city of Corrientes was fanned by a student death and flamed into further student protests and further deaths at Rosario and a major labor protest against inflation and police brutality at the industrial city of Córdoba. Fierce street fighting broke out at the end of May in Córdoba, and a general strike largely paralyzed the country. Onganía responded with a major cabinet shake-up and promises that the 1966 Revolution had completed its economic rebuilding phase and would now stress solutions to social problems. Nelson Rockefeller's ill-timed visit as part of his Latin American fact-finding mission provided provocateurs at this crisis moment the chance to firebomb and destroy a number of supermarkets in Buenos Aires connected with his financial interests. At the same time, the depth of labor disturbances was forcefully underlined by the assassination at his headquarters of Augusto Vandor, the leading labor organizer who favored a conciliatory policy toward the government. Scattered incidents of violence continued: attacks on sentinel posts, bombings of selected foreign

companies, kidnapping of certain diplomats and key officials. Although
an uneasy calm prevailed at Buenos Aires and other major cities after the
May and June explosions, the rumor market once again was rife with
speculation as to who actually held the reins of government. The labor
leader who sparked the Córdoba riots was in jail. An attempted coup by
a clique of colonels with Peronist leanings, who earned their nickname
of *peruanistas* from the army takeover in Peru in 1968, was squashed.
But still doubts remained, to flourish with every financial upset, with
every troop movement, with every public utterance by a cabinet member, with every gesture by the military high command.

The prognosticators finally had their day in June 1970. Onganía fell.
Former president Aramburu had been kidnapped and shot at the end of
May. According to some versions, Peronists thus sought revenge for the
executions which Aramburu had ordered in June 1956 following a Peronist coup; other more sinister explanations also flourished which impli-
cated elements within the existing Onganía regime. Key officers within
the armed forces finally judged that Onganía had not been able to regain
control of the situation so badly shattered the year before by student
and labor upheavals and that both economic development and social
reform were lagging. Also under fire were Onganía's political efforts to
replace representative democracy with a neo-corporativist system.

A new general, Roberto M. Levingston, emerged as chief executive,
named by the commanders of the three services. But devaluation of the
peso, reconstitution of the cabinet, and promises of future elections re-
assured few. Bombings, assassinations, kidnappings, and cabinet crises
continued to splash across the headlines. High ranking officials began
to hint at further neo-corporative experiments, creation of an official
government political party, or other measures which once again seemed
to push any return to democratically elected government off for a number of years. The abrupt intervention by the commanders-in-chief of
the armed forces in March 1971 removed Levingston from office and
served once again to underline the degree of military dominance of the
contemporary scene. Some found in the periodic violence and particularly in the new stirrings by labor at Córdoba, Tucumán, and Rosario
the signs of structural upheaval and perhaps revolutionary change.

To the average Argentine, however, the crisis environment had become commonplace. In actuality the Argentine body politic evinced no basic interest in radical or revolutionary change and indeed recoiled when drastic revision was proposed. Argentines might still occasionally hope a great future lay ahead, but they were prepared to muddle along with middle-of-the-road political and economic experiments, be these designs of generals, economists, lawyers, medical doctors, or educators. As a corollary, the interested observer of Argentine affairs can predict that the armed forces will continue for several years and perhaps for several decades to exert the predominant political role in Argentina and to act as an authority above civilian government.

Since 1945 constant turmoil and change seem to characterize the Argentine scene. Nationalism and militarism still constitute major elements in the nation's contemporary crisis. But more lasting and certainly more revolutionary in their eventual impact have been the continuing trends toward industrialization and the rise of the lower classes.

Europe's Industrial Revolution encouraged the New World to expand far beyond the economic horizons of gold and silver, or of sugar, indigo, and tobacco, into the production and export of a wide variety of mineral and agricultural raw materials. The New World's Industrial Revolution, still in its infancy in many parts of Latin America, arose largely as a result of the disadvantageous position in which the new nations found themselves with regard to the major industrial powers. The answer to the obvious question of why Argentina did not follow the United States, which it resembled in so many ways, to early supremacy in this field is found only too clearly in the manner of its agricultural revolution. In the course of half a century the country which in 1870 had a population barely equal to that of Chile, an established reputation for revolution and insecurity, and a humble economy based on hides and wool became the economic and cultural leader of Latin America. But modern Argentina was built on the development of only one agricultural zone. The structure of national prosperity and the elite class itself conspired to subordinate everything to the exploitation of the pampas. Railroads radiating from the ports drew the products of the pampas to the coast for rapid transit to Europe, but construction of roads and connecting railroad links was neglected. One metropolis effectively monopolized all negotiations and decisions and served as the only connection to Europe. Mining or manufacturing activities not directly related to the pampas' agricultural primacy were abandoned. It was as if, long before the Civil War, the South had emerged as the dominant and only area of United States expansion, with its capital at Savannah or Charleston, an economy based entirely on cotton exported to British mills, and an oligarchy composed of plantation owners and merchants.

Any major readjustment in such an agricultural export economy was bound to be painful—the more so in Argentina where, by the early twentieth century, the majority of the population was accustomed to a relatively high standard of living. Yet the changes brought about by two world wars and a world depression left Argentina no alternative. Just as the decline of the Potosí mines and the collapse of the Spanish Empire altered the orientation of the Río de la Plata colony, so the falling prices of raw materials and the collapse of the British free trade system shifted the focus for modern Argentina. No longer could the increasing urbanization and the expectations of the growing middle and lower classes be supported by traditional agricultural exports. For Argentines of the mid-twentieth century the solution lay with industrialization.

The economic prospects for Argentina in 1945 appeared promising. Industry had enjoyed protection for more than a decade through tariffs and through reduction of imports due to depression and wartime shortages. Manufacturing contributed 30 per cent of the country's gross national product as compared with 26 per cent in 1935. At the same time Argentina's production of wool, meat, hides, and cereals for the Allies had netted the country a substantial dollar and sterling reserve —a forced saving of 1.7 billion dollars accumulated during the war years when consumer and capital goods from abroad were unavailable. Presumably Argentina possessed the funds to purchase the heavy equipment needed for industrialization, while continuing to earn substantial sums from feeding war-torn Europe.

There were, however, shadows in this rosy picture, many of them inherited from the depression and war years. Despite efforts in the

1930's to begin construction of a highway system, commerce and industry remained shackled to railroads designed to handle the commerce of the pampas but inadequate for a country with industrial aspirations. In 1945 less than 5,000 miles of the 38,000 miles of roads had any kind of surfacing, and nearly half the trucks in service were more than fifteen years old. The railroads themselves suffered from lack of replacements. It had been almost thirty-five years since the British owners had made any significant investments in rails, locomotives, or cars. As industry and transport demanded ever larger quantities of petroleum, the rising domestic output continued to meet only half the country's consumption needs. Coal and steel imports, held in abeyance during the war, likewise ate up exchange credits since large annual imports were required after the war. Finally Argentina found itself in much the same predicament it had faced during the depression: the profits from agriculture did not stretch as far as before in the purchase of capital goods and machinery. With the relaxation of price controls and rationing in industrial nations and the sharp price rise of capital goods in the world market, exchange reserves rapidly dwindled. The full implication of these developments was not realized in Argentina until the 1950's, largely because during the first postwar years world prices for meats, cereals, hides, and wool remained high. Extensive government controls and interference in the economy also disguised the deteriorating situation both within the country and in international trade.

The military regime which replaced the Conservatives in 1943 had looked to industrialization as the means to achieve Argentine self-sufficiency and supremacy in South America. But wartime curtailment of imports, although strengthening many consumer goods industries, prevented Argentina from acquiring much needed industrial equipment. Furthermore, the evident pro-Axis bent of the country's rulers cut Argentina off from United States aid. While Brazil, Argentina's traditional rival in Río de la Plata politics, received tanks and warships, steel and oil, blast furnaces and factories, and even the potential to build airplane engines, Argentina's industrial plant deteriorated and its heavy industry remained a dream.

With the end of the war Argentina attempted to compensate for these lean years in its industrial formation. Under the guidance of

Perón, who was elected president in 1946, the country embarked on a program of rapid industrialization, and the government became the principal arbiter of economic development. The government's overall planning placed primary emphasis on industrial expansion. Perón's first Five-Year Plan (1947-51) aspired to many advances, especially in the output of coal, oil, steel, and electric power, but, above all, it aimed at increasing the country's manufacturing capacity. At the core of this program was IAPI (Instituto Argentino de Promoción del Intercambio, or the State Institute for Trade Promotion), a mammoth bureaucracy that purchased agricultural products at fixed prices from farmers and *estancieros,* sold these products on the world market, and at the same time handled a substantial share of Argentine imports. In theory the Institute could act as a buffer against fluctuations in world prices, and from 1953 to 1955 it actually lost millions of dollars in futile attempts to protect Argentine producers in a falling world market. But during the course of the first Five-Year Plan, the Institute bought the products of the land at absurdly low prices and sold them at the highest possible level to hungry European nations. Argentina thereby earned an unsavory reputation with its unwillingness to gamble on European recovery. Typical was the statement made to European buyers by one of Perón's principal economic advisers: "Either you pay our prices or you don't eat." The profits thus realized went to the state, not to the farmers. Government, aside from indeterminate losses due to graft and bureaucratic waste, plowed these profits into industrialization: into credits, import licenses, and favorable exchange rates for manufacturers of consumer goods; into subsidies, airplanes, and ships for the national airline and merchant marine; into the so-called military factories which administered the infant steel industry and the German properties seized at the very end of the war; into exploration for coal resources and construction of several hydroelectric projects; into limited purchases of railroad and oil-drilling equipment; and into illusory atomic energy experiments which utilized the talents of the few German scientists not working for Russia or the United States.

Argentina also invested heavily during these immediate postwar years in transport and public utilities, unfortunately not through modernization of existing facilities but merely through the purchase of these facilities from foreign ownership. The deterioration of the railroads had appeared to justify demands that the state appropriate and control the national transport and communication system. Public opinion rallied to Perón's pronouncement that the purchase of foreign railroads constituted the economic complement to San Martín's political liberation of Argentina. Having given fair and even generous payments for the British and French lines, Argentina also bought the foreign-owned gasworks and telephone system—a total outlay that absorbed 45 per cent of the country's postwar foreign exchange. But no matter how dramatically the acquisition of railroads, telephones, and utilities might assuage the demands of economic nationalism, the burdens of renovation, expansion, and wage increases weighed heavily on the country's budget after 1947.

Dollar reserves also disappeared into less productive areas. War surplus tanks and planes were purchased from the United States in order to satisfy colonels and generals who unhappily contemplated Brazil's modern military establishment. In an attempt to encourage diversification and development of Patagonia, the government in 1945 declared the region south of the 42° parallel a duty-free zone. But the objective was frustrated by the tendency to import luxury items and passenger cars for subsequent shipment north to Buenos Aires, instead of importing the essentials for Patagonian development.

The emphasis on industry did not solve Argentina's problems in the post-1945 world. Indeed, it accentuated some of the pre-existing trends. During the Perón administration, which deliberately depreciated rural occupations and promised bread and circuses for the urban masses, the movement of population continued to be toward the cities, particularly toward the city of Buenos Aires. Although the national rate of population growth now amounted to less than 2 per cent a year (in contrast to the 3 and 4 per cent of the first decades of the twentieth century), the population of Greater Buenos Aires rose from 2 million in 1914, to 4.6 million in 1947, to 6.8 million by 1960, and to approximately 8 million by 1970. A new wave of Italian and Spanish immigrants reached Argentina in the postwar years and settled almost entirely in the cities; only east Europeans and Germans headed for agricultural frontiers in

Río Negro, the Chaco, and Misiones. The bulk of city dwellers came from the interior and countryside of Argentina itself. Prior to 1935 approximately 8,000 persons a year migrated from the interior to Greater Buenos Aires. During the war years the yearly average rose to 100,000, and from 1947 to 1951 it climbed to nearly 200,000 a year. But industry was unable to employ these unskilled and often illiterate peasants from the Argentine hinterland, and those who remained often entered the service occupations as laborers in transport, commerce, and government. While the percentage of the economically active population employed in agriculture declined and that in industry remained relatively stable, the percentage in the services showed a marked rise. Related to these economic adjustments was the very slow increase in Argentina's gross national product, averaging 1.8 per cent a year since 1930 or, in terms of per capita production, amounting to virtual stagnation. Here was serious trouble for an economy which needed to expand its ability to produce and to consume if industrialization were to succeed.

The accomplishments of the first Five-Year Plan were modest. Support given to the manufacturing industries served to increase Argentine self-sufficiency in consumer goods, and by 1955 local industry produced 99 per cent of the consumer goods used in the country. The use of foreign exchange for shipping charges was reduced by expansion of the merchant marine which by the early 1950's carried between one-fifth and one-fourth of the nation's trade. The national airline, Aerolíneas Argentinas, covered Argentina with an extensive network of local flights and reached London and New York with its international service. In 1949 the government anticipated the jet age with the completion of the enormous and extravagant international airport of Ezeiza, thirteen miles southwest of the city of Buenos Aires. Although plans drawn up in 1947 for a steel mill at San Nicolás had not progressed, two blast furnaces in Jujuy were processing ore from local mines. There were also promising signs of development of energy resources. Low-grade but sizable coal reserves at Río Turbio in the Andes of southern Patagonia were linked by railroad to the port of Río Gallegos. Plans were traced for hydroelectric projects to utilize several rivers in Córdoba, Mendoza, and Río Negro. Finally, the completion of a natural gas pipeline from

Comodoro Rivadavia to Buenos Aires in 1949 forecast a new era in the exploitation of petroleum resources.

These achievements did not disguise the painful transition, through depression, world wars, and government controls, from an agricultural economy dependent on world markets to an industrial economy dependent on internal markets. By 1949 Argentina had spent more than a billion dollars (over 60 per cent) of its foreign exchange reserve. The remainder consisted largely of frozen sterling credits at a time when demand was shifting from British pounds to United States dollars. Profits from agricultural exports were threatened by IAPI, which drained all profits from agriculture without returning either investment or incentive, and by falling world prices, resulting from increased European and United States farm production. Droughts in 1949-50 and 1951-52 added their toll. The value of agricultural exports, which since 1910 had fluctuated well above the billion-dollar level (1960 value of the dollar), dropped sharply, especially in 1952. Per capita foreign investment and capital accumulation likewise fell at that time to their lowest levels in almost fifty years. Such declines brought a re-evaluation of economic policy, and the second Five-Year Plan (1953-57) announced that agricultural investment and development would henceforth be favored. Nevertheless, agriculture significantly received a mere 3 per cent of the funds to be expended under the second Five-Year Plan.

Confronted with enormous and vital expenditures for transportation, steel, and energy, the government turned to the printing press to provide funds. The rise of currency in circulation—from 3.2 billion pesos at the end of 1945, to 13 billion in 1950, to 33 billion in September 1955—launched an inflationary spiral. The cost of living in Buenos Aires rose from a base of 100 in 1943 to 680 by 1955. (Recent investigations, using a base of 100 in 1960, give 3 for 1943 and 20 for 1955.) Despite exchange controls, the peso, which long stood at four to the dollar, reached a free market valuation of thirty to the dollar by the end of the Perón era. Real wages for industrial and urban workers, which increased after the 1943 coup and during the early years of the Perón administration, now sagged, while Perón sought to take his followers' minds off climbing food costs by paid vacations, sports events, and demagoguery.

Progress toward providing the fundamental elements of an industrialized nation moved at a snail's pace. Inflation and government
subsidization of the industrial sector caused Argentina to dip ever
deeper into its gold and foreign exchange reserves. Electric power for
the coastal region still came from generators fueled by oil or coal. Despite increasing oil production, industrial and public demand grew even
more rapidly. By 1955 Argentina had to import 60 per cent of its oil,
and this alone accounted for nearly one-fifth the value of all Argentine
imports. The low-grade coal mined in Río Turbio met only 10 per cent
of the country's needs. In 1955 the Export-Import Bank made a loan of
60 million dollars which was to be applied to the San Nicolás steel mill,
but under the best of conditions industry would still have to rely on imported steel for another two decades. Meanwhile, little was done to expand or even to maintain the road system, and total highway mileage
actually showed a loss during the decade 1945-55. Railroads continued
to deteriorate without replacements of equipment, and service worsened. As featherbedding increased the number of employees, efficiency
declined. Perón could not even boast that he had made the trains run
on time, and politically the government could not afford to raise rates to
cover operating expenses.

It remained for Perón's successors to bear the brunt of the country's
industrialization crisis. The Prebisch reports, drafted in 1955-56 by Argentina's leading economist on the United Nations' Economic Commission for Latin America, pointed to the run-down and antiquated
transportation system, the insufficient sources of fuel and energy, and
the absence of a steel industry, and concluded: "Argentina has sought
to increase consumption without sufficiently increasing its production."
The two constitutionally elected regimes from 1958 to 1962 and from
1963 to 1966, along with the military caretakers who ruled during the
remaining years, have consequently had to face many of the same problems which gave rise to the five-year plans.

Industry desperately needed the foreign exchange which only agricultural exports could earn. In an effort to stimulate the agrarian sector,
the official exchange rate in 1955 was changed from 7.5 to 18 pesos to

the dollar,* and the cumbersome apparatus of IAPI was dismantled. Three years later the government further encouraged agriculture by adopting the free market rate, then approximately seventy pesos to the dollar, as the official rate. But other serious obstacles hampered rural recovery. World agricultural prices continued to decline, and the specter of United States wheat surpluses and Commonwealth and European Common Market discrimination loomed on the horizon. Farm techniques lagged far behind those of major competitors. The farmer suffered from lack of capital, credit, and equipment and from living conditions which had not improved over the past fifty years. Except on remote frontiers where few were willing to venture, ownership of the land was beyond the grasp of nearly two-thirds of Argentine farmers.

Industrialization also required investment and credit from abroad. Argentina's military caretakers limited themselves to refunding the foreign debt. But the nationalistic and leftist Frondizi, inaugurated as president in May 1958, boldly adopted measures to attract foreign capital. He believed economic development to be the only solution to the country's problems. Unable to impose forced savings at home, he turned to foreign sources for the needed funds. In contradiction to his own writings and the Radical Party platform and without congressional authorization, his administration invited foreign companies to develop Argentine petroleum resources under the supervision of the national oil agency. The hopes of encouraging foreign investment and securing foreign loans likewise caused the government to accept many of the conservative financial dictates of the International Monetary Fund and the United States Treasury.

At first the results were encouraging. Large sums of private capital from the United States, Switzerland, Holland, and Germany entered Argentina during 1959 and 1960. Favored were the petroleum and automotive fields. United States capital and technicians contributed to the completion of natural gas and oil pipelines from the Campo Durán

* The Perón administration maintained various official rates, ranging from 5 to 14 pesos to the dollar. By 1955 the free market quotation reached 30. Since the Central Bank controlled all official exchange transactions, this had meant a government subsidy directed to approved imports for industrial development.

fields in Salta to the coast in 1960, and by 1962 Argentina achieved virtual self-sufficiency in petroleum. Less beneficial was the over-expansion of the automotive industry. In the mid-fifties the Kaiser factory at Córdoba established a precedent with its jeeps and sedans largely built in Argentina. But the lifting of certain import restrictions in 1959-60 and the promise of short-term profits in this car-starved land flooded Argentina with more than twenty European and United States firms which merely assembled imported parts. Argentine industry thereby received no stimulus for producing components locally, and, although some companies, such as Fiat, promised tractor and locomotive production, the importation of parts created serious drains on foreign exchange.

International loans spurred other sectors of the economy. The output of coal from the Río Turbio mines increased to cover nearly one-fifth of Argentine needs by 1960. The San Nicolás steel mill, helped along by additional Export-Import Bank credits, began limited production in 1960. Discovery of new iron ore deposits in the Sierra Grande region of Río Negro reinforced dreams that Argentina might one day possess a heavy industry of its own. In the field of electric power, Swiss and Belgian investments were merged into a public-service company to increase the supply of energy for the city of Buenos Aires, and construction began on a major thermoelectric plant to service the southern industrial area of Greater Buenos Aires. Several dams were completed in Mendoza and Córdoba, and plans were laid to harness the rapids and falls of the upper Paraná and Uruguay rivers. The ambitious Chocón hydroelectric project, located on the Río Limay eight hundred miles southwest of Buenos Aires, was stalled for lack of funds, but government planners pinned hopes on the newly established Inter-American Bank and on European private capital. Alliance for Progress funds also promised to supplement the loans already extended by the World Bank, or the International Bank for Reconstruction and Development, for the pressing needs in railroad modernization, highway construction, and low-cost housing.

By late 1962, the Argentine economy had entered another of its periodic slumps. Economists now began to point to acute shortages of foreign exchange as the cause for these crises which seemed to repeat themselves every three or four years. Since the authorities took little effective action to maintain or increase the level of agricultural exports, which still earned 85 to 90 per cent of the country's foreign exchange, Argentina lacked the exchange earnings usually relied upon in other Western nations to develop the costly infrastructure and expanding markets for industrialization. Although regimes since 1930 had stressed import substitution—local manufacture of consumer goods—this fell far short of a consistent long-range industrialization program. A nation with industrial tastes and aspirations had emerged, but in world trade Argentina still depended on its agriculture. The delicate balance of inflation, foreign loans, and subsidies showed itself particularly vulnerable, therefore, to drought years, political crises, or overextended imports. If Argentina were to buy machinery to continue expanding its factories, to secure industrial raw materials not produced within its borders, to renovate and modernize its transportation and electric power infrastructure, and at the same time to stimulate and increase internal demands for its consumer and industrial products, the economy needed vast amounts of foreign exchange. Clearly the labor force, vocal and organized, could not be excessively taxed by means of a drop in real wages. In face of economic nationalism, only limited use could be made of foreign loans and investments. Though it appealed to the national ego, the Raúl Prebisch thesis, that agricultural exporters were at the mercy of industrial nations because export prices for primary products had declined since 1929 while those for manufactures and capital goods had increased, provided no specific remedies. Thus the only substantial source for foreign exchange earnings seemed to be agriculture. Yet it was exactly in this sector that investments in infrastructure—transport, storage, extension research, and disease control—and in equipment and modernization had lagged drastically behind its agricultural competitors in Australia, Canada, and the United States during the previous forty years.

The immediate cause for the downturn in 1962-63 apparently resulted from excessive reallocation of resources to the secondary or industrial sector along with major and costly investments in transport, power, and steel. The agriculture-based export economy just could not provide sufficient foreign exchange earnings for such sustained expenditures, and recession and devaluation followed. Externally Argentina had lived beyond its productive means with trade deficits (in value of 1960 prices) that amounted to 170 million dollars in 1960, 498 million in 1961, and 141 million in 1962. Internally the government continued to rely on inflation. Money in circulation, which had amounted to 33 billion pesos in 1955, rose to 153 billion in 1962.

Rather than face the simple though harsh economic realities, the Illia administration honestly believed that politics constituted the country's major problem and that the less action taken in the economic or social field the better. The new president made only one major economic decision, and that was politically inspired and economically disastrous. In response to his campaign pledges, he cancelled contracts with the foreign oil companies. He viewed these contracts not only as unconstitutional but also as illegal because congress had not approved them. Thus the daring move by Frondizi to attract foreign capital and to develop the country's substantial petroleum and natural gas resources was lost just as it had begun to pay dividends in self-sufficiency. Furthermore Argentina now had to pay over 300 million dollars in compensation to the foreign companies.

Nevertheless, the Illia formula of "hands-off" seemed to work at first. Devaluation of the peso stimulated agricultural exports, and two good harvests added to foreign currency earnings. But the government took no action to support the agricultural sector and provided no direction for business, industry, and above all labor.

Despite pronouncements that wages and cost-of-living would be held down, the government surrendered its efforts to reduce featherbedding in the railroad system and responded to labor pressure by permitting repeated wage hikes. The conciliatory—some called it spineless—attitude of the Illia government had certain merits. The Peronists who dominated the largest labor organization, the C.G.T. (Confederación General de Trabajo, or General Labor Confederation), demanded price controls, minimum wage levels, elimination of unemployment, and worker participation in plant management. In early 1964 they embarked on a "battle plan" to demonstrate their strength. Illia clearly wanted to avoid a confrontation, so he dealt with the seizure of plants and transport facilities through the courts rather than by violent police or military action. The struggle between rival labor factions—those favoring Perón's return from exile in Spain, those attempting to establish a moderate independent position, and those in favor of extreme social revolution—further complicated the government's role. Since Illia's initial goal, at least until 1966, was incorporation of the Peronists within the political system, conciliation remained crucial and undoubtedly facilitated the capture of the Peronist movement by moderate elements.

At the same time entrepreneurs and military men found little to praise in the drifting, deteriorating economic scene. Inflation had not been halted, and cost-of-living indices were climbing at more than 30 per cent a year. The potential for economic expansion in the previous two years had been more than offset by rising domestic and foreign debts. Indeed the government seemed unable to take any constructive action beyond repeated devaluations of the peso.

Economically, therefore, as well as politically, few mourned the overthrow of the Illia administration in 1966. The military, with its technological and developmentalist orientation, was expected to provide the plans and discipline to snap the economy out of its drift and periodic recessions.

The four years of Onganía proved once again that building an industrial base to support a highly urbanized population in an agricultural export economy is fraught with obstacles and pitfalls. Although few will want to venture that Argentina is locked into a cyclical pattern in which governments fall every three or four years in response to economic crises and foreign currency shortages, the economy clearly suffers from insufficient export capacity in the short term to pay the heavy costs of an industrial infrastructure as well as social improvements increasingly demanded by the working population. Simultaneously, the economy has been unable to generate sufficient internal demand to utilize its existing consumer and capital goods industries at full capacity.

After nearly six months of economic hesitation, rising budget deficits, and worsening inflation, the appointment of a new Minister of Economics and Labor in December 1966 signaled a liberal, free-enterprise attempt to correct the country's imbalances. But accompanying this economic liberalism was a heavy dose of development planning, carried out by CONADE (Consejo Nacional de Desarrollo, or National Development Council). A massive, and it was hoped final, currency devaluation brought the peso to 350 to the dollar in March 1967. Protective tariff rates were cut. Substantial programs to build roads, housing, and power facilities were implemented. Foreign capital once more entered the petroleum fields, as well as the cigarette industry, chemicals, and banking.

At the outset the indicators were encouraging. Annual inflation dropped below 10 per cent. Gross national product spurted ahead, to 7 per cent in the first half of 1969, with particularly sharp rises in construction, commerce, and chemical industries. Foreign exchange holdings quadrupled in two years. A hard line with labor temporarily quelled obstruction from that sector, while entrepreneurs and businessmen hailed the return to normalcy. The government reflected new optimism in its plans to develop Patagonia and to further industrial expansion in the interior provinces.

The violent labor reaction to the Onganía regime in May and June 1969 had no clear economic justification, except insofar as stabilization meant worsening living standards for the working classes. Nevertheless, the watch-and-wait attitude which the labor unions had adopted after the collapse of the C.G.T. strikes in early 1967 could not last indefinitely, especially in face of rising divisions and tensions within the labor movement itself. The moderate independents who had influenced the C.G.T. and the Peronist movement since 1965 faced serious challenges from more radical voices. Formal organization of outright opposition to the government took place in March 1968 when a new C.G.T. came into existence, identified with its location on Paseo Colón and opposed to the C.G.T. headquarters on Azopardo in Buenos Aires. This new organization strongly supported a major walkout by Y.P.F.

refinery workers in La Plata against the change from a six-hour to an eight-hour day and began to capitalize on discontent in the depressed wine and sugar industries in Mendoza and Tucumán. In May 1969 it took a leading role in organizing the violent reaction in Córdoba, activities which sent its secretary general to jail. The assassination the following month of the principal spokesman for a moderate Peronist position, independent of Perón's direct guidance, did nothing to calm labor agitation. This event also led to continued questioning of the government's ability to control the situation. Violence on the labor front continued into 1970 and reached another climax in August with the assassination of the leading organizer who had favored Perón's direct control of the movement.

Despite an initial growth spurt in 1967-69, economic indicators revealed that labor problems were not the only difficulties faced by Argentina. Onganía and his ministers had proved incapable of galvanizing the agricultural sector into more than an annual 2 per cent growth rate. Although the pace of inflation had slowed down and many business groups prospered, Argentina still lacked the foreign currency earnings to restructure its economy along the lines of heavy industry and simultaneously to meet the aspirations and demands of its working classes. The appointment of an orthodox economist as Minister of Economics and Labor in June 1969 and the issuance of a new peso in January 1970 to replace the old devalued currency at 1 to 100, represented brave but superficial attempts to recapture public confidence and to create a balanced economy.

After Levingston replaced Onganía in June 1970 more dramatic acts were required in face of rising living costs, serious labor agitation, and financial losses, particularly by the meat-packing industries. A new devaluation brought the peso to 4 new (or 400 old) pesos to the dollar. In mid-October the reshuffling of the cabinet placed a noted economist, Aldo Ferrer, in charge of the Ministry of Economics and Labor. His policy, soon made explicit in official pronouncements, envisaged reducing Argentina's dependence on foreign capital while at the same time encouraging Argentine industrial initiative and technology. By the end of the year the program of "Buy National," which required private as well as state enterprises to purchase Argentine-made equipment wherever possible, and the unveiling of a new development plan for 1971-75 gave evidence of Ferrer's determination. But the fall of the Levingston regime three months later, in March 1971, reemphasized the difficulties facing any implementation of development programs and long-range plans in Argentina.

Regardless of the program pursued, however, the fitful nature of economic expansion in the 1960's demonstrated that many other factors beyond purely economic development affected Argentina's future. Any transition from an agricultural base to an industrial one would eventually require basic readjustments for Argentine society.

The sparse population of the mid-nineteenth century developed into urbanized, nationalistic, and ambitious Argentines of the twentieth. By 1940 nearly half these people enjoyed middle-class standards of secondary education, white-collar employment, and decent clothing. Even though excessive consumption of animal fats and fried food contributed to ailments of the liver, or *hígado,* and malnutrition and starvation were prevalent in the villages of Tucumán or Santiago del Estero, the Argentines as a whole were still among the world's best-fed people. Their cities, their artistic and literary productivity, and their way of life were the envy of South Americans and of not a few Europeans and North Americans.

Until World War II this society faced few revolutionary changes. The immigrant was absorbed with remarkable facility. The oligarchy, despite the Yrigoyen interlude, retained control over the nation's economic and political life. New middle classes emerged, particularly in the cities, but in an expanding economy they were able to achieve security and advancement without disturbing the upper or lower classes. The urban laboring classes enjoyed a gradual improvement in status and living conditions, while in the countryside the lower classes showed little inclination to rebel against poverty and isolation.

The sudden acceleration of industrialization and urbanization during World War II introduced, as well as exposed, conflicts within this complacent society. The flood of migrants from the countryside to the cities and from the interior to Buenos Aires and the postwar immigration from Europe emphasized class awareness as never before. Increasingly, the ragged, the illiterate, the dark-skinned, and the unemployed made their presence felt in the coastal cities. At the same time, the middle classes had to contend with the slowly rising tide of inflation that threatened their ability to maintain standards of education for their children, professional or white-collar employment, fastidious and conservative dress, and adequate entertainment and housing. The war brought prosperity to many and a general expansion of the economy, but with it came a preview of shortages in housing, imported consumer goods, electric power, and public transportation. These were pressures, frustrations, and differences which concentration of population in urban centers served only to magnify.

Since 1945 the slow transition from an agricultural to an industrial economy has been paralleled by a crisis in Argentine society frequently characterized as "the emergence of the lower classes," "the overthrow of the oligarchy," "the society of the masses," or "the era of the common man." Fundamentally it represented the aspiration of new groups to a share in government and economic profits, much as the creoles of 1810 or the middle classes of 1890 protested against the existing order. Complicating any analysis of this process, however, was the political challenge of "Peronismo," a doctrine and a political movement which emphasized the importance of the working man. In its most sophisticated terms, as its label of *Justicialismo* indicated, it aspired to a form of social democracy. It claimed to steer a middle course between communism and capitalism and between collectivism and individualism, to establish a third position between Russia and the United States, and to maintain an equitable balance between the various sectors of society. In more practical terms, it was the vindication of the lower classes used as a political weapon by an astute caudillo.

Perón was not the originator of social change; he merely capitalized on existing trends. Among the small group of army officers which seized control in June 1943, he alone recognized the potential of Argentina's working classes. Within a year he built the insignificant Department of Labor and Social Welfare, which he headed, into the defender and leader of the country's divided and disoriented industrial laborers. Major unions in the meat-packing and transportation fields became his disciplined followers, and membership increased rapidly as the government for the first time helped labor to win concrete advantages. Through policies and programs which he continued as president, Perón became the savior of the *descamisados* or "shirtless ones."* Laborers now benefited from broad social security coverage. For several years, at least until overwhelmed by the tide of inflation, the total increases in the working man's real wages ranged from 10 to 50 per cent. Labor's share of the national income rose from 45 per cent in 1945 to over 60 per cent by 1950. Workers began to enjoy unprecedented privileges. The factory laborer and his family received paid vacations and special excursions which permitted them to visit the beaches of Mar del Plata or the scenic beauties of Córdoba and Bariloche. Working hours became shorter while retirement and medical benefits increased. Ceilings were placed on food and transportation prices and the government began building low-cost housing projects. The working man could now own a locally made bicycle, radio, refrigerator, or washing machine.

Peronismo also increased the political consciousness of the lower classes. Perón and especially his wife, Eva Duarte, or Evita, constantly made appeals to the *descamisados*. For the first time the working man was made to feel important. Government controls over newspapers, radios, and education facilitated a propaganda campaign that reached large sections of the public previously ignored or overlooked by the oligarchy and the Radicals. Laborers won seats in congress and even held cabinet posts. Evita organized a vast state welfare agency which monopolized all charitable activity and lost no opportunity to publicize Perón's concern for the underprivileged. Meanwhile, the drift of population toward the coast and the cities was spurred by official encouragement of industry over agriculture and by the rising living standards available only in the urban centers. The *cabecitas negras*† from the interior added to the number of laborers and servants in Buenos

---

* The term was first used by the well-to-do to depreciate the urban rabble that assembled in a mass demonstration in the Plaza de Mayo on October 17, 1945, to demand the release of Perón from arrest by certain military groups. Perón subsequently seized upon the term as a rallying cry for the common man.

† This derogatory term for lower-class workers, often of mestizo stock, which came from the name of a common Argentine sparrow, suffered the opposite fate of *descamisado* and became virtually a forbidden expression under the Perón regime.

Aires and Rosario and provided vigorous support for their benefactor at rallies and demonstrations.

The city masses and the industrial workers consequently became the principal supporters of Peronismo. But if Perón did not do as much for the rural laborer or the humble inhabitant in the remote provinces, he still managed to create a bright public image even for these groups. To the exploited laborers of the Tucumán sugar fields and factories and the Chaco forests he gave a rudimentary labor organization and the promise of higher wages and better working conditions. He seized the estates of several political enemies and subdivided the land among tenants. He extended credit to small farmers, encouraged co-operatives, and publicized widely scattered irrigation works, school and hospital construction, and community housing projects. Peronismo thereby encouraged aspirations for improvement in all the lower economic and social strata, and, although instigated primarily for political ends, these sentiments soon solidified into permanent features of the Argentine make-up.

The bountiful years of this revolution in social expectations lasted through 1948, that is, until readily available wartime credits were exhausted and hungry Europe once more began to fill its own larder. The ensuing difficulties of industrialization, the severe droughts, the inflation, and the rising cost of living checked further advances for the lower classes. Financial problems forced Perón to revise not only his economic but also his social programs. Evita had been the principal champion of the *descamisado,* and after her death in July 1952 Perón gradually turned away from labor. He took a firm line against strikes and further wage increases, and his speeches were sprinkled with exhortations to work and produce. He even attempted to organize white-collar employees as a counterbalance to the industrial unions.

In the end neither the Perón regime nor its successors have developed any reliable method to increase productivity and consumption, to co-ordinate the industrial and agricultural sectors, or to meet the insistent demands of the lower classes for status and prosperity. Peronismo could be blamed by economists for voicing primarily popular appeals and neglecting capital formation and economic development. The ensuing approaches which intermittently favored investors and entrepreneurs at the expense of labor proved equally disastrous. The Argentines as a people proved unreceptive to any degree of "belt-tightening" in the interests of their country's future development. The qualities of leadership displayed by Aramburu, Frondizi, Illia, and Onganía aroused no devoted following. None possessed charismatic or even popular images. Ordered discipline, intellectual sharpness, bumbling goodwill, and cold impersonality seemed to be the dominant traits projected in succession by these four presidents.

At the same time the aspirations and desires of the lower classes have been stimulated without simultaneous growth of the country's capacity to support such ambitions. Characteristic of this imbalance between capabilities and realization is the growth in and around major cities of *villas miserias*, or shanty towns—acre on acre of shacks inhabited by workers' families. These are not the very poor, although they live as such. Families remain small with an average of less than two children per family. Common-law marriages are almost as prevalent as legal wedlock, but households are remarkably stable. Nearly 85 per cent of family heads are employed as construction, industrial, or office workers, and employment levels equate with those of the economy as a whole. Family incomes in the *villas miserias* also compare surprisingly well with the rest of the urban population. A study completed in 1965 suggested that at least two-thirds of these families had sufficient income to enable them to buy housing, had credit and facilities been available. The housing was lacking, however, especially in the urban centers which in recent years had attracted so much internal migration. By 1968 Argentina already suffered from a deficit of 1,400,000 housing units, and the gap between supply and need has continued to widen at 150,000 units a year.

Compounding the shortages in adequate housing were the constant inflationary pressures which weighed particularly on white-collar workers, unorganized labor, the self-employed, and the pensioned. Labor's share of gross domestic income, which had hovered around 40 per cent at the advent of Perón and had climbed to 50 per cent by 1952, fell back during the 1960's to 41 per cent of the total. Although it can be demonstrated that the real wages of industrial labor have remained constant or have fallen only slightly (depending on the indices or statistical methods used) and that food intake, particularly of beef, has not declined appreciably since the heyday of Perón, the popular assessment is quite different. Ultimately the man on the street talks to his neighbor and weighs the impact on his pocketbook in personal terms—not necessarily in line with those used by the statistician or economist. During the 1960's, that man on the street, whether from the ranks of organized labor or not, concluded that the government and the economy were doing remarkably little to improve his economic or social situation. The cost-of-living index in Buenos Aires had been multiplied by a factor of sixty between 1943 and 1963. Despite a temporary slowing of the inflationary rate in 1967-68, the index had risen from a base of 100 in 1960 to 687 by 1970.

Less easy to assess were the frustrations and tensions which occurred every time the common man waited hours for a bus or train, found his hot water, telephone, or electricity turned off, lined up to buy the ever more expensive groceries, and picked his way around gaping holes in the sidewalks. Graft, inefficiency, and conspicuous consumption were to be seen on every hand, at the same time that the government asked citizens to tighten their belts in order to permit extra meat exports and postponed payment of social security pensions with the excuse that funds were unavailable. Manual laborers—from the oil rigger in Salta to the sheepherder in Río Negro, from the mill hand in Tucumán to the stevedore in Buenos Aires—remembered the early years of Perón and were unhappy. Office workers and professional classes, although recalling the Perón years in less rosy colors, joined the chorus of discontent. Crowded and costly apartment living, the rising prices of clothing and food, and inelastic salaries threatened to drag the middle classes downward. Only through constant borrowing and real sacrifices in housing, food, and entertainment were the most basic symbols of education and dress maintained.

The frustration of this environment and the lack of dramatic national leadership to remedy the situation encouraged some to look for revolutionary solutions. Since the Revolution of 1930, no leader has long resisted that delicately balanced barometer—the consensus of the country's military commanders. This, in turn, has demanded that the military and the state take increasingly important roles in every aspect of life. Partly in reaction, socially concerned individuals from the Church, labor unions, and universities have argued in recent years for rapid and forceful changes in the social and economic structure.

The most dramatic and certainly the most significant developments occurred in the uprisings in Córdoba, and to a lesser degree in those in Rosario, in May 1969. The workers who momentarily seized control of downtown Córdoba on May 29 bore little resemblance to the lumpen proletariat or the descamisados who had been stirred and guided by Perón's harangues. These skilled industrial workers from automotive factories, led by sophisticated labor organizers, sought rational structural changes in Argentine society and politics. Student groups both at the secondary and university levels and even some priests quickly joined the organized laborers. Although army units finally restored order to the city, the explosion left behind it an awareness that major reforms were indeed necessary. As noted earlier, even the Onganía government responded with promises that the social phase of the 1966 Revolution must now be implemented. Córdoba's upheaval, however, introduced a new factor in the Argentine situation: the presence of organized industrial labor as a force to be reckoned with. Perón perhaps had given the working man dignity and importance. In the subsequent years, the labor movement had matured, and at Córdoba, albeit unsuccessfully and chaotically, it had shown its courage and potential.

Beyond these very significant events in Córdoba, other unrelated movements have increasingly unleashed violent attacks in 1970, often on selected targets. Rural guerrilla movements have spluttered periodically in the northwest of Argentina. The *Uturunko* in Tucumán, the *Ejército Guerrilla* in Salta and Jujuy, or the *Montoneros* in Córdoba remained, however, pale reflections of Che Guevara and Fidel Castro. From the right, the earlier *Tacuara* youth organization still occasionally raised its anti-Semitic head but received little popular or official encouragement. The greatest threat to stability and development comes—as forcefully demonstrated in recent years in the United States or more immediately just across the estuary in Montevideo—from extremist urban-based groups which strike selected targets by bombing, robbery, kidnapping, or assassination. Whether for the limited political objective of discrediting a particular regime or in hopes of provoking a major social revolution, these acts threaten established interests and as such provoke added repression. Increasingly during 1970 these direct action groups, including the *Fuerzas Armadas Peronistas, Fuerzas Armadas de Liberación,* and *Fuerzas Argentinas Revolucionarias,* struck at banks, police stations, garrisons, and trains. Nevertheless, although governmental reaction may drive a few others to conclude that only violence can introduce significant changes, the overwhelming weight of Argentine values and attitudes seems to support peaceful change within existing structures.

The rise of the lower classes which is taking place in Argentina precludes any return to the pre-1940 economy or society, but its eventual impact on national development remains far from clear. The frustrations and discontent so far have not generated sustained upheavals or even effective political action. Instead, creeping apathy settles over an increasing number of Argentines. Any incentive to save or to build for the future disappears with snowballing inflation. Honesty, hard work, and planning receive little material reward or social encouragement. More and more, the population gives vent to negative judgments without supporting positive alternatives. At best, the people appear resigned to bear a long and painful period of adjustment that accompanies the industrialization of their country.

The crisis of the contemporary scene resembles two other moments of profound change in Argentina. The events of 1770 to 1820 and of 1870 to 1920 marked the end of old orders and the emergence of new ones. Declining silver production, imperial rivalries, and Europe's Industrial Revolution turned the stepchild of the Spanish Empire toward the Atlantic and laid the foundations for an independent Argentina. British free trade, agricultural exports, and European immigration in the nineteenth century contributed to the formation of an Argentine nation. Today, industrialization and the lower classes create equally challenging prospects. Despite the chaos, bitterness, and apathy that threaten Argentina in the 1970's, these people once more stand on the threshold of great economic and social change which may bring them closer to fulfilling their dreams of prosperity and progress.

Political Chronology

I. DISCOVERY AND CONQUEST: 1516-1600

1516   JUAN DÍAZ DE SOLIS, one of Spain's chief navigators, enters the estuary of the Río de la Plata and is killed on its banks by Indians.

1520   Magellan and his expedition winter on the Patagonian coast before proceeding on through the Strait.

1527   Sebastian Cabot's expedition establishes a short-lived settlement on the lower Paraná at the mouth of the Carcarañá River.

1536   PEDRO DE MENDOZA, with a major expedition from Spain, establishes the first settlement at Buenos Aires (in the vicinity of the present-day La Boca section). Spaniards settle Asunción in 1537, and in 1541 the Buenos Aires settlement is abandoned.

1553   Santiago del Estero, first permanent Spanish town within the boundaries of present-day Argentina, is established by settlers from Peru.

1561-62   Spanish towns are established at Mendoza (1561) and San Juan (1562) by expeditions from Chile.

1563   The governorship of Tucumán, with its capital at Santiago del Estero, is established as a dependency of the *audiencia,* or administrative court, of Charcas.

1565   Settlement of the town of Tucumán.

1570   Establishment of the bishopric of Tucumán with seat at Santiago del Estero. Later (1699) moved to Córdoba.

1573   Establishment of Spanish settlements at Córdoba, by an expedition from the northwestern towns, and at Santa Fe, by an expedition from Asunción.

1580   Re-establishment of Spanish settlement at Buenos Aires by an expedition from Asunción under JUAN DE GARAY.

II. COLONIAL PERIOD: 1600-1810

1613-14   Inauguration of a Jesuit college at Córdoba, later (1622) reorganized as the University of Córdoba.

1617   Area of Buenos Aires established as a governorship, separate from Asunción.

1620   Creation of a bishopric at Buenos Aires.

1622   Establishment of an inland customhouse at Córdoba to discourage shipment of imported goods from Buenos Aires to the interior. Removed to Salta (1671).

1661   Creation of a temporary *audiencia* at Buenos Aires. Suppressed in 1671.

1680   Establishment of a Portuguese base and port, Colônia do Sacramento, across the estuary from Buenos Aires. Captured by porteño forces in 1702, only to be returned to Portugal by the Treaty of Utrecht (1713). Captured again by porteño forces in 1762 and returned by the Treaty of Paris (1763). Finally surrendered to Buenos Aires, after capture, by the Treaty of San Ildefonso (1777).

1729   Spanish settlement officially established at Montevideo.

1766-74   Disputes with England over possession of the Malvinas, or Falkland Islands. English abandon islands and do not reassert control until 1833.

1767   Expulsion of Jesuits from Spanish realms, affecting the University of Córdoba and the Misiones settlements.

1776   Establishment of the Viceroyalty of the Río de la Plata, with seat at Buenos Aires, in conjunction with the military expedition led by Pedro Cevallos, the first viceroy (1776-78), to check Portuguese expansion southward.

1777   Viceroyalty given permanence with appointment of Juan José de Vértiz as viceroy (1778-84).

1778   Royal decree ends Seville monopoly and permits trade between
       several Spanish ports and the colonial ports of the Americas.
       Customhouse established at Buenos Aires (1779).

1782   Royal supervision increased by the extension of the intendancy
       system to the Río de la Plata. Creation of eight intendancies with
       military and fiscal responsibilities.

1785   Installation of an *audiencia* at Buenos Aires (decreed in 1783).

1794   Installation of a *consulado,* or corporation of merchants, at
       Buenos Aires.

1795   Royal decree permits trade with colonies of Spain's allies. Com-
       mercial restrictions further relaxed in 1797 to permit neutral
       shipping to enter Spanish American ports.

1801   First newspaper, *El Telégrafo Mercantil* (1801-02), in Buenos
       Aires, followed by *El Semanario de Agricultura* (1802-07).

1806   British expedition under Sir Home Popham on return from
       South Africa occupies Buenos Aires (June-August). Viceroy
       Rafael de Sobremonte flees toward Córdoba. Colonial militia led
       by SANTIAGO LINIERS forces British to surrender. Liniers
       is elected viceroy by a gathering of the principal citizenry.

1807   Second British expedition under General John Whitelocke occu-
       pies Montevideo (February-July) and attacks Buenos Aires
       (June-July), but Liniers again forces British to capitulate.

1809   Liniers survives conservative coup to oust him from viceroyship
       (January) but is replaced later in year by Viceroy Baltasar
       Hidalgo de Cisneros, appointed by the Junta in Spain.

III. POLITICAL CONSOLIDATION: 1810-1880

1810   May 25. Following the news of the dissolution of the Central
       Junta in Spain, the viceroy and municipal council turn authority
       over to a provisional junta ruling in the name of Ferdinand VII.
       Provisional junta, dominated by MARIANO MORENO, rejects
       authority of provisional government in Spain and unsuccessfully
       attempts to extend porteño control to Montevideo and Asunción.
       Montevideo remains in Spanish hands, while José Artigas, leader
       of Uruguayan autonomy, gains control of rural areas. Paraguay
       rejects "liberating" column from Buenos Aires and under José
       Gaspar de Francia declares independence (1813).

1810-11 Delegates from interior provinces gradually join the provisional
         junta in Buenos Aires, supplanting Moreno's influence. Moreno

resigns, dies at sea on a mission to England (1811). Conservative triumvirate replaces junta (1811).

1812 MANUEL BELGRANO, in charge of porteño forces in northwestern provinces, checks royalist attacks at Tucumán and Salta, but his subsequent invasion of Upper Peru (1813) fails. A second triumvirate is organized at Buenos Aires.

1813 Assembly of provincial representatives meeting at Buenos Aires approves resolutions abolishing slavery, extending equal rights to all citizens, and creating office of Supreme Director to replace triumvirate. First director is Gervasio Posadas (January 1814–January 1815).

1814 JOSÉ DE SAN MARTÍN assumes command of army in north and subsequently (1815) begins organization of army at Mendoza for attack on Spanish forces in Chile.

1815 Changes in Supreme Directors: Carlos de Alvear (January-April) and José Rondeau (April 1815–April 1816).

1816 July 9. Congress of provincial representatives, meeting at Tucumán, declares independence from Spain. JUAN MARTÍN DE PUEYRREDÓN named Supreme Director.

1819 Congress of Tucumán, having moved to Buenos Aires, drafts centralist constitution which is overwhelmingly rejected by autonomist sentiment in the provinces. Collapse of centralist authority at Buenos Aires (1820).

1821-24 Governorship of Martín Rodríguez at Buenos Aires; minister of government is BERNARDINO RIVADAVIA. Period of progressive measures at Buenos Aires: British loans and commercial treaty, immigration projects, limited separation of Church and State, formation of the University of Buenos Aires (1821), and agricultural development.

1825-28 Following Brazilian annexation of Uruguay (1821), Buenos Aires supports political revolt in Banda Oriental and declares war on Brazil. Brazilian forces defeated at Ituzaingó (1827). Uruguay is established as independent buffer state under British auspices.

1826 Congress of provincial representatives meeting at Buenos Aires draws up another centralist constitution and elects Rivadavia as president (February 1826–July 1827).

1827 Constitution is rejected by provinces and Rivadavia resigns.

Manuel Dorrego, an autonomist, is elected governor of Buenos Aires.

1828-29   Civil war between autonomists under Dorrego and centralists led by General Juan Lavalle. Dorrego captured and shot (December 1828). JUAN MANUEL DE ROSAS capitalizes on reaction to Dorrego's execution, restores order under the autonomist banner, and is elected governor (1829-31).

1831   Pact of the Littoral, signed by the provinces of Buenos Aires, Entre Ríos, and Santa Fe (subsequently joined by Corrientes), provides limited concept of national unity.

1833   Rosas pushes Indian frontier south to the Río Colorado.

1835   Rosas is elected governor with "supreme and absolute powers" and confirmed by a plebiscite.

1837-38   Rosas breaks relations with and declares war on Bolivian-Peruvian Confederation. Continued centralist-autonomist conflict in interior.

1838-51   Rosas enters the civil war in Uruguay and besieges Montevideo.

1838-40   Following disputes over treatment of French subjects, France establishes blockade of Buenos Aires and extends military assistance to forces opposing Rosas in both Uruguay and Argentina.

1839-42   Intensified civil conflict within Argentina. Severe repressions in Buenos Aires.

1845-48   Following disputes with England and France concerning porteño intervention in Uruguay and navigation of the Paraná River, Buenos Aires is again blockaded.

1851   Open rebellion against Rosas by JUSTO JOSÉ DE URQUIZA, governor of Entre Ríos, who forms an alliance with Brazilian and Uruguayan forces. Rosas is defeated at Caseros (1852) and flees to asylum in England.

1852-61   Intermittent civil war between Buenos Aires and the other provinces. Buenos Aires rebels against Urquiza's Confederation (September 1852) and adopts a separate constitution (1854). Confederation adopts national constitution (May 1853), and Urquiza is elected president (1854-60). Porteño forces are defeated by Urquiza at Cepeda (1859), and Buenos Aires agrees to join Confederation. Santiago Derqui elected as Urquiza's successor (1860-61). New difficulties between Buenos Aires and the provinces; porteño forces defeat Confederation army at Pavón (1861).

1862-68   Porteño governor, BARTOLOMÉ MITRE, establishes provisional national government and then is inaugurated president (October 1862). Buenos Aires is declared provisional capital. Insurrections in interior suppressed (1863, 1866-68).

1865-70 Paraguayan War. A surprise Paraguayan attack on Corrientes draws Argentina into alliance with Uruguay and Brazil in their war against Paraguay, begun in 1864. Mitre commands allied forces until 1867.

1868-74 Administration of DOMINGO F. SARMIENTO. Education and immigration are stimulated. Serious rebellions in Entre Ríos are suppressed (1870, 1872). Rosario-Córdoba Railroad is completed (1870).

1874-80 Administration of NICOLÁS AVELLANEDA. Revolt by Mitre is suppressed (1874). Agricultural colonies expand in Santa Fe; immigration increases; first shipments of frozen meat are sent to Europe. Conquest of the Desert eliminates Indian menace (1879-80). City of Buenos Aires is federalized as national capital after brief civil war (June 1880).

IV. MODERN ARGENTINA: 1880-present

1880-86 Administration of JULIO ROCA. Consolidation of the oligarchy and of National Autonomist, or Conservative, Party. Provincial capital of Buenos Aires established at La Plata (1882). Continued southward expansion of frontier against Indians. Beginning of economic boom of 1882-89, with land speculation, railroad building, immigration, agricultural development, meat packing, and public works.

1886-92 Administrations of MIGUEL JUÁREZ CELMAN and Carlos Pellegrini. Speculation and corruption are followed by depression in 1890. Middle and professional classes protest in Buenos Aires. Civil-military revolt (July 1890) is defeated, but Juárez Celman resigns and is replaced by Vice President Pellegrini. Efforts to rebuild Argentine credit and financial stability. Roca-Mitre entente (1891) for next presidential campaign. Radical Party emerges under Leandro Alem and HIPÓLITO YRIGO-YEN, pledged to political reform, universal male suffrage, and no compromise with Conservatives. Luis Saenz Peña, supported by Roca and Mitre, is nominated by Conservatives to eliminate the candidacy of his less manageable son, Roque.

1892-98 Administrations of Luis Saenz Peña and José E. Uriburu. Radical Party revolts (1893, 1895) suppressed. Socialist Party formed

(1894-96). Vice President Uriburu assumes presidency upon resignation of Luis Saenz Peña in 1895. Period of rebuilding from depression; construction of Buenos Aires and La Plata port works.

1898-   Second administration of Julio Roca. Dispute with Chile over
1904   Patagonian border is settled by arbitration (1899-1902). Peso set at 0.44 of gold peso in 1899 and financial stability returns. Labor unrest and anarchist agitation; Foreigners' Residence Law (1903) aimed at expulsion of undesirable aliens.

1904-10   Administrations of Manuel Quintana and José Figueroa Alcorta. Economic boom of 1904-12, with railroad construction, immigration, public works, and growth of cities. Radical Party revolt (1905); continued labor and anarchist agitation. Vice President Figueroa Alcorta assumes presidency on death of Quintana (1906). Centennial celebrations (1910).

1910-16   Administrations of ROQUE SAENZ PEÑA and Victorino de la Plaza. Compulsory male suffrage through the Saenz Peña Law (1912). Depression and economic difficulties sharpened with the outbreak of World War I. Vice President De la Plaza assumes presidency on death of Saenz Peña (1914).

1916-22   Administration of Hipólito Yrigoyen. Strict adherence to neutrality, despite sinking of Argentine ships by German submarines. Economic recovery with meat shipments to Allies; stimulus to local manufacturing with reduction of consumer goods imports. Attempted social and labor legislation largely nullified by postwar depression; labor unrest and Semana Trágica (January 1919). Withdrawal from League of Nations (1921). Creation of national oil agency, Y.P.F. (1922).

1922-28   Administration of Marcelo T. de Alvear. Economic prosperity returns on basis of cereal and meat production; immigration increases. Split in Radical Party; formation of the conservative or "anti-Yrigoyen" wing (1924).

1928-30   Re-election of Yrigoyen as president. Accusations against him and impact of world depression (falling cereal and meat prices, devaluation of the peso, and unemployment) lead to chaos in government.

1930   September 6. Military forces under General José F. Uriburu (nephew of former president José E. Uriburu) take control of government and establish *de facto* regime until 1932. Radical Party electoral victories in Buenos Aires annulled, and national elections postponed (April 1931). Radical Party boycotts presidential elections in November 1931.

1932-38   Administration of AGUSTÍN P. JUSTO. Justo, an anti-Yrigoyen Radical, heads a Conservative regime which maintains itself in power by controlled elections and fraud. Radical Party revolt in Entre Ríos is suppressed (1932). National economic recovery program, with commercial controls, worker benefits, monetary reforms, Roca-Runciman Pact to guarantee British market (1933, renewed 1936), British monopoly of porteño transport system. Argentina resumes full membership in League of Nations (1933).

1938-43   Administrations of Roberto M. Ortiz and Ramon S. Castillo. Ortiz, an anti-Yrigoyen Radical, is selected to continue the Conservative regime. Ortiz attempts a return to free elections, but failing health forces him to delegate powers to Vice President Castillo (July 1940; resignation June 1942). Increasing industrialization and profits from meat production result from World War II. Pressure of certain military groups turns Argentina toward Axis side. Castillo declares state of siege (December 1941) and favors Axis.

1943   June 4. Generals Rawson and Ramírez seize control of government to prevent succession of pro-British Conservative candidate to presidency. Military authorities remain in control until 1946. Ramírez breaks relations with the Axis and is replaced by General Farrell (1944). JUAN DOMINGO PERÓN emerges as vice president (1944). Argentina declares war on Germany and Japan (March 1945), signs the Act of Chapultepec, and once more becomes member in good standing of the Pan American Union. Increasing civilian discontent with military rule.

1945   October. Perón is forced to resign and is placed under arrest on island of Martín García. He is called back to control mass rally of workers and followers in city of Buenos Aires (October 17), then nominated for presidency by hastily assembled Labor Party.

1946-52   Administration of Perón. Creation of IAPI to control trade; nationalization of telephones, gasworks, and railroads (1946-48); first Five-Year Plan (1947-51) geared to industrialization. Female suffrage (1947). Economic difficulties and inflation accentuated as wartime reserves dwindle, agricultural exports decline, and imports for industry and consumption rise. Serious droughts (1949, 1952). Formation of Peronist Party (1949). Constitution of 1949 alters Constitution of 1853 to include social welfare measures and provision allowing for immediate re-election of presidents. *La Prensa* closed and expropriated as climax to press-control measures (1951). Military revolt against Perón suppressed and "state of internal war" declared by government (September 1951).

1952-55   Second administration of Perón. Eva Duarte de Perón dies (1952). Economic difficulties continue. Second Five-Year Plan (1953-57) attempts to balance agricultural and industrial expansion on basis of development of oil reserves and energy resources. Government-instigated violence against opposition burns the Jockey Club and various political party headquarters (1953). Oil negotiations opened with Standard Oil of California (1953). Conflict with Church sharpened with sanction of divorce law (1954). Military revolt suppressed; churches burned in Buenos Aires (June 1955).

1955   September. Military revolt overthrows Perón. Provisional government under General Eduardo Lonardi (September-November). Return to Constitution of 1853. "State of war" suspended.

1955-58   Provisional presidency of General PEDRO E. ARAMBURU. Lonardi replaced as certain military groups seek to eliminate Peronismo from political scene. Peronist revolt is crushed (June 1956). Constituent Assembly dissolves without reforming 1853 Constitution (1957). Little progress in implementing economic reforms or development programs.

1958-62   Administration of ARTURO FRONDIZI. Frondizi, an Intransigent Radical, is elected with Peronist votes, inaugurated (May 1958). Contracts with foreign oil companies for exploitation of Argentine reserves (1958). Vice President Alejandro Gómez resigns when his coup to assume executive powers fails; state of siege imposed (November 1958). Efforts to stabilize peso, promote agriculture, and reduce imports (December 1958). Serious military coup suppressed (June 1959). Intervention in Córdoba and suppression of military-civil coup in San Luis (June 1960). Self-sufficiency in petroleum attained by 1962. Peronist candidates permitted to run in 1962 elections; win nearly half the vacancies in the Chamber of Deputies and more than half the provincial governorships. Military remove Frondizi from power, place him under arrest on island of Martín García, and annul elections (March 1962).

1962-63 Administration of José M. Guido. President of Senate installed as provisional executive by the military (March 1962). Conflict between *Azul* (favoring non-political professional military) and *Colorado* (tutelary role of military over government) factions in army leads to clashes and crisis in military high command. General JUAN CARLOS ONGANÍA, leader of *Azul* group, emerges as new army commander-in-chief (September 1962). Serious naval revolt, supported by Colorado elements in army, is crushed (April 1963). Presidential, gubernatorial, and congressional elections held and ARTURO ILLIA, candidate of the conservative wing of the Radical Party, wins the presidency with 25 per cent of the popular vote (July 1963).

1963-66 Administration of Illia. Inauguration as president (October 1963). Annulment of petroleum contracts with foreign companies (November 1963). Threatened Air Force revolt averted (December 1963). Peronist "Battle Plan" to occupy temporarily industrial and transportation facilities dealt with gently (May-June 1964). Moderate elements under Augusto Vandor win over extremists under Andrés Framini to organize and control Justicialista Party; Peronist movement aspires to legal recognition and eschews direct control by Perón from Madrid (July 1964). Perón attempts to return from Madrid but is turned back by police at Rio de Janeiro (December 1964). In congressional elections, Peronists win 44 of 99 seats and poll 38 per cent of national vote as contrasted to 30 per cent for Illia's party (March 1965). Increasing conflict within Peronist movement between Vandor (Peronismo without Perón) and José Alonso (De pie junto con Perón or Stand Up for Perón) fanned by visit of Perón's wife, Isabel Martínez de Perón (October 1965-July 1966). Resignation of Onganía as army commander-in-chief (November 1965). Two Peronist candidates poll 41 per cent of vote in Mendoza's gubernatorial contest, although they lose to traditional conservative group because of Alonso-Vandor split (April 1966). Peronists win control of Catamarca's provincial legislature (May 1966).

1966-70 Administration of Onganía. Bloodless coup by military junta under General Pascual A. Pistarini deposes Illia, proclaims Estatuo de la Revolución Argentina or Statute of the Argentine Revolution, dissolves congress, provincial legislatures, and political parties, replaces judges and governors, and installs Onganía as president (June 28-29, 1966). Intervention of all eight national universities ends autonomy and terminates tripartite government by students, faculty, and alumni in university councils; humorous satirical weekly, *Tía Vicenta,* closed, replaced by *María Belem* (July 1966). Vandor gains control of the C.G.T.—Confederación General de Trabajo or General Labor Confederation—(October 1966). Major cabinet reshuffle with appointment of Adalbert Krieger Vasena as Minister of Economy and Guillermo Antonio Borda as Minister of Interior (December 1966). Krieger Vasena's stabilization program launched; devaluation of peso to 350 to dollar; C.G.T. general strike largely unsuccessful (March 1967). Following strong government measures against strike leaders, general truce between labor and government authorities (May 1967-March 1968). Creation of rival C.G.T.-Paseo Colón under Raimundo Ongaro to oppose Vandor's group, C.G.T.-Azopardo (March 1968). Rumors of coup result in replacement of commanders-in-chief of three services (August 1968). Petroleum workers' strike against La Plata Y.P.F. refinery finally collapses (October-November 1968). Violence and the death of a student in Corrientes strike trigger protests throughout Argentina (mid-May 1969). Bloody riots in city of Córdoba and nation-wide general strike (May 29-30, 1969). Major cabinet reshuffle with appointment of José María Dagnino Pastore as Minister of Economy and Francisco Antonio Imaz as Minister of Interior; Nelson Rockefeller's visit to Buenos Aires accompanied by fire-bombing of several supermarkets linked to his financial interests; assassination of Vandor at his labor headquarters (June 1969). Coup by army officers with Peronist leanings who attempt to imitate Peruvian military takeover of 1968—nicknamed *peruanistas*—is thwarted (October 1969). Further divisions and conflicts within the labor union movement; increasing numbers of strikes by professional and labor groups; establishment of new peso worth 100 of former currency (January 1970). Major strike by workers at the Chocón hydroelectric complex (February-March 1970). Increasing student agitation in Córdoba, Rosario, and Tucumán; repeated incidents of violence, including the kidnapping of a Paraguayan consul and two Russian diplomats and an organized wave of bank robberies; isolated attacks by extremist groups on police and military guard posts (March-April 1970). Kidnapping of Aramburu (late May 1970).

1970-71 Administration of Roberto M. Levingston. Onganía is removed from power by the military commanders-in-chief, Pedro Gnavi, ALEJANDRO LANUSSE, and Carlos Rey; pro-democratic pronouncements that elections would be scheduled in the near future; designation of Levingston as president and reorganization of cabinet (June 1970). Devaluation of peso to 4 new (400 old) pesos to dollar provokes intense labor agitation (June-July 1970). Discovery of Aramburu's body; increasing conflict within the faculties of the national universities (July 1970). Hit-and-run assaults on police headquarters, banks, and communications centers; assassination of José Alonso, leading Peronist labor union leader (August 1970). Cabinet reshuffling places Aldo Ferrer in Ministry of Economy; foreign exchange market closed; increasing labor union protest against inflation and demands for wage increases; serious financial difficulties affect meat producers and packing houses, including Swift, Anglo, and Bovril (October 1970). Postponement of a return to an elective political system generally rejected by armed forces and public; announcement of new development plan for 1971-75, along with "Buy National" legislation requiring private as well as state enterprises to purchase Argentine-made equipment in preference to imported goods (December 1970). Continued unrest in Córdoba and Tucumán, strikes and disorders (January-February 1971). Levingston clashes with the military commanders-in-chief and is removed from power by them (March 1971).

1971- Administration of Alejandro Lanusse. Lanusse sworn in as president; retains most of cabinet, including Ferrer (March 1971). Plans discussed for reform of constitution and return to representative government by 1973-74; relations and negotiations with Perón and Peronists remain confused; continued economic crisis with rampant inflation, declining exports, meat shortages, and small devaluations of the peso (April 1971).

A Selective Guide to the
Literature on Argentina

This bibliography is an invitation to the general reader as well as to the specialist to venture more deeply into the study of Argentina. The objective is to provide a guide to the major works in English and Spanish (with occasional references in other languages) useful for a broad understanding of the area. General works appear first, followed by more specialized studies. The first section lists readily available and pertinent material for the general reader. Major contributions by travelers to Argentina, from the sixteenth century to the present day, are outlined in Section II, followed by the principal reference materials for the study of geography and economics, topically organized. The fourth section on society and culture includes studies on anthropology, sociology, intellectual and artistic trends, and literature, and a list of the outstanding literary works. Essential bibliographic and reference items introduce a review of writings on the various periods of Argentine history, followed by a section on government and foreign affairs. Particularly useful for the investigator is the final section which lists bibliographies for both topical studies and current publications and suggests newspapers and important journals in the fields of economics, history, and cultural affairs.

I. SELECTED STUDIES IN ENGLISH

A list of introductory works might well be headed by the balanced and judicious assessment of twentieth-century political and economic development found in Henry S. Ferns, *Argentina* (New York, 1969). Also useful for the layman are three studies which stress recent political and economic events, Robert J. Alexander, *An Introduction to Argentina* (New York, 1969), George Pendle, *Argentina* (London, 1955; 3d ed., 1963), and Arthur P. Whitaker, *Argentina* (Englewood Cliffs, 1964), and the geographical emphasis presented by Thomas F. McGann, *Argentina: The Divided Land* (Princeton, 1966). Ysabel F. Rennie, *The Argentine Republic* (New York, 1945) provides a highly readable account of late nineteenth-century economic growth and of the rise of Perón. A brief historical survey of Argentine development along with a study of inter-American relations emerge in Arthur P. Whitaker, *The United States and Argentina* (Cambridge, Mass., 1954; Sp. transl., Bs As, 1956). Major economic and political themes are developed in José L. Romero, *A History of Argentine Political Thought,* transl. from 3d ed. by Thomas F. McGann (Stanford, 1963; 2d ed., 1968). Nineteenth-century political events are summarized in Frederick A. Kirkpatrick, *A History of the Argentine Republic* (Cambridge, England, 1931), which can be complemented by an Argentine textbook, Ricardo Levene, *A History of Argentina,* transl. by William S. Robertson (Chapel Hill, 1937; reprint, 1963), emphasizing the colonial and revolutionary periods. For a comprehensive, popularized account, see John W. White, *Argentina: The Life Story of a Nation* (New York, 1942).

Excellent background for Argentine economic history as well as for current economic planning can be found in the work of an economist who became Minister of Economics in late 1970, Aldo Ferrer, *The Argentine Economy,* transl. by Marjory M. Urquidi (Berkeley, 1967). Particular problems of recent economic development are treated with great detail and understanding in Carlos F. Díaz Alejandro, *Essays on the Economic History of the Argentine Republic* (New Haven, 1970). An outstanding but dated study in geography and economics, Pierre Denis, *The Argentine Republic: Its Development and Progress,* transl. from Fr. by Joseph McCabe (London & New York, 1922), should be supplemented by chapters from Preston E. James, *Latin America* (New York, 1942; 3d ed., 1959). For a review of the meat trade consult Simon G. Hanson, *Argentine Meat and the British Market* (Stanford, 1938). Aspects of rural development are examined in Carl C. Taylor's economic and sociological study of farm life, *Rural Life in Argentina* (Baton Rouge, 1948), in the American Geographical Society's publication, Mark Jefferson, *Peopling the Argentine Pampa* (New York, 1926; reprint, 1971), and in James R. Scobie, *Revolution on the Pampas; A Social History of Argentine Wheat, 1860-1910* (Austin, 1964; Sp. transl., Bs As, 1968).

Valuable historical monographs include Samuel L. Baily, *Labor, Nationalism and Politics in Argentina* (New Brunswick, 1967; Sp. transl., Bs As, 1971), focused on the 1930's and 1940's; Allison W. Bunkley, *The Life of Sarmiento* (Princeton, 1952; reprint, 1970; Sp. transl., Bs As, 1966), which emphasizes the early years of this great educator and writer; Miron Burgin, *The Economic Aspects of Argentine Federalism, 1820-1852* (Cambridge, Mass., 1946; Sp. transl., Bs As, 1960), an outstanding study of economics behind the Rosas regime; Henry S. Ferns, *Britain and Argentina in the Nineteenth Century* (Oxford, 1960; Sp. transl., Bs As, 1966), a detailed review of economic and diplomatic relations compiled from British sources; Thomas F. McGann, *Argentina, the United States, and the Inter-American System, 1880-1914* (Cambridge, Mass., 1957; Sp. transl., Bs As, 1961), especially for the introductory chapters on the Generation of 1880; Robert A. Potash, *The Army and Politics in Argentina, 1928-1945: Yrigoyen to Perón* (Stanford, 1969), a detailed examination of the origins and attitudes of the officer corps; and Peter H. Smith, *Politics and Beef in Argentina: Patterns of Conflict and Change* (New York, 1969; Sp. transl., Bs As, 1969), a significant social science examination of pressures and alignments involved in one of Argentina's great industries from 1900 to 1946. A useful assessment of Perón's rise to power, Joseph R. Barager, ed., *Why Perón Came to Power: The Background to Peronism in Argentina* (New York, 1968) can be supplemented by Robert J. Alexander, *The Perón Era* (New York, 1951; reprint, 1965), still the best summary of the early Perón years, and George I. Blanksten, *Perón's Argentina* (Chicago, 1953; reprint, 1967).

For Argentine literature, there is that masterpiece of Latin American letters, Sarmiento's *Facundo*, which appeared in English as *Life in the Argentine Republic in the Days of the Tyrants; or, Civilization and Barbarism,* transl. by Mrs. Horace Mann (New York, 1868; Boston, 1960; New York, 1961). William H. Hudson, an Englishman of long residence in the Río de la Plata and well known for *Green Mansions* and for his description of Uruguay in *Purple Land,* brings the pampas to life in his *Far Away and Long Ago: A History of My Early Life* (New York & London, 1918; Sp. transl., Bs As, 1958). Ricardo Güiraldes, *Don Segundo Sombra,* transl. by Harriet de Onís (New York & London, 1935), the tale of a boy befriended by an old gaucho, stands as a classic among Argentine novels.

II. ACCOUNTS BY TRAVELERS

During four centuries travelers and foreign observers have contributed fascinating and occasionally invaluable insights into Argentina. Among the valuable bibliographical studies are: Tom B. Jones, *South America Redis-*

covered (Minneapolis, 1949), an anthology for the larger area covering the period 1810 to 1870; José E. Uriburu, *La República Argentina a través de las obras de escritores ingleses* (Bs As, 1948); and the excellently annotated Santo S. Trifilo, *La Argentina visto por viajeros ingleses, 1810-1860* (Bs As, 1959).

An enlightening and exciting narrative of Pedro de Mendoza's expedition is that of a German sergeant, Ulrich Schmidel, whose memoirs were first published in German in 1567. An English translation was printed by the Hakluyt Society, *The Conquest of the River Plate, 1535-1555*, Vol. 81, Part I, *Voyage of Ulrich Schmidt to the Rivers La Plata and Paraguai* (London, 1891), and the definitive Spanish translation by Edmundo Wernicke appeared as *Derrotero y viaje a España y las Indias* (Santa Fe, Argentina, 1938; various eds.). The epic poem of the conquest period, Martín del Barco Centenera, *Argentina y conquista del Río de la Plata* (Lisbon, 1602; fasc. ed., 1912; various eds.), was written as propaganda to publicize the riches and potential of the Río de la Plata. The first historical chronicle to emerge from the area of future Argentina, Ruy Díaz de Guzmán, *La Argentina*, ed. by Enrique de Gandía (Bs As, 1943), dates from 1612.

One of the earliest travelogues is Acarete du Biscay, *An Account of a Voyage up the River de la Plata and Thence over Land to Peru* (London, 1698; various eds.; Sp. transl., Bs As, 1943). Among the many accounts left by the religious orders are two important eighteenth-century documents: Fray Pedro J. de Parras, *Diario y derrotero de sus viajes, 1749-1753. España, Río de la Plata, Córdoba, Paraguay*, ed., José L. Busaniche (Bs As, 1943) and Thomas Falkner, *A Description of Patagonia, and the Adjoining Parts of South America* (London, 1774; Chicago, 1935; Sp. transl., Bs As, 1911, 1957), by an English doctor turned Jesuit. Famed as a contemporary guidebook and as a literary masterpiece is Calixto Bustamante Carlos (pseud., Concolocorvo), *El lazarillo de ciegos caminantes desde Buenos Aires hasta Lima* (Gijón, 1773; Bs As, 1942; various eds.). Late eighteenth-century scientific expeditions to the New World produced several valuable studies of contemporary life and manners in the Viceroyalty: the sketches and narrative of Alejandro Malaspina, *Viaje al río de la Plata en el siglo XVIII*, ed., Hector R. Ratto (Bs As, 1938); the observations of a Spanish official sent to survey boundaries with the Portuguese possessions, Félix de Azara, *Voyages dans l'Amérique méridionale dépuis 1781 jusqu'en 1801* (4 vols. & atlas; Paris, 1809; Sp. transl., Bs As, 1923); and the subsequent amplification in a posthumous work edited by his nephew, Agustín de Azara, *Descripción e historia del Paraguay y del Río de la Plata* . . . (2 vols.; Madrid, 1847; 3d ed., Bs As, 1943).

Emeric E. Vidal, *Picturesque Illustrations of Buenos Ayres and Monte-video* . . . (London, 1820; various facs. and Sp. eds.), an outstanding set of aquatints and word pictures, introduces the Buenos Aires of the early nineteenth century. The ill-fated British expeditions added the memoirs of one of the captured officers, Alexander Gillespie, *Gleanings and Remarks, Collected During Many Months of Residence at Buenos Aires and Within the Upper Country* . . . (Leeds, 1818; Sp. transl., Bs As, 1921). Henry M. Brackenridge, *Voyage to South America, Performed by Order of the American Government in the years 1817 and 1818* . . . (2 vols.; Baltimore, 1819, London, 1820; Sp. transl., Bs As, 1927) records the observations of the secretary to a United States commission sent to the Río de la Plata. A noteworthy account by a Swedish traveler appeared in Spanish translation as Jean A. Graaner, *Las provincias del Río de la Plata en 1816; informe dirigido al príncipe Bernadotte* (Bs As, 1949). Several British accounts merit special attention for their comprehensive view of the land and people: J. A. B. Beaumont, *Travels in Buenos Ayres and the Adjacent Provinces of Río de la Plata* . . . (London, 1828; Sp. transl., Bs As, 1957); Francis B. Head, *Rough Notes Taken During Some Rapid Journeys Across the Pampas and Among the Andes* (London, 1826; 3d ed., 1828; reprint, 1967; Sp. transl., Bs As, 1920); Joseph Andrews, *Journey from Buenos Ayres Through the Provinces of Cordova, Tucuman, and Salta to Potosi* . . . (2 vols.; London, 1827; Sp. transl., Bs As, 1920); by an anonymous Englishman (actually Thomas G. Love, director of *The British Packet* in Buenos Aires), *A Five Years' Residence in Buenos Ayres During the Years 1820-1825* (London, 1825; 2d ed., 1827; Sp. transl., Bs As, 1942, 1962); and John P. and William P. Robertson, *Letters on South America: Comprising Travels on the Banks of the Paraná and Río de la Plata* (3 vols.; London, 1843; Sp. transl., Bs As, 1952). Recently the interesting notes and correspondence of an early United States commercial agent have been published in Spanish: John M. Forbes, *Once años en Buenos Aires, 1820-1831*, comp. and transl. by Felipe A. Espil (Bs As, 1956).

The physical aspects of the Argentina of Rosas are faithfully set down in the famous journal of Charles Darwin, *The Voyage of the Beagle* (London, 1839; numerous eds.). A French account adds perspective to the early 1830's, Arsène Isabelle, *Voyage à Buenos Ayres et à Porto Alègre, par la Banda Oriental, les missions d'Uruguay, et la province de Rio-Grande-de-Sul, de 1830 à 1834* (Havre, 1835; Sp. transl., Bs As, 1943). The British consul-general in Buenos Aires, a friend of Rosas and long a resident of Argentina, presents an extensive, although biased, history of the period: Woodbine Parish, *Buenos Ayres and the Provinces of the Río de la Plata* . . . (London, 1839; 2d ed., 1852; Sp. transl., Bs As, 1854, 1958). John A. King, *Twenty-four Years in the Argentine Republic* . . . (New York, Philadelphia, & London, 1846; Sp. transl., Bs As, 1921) emphasizes rural life, while William MacCann, *Two Thousand Miles' Ride Through the Argentine Provinces* (2 vols.; London, 1853; Sp. transl., Bs As, 1939; 2d ed., 1969) acquaints the reader with the far-flung Indian frontier. The observations of a British naval officer who participated in the 1846 blockade of Buenos Aires are found in Lauchlan B. Mackinnon, *Steam Warfare in the Parana* (2 vols.; London, 1848; Sp. transl., Bs As, 1957). The brief reminiscences of a Russian nobleman, only recently translated, adds some further fragments, Platon A. Chikhachev, *A Trip Across the Pampas of Buenos Aires, 1836-1837*, transl. by Jack Weiner (Lawrence, Kansas, 1967).

From the 1850's and 1860's came a great number of works which sought to inform Europe about the new opportunities for commerce and agriculture, including: Hermann Burmeister, *Reise durch die La Plata-staaten, mit besonderer Rüchsicht auf die physische Beschaffenheit und den Culturzustand der Argentinischen Republik* (2 vols.; Halle, 1861; Sp. transl., Bs As, 3 vols., 1943-44); the extensive, though uneven, labors of the French geographer Victor Martin de Moussy, *Description géographique et statistique de la Confédération argentine* (3 vols. & atlas; Paris, 1860-73); the summary by Charles Beck-Bernard, director of one of Argentina's first agricultural colonies, *La République argentine* (Lausanne, 1865); and the delightful reminiscences of his wife, Lina Beck-Bernard, *Le Río Parana: Cinq années de séjour dans la République Argentine* (Paris, 1864; Sp. transl., Bs As, 1935). Perhaps most valuable for impressions following the overthrow of Rosas are Charles B. Mansfield, *Paraguay, Brazil and the Plate: Letters Written in 1852-1853* (Cambridge, Eng., 1856) and William Hadfield, *Brazil, the River Plate, and the Falkland Islands* (London, 1854; Sp. transl., Bs As 1943). Fifteen years later, Hadfield drew interesting comparisons with his earlier observations in *Brazil and the River Plate in 1868* . . . (London, 1869). The British consul at Rosario, Thomas J. Hutchinson, also contributed a pair of volumes filled with personal commentary, *Buenos Aires and Argentine Gleanings, With Extracts from a Diary of Salado Exploration in 1862 and 1863* (London, 1865; Sp. transl., Bs As, 1945) and *The Paraná, With Incidents of the Paraguayan War, and South American recollections from 1861 to 1868* (London, 1868). The editors of the English newspaper in Buenos Aires, *The Standard*, regularly issued a *Handbook of the River Plate*, eds., Michael G. and Edward T. Mulhall (Bs As, 1863; numerous eds.), which reached its sixth edition before the end of the century. Two works, written by Englishmen with residence and experience in Argentina, are especially valuable for their description of agricultural activities: Wilfrid Latham, *The States of the River Plate* (London, 1866; 2d ed., 1868; Sp. transl., Bs As, 1867), a treatise on sheep raising, and Richard A. Seymour, *Pioneering in the Pampas; or, the first Four Years of a Settler's Experience in the La Plata Camps* (London, 1869; 2d ed., 1870; Sp. transl., Bs As, 1947). North American scientific expeditions added other accounts: Thomas J. Page, *La Plata, the Argentine Confederation, and Paraguay* (New York, 1859; Sp. transl. of first five chs., Paraná, 1954) and Archibald MacRae, *Report of Journeys Across the Andes and Pampas of the Argentine Provinces*, Vol. II of *United States Naval Astronomical Expedition to Southern Hemisphere, 1849-1852* (3 vols.; Washington, D.C., 1855-56).

Argentina's rapid economic expansion in the 1880's encouraged an ever larger flow of guidebooks, travelogues, and official propaganda, but those of high quality and reliability became increasingly rare. In the field of personal reminiscences William H. Hudson, *Idle Days in Patagonia* (London, 1893; New York, 1917; various eds.; Sp. transl., Bs As, 1940) should be added to his *Far Away and Long Ago*. An understanding French traveler, Émile Daireaux, provides undoubtedly the best synthesis of Argentina before the end of the century in *La vie et les moeurs à la Plata* (2 vols.; Paris, 1888; various Sp. eds.). Sir Horace Rumbold, British minister to Argentina, continues the tradition of Parish and Hutchinson in *The Great Silver River: Notes of a Residence in Buenos Ayres in 1880 and 1881* (London, 1887). The rise and fall of the 1890's are portrayed in two acute and often sarcastic British accounts: Thomas A. Turner, *Argentina and the Argentines: Notes and Impressions of a Five Years' Sojourn in the Argentine Republic, 1885-90* (London, 1892) and Charles E. Akers, *Argentine, Patagonian, and Chilian Sketches, With a Few Notes on Uruguay* (London, 1893). One of the representatives on the British arbitration commission which determined the Argentine-Chilean boundary contributed Thomas H. Holdich, *The Countries of the King's Award* (London, 1904). These same frontiers are recalled in George C. Musters, *At Home with the Patagonians: A Year's Wanderings over Untrodden Ground from the Straits of Magellan to the Río Negro* (London, 1897; reprint, 1970).

Interest in Argentina continued as the nation enjoyed another economic boom at the beginning of the twentieth century. James B. Bryce, *South America: Observations and Impressions* (New York & London, 1912) presents fascinating material on social and economic development. Another famous visitor, George E. B. Clemenceau, edited his laudatory comments in English as well as French in *South America Today: A Study of Conditions, Social, Political, and Commercial in Argentina, Uruguay and Brazil* (New York & London, 1911). A Spaniard, Adolfo Posada, provides a brief, but stimulating, set of essays in *La República Argentina: Impresiones y comentarios* (Madrid, 1912). Adolf N. Schuster, *Argentinien: Land, Volk, Wirtschaftsleben und Kolonisation* (2 vols.; Munich, 1913) is a thorough analysis of the economy. Other valuable works include John A. Hammerton, *The Real Argentine: Notes and Impressions of a Year in the Argentine and Uruguay* (New York, 1915), A. Stuart Pennington, *The Argentine Republic: Its Physical Features, History* . . . (Bs As & New York, 1910), and William H. Koebel, *Argentina, Past and Present* (London, 1910; 2d ed., 1914). The most thorough and penetrating analysis of society and culture is again the work of a Frenchman, Jules Huret, *En Argentine: De Buenos-Aires au Gran Chaco* (Paris, 1911; Sp. transl., Paris, 1913) and *En Argentine: De la Plata à la Cordillère des Andes* (Paris, 1913).

The challenging frontier of Patagonia and Tierra del Fuego has inspired a literature of its own. There is a thorough study of the people and geography by Father Alberto M. de Agostini, *Trent' anni nella Terra del Fuoco* (Turin, 1955; Sp. transl., Bs As, 1956). A North American recounts his adventures on scientific missions in Bailey Willis, *A Yanqui in Patagonia* (Stanford, 1947). E. Lucas Bridges, *Uttermost Part of the Earth* (London, 1948; N.Y., 1949; Sp. transl., Bs As, 1952) and Raúl Bustos Berrondo, *Huellas en los mares del sur* (Bs As, 1959) provide fascinating personal accounts of life in these southern lands.

Several of the works mentioned in Section I were products of twentieth-century experience in Argentina. Jefferson, *Peopling the Argentine Pampa*, resulted from long years in Tucumán and Buenos Aires, and White, *Argentina: The Life Story of a Nation,* was based on a lengthy period of residence. A former United States ambassador, James Bruce, conveys sympathetic but superficial impressions in *Those Perplexing Argentines* (New York, 1953; London, 1954). Of recent syntheses none is so penetrating and complete as René Marill (pseud., René M. Albérès), *Argentine, un monde, une ville* (Paris, 1957).

III. GEOGRAPHY AND ECONOMICS

James, *Latin America,* and Denis, *The Argentine Republic,* serve as adequate introductions to Argentine geography. A wealth of information and detail has been brought together in Francisco de Aparicio and Horacio A. Difrieri, eds., *La Argentina: Suma de geografía* (9 vols.; Bs As, 1958-63). Considerably more manageable, yet thorough, is Federico A. Daus, *Geografía de la República Argentina* (2 vols.; Bs As, 1945; various eds.), Vol. I dealing with physical geography and Vol. II with economic and political problems. Somewhat dated, though still excellent, is Franz H. Kühn, *Geografía de la Argentina* (Barcelona, 1930; 2d ed., 1941). Romain Gaignard, *Geografía económica de la Argentina* (Bs As, in preparation) will provide an up-to-date and useful summary.

A number of official and private organizations provide information and analysis of the contemporary economic scene: Consejo Nacional de Desarrollo (CONADE) periodically publishes the official five-year development plans of the Argentine government; Consejo Federal de Inversiones in conjunction with the Instituto Torcuato di Tella prepared a wealth of data in *Relevamiento de la estructura regional de la economía argentina* (5 vols.; Bs As, 1965); the Italian industrial complex, Fabbrica Italiana Automobili Torino (FIAT) systematically analyzes Argentine conditions in *Argentina, síntesis económica y financiera* (Bs As, No. 1, 1959; No. 2, 1966; No. 3, in preparation); the Organization for Economic Cooperation and Development reported on educational and development problems in *Education, Human Resources and Development in Argentina* (2 vols.; Washington, D.C. and Paris, Eng. and Fr. eds., 1967-68); and the Economic and Social Council of the Organization of American States published a brief country survey as *Desarrollo económico y social de la Argentina* (2 vols.; Washington, D.C., Eng., Sp. and Port. eds., 1962). The excellent work of the United Nations' Economic Commission for Latin America (ECLA), *El desarrollo económico de la Argentina* (3 vols.; Mexico, D.F., 1959) has been continued with *El desarrollo económico y la distribución del ingreso en la Argentina* (New York, 1968; Eng. ed., 1969) which emphasizes postwar economic policies. ECLA's semiannual *Economic Bulletin for Latin America* carries an occasional article on Argentina. Particularly useful are the reports of *The Economist,* Intelligence Unit, *Three-Monthly Economic Review: Argentina,* and the publications of Great Britain's Board of Trade, Commercial Relations and Export Department, *Overseas Economic Surveys.* Also helpful are the *Overseas Business Reports* (formerly *World Trade Information Service*) of the United States Department of Commerce; the periodic reports on crops, marketing, and industries by the United States Department of Agriculture; the special statistical number each October of the bulletin, *Comments on Argentine Trade,* published by the Chamber of Commerce of the United States in the Argentine Republic; as well as the numerous bulletins listed under Section VII of this bibliography.

In addition to Ferrer, *The Argentine Economy,* and Díaz Alejandro, *Essays on the Economic History of the Argentine Republic,* listed in Section I, the student of economic history and development should consult the following: a basic analysis in Rostovian terms, Guido Di Tella and Manuel

Zymelman, *Las etapas del desarrollo económico argentino* (Bs As, 1967); an in-depth study of the contemporary rural sector, Darrell F. Fienup, Russell H. Brannon, and Frank A. Fender, *The Agricultural Development of Argentina: A Policy and Development Perspective* (New York, 1969); a handy textbook-style reference work, Isidro J. Carlevari, *La Argentina* (Bs As, 1960; 3d ed., 1967); and general socio-economic introductions such as Estéban Dufourq (h.), *El país de los argentinos* (Bs As, 1966) and Marcelo Isacovich, *Argentina económica y social* (Bs As, 1961; 3d ed., 1965). A wealth of economic detail is included in chapters written by specialists under the direction of Gino Miniati, *Argentina económica y financiera* (Bs As, 1960; 2d ed., 1966; 3d ed., in preparation). In spite of their Marxist orientations, Benito Marianetti, *Argentina: realidad y perspectivas* (Bs As, 1964), Ricardo M. Ortiz, *Historia económica de la Argentina, 1850-1930* (2 vols.; Bs As, 1955), and Leopoldo Portnoy, *Análisis crítico de la economía* (Mexico, D.F. and Bs As, 1961) also provide valuable information and provocative ideas. More dated but still useful general studies include Rafael García Mata and Emilio Llorens, *Argentina económica* (Bs As, 1939), Lus R. Gondra, *Historia económica de la República Argentina* (Bs As, 1943), and Carlos Moyano Llerena, *Argentina social y económica* (Bs As, 1950). Of the many summaries prepared for foreign investors in the early twentieth century, two still have historical value: Albert B. Martínez and Maurice Lewandowski, *The Argentine in the Twentieth Century* (London, 1911; several eds.) and *Economic Development of the Argentine Republic in the Last Fifty Years* (Bs As, 1919), edited in several languages by the banking firm of Ernesto Tornquist & Cía. The classical economic history and analysis, Alejandro E. Bunge, *La economía argentina* (4 vols.; Bs As, 1928-30) also continues to be consulted.

There is no definitive study of the development of agricultural and livestock industries. The legal and historical aspects of landownership are explored by Miguel A. Cárcano, *Evolución histórica del régimen de la tierra pública, 1810-1916* (Bs As, 1917; 2d ed., 1925). The specific issue of large landholdings is investigated in partisan studies by Emilio A. Coni, *La verdad sobre la enfiteusis de Rivadavia* (Bs As, 1927) and Jacinto Oddone, *La burguesía terrateniente argentina* (Bs As, 1930; 3d ed., 1956). Some of the social problems of land tenure appear in José P. Podestá "La pequeña propiedad rural en la República Argentina," in *Investigaciones de seminario: Facultad de ciencias económicas de la Universidad de Buenos Aires,* III, 1923, pp. 3-144, Juan L. Tenembaum, *Orientación económica de la agricultura argentina* (Bs As, 1946), Nemesio de Olariaga, *El ruralismo argentino* (Bs As, 1943), Roland Hume, *Nuevo enfoque agrario*

(Santa Fe, 1956), and Pedro de Paoli, *La reforma agraria* (Bs As, 1960).
The early development of the cattle industry has been explored in Emilio
A. Coni, *Historia de las vaquerías del Río de la Plata*, 1555-1750 (Madrid,
1930; 2d ed., Bs As, 1956) and in his unsympathetic portrayal in *El
gaucho: Argentina, Brasil, Uruguay* (Bs As, 1945; 2d ed., 1969). Horacio
C. E. Giberti, *Historia económica de la ganadería argentina* (Bs As, 1954;
2d ed., 1961), an excellent synthesis of the cattle industry, should be accompanied by Ricardo Rodríguez Molas, *Historia social del gaucho* (Bs As,
1968). Closely related problems of the salted-meat industry, fencing, and
water are examined in brief but competent monographs: Alfredo Montoya,
Historia de los saladeros argentinos (Bs As, 1956), Noel H. Sbarra, *Historia del alambrado en Argentina* (Bs As, 1955; 2d ed., 1964), and the
latter's *Historia de las aguadas y el molino* (La Plata, 1961). Dated
summaries of sheep raising are found in Latham, *The States of the River
Plate*, and in Herbert Gibson, *The History and Present State of the
Sheep-Breeding Industry in the Argentine Republic* (Bs As, 1893).

Aspects of agricultural development are examined in Florencio T. Mo-
linas, *La colonización argentina y las industrias agropecuarias*, in Roberto
Schopflocher, *Historia de la colonización agrícola en Argentina* (Bs As,
1955), in Gaston Gori, *El pan nuestro* (Bs As, 1958), and in Taylor,
Rural Life in Argentina, and Scobie, *Revolution on the Pampas*. An excellent synthesis of development of the coastal region is presented by Horacio
C. E. Giberti, *El desarrollo agrario argentino: Estudio de la región pam-
peana* (Bs As, 1964).

Publications by an early director of the Argentine immigration office,
Juan A. Alsina, serve as an introduction to immigration, especially his *La
inmigración en el primer siglo de la independencia* (Bs As, 1910). New
materials, particularly from literary sources, have been uncovered in Carl
Solberg, *Immigration and Nationalism: Argentina and Chile, 1890-1914*
(Austin, 1970). Swiss immigration has been investigated in detail by
Juan Schobinger, *Inmigración y colonización suizas en la República Argentina en el siglo XIX* (Bs As, 1957), while a brief monograph, Morton
D. Winsberg, *Colonia Baron Hirsch: A Jewish Agricultural Colony in
Argentina* (Gainesville, Fla., 1964) explores the Russian-Jewish colonization experience. Niccolò Cuneo, *Storia dell'emigrazione italiana in Argentina, 1810-1870* (Milan, 1940) examines the early years of Italian influence. The economist Alejandro E. Bunge provides a now dated pessimistic
forecast of immigration and population expansion in *Una nueva Argentina*
(Bs As, 1940). Dardo Cúneo has brought together a suggestive set of essays in *Inmigración y nacionalidad* (Bs As, 1967) which advances new
insights and hypotheses for future research.

The broad field of communications has barely been touched. A brief survey of colonial and early national origins is found in Enrique M. Barba, *Rastrilladas, huellas y caminos* (Bs As, 1956). No satisfactory history of railroad development has yet appeared, although Horacio J. Cuccorese, *Historia de los ferrocarriles en la Argentina* (Bs As, 1969) provides a synthesis and overview; the earlier studies by Ricardo M. Ortiz, Raul Scalabrini Ortiz, and Alejandro E. Bunge on the subject are either superficial or excessively biased. A lengthy monograph by Ramón J. Cárcano, *Historia de los medios de comunicación y transporte en la República Argentina* (2 vols.; Bs As, 1893) deals entirely with the colonial period.

Specific questions in Argentine trade and finances have been reviewed in Hanson, *Argentine Meat and the British Market;* John H. Williams, *Argentine International Trade Under Inconvertible Paper Money, 1880-1900* (Cambridge, Mass., 1920; reprint, 1969); Alec G. Ford, *The Gold Standard, 1880-1914: Britain and Argentina* (Oxford, 1962; Sp. transl., Bs As, 1966); Ernesto J. Fitte, *Histora de un empréstito: La emisión de Baring Brothers en 1824* (Bs As, 1962); Vernon L. Phelps, *The International Economic Position of Argentina* (Philadelphia, 1938); Harold E. Peters, *The Foreign Debt of the Argentine Republic* (Baltimore, 1934), with emphasis on the period 1880-1929; Virgil Salera, *Exchange Control and the Argentine Market* (New York, 1941); Walter Beveraggi Allende, *El servicio del capital extranjero y el control de cambios: La experiencia argentina de 1900 a 1943* (Mexico, D.F., 1954); Carlos F. Díaz Alejandro, *Devaluación de la tasa de cambio en un país semi-industrializado: La experiencia de la Argentina, 1955-1961* (Bs As, 1966); Emilio Hansen, *La moneda argentina* (Bs As, 1916); Norberto Piñeiro, *La moneda de crédito y los bancos en la Argentina* (Bs As, 1921); Ildefonso Cavagna Martínez, *Sistema bancario argentino* (Bs As, 1954); and Rafael Olarra Jiménez, *Evolución monetaria argentina* (Bs As, 1968).

The most neglected area of economic investigation is that of industry. The standard works by Adolfo Dorfman, *Historia de la industria argentina* (Bs As, 1942; 2d ed., 1971) and *Evolución industrial argentina* (Bs As, 1942) are little more than textbooks. A brief discussion of agricultural versus industrial interests appears in Felix J. Weil, *Argentine Riddle* (New York, 1944). New ideas and methods of investigation have been suggested in pioneer studies by Thomas C. Cochran and Ruben E. Reina, *Entrepreneurship in Argentine Culture: Torcuato Di Tella and S.I.A.M.* (Philadelphia, 1962), FIAT, Oficina de estudios, *Importación, industrialización, desarrollo económico en la Argentina: Evolución y perspectivas* (2 vols.; Bs As, 1963), Jorge M. Katz, *Production Functions, Foreign Investment, and Growth: A Study Based on the Argentine Manufacturing Sector, 1946-1961* (Amsterdam and London, 1969), and Tomás R. Fillol, *Social Factors in Economic Development: The Argentine Case* (Cambridge, Mass., 1961). The related field of labor organization has been explored in Sebastián Marotta, *El movimiento sindical argentino* (3 vols. of projected 4 vols.; Bs As, 1960-70), and in Luis Ramicone, *La organización gremial obrera en la actualidad* (Bs As, 1963). The profitable direction of investigations into labor history also have been outlined in an excellent collection of documents accompanied by a lengthy introductory essay, Hobart A. Spalding, Jr., ed., *Historia de la clase trabajadora argentina, 1890-1912* (Bs As, 1970); in a series of essays edited by Torcuato di Tella, ed., *Estructuras sindicales* (Bs As, 1969); in the posthumous work of Celia Durruty, *Clase obrera y peronismo* (Córdoba, 1969); in Hilda Iparraguirre and Ofelia Pianetto, *La organización de la clase obrera en Córdoba, 1870-1895* (Córdoba, 1968); and in a synthesis by José Panettieri, *Los trabajadores* (Bs As, 1967), an outgrowth of his dissertation at the National University of La Plata.

IV. SOCIETY AND CULTURE

Under this broad heading it is possible to suggest only some of the most important and readily available literature. In the absence of satisfactory general studies, the *ensayistas* provide an interesting assortment of ideas interpreting, defending, or criticizing Argentine psychology and manners: Joaquín V. González, *La tradición nacional* (Bs As, 1888; various eds.); Juan Álvarez, *Estudios sobre las guerras civiles argentinas* (Bs As, 1914; various eds.); Agustín Álvarez, *South America: Ensayo de psicología política* (Bs As, 1894; various eds.); Lucas Ayarragaray, *La anarquía argentina y el caudillismo* (Bs As, 1904; various eds.); Carlos O. Bunge, *Nuestra América: Ensayo de psicología política* (Bs As, 1903; various eds.); Ricardo Rojas, *Las provincias* (Bs As, 1927; various eds.) and *Eurindia* (Bs As, 1924; various eds.); Juan B. Terán, *La formación de la inteligencia argentina* (Bs As, 1933); Raúl Scalabrini Ortiz, *El hombre que está solo y espera* (Bs As, 1931); and Ezequiel Martínez Estrada, *Radiografía de la pampa* (2 vols.; Bs As, 1933; various eds.), *Cabeza de Goliat: Microscopía de Buenos Aires* (Bs As, 1940; 3d ed., 1957), and *Muerte y transfiguración de Martín Fierro* (2 vols.; Mexico, D.F., 1948; 2d ed., 1960).

More recently authors in the *ensayista* tradition have addressed themselves increasingly to the problem of national identity and purpose. One of Argentina's leading literary figures has edited a collection of such essays, Jorge L. Borges, ed., *¿Qué es la Argentina?* (Bs As, 1970); another handy anthology of such approaches appears in H. Ernesto Lewald, comp., *Argentina: Análisis y autoanálisis* (Bs As, 1969). A generational analysis, utilizing the theories of Ortega y Gasset, serves as the basis of Jaime Perriaux, *Las generaciones argentinas* (Bs As, 1970), while Antonio J. Pérez Amuchástegui provides a challenging review of changing attitudes in *Mentalidades argentinas, 1860-1930* (Bs As, 1965; 2d ed., 1970). Less rigorous in methodology and data, but still useful for their insights are Arturo Jauretche, *El medio pelo en la sociedad argentina: apuntes para una sociología nacional* (Bs As, 1967), Julio Mafud, *El desarraigo argentino* (Bs As, 1959), *Psicología de la viveza criolla: contribuciones para una interpretación de la realidad social argentina y americana* (Bs As, 1965), and *Los argentinos y el status* (Bs As, 1969), and a challenging linking of literature and politics in David Viñas, *Literatura argentina y realidad política* (Bs As, 1964).

Numerous reminiscences also seek to recall society and culture of past years. Particularly useful for their insights are works such as José A. Wilde, *Buenos Aires desde sesenta años atrás* (Bs As, 1881; various eds.), Pastor Obligado, *Tradiciones argentinas* (4 vols.; Bs As, 1888-1900; selections, 1955), Vicente G. Quesada (pseud., Víctor Gálvez), *Memorias de un viejo: Escenas de costumbres de la República Argentina* (3 vols.; Bs As, 1889; 1 vol., 1942), Ramón J. Cárcano, *Mis primeros 80 años* (Bs As, 1943; 2d ed., 1965), Carlos Ibarguren, *La historia que he vivido* (Bs As, 1955; 2d ed., 1969), Zelmira Garrigós, *Memorias de mi lejana infancia; el barrio de la Merced en 1880* (Bs As, 1964), Julia V. Bunge, *Vida: Época maravillosa, 1903-1911* (Bs As, 1965), and Juan F. Marsal, ed., *Hacer la América: Autobiografía de un inmigrante español en la Argentina* (Bs As, 1969).

Anthropology and sociology are still young sciences in Argentina, although the latter has been making remarkable strides in recent years. Demographic problems for the larger area are explored in Fernando Márquez Miranda, *Región meridional de América del Sur: Período indígena* (Mexico, D.F., 1954) and Angel Rosenblat, *La población indígena y el mestizaje en América* (2 vols.; Bs As, 1954). Of particular interest for the nonspecialist are Salvador Canals Frau, *Las poblaciones indígenas de la Argentina: Su origen, su pasado, su presente* (Bs As, 1953) and Antonio Serrano, *Los pueblos y culturas indígenas del litoral* (Santa Fe, 1955). Two brief monographs assemble considerable demographic material, Jorge Comadrán Ruiz, *Evolución demográfica argentina durante el período hispano, 1535-1810* (Bs As, 1969), and Ernesto J. A. Maeder, *Evolución demográfica argentina de 1810 a 1869* (Bs As, 1969). In the tradition of the *ensayistas,* Juan A. García has examined colonial society in *La ciudad indiana: Buenos Aires desde 1600 hasta mediados del siglo XVIII* (Bs As, 1900; various eds.). For a better understanding of the gaucho as a social phenomenon one should consult Justo P. Sáenz (h.),

Equitación gaucha en la pampa y mesopotamia (Bs As, 1942; 4th ed., 1960), as well as Rodríguez Molas, *Historia social del gaucho,* mentioned in Section III. For folklore, one cannot overlook the masterful work by José Imbelloni, and others, *Folklore argentino* (Bs As, 1959).

Sociological investigations have received significant emphasis in the 1960's, following the pioneering thrust of Gino Germani, *Estructura social de la Argentina* (Bs As, 1955) and *Política y sociedad en una época de transición de la sociedad tradicional a la sociedad de las masas* (Bs As, 1962; several eds.). Sergio Bagú has outlined the field of social stratification in *Evolución histórica de la estratificación social en la Argentina* (Caracas, 1969). Significant studies of elites appear in José Luis de Imaz, *Los que mandan* (Bs As, 1964; Eng. transl., Albany, 1970) and in Juan Carlos Agulla, *Eclipse de una aristocracia: una investigación sobre elites dirigentes de la ciudad de Córdoba* (Bs As, 1968). Backgrounds of congressmen emerge in the excellent study by Darío Cantón, *El parlamento argentino en épocas de cambio: 1890, 1916 y 1946* (Bs As, 1966), while Mario Margulis, *Migración y marginalidad en la sociedad argentina* (Bs As, 1968) provides preliminary data on marginal groups. Two excellent collections of essays provide further information on new research trends, Torcuato S. di Tella, and others, *Argentina, sociedad de masas* (Bs As, 1965), and Norberto Rodríguez Bustamante, and others, *Los intelectuales y su sociedad* (Bs As, 1967). Rich resources also exist in the numerous mimeographed *Documentos de Trabajo,* issued by the Centro de Investigaciones Sociales, Instituto Torcuato di Tella.

For the history of cultural development one can consult Manuel H. Solari, *Historia de la cultura argentina* (Bs As, 1951; 2d ed., 1954), Miguel Solá, *Compendio de historia de la cultura argentina* (La Plata, 1959), the suggestive essays of José L. Romero, *Argentina: Imágenes y perspectivas* (Bs As, 1956), Roberto F. Giusti, *Momentos y aspectos de la cultura argentina* (Bs As, 1954), Juan C. Zuretti, *Historia de la cultura argentina* (Bs As, 1952; various eds.), José L. Trenti Rocamora, *La cultura en Buenos Aires hasta 1810* (Bs As, 1948), and José Babini, *Historia de la ciencia argentina* (Mexico, D.F., 1949).

The principal investigations into educational, intellectual, and artistic activities have concerned themselves with the colonial period when the role of the Church was fundamental to all such endeavors. Among the important studies are Juan M. Gutiérrez' classic *Noticias históricas sobre el origen y desarrollo de la enseñanza superior en Buenos Aires . . .* (Bs As, 1868; 3d ed., 1915); Abel Chanetón, *La instrucción primaria en la época colonial* (Bs As, 1936; 2d ed., 1942); the work of the Chilean historian, José T. Medina, *El tribunal del Santo Oficio de la Inquisición en las pro-*

vincias del Plata (Santiago de Chile, 1899; Bs As, 1945); and Rómulo D. Carbía, *Historia eclesiástica del Río de la Plata* (Bs As, 1914). The principal authority on the Church dominance of colonial cultural developments undoubtedly is Guillermo Fúrlong Cárdiff, with works such as *Historia del Colegio del Salvador y de sus irradiaciones culturales y espirituales en la ciudad de Buenos Aires, 1617-1943* (2 vols.; Bs As, 1944), his comprehensive and controversial *Nacimiento y desarrollo de la filosofía en el Río de la Plata, 1536-1810* (Bs As, 1952), the partisan though thorough examination of his own order, *Los jesuitas y la cultura rioplatense* (Montevideo, 1933; Bs As, 1946), and the synthesis of his contributions brought together as *Historia social y cultural del Río de la Plata, 1536-1810* (2 vols.; Bs As, 1969). Another major Church history is now emerging under the pen of Cayetano Bruno, *Historia de la Iglesia en la Argentina* (6 vols. of projected 12 vols.; Bs As, 1966-70). Invaluable for appreciation of artistic accomplishments are Mario J. Buschiazzo, *Historia de la arquitectura colonial en Iberoamérica* (Bs As, 1961); the various publications by Alfredo Taullard, such as *Platería sudamericana* (Bs As, 1947), *El mueble colonial sudamericano* (Bs As, 1949), or *Tejidos y ponchos indígenas de Sudamérica* (Bs As, 1949); Adolfo L. Ribera, *La platería en el Río de la Plata* (Bs As, 1955); and Héctor Schenone and Adolfo L. Ribera, *El arte de la imaginería en el Río de la Plata* (Bs As, 1948).

For the national period there are scattered but significant studies of cultural development, several reaching back into colonial origins: the brilliant blending of sociology, philosophy, and politics in José Ingenieros, *La evolución de las ideas argentinas* (2 vols.; Bs As, 1918-20; various eds.); Alejandro Korn, *Las influencias filosóficas en la evolución nacional* (Bs As, 1936); Juan C. Torchía Estrada, *La filosofía en la Argentina* (Washington, D.C., 1961); Tulio Halperín Donghi, *Historia de la Universidad de Buenos Aires* (Bs As, 1962); and Vicente Gesualdo, *Historia de la música en la Argentina* (2 vols.; Bs As, 1961). Architects recently have contributed several studies including Mario J. Buschiazzo, *La arquitectura en la República Argentina, 1810-1930* (Bs As, 1966); Federico F. Ortiz, and others, *La arquitectura del liberalismo en la Argentina* (Bs As, 1969); José X. Martini and José M. Peña, *La ornamentación en la arquitectura de Buenos Aires* (2 vols.; Bs As, 1966-67); Jorge O. Gazaneo and Mabel M. Scarone, *Arquitectura de la revolución industrial* (Bs As, 1966); and Francisco Bullrich, *Arquitectura argentina contemporanea: panorama de la arquitectura argentina, 1950-1963* (Bs As, 1963). For summaries of art one can turn to the classical studies of José L. Pagano, *El arte de los argentinos* (3 vols.; Bs As, 1937-40) and Eduardo Schiaffino, *La pintura y la escultura en la Argentina* (Paris, 1933); to two excellent summaries, the introduction by Manuel Mújica Láinez, *Argentina* (Washington, D.C., 1961) and the more comprehensive review by Romualdo Brughetti, *Historia del arte en Argentina* (Mexico, D.F., 1965); as well as to specialized studies such as Aldo Pellegrini, *Panorama de la pintura argentina contemporánea* (Bs As, 1967), and Cayetano Córdova Iturburu, *La pintura argentina del siglo XX* (Bs As, 1958), and his study of Argentina's leading cubist, *Pettoruti* (Bs As, 1963).

Two fundamental surveys of Argentine literature are Ricardo Rojas, *Historia de la literatura argentina* (4 vols.; Bs As, 1917-22; 4th ed., 9 vols., 1957) and Rafael A. Arrieta, ed., *Historia de la literatura argentina* (6 vols.; Bs As, 1958-59). Argentine theater is analyzed in Ernesto Morales, *Historia del teatro argentino* (Bs As, 1944), Luis Ordaz, *El teatro en el Río de la Plata, desde sus orígenes hasta nuestros días* (Bs As, 1946; 2d ed., 1957), Raúl H. Castagnino, *El circo criollo* (Bs As, 1953), and his *Literatura dramática argentina, 1717-1967* (Bs As, 1968). The novel and the immigrant have provided subject matter for Myron I. Lichtblau, *The Argentine Novel in the Nineteenth Century* (New York, 1959), and more recently, Gladys S. Onega, *La inmigración en la literatura argentina* (Bs As, 1968), and Germán García, *El inmigrante en la novela argentina* (Bs As, 1970). The theme of the gaucho has inspired considerable analysis: a bibliographical study by Madaline W. Nichols, *The Gaucho: Cattle Hunter, Cavalryman, Ideal of Romance* (Durham, 1942; Sp. transl., 1953); Edward L. Tinker, *Los jinetes de las Américas y la literatura por ellos inspirada* (Bs As, 1952); Raúl A. Cortazar, *Indios y gauchos en la literatura argentina* (Bs As, 1956); Enrique Williams Alzaga, *La pampa en la novela argentina* (Bs As, 1955); a linguistic study by Tito Saubidet Gache, *Vocabulario y refranero criollo* (Bs As, 1943; 5th ed., 1958); and a reference work, Félix Coluccio, *Diccionario folklórico argentino* (Bs As, 1948; 2d ed., 1950).

The following is a brief list of significant, enjoyable, and representative works of literature: Sarmiento's previously mentioned *Facundo* (Santiago de Chile, 1845; critical eds., 1938, 1940, 1955; Eng. transl., 1868, 1960, 1961); the epic poem *El gaucho Martín Fierro y la vuelta de Martín Fierro* by José Hernández (Bs As, 1872, 1879; critical eds., 1945, 1951, 1961; Eng. transl., New York, 1936, 1948, 1960, 1968); Esteban Echeverría's evocation of the Rosas period in *El matadero* (Bs As, 1871; critical ed., 1958); José Mármol's romantic novel, *Amalia* (Montevideo, 1844, 1850; numerous eds.; Eng. transl., New York, 1919); the school-day reminiscences in Miguel Cané, *Juvenilia* (Vienna, 1884; numerous eds.); the porteño society of former days in Lucio V. López, *La gran aldea* (Bs As, 1884; numerous eds.); the Buenos Aires of boom and depression in the late 1880's in José Miró (pseud., Julián Martel), *La Bolsa* (Bs As, 1891; various eds.); the previously mentioned works of William H. Hudson, *Far Away and Long Ago* and *Idle Days in Patagonia*, and of Ricardo Güiraldes, *Don Segundo Sombra* (Bs As, 1926; several eds.; Eng. transl., New York, 1935, 1948); the delicate painting of rural life in Buenos Aires by Benito Lynch, *El inglés de los güesos* (Madrid, 1924; several eds.); the masterful portrayal of society and politics in a small rural town in Roberto J. Payró, *Divertidas aventuras del nieto de Juan Moreira* (Bs As, 1911; several eds.); the verses of Leopoldo Lugones in *Romances del Río Seco* (Bs As, 1938; several eds.); Ricardo Rojas, *El país de la selva* (Paris, 1907; various eds.); Joaquín V. González, *Mis montañas* (Bs As, 1893; various eds.); Manuel Gálvez, *Nacha Regules* (Bs As, 1920; various eds.; Eng. transl., New York, 1922), a novel of prostitution and the porteño waterfront; Eduardo Mallea's semi-autobiographical *La bahía del silencio* (Bs As, 1940; various eds.; Eng. transl., New York, 1944), his *Obras completas* (2 vols.; Bs As, 1961-65), and his recent *La penúltima puerta* (Bs As, 1969); the purely imaginative novel of Adolfo Bioy Casares, *La invención de Morel* (Bs As, 1940; 2d ed., 1948; Eng. transl., Austin, 1964); and his selection of short stories, *El gran serafín* (Bs As, 1967); the psychological novel of Ernesto Sábato, *El tunel* (Bs As, 1948; several eds.; Eng. transl., New York, 1950), and his complex historical and psychological novel, *Sobre héroes y tumbas* (Bs As, 1961; various eds.); Julio Cortázar's unusual and universally acclaimed psychological novels, *Los premios* (Bs As, 1960; various eds.; Eng. transl., New York, 1965), *Rayuela* (Bs As, 1963; various eds.; Eng. transl., New York, 1966), *Último round* (Mexico, D.F., 1969), and his short stories, *Final del juego* (Bs As, 1964; Eng. transl., New York, 1967) and *Todos los fuegos el fuego* (Bs As, 1966); and the poems, essays, and novels of Jorge L. Borges, the leading man of contemporary letters, in *Obras completas* (9 vols.; Bs As, 1954-63; Eng. transl. of numerous individual works) and his recent *Elogio de la sombra* (Bs As, 1969) and *El informe a Brodie* (Bs As, 1970). Despite their Uruguayan antecedents, the plays of Florencio Sánchez, especially *Barranca abajo* (1905) and *M'hijo el dotor* (1903), and the short stories of Horacio Quiroga, such as "El regreso de Anaconda" or "Los desterrados," must be ranked in the forefront of Argentine literature.

Recent political events form the basis for the novels of Silvina Bullrich, *Los salvadores de la patria* (Bs As, 1965), *La creciente* (Bs As, 1967), and *Mañana digo basta* (Bs As, 1968), of Beatriz Guido, *Fin de fiesta* (Bs As, 1958), *El incendio y las vísperas* (Bs As, 1964; Eng. transl., New York, 1966), and *Escándalos y soledades* (Bs As, 1970), and of Manuel Peyrou, *Las leyes del juego* (Bs As, 1959), *Acto y ceniza* (Bs As, 1963), and *Se*

vuelvan contra nosotros (Bs As, 1966). The "angry young men and
women" of Argentina also are contributing significant works of literature
which take their inspiration from contemporary and agonizing social and
political problems: Iverna Codina de Giannoni, *La enlutada* (Bs As, 1966)
and *Los guerrilleros* (Bs As, 1968); Dalmiro Sáenz, *El pecado necesario*
(Bs As, 1964) and *Hay hambre dentro de tu pan* (Bs As, 1963); and
David Viñas, *Dar la cara* (Bs As, 1962), *Los duenos de la tierra* (Bs As,
1959), and *Los hombres de a caballo* (La Habana, 1967). The younger
writers, both playwrights and novelists, have effectively utilized the humor
as well as the drabness of daily life for subject matter: in the plays of Gri-
selda Gambaro, *El campo* (Bs As, 1967), of Carlos Gorostiza, *¿A qué
jugamos?* (Bs As, 1969), of Roberto Cossa, *Nuestro fin de semana* (Bs
As, 1964), and Ricardo Talesnick, *La fiaca* (Bs As, 1967); and in the
novels of Sara Gallardo, *Los galgos, los galgos* (Bs As, 1968) and Eduardo
Gudiño Kieffer, *Carta abierta a Buenos Aires violenta* (Bs As, 1970).
Among the numerous anthologies of Argentine poetry are Horacio J.
Becco, comp., *Cancionero tradicional argentino* (Bs As, 1960); Jorge
L. Borges and Adolfo Bioy Casares, comps., *Poesía gauchesca* (2 vols.;
Mexico, D.F., 1955), including works by Estanislao del Campo, Hilario
Ascasubi, and José Hernández; Julio Noé, comp., *Antología de la poesía
argentina moderna* (Bs As, 1926; 2d ed., 1931); Juan C. Ghiano, *Poesía
argentina del siglo XX* (Mexico, D.F., 1957); Instituto Torcuato di Tella,
Poesía argentina (Bs As, 1963); and Guillermo Ara, *Suma de poesía argentina* (Bs As, 1970). One may also consult Editorial Losada's prestigious
collection, "Poetas de Ayer y de Hoy," which has published nearly 100
titles of Argentine poets since its start in 1938. The student of literary reviews will want to utilize Héctor R. Lafleur, and others, *Las revistas literarias argentinas, 1893-1967* (Bs As, 1962; 2d ed., 1969) as well as the
collection begun in 1968 by Editorial Galerna, including Noemi Ulla,
Nosotros (Bs As, 1969), Adolfo Prieto, *El periódico Martín Fierro* (Bs As,
1968), and Jorge Rufinelli, *La revista Cara y Caretas* (Bs As, 1968). The
low-priced collection "Serie del Siglo y Medio" of EUDEBA (Bs As) has
published 120 volumes between 1960 and 1970, including many of the
above-mentioned works.

v. HISTORY (Developments since 1930 are treated in Section vi)

The basic handbook of Argentine historiography, Rómulo D. Carbía, *Historia crítica de la historiografía argentina, desde sus orígenes en el siglo
XVI* (La Plata, 1925; 2d ed., 1939; Bs As, 1940), should be supplemented
by Ricardo Caillet-Bois, "La historiografía," in Arrieta, *Historia de la literatura argentina,* VI, pp. 19-198, and, for the national period, by Joseph

Barager, "Historiography of the Río de la Plata Area," *Hispanic American Historical Review*, Nov. 1959, pp. 588-642.

Among useful reference tools are Ricardo Piccirilli, Francisco L. Romay, and Leoncio Gianello, eds., *Diccionario histórico argentino* (6 vols.; Bs As, 1953-55), Diego Abad de Santillán, ed., *Gran enciclopedia argentina* (9 vols.; Bs As, 1956-63), and Enrique Udaondo, *Diccionario biográfico argentino* (Bs As, 1938), *Diccionario biográfico colonial argentino* (Bs As, 1945), and *Grandes hombres de nuestra patria* (3 vols.; Bs As, 1968), and a newly started project, Vicente O. Cutolo, *Nuevo diccionario biográfico argentino, 1750-1930* (2 vols. of projected 8 vols., ltrs, A-E; Bs As, 1968-69). The multi-volume histories have certain obvious limitations, although they are valuable for reference. Best known is the publication of the Academia Nacional de la Historia, ed., Ricardo Levene, *Historia de la nación argentina* (10 vols.; Bs As, 1936-42; 2d ed., 1939-47; 3d ed., 15 vols., 1963). The quality of the volumes is uneven, and much research and interpretation are outdated. To cover the period 1862-1930 the Academia has recently published the *Historia argentina contemporanea* (7 vols.; Bs As, 1963-67). Vicente D. Sierra, ed., *Historia de la Argentina* (8 vols. of projected 15 vols.; Bs As, 1956-69), is a profusely illustrated, elegantly presented study by a group of conservative historians. Among other important multi-volume studies, one should be aware of the collaborative work from the traditional "liberal" school of historians, Roberto Levillier, ed., *Historia argentina* (5 vols.; Bs As, 1969); a "middle-of-the-road" interpretation, Diego Abad de Santillán, ed., *Historia argentina* (3 vols.; Bs As, 1965-66); the revisionist work of José M. Rosa, *Historia argentina* (5 vols.; Bs As, 1965); and the beginnings of a Marxist analysis, Liborio Justo, *Nuestra patria vasalla* (1 vol. of projected 4 vols.; Bs As, 1968). Also useful for the more recent period is the challenging Marxist interpretation, Jorge A. Ramos, *Revolución y contrarrevolución en la Argentina* (Bs As, 1957; 3d ed., 2 vols., 1965). One of the classics of Argentine history has recently been reprinted: Vicente F. López, *Historia de la República Argentina* (10 vols.; Bs As, 1883-93; 5th ed., 8 vols., 1957). In the more specialized area of legal history, Ricardo Levene, ed., *Historia del derecho argentino* (11 vols.; Bs As, 1945-58) stands as a masterpiece.

Satisfactory one-volume summaries are rare indeed. The textbook summary by Ricardo Levene and the stimulating review by José L. Romero, mentioned in Section I, can be profitably supplemented by Carlos Sánchez Viamonte, *Historia institucional de Argentina* (Mexico, D.F., 1948; 2d ed., 1957), Ricardo Zorraquín Becú, *El federalismo argentino* (Bs As, 1939), Ruben F. Mayer, *El país que se busca a si mismo: Historia social argentina* (Bs As, 1944), and Gustavo G. Levene, *La Argentina se hizo así*

(Bs As, 1960). Russian scholars have lately devoted increasing attention to Latin America; the major Marxist interpretation of Argentine history by Russian authors is accompanied by a good bibliography, V. I. Ermolaev, and others, *Ocherki istorii Argentiny* (Moscow, 1961).

The study of colonial history has yielded a rich and extensive bibliography. Two works by Ricardo Zorraquín Becú trace the development of judicial and political institutions: *La organización judicial argentina en el período hispánico* (Bs As, 1952) and *La organización política argentina en el período hispánico* (Bs As, 1959; 2d ed., 1962). Economic problems are defined in a study of pastoral expansion by Julio V. González, *Historia argentina: La era colonial* (Mexico, D.F., & Bs As, 1957) and in Giberti, *Historia económica de la ganadería argentina*, and Cárcano, *Historia de los medios de comunicación y transporte en la República Argentina*. For colonial society, in addition to the works by Fúrlong Cárdiff mentioned in Section IV, one should consult José Torre Revello, *La sociedad colonial: Buenos Aires entre los siglos XVI y XIX* (Bs As, 1970).

The exploration of the Río de la Plata and the two foundings of Buenos Aires were first described in 1612 by Argentina's first historian, Ruy Díaz de Guzmán, in *La Argentina*. Gregorio Funes, *Ensayo de la historia civil de Buenos Aires, Tucumán y Paraguay* (3 vols.; Bs As, 1816-17; 3d ed., 2 vols., 1910-11) and Pedro Lozano, *Historia de la conquista del Paraguay, Río de la Plata y Tucumán* (5 vols.; Bs As, 1873-75) are two important and serious studies written by churchmen. The epic of the conquest has been retold with literary flourishes by R. B. C. Graham, *The Conquest of the River Plate* (London & New York, 1924; reprint, 1968; Sp. transl., 1928). The Frenchman Paul Groussac, famed as director of the Biblioteca Nacional in Buenos Aires, has contributed *Mendoza y Garay* (Bs As, 1916; 2 vols., 1949-50). The broad themes of exploration and settlement are brought together in Julián M. Rubio, *Exploración y conquista del Río de la Plata, siglos XVI y XVII*, Vol. 8 in *Historia de América*, ed., Antonio Ballesteros y Berreta (Barcelona & Bs As, 1942). For the principal avenues of settlement from Chile and Peru, see the extensive investigations of Roberto Levillier, *Nueva crónica de la conquista del Tucumán* (3 vols.; Madrid, 1926-28).

Noteworthy economic studies on seventeenth-century Río de la Plata development include Alice P. Canabrava, *O comercio portugues no Rio da Prata, 1580-1640* (São Paulo, 1944) and Magnus Mörner, *The Political and Economic Activities of the Jesuits in the La Plata Region, Hapsburg Era*, transl. by Albert Read (Stockholm, 1953).

The economic history of the eighteenth century still relies on the fundamental work by Ricardo Levene, *Investigaciones acerca de la historia económica del virreinato del Plata* (2 vols.; La Plata, 1927-28; 2d ed., 1952). The decline of Lima in the last century of colonial rule is emphasized in Guillermo Céspedes del Castillo, *Lima y Buenos Aires: Repercusiones económicas y políticas de la creación del virreinato del Río de la Plata* (Seville, 1946-47). Further basic monographic work has been contributed by Edberto O. Acevedo, *La intendencia de Salta del Tucumán en el virreinato del Río de la Plata* (Mendoza, 1965), José M. Mariluz Urquijo, *El virreinato del Río de la Plata en la época del Marqués de Avilés* (Bs As, 1964), Pedro S. Martínez, *Historia económica de Mendoza durante el virreinato, 1776-1810* (Madrid, 1961), and *Las industrias durante el virreinato, 1776-1810* (Bs As, 1969), Sergio Villalobos R., *Comercio y contrabando en el Río de la Plata y Chile, 1700-1811* (Bs As, 1965), and Enrique Wedovoy, *La evolución económica rioplatense a fines del siglo XVIII y principios del siglo XIX a la luz de la historia del seguro* (La Plata, 1967). Slave trade and its close connection with porteño development has been explored in Diego L. Molinari, *La trata de Negros: Datos para su estudio en el Río de la Plata* (Bs As, 1916; 2d ed., 1944) and in Elena F. Scheuss de Studer, *La trata de Negros en el Río de la Plata durante el siglo XVIII* (Bs As, 1958). Germán O. E. Tjarks, *El Consulado de Buenos Aires y sus proyecciones en la historia del Río de la Plata* (2 vols.; Bs As, 1962) investigates the role of this important trade organization.

In political matters of the eighteenth century, in addition to the abovementioned works by Zorraquín Becú, one should consult the still standard biography by Enrique Barba, *Don Pedro de Cevallos, gobernador de Buenos Aires y virrey del Río de la Plata* (Bs As, 1937) and the excellent survey of Bourbon administrative reform in John Lynch, *Spanish Colonial Administration, 1782-1810: The Intendant System in the Viceroyalty of the Río de la Plata* (London, 1958; reprint, 1970; Sp. transl., Bs As, 1962). The larger field of international relationships has been examined by Octavio Gil Munilla, *El Río de la Plata en la política internacional: Génesis del virreinato* (Seville, 1949).

The Río de la Plata's separation from the Spanish Empire has recently been thrown into relief by the sesquicentennial celebrations of 1960, especially in the publication of bibliography and documents. Most analysis of the troubled years 1800 to 1830 has centered on political history and on major personalities, a pattern first established by the classical and still valuable studies of Bartolomé Mitre, *Historia de Belgrano* (2 vols.; Bs As, 1859; definitive ed., 1887; several eds.) and *Historia de San Martín y de la emancipación sudamericana* (3 vols.; Bs As, 1887-89; several eds.; abridged transl., 1893; reprint, 1969). On San Martín the most valuable works are

José P. Otero, *Historia del libertador don José de San Martín* (4 vols.; Bs As, 1932; 8 vols., 1944-45), Augusto Barcia Trelles, *Antécedentes para estudiar la personalidad y la obra de José de San Martín* (5 vols.; Bs As, 1941-45), Ricardo Piccirilli, *San Martín y la política de los pueblos* (Bs As, 1957), and Enrique de Gandía, *San Martín: su pensamiento político* (Bs As, 1964). In English there are J.C. J. Metford, *San Martín, the Liberator* (Oxford, 1950; reprint, 1970) and Ricardo Rojas, *San Martín, Knight of the Andes,* transl. by Herschel Brickell and Carlos Videla (New York, 1945). Interpretations of Belgrano include *Historia de Belgrano* (Bs As, 1927; 2d ed., 1944) by a descendent, Mario Belgrano, and Luis R. Gondra, *Las ideas económicas de Manuel Belgrano* (Bs As, 1923; 2d ed., 1927). Contrasting evaluations of Moreno are presented by Diego L. Molinari, *La "Representación de los Hacendados" de Mariano Moreno: Su ninguna influencia en la vida económica del país y en los sucesos de mayo de 1810* (Bs As, 1914; 2d ed., 1939) and Ricardo Levene, *Ensayo histórico sobre la Revolución de Mayo y Mariano Moreno* (2 vols.; Bs As, 1920-21; 4th ed., 3 vols., 1960). The Spanish administrators have been examined by José Torre Revello, *El marqués de Sobre Monte, gobernador intendente de Córdoba y virrey del Río de la Plata* (Bs As, 1946) and Paul Groussac, *Santiago de Liniers* (Bs As, 1907; several eds.). Enrique Ruiz Guiñazú, *El presidente Saavedra y el pueblo soberano de 1810* (Bs As, 1960), Julio C. Raffo de la Reta, *Historia de Juan Martín de Pueyrredón* (Bs As, 1948), Hialmar E. Gammalsson, *Juan Martín de Pueyrredón* (Bs As, 1968), and Mariano de Vedia y Mitre, *La vida de Monteagudo* (3 vols.; Bs As, 1950) place these major figures against the broad background of ideas and events. Ricardo Piccirilli, *Rivadavia y su tiempo* (2 vols.; Bs As, 1943; 2d ed., 3 vols., 1960) and Alberto Palcos, *Rivadavia, ejecutor del pensamiento de Mayo* (2 vols.; La Plata, 1960) provide a composite picture of this statesman. Roger M. Haigh, *Martín Güemes: Tyrant or Tool. A Study of the Sources of Power of an Argentine Caudillo* (Ft. Worth, 1968) experiments with new techniques for the study of a provincial leader of Salta. The standard biography of the naval hero of independence, *Historia de Brown* by Héctor R. Ratto (2 vols.; Bs As, 1939), should be supplemented with the principal Argentine naval histories, Teodoro Caillet-Bois, *Historia naval argentina* (Bs As, 1944), and Humberto F. Burzio, *Armada nacional: reseña histórica de su orígen y desarrollo orgánico* (Bs As, 1960).

Some of the background material of separation from Spain has been explored by Julio V. González, *Filación histórica del gobierno representativo argentino* (2 vols.; Bs As, 1937-38), Enrique O. Corbellini, *La Revolución de Mayo y sus antecedentes desde las invasiones inglesas al Río de la Plata* (2 vols.; Bs As, 1950), and Tulio Halperin Donghi, *Tradición política española e ideología revolucionaria de Mayo* (Bs As, 1961). Uruguayan relationships are studied in John Street, *Artigas and the Emancipation of Uruguay* (Cambridge, Eng., 1959). The British influence has been critically analyzed by Enrique Ruiz Guiñazú, *Lord Strangford y la Revolución de Mayo* (Bs As, 1937). Benjamin Keene has provided a biography of an early United States commercial agent in *David Curtis DeForest and the Revolution of Buenos Aires* (New Haven, 1947; reprint, 1970). Still other influences are traced in Juan Canter, *Las sociedades secretas, políticas y literarias, 1810-1815* (Bs As, 1942) and Martín V. Lazcano, *Las sociedades secretas, políticas y masónicas en Buenos Aires* (2 vols.; Bs As, 1927). The narrative of the revolution itself is given in Carlos A. Pueyrredón, *1810: La Revolución de Mayo* (Bs As, 1953), and in Roberto H. Marfany, *Episodios de la Revolución de Mayo* (Bs As, 1966). A solid factual work on the Congress of Tucumán has appeared in Leoncio Gianello, *Historia del Congreso de Tucumán* (Bs As, 1966), while an interesting but more questionable revisionist interpretation emerges in René Orsi, *Historia de la desegregación rioplatense, 1808-1816* (Bs As, 1969). Fundamental economic questions surrounding independence and the immediate post-independence period receive thorough investigation in Sergio Bagú, *El plan económico del grupo rivadaviano, 1811-1827: su sentido y sus contradicciones, sus proyecciones sociales, sus enemigos* (Rosario, 1966), Horacio W. Bliss, *Del virreinato a Rosas: ensayo de historia económica argentina, 1776-1829* (Tucumán, 1959), and Ernesto J. Fitte, *Historia de un empréstito: la emisión de Baring Brothers en 1824* (Bs As, 1962). José M. Mariluz Urquijo has thoroughly investigated the Spanish reaction in *Los proyectos españoles para reconquistar el Río de la Plata, 1820-1833* (Bs As, 1958). Military campaigns, extending up to the Conquest of the Desert, have been neatly summarized in Félix Best, *Historia de las guerras argentinas* (2 vols.; Bs As, 1960), a valuable addition to the classical studies by Juan Beverina, *La guerra del Paraguay* (7 vols.; Bs As, 1921-33), and the latter's *Las invasiones inglesas al Río de la Plata* (2 vols.; Bs As, 1939).

Rosas dominates Argentine historiography in a manner that admits little chance for dispassionate historical analysis. A useful introduction to these problems is provided by Clifton B. Kroeber, *Rosas y la revisión de la historia argentina* (Bs As, 1965), an expanded version of an earlier article in English published in *Inter-American Review of Bibliography*, No. 10, Jan.-March 1960, pp. 3-25. Those who replaced Rosas in power initially wrote the history of this period, and the spirit of *Facundo* permeated much of the nineteenth-century conclusions. The first major attempt to rehabilitate Rosas, Adolfo Saldías, *Historia de Rozas y su época* (5 vols.; Paris, 1881-87; subsequent eds. with title *Historia de la Confederación Argentina*), was brought to scholarly fruition by Ernesto Quesada in *La época de Rosas* (Bs As, 1898; various eds.), an attempt to understand Rosas in the light of his times. Discarding wholly polemical works, the case against Rosas has been presented by Antonio Dellepiane, *Rosas* (Bs As, 1950; 2d ed., 1956), Luis L. Franco, *El otro Rosas* (Bs As, 1945; 2d ed., 1968), and Ernesto H. Celesia, *Rosas: Aportes para su historia* (2 vols.; Bs As, 1954-68). These works should be complemented by Carlos Ibarguren, *Juan Manuel de Rosas: Su vida, su tiempo, su drama* (Bs As, 1930; various eds.), Lucio V. Mansilla, *Rosas: Ensayo histórico-psicológico* (Paris, 1898; several eds.), and Julio Irazusta, *Vida política de Juan Manuel de Rosas a través de su correspondencia* (5 vols. of incomplete ed.; Bs As, 1941-61; 2d ed., 8 vols.; Bs As, 1970). A valuable summary, incorporating distinct viewpoints, was published as the second number of the short-lived *Revista de Historia* (Bs As, 1957), dedicated to "Unitarios y Federales." Recently a series of essays by one of the most judicious scholars of the early nineteenth century have appeared in a posthumous collection, Emilio Ravignani, *Rosas: interpretación real y moderna* (Bs As, 1970). Another attempt at dispassionate assessment appears in Hebe Clementi, *Rosas en la historia nacional* (Bs As, 1970).

Besides Burgin, *Economic Aspects of Argentine Federalism*, the economic scene has been studied by Clifton Kroeber, *The Growth of the Shipping Industry in the Río de la Plata Region, 1794-1860* (Madison, 1957; Sp. transl., Bs As, 1967). Foreign intervention was first scrutinized by John F. Cady, *Foreign Interventions in the Río de la Plata, 1838-1850* (Philadelphia & London, 1929; Sp. transl., Bs As, 1943) and re-explored from the *rosista* point of view in Gabriel A. Puentes, *La intervención francesa en el Río de la Plata* (Bs As, 1958). Also valuable are José M. Rosa, *La caída de Rosas* (Madrid, 1958) and José L. Muñoz Azpiri, *Rosas frente al Imperio Inglés* (Bs As, 1960).

Leading political and military figures have again provided the basis for many of the studies of the Rosas period. Significant biographies of the caudillos include José L. Busaniche, *Estanislao López y el federalismo del litoral* (Bs As, 1926; 3d ed., 1969); Ramón J. Cárcano, *Juan Facundo Quiroga: Simulación, infidencia, tragedia* (Bs As, 1931; several eds.); David Peña, *Juan Facundo Quiroga* (Bs As, 1906); Pedro de Paoli, *Facundo: Vida del brigadier general don Juan Facundo Quiroga, víctima suprema de la impostura* (Bs As, 1952; 2d ed., 1960); the major Marxist and revisionist interpretation, Rodolfo Ortega Peña and Eduardo L. Duhalde, *Facundo y la montonera: Historia de la resistencia nacional a la penetración británica* (Bs As, 1968); and Carlos A. Fernández Pardo, *Nazario Benavídez, caudillo federal* (Bs As, 1969). The major military figure opposing Rosas has been treated in Juan B. Terán, *José María Paz, 1791-1854* (Bs As, 1936) and in Luis L. Franco, *El general Paz y los dos caudil-*

lajes (Bs As, 1961). Julio Irazusta, *Tomás de Anchorena o la emancipación américana a la luz de las circunstancias históricas* (Bs As, 1950; 2d ed., 1962) studies one of the key entrepreneurs and landowners of the Rosas period. The independence and Rosas periods also appear in a careful study by Armando A. Piñeiro, *Historia del general Viamonte y su época* (Bs As, 1959; 2d ed., 1970). The diplomatic career of Argentina's first minister to the United States is outlined in Thomas B. Davis, Jr., *Carlos de Alvear: Man of Revolution* (Durham, 1955; Sp. transl., Bs As, 1964). A major study of the legal and political implications of the period is contained in Victor Tau Anzoátegui, *Formación del estado federal argentino, 1820-1852: la intervención del gobierno de Buenos Aires en los asuntos nacionales* (Bs As, 1965).

The period of national organization from 1852 to 1880 has produced few definitive evaluations. Among the survey materials are Mariano de Vedia y Mitre, *Historia de la unidad nacional* (Bs As, 1952) and Rodolfo Rivarola's frank plea for centralization in *Del régimen federativo al unitario: Estudio sobre la organización política de la Argentina* (Bs As, 1908). The decade of struggle between Buenos Aires and the Confederation was first studied seriously by Ramón J. Cárcano, *De Caseros al 11 de septiembre* (Bs As, 1918; several eds.) and *Del sitio de Buenos Aires al campo de Cepeda* (Bs As, 1921; several eds.) and by Juan A. González Calderón, *El general Urquiza y la organización nacional* (Bs As, 1940). The narrative has been brought up to date with new materials by James R. Scobie, *La lucha por la consolidación de la nacionalidad argentina, 1852-1862* (Bs As, 1964). On Argentine involvement in the Paraguayan War there are such valuable studies as Pelham H. Box, *The Origins of the Paraguayan War* (Urbana, 1929; reprint, 1967; Sp. transl., Bs As, 1958), Efraím Cardozo, *Vísperas de la guerra del Paraguay* (Bs As, 1954) and his *El Imperio del Brasil y el Río de la Plata* (Bs As, 1961), Ramón J. Cárcano, *Guerra del Paraguay* (3 vols.; Bs As, 1939-41), and a revisionist assessment in José M. Rosas, *La guerra del Paraguay y las montoneras argentinas* (Bs As, 1964). The principal biographies of the period include Luis B. Calderón, *Urquiza: Síntesis histórica de su época, su actuación y su obra* (Bs As, 1949; 2d ed., Paraná, 1951); a briefer synthesis in Beatriz Bosch, *Urquiza, el organizador* (Bs As, 1963); Jorge Mayer, *Alberdi y su tiempo* (Bs As, 1963); Abel Chanetón, *Historia de Vélez Sársfield* (2 vols.; Bs As, 1937; 3d ed., 1 vol., 1970); the revisionist study of Fermín Chávez, *Vida de Chacho; Ángel Vicente Peñaloza, General de la Confederación* (Bs As, 1962; 2d ed., 1967); and José S. Campobassi, *Sarmiento y Mitre: Hombres de Mayo y Caseros* (Bs As, 1962). William H. Jeffrey, *Mitre and Argentina* (New York, 1952) summarizes eulogistic Argentine literature on Mitre. Sarmiento, like Rosas, has aroused two distinct interpretations. The sympathetic portrayals by Alberto Palcos, *Sarmiento; La vida, la obra, las ideas, el genio* (Bs As, 1929; several eds.) and Ricardo Rojas, *El profeta de la pampa. Vida de Sarmiento* (Bs As, 1945) should be balanced by Leopoldo Lugones, *Historia de Sarmiento* (Bs As, 1911; several eds.), Manuel Gálvez, *Vida de Sarmiento, el hombre de autoridad* (Bs As, 1945), and the revisionist work by Roberto Tamagno, *Sarmiento, los liberales y el imperialismo inglés* (Bs As, 1963). For scholarly and balanced appraisals one may read Bunkley, *The Life of Sarmiento,* mentioned in Section I, and the French literary examination in Paul Verdevoye, *Domingo Faustino Sarmiento, educateur et publiciste, entre 1839 et 1852* (Paris, 1963).

The 1880's ushered in a new Argentina. To capture some of the flavor of the Indian frontier one should read the literary classic of Lucio V. Mansilla, *Una excursión a los indios ranqueles* (2 vols.; Bs As, 1870; several eds.), Álvaro Barros, *Fronteras y territorios federales de las pampas del sur* (Bs As, 1872; 2d ed., 1957), Alfredo Ebelot, *Recuerdos y relatos de la frontera* (Bs As, 1968), Juan C. Walther, *La conquista del desierto* (2 vols.; Bs As, 1947-48; 3d ed., 1 vol., 1970), Juan M. Raone, *Fortines del desierto: Mojones de civilización* (3 vols.; Bs As, 1969), and Dionisio Schoo Lastra, *El indio del desierto, 1535-1879* (Bs As, 1928; various eds.). McGann's initial chapters on the Generation of 1880 in *Argentina, the United States and the Inter-American System* can be supplemented by Carlos A. D'Amico (pseud., Carlos Martínez), *Buenos Aires: Su naturaleza, sus costumbres, sus hombres* (Mexico, D.F., 1890; several eds.), the biased, but interesting, observations written by an ex-governor of Buenos Aires in exile; by José Arce, *Roca, 1843-1914: Su vida, su obra* (2 vols.; Bs As, 1960-61); and by Agustín P. Rivero Astengo, *Juárez Celman, 1844-1909* (Bs As, 1944) and his biography of Carlos Pellegrini, published in the first two volumes of Carlos Pellegrini, *Obras* (5 vols.; Bs As, 1941). A detailed narrative, Bartolomé Galíndez, *Historia política argentina: La revolución del 80* (Bs As, 1945), reviews the federalization of the city of Buenos Aires while Lía E. M. Sanucci, *La renovación presidencial del 1880* (La Plata, 1959) examines the politics of Nicolás Avellaneda's presidency. On interventions there is Luis H. Sommariva, *Historia de las intervenciones federales en las provincias* (2 vols.; Bs As, 1929-31).

Argentine historiography has barely penetrated beyond 1890. Some new directions have been opened up in Di Tella, *Argentina, sociedad de masas,* Bagú, *Evolución histórica de la estratificación social en la Argentina,* Cantón, *El parlamento argentino en épocas de cambio, 1890, 1916, y 1946,* mentioned in Section IV; in the challenging synthesis of the years 1870 to 1914 in Roberto Cortés Conde and Ezequiel Gallo, *La formación de la Argentina moderna* (Bs As, 1967); in José L. Romero, *El desarrollo de las ideas en la sociedad argentina del siglo XX* (Mexico, D.F., 1965); and in tentative hypotheses on urban history in James R. Scobie, *Buenos Aires hacia 1900* (Bs As, 1971). More traditional political history appears in Miguel A. Cárcano, *Sáenz Peña: La revolución por los comicios* (Bs As, 1963), Exequiel C. Ortega, "*¿Quiere el pueblo votar?*" *Historia electoral argentina desde la Revolución de Mayo, a la ley Sáenz Peña, 1810-1912* (Bahía Blanca, 1963), and Roberto Etchepareborda, *Tres revoluciones: 1890, 1893, 1905* (Bs As, 1968). The revolution of 1890 has been studied in Mariano de Vedia y Mitre, *La revolución del 90* (Bs As, 1929), Juan Balestra, *El Noventa: Una evolución política argentina* (Bs As, 1934; 3d ed., 1959), and the first issue of *Revista de Historia*, 1957, devoted to "La crisis del 90." Biography has remained a standard tool: Juan A. Noble, *Cien años, dos vidas* (Bs As, 1960), a study of Leandro Alem and Lisandro De la Torre; Arístides Gandolfi Herrero (pseud., Álvaro Yunque), *Leandro N. Alem, el hombre de la multitud* (Bs As, 1946; 2d ed., 1953); Roberto Farías Alem, *Alem y la democracia argentina* (Bs As, 1957); Manuel Gálvez, *Vida de Hipólito Yrigoyen, el hombre de misterio* (Bs As, 1939); Luis V. Sommi, *Hipólito Yrigoyen: Su época y su vida* (Bs As, 1947); Félix Luna, *Yrigoyen, el templario de la libertad* (Bs As, 1954) and his *Alvear* (Bs As, 1958); and Ricardo Sáenz Hayes, *Ramón J. Cárcano: En las letras, el gobierno, y la diplomacia, 1860-1946* (Bs As, 1960). Also valuable are the reminiscences of congressional politics by the Socialist Party leader, Nicolás Repetto, *Mi paso por la política: De Roca a Yrigoyen* (Bs As, 1956), continued for the subsequent period as *Mi paso por la política: De Uriburu a Perón* (Bs As, 1957), and summarized in *Mis noventa años* (Bs As, 1962).

VI. GOVERNMENT AND FOREIGN AFFAIRS

There is no up-to-date study of the structure of Argentine government. Outlines have been provided by Leo S. Rowe, *The Federal System of the Argentine Republic* (Washington, D.C., 1921), Austin F. Macdonald, *Government of the Argentine Republic* (New York, 1942), and Santos P. Amadeo, *Argentine Constitutional Law* (New York, 1943). The classical account by José N. Matienzo, *El gobierno representativo federal en la· República Argentina* (Bs As, 1910), can be supplemented by the thorough examination of Segundo V. Linares Quintana's *Gobierno y administración de la República Argentina* (2 vols.; Bs As, 1946) and by Ricardo Levene's digest, *Manual de historia del derecho argentino* (Bs As, 1952; 2d ed., 1957). Early studies of legal and constitutional history include Luis V. Varela, *Historia constitucional de la República Argentina* (4 vols.; Bs As, 1910), Juan A.·González Calderón, *Derecho constitucional argentino* (3 vols.; Bs As, 1917-23), and the transcribed lecture notes of Emilio Ravignani, *Historia constitucional de la República Argentina* (3 vols.; Bs As, 1926-27).

The study of political parties has been summarized in Alfredo Galletti, *La política y los partidos* (Mexico, D.F., & Bs As, 1961) and in Carlos F. Melo, *Los partidos políticos* (Bs As, 1943; 4th ed., 1970). For a Marxist orientation, Rodolfo Puiggrós, *Historia crítica de los partidos políticos argentinos* (Bs As, 1956; 3d ed., 5 vols. of projected 6 vols., 1965-69) provides an interesting review of developments from 1890 to 1945. The valuable and balanced treatment of the complex 1930's and 1940's found in Alberto Ciria, *Partidos y poder en la Argentina moderna, 1930-1946* (Bs As, 1964; 2d ed., 1968), can be supplemented by Marysa Navarro Gerassi, *Los nacionalistas* (Bs As, 1969) and Dardo Cúneo, *El desencuento argentino, 1930-1955* (Bs As, 1965). Silvio Frondizi, *La realidad argentina* (2 vols.; Bs As, 1955-56; 2d ed., 1957) analyzes the application of Marxism to Latin America and to Argentina. The Radical Party's growth has been examined in three volumes by Gabriel del Mazo, *El radicalismo: Ensayo sobre su historia y doctrina* (Bs As, 1951), *El radicalismo: Notas sobre su historia y doctrina, 1922-52* (Bs As, 1955), and *El radicalismo: El movimiento de intransigencia y renovación, 1945-1957* (Bs As, 1957). A similar review for the Socialist Party appears in Jacinto Oddone, *Historia del socialismo argentino* (2 vols.; Bs As, 1934). In English the Radical Party has been studied by Peter G. Snow, *Argentine Radicalism: The History and Doctrine of the Radical Civic Union* (Ames, 1965). Valuable political memoirs include the previously mentioned volumes by Nicolás Repetto (p. 293), Enrique Dickmann, *Recuerdos de un militante socialista* (Bs As, 1949), Federico Pinedo, *En tiempos de la República* (5 vols.; Bs As, 1946-48), Juan E. Carulla, *Al filo del medio siglo* (Paraná, 1951), Juan J. Real, *30 años de historia argentina* (Bs As, 1962), and José M. Sarobe, *Memorias sobre la revolución del 6 de septiembre de 1930* (Bs As, 1957). The Revolution of 1930 appears in narrative in J. Beresford Crawkes, *533 días de historia argentina: 6 de septiembre de 1930–20 de febrero de 1932* (Bs As, 1932) and in careful analysis in the third issue of *Revista de Historia*, 1957, dedicated to "La crisis del 1930." Treatment of other factors which influence the political scene appears in appropriate chapters of John J. Johnson, *Political Change in Latin America: The Emergence of the Middle Sectors* (Stanford, 1958; Sp. transl., Bs As, 1961), and his *The Military and Society in Latin America* (Stanford, 1964), Edwin Lieuwen, *Arms and Politics in Latin America* (N.Y., 1960; 2d ed., 1961), in the previously mentioned volumes by Gino Germani, *Estructura social de la argentina* and *Política y sociedad en una época de transición,* and in John J. Kennedy,

Catholicism, Nationalism and Democracy in Argentina (Notre Dame, 1958). For a review of military influences, one can probe beyond Potash, *The Army and Politics in Argentina, 1928-1945,* mentioned in Section I, into Juan V. Oroña, *La logia militar que enfrentó a Hipólito Yrigoyen* (Bs As, 1965), *La revolución del 6 de septiembre* (Bs As, 1966), and *La logia militar que derrocó a Castillo* (Bs As, 1967). The highly crucial role of students and the Reform Movement in the universities has been examined by Alberto Ciria and Horacio Sanguinetti, *Los reformistas* (Bs As, 1968), and surveyed in English by Richard J. Walter, *Student Politics in Argentina: The Reform and its Effects, 1918-1964* (New York, 1968).

The history of Perón is still being written, and no definitive treatments have yet emerged. Encouraging new materials, however, are being developed beyond the initial assessments by Alexander, *The Perón Era,* and Blanksten, *Perón's Argentina,* in works such as Alberto Ciria, *Perón y el justicialismo* (Mexico, D. F. and Bs As, 1971) and Pedro C. Lux-Wurm, *Le péronisme* (Paris, 1965). The early partisan literature is surveyed in Fritz L. Hoffman, "Perón and After," *Hispanic American Historical Review,* Nov. 1956, pp. 510-28, and May 1959, pp. 212-33. Two journalistic accounts, Ruth and Leonard Greenup, *Revolution Before Breakfast: Argentina, 1941-1946* (Chapel Hill, 1947) and Ray Josephs, *Argentine Diary: The Inside Story of the Coming of Fascism* (New York, 1944) should be supplemented by Félix Luna, *El 45: crónica de un año decisivo* (Bs As, 1969), a fascinating account of the conflicting forces behind Perón's return on October 17, 1945. A popularized type of anti-Peronist propaganda is represented by Mary F. Main (pseud., María Flores), *Woman with the Whip: Eva Perón* (New York, 1952) and *The Call from Calle Moreno* (New York, 1955), an exposure of secret police atrocities. Important among the numerous Peronist items is Juan D. Perón, *El pueblo quiere saber de qué se trata* (Bs As, 1944) and his (pseud., Descartes) *Política y estrategia* (Bs As, 1951, 1952). Eva Duarte de Perón, *La razón de mi vida* (Bs As, 1951; Eng. transl., New York, 1953) is a ghost-written autobiographical exhortation to Argentines to be good Peronists. Among the more articulate defenses of Peronismo are Antonio F. Cafiero, *Cinco años después* (Bs As, 1961), which presents the period 1955-60 as one of regression when contrasted with the Perón years, Juan J. Hernández Arregui, *La formación de la conciencia nacional, 1930-1960* (Bs As, 1960), a persuasive Marxist study of the mass society; an intelligent and critical examination of Peronist labor policy in Miguel Gazzera and Norberto Ceresole, *Peronismo, autocrítica y perspectivas* (Bs As, 1970); and a militant Third World review in Gonzálo H. Cárdenas, and others, *El peronismo* (Bs As, 1969). Arthur P. Whitaker, *Argentine Upheaval: Perón's Fall and the New Regime* (New York & London, 1956) reassesses the political scene as a supplement to his *The United States and Argentina;* while Juan C. Torres and Santiago Senén González, *Ejército y sindicatos: los 60 días de Lonardi* (Bs As, 1969) provide the chronology for the period immediately following the fall of Perón.

Neither volume nor partisanship have diminished with the contemporary scene, but a number of works can be recommended that summarize developments for the general reader: a brave but uneven attempt by the publishing house Sur in *Argentina, 1930-1960,* comp. by Jorge A. Paita (Bs As, 1961); Mariano Montemayor, *Claves para entender a un gobierno* (Bs As, 1960); José M. Saravia, *Argentina, 1959: Un estudio sociológico* (Bs As, 1959); Eduardo Tiscornia, *¿Qué pasa con la Argentina?* (Bs As, 1962); the observations of a Brazilian newspaperman, Emilio Perina, *Detrás de la crisis* (Bs As, 1960); Bonifacio del Carril, *¿Qué nos pasa a los argentinos?* (Bs As, 1963); the previously mentioned Mafud, *El desarraigo argentino;* a scholarly French study of the Radical Party from 1955 to 1962 in Alain Rouquié, *Le movement Frondizi et le radicalisme argentin* (Paris, 1967); a Third World analysis, Gonzálo H. Cárdenas, *Las luchas nacionales contra la dependencia: historia social argentina* (Bs As, 1969); a thoughtful examination of the business class in Dardo Cúneo, *Comportamiento y crisis de la clase empresaria* (Bs As, 1967); an assessment of the effects of urbanization in Juan C. Rubinstein, *Desarrollo y discontinuidad política en Argentina* (Bs As, 1968); a businessman's formulation of the policy needed in order to break out of the cycle of economic stagnation in Francisco J. Sánchez Jáuregui, *El desaliento argentino* (Bs As, 1968); Raúl Bustos Fierro, *Desde Perón hasta Onganía* (Bs As, 1969); the brief chronology presented by Kenneth F. Johnson, *Argentina's Mosaic of Discord, 1966-1968* (Washington, D.C., 1969); and a highly polemical discussion of divisions within the labor movement in Rodolfo Walsh, *¿Quién mató a Rosendo?* (Bs As, 1969).

Argentina's role in international relations has received relatively little attention or investigation. Some historical perspective is provided by Ricardo R. Caillet-Bois, *Cuestiones internacionales, 1852-1966* (Bs As, 1970), Isidoro Ruiz Moreno, *Historia de las relaciones exteriores argentinas, 1810-1955* (Bs As, 1961), and by the discussion of Argentina's position in current world tensions in Sergio Bagú, *Argentina en el mundo* (Mexico, D.F., & Bs As, 1961). Recently, Harold F. Peterson, *Argentina and the United States, 1810-1960* (New York, 1964) has been added to Clarence H. Haring's pioneer *Argentina and the United States* (Boston, 1941). Whitaker, *The United States and Argentina,* Ferns, *Britain and Argentina in the Nineteenth Century,* McGann, *Argentina, the United States, and the Inter-American System, 1880-1914,* Alberto A. Conil Paz and Gustavo E. Ferrari, *Argentina's Foreign Policy, 1930-1962,* transl. by Joseph J. Kennedy (Notre

Dame, 1966), and Gustavo Ferrari, *Conflicto y paz con Chile, 1898-1903* (Bs As, 1968) provide reliable information on particular problems. Sources for the study of the long-standing Malvinas, or Falkland Islands, dispute are reviewed in José Torre Revello, *Bibliografía de las Islas Malvinas: Obras, mapas y documentos* (Bs As, 1953). A thorough investigation of the question appears in Julius Goebel, Jr., *The Struggle for the Falkland Islands* (New Haven & London, 1927; reprint, 1971). Significant Argentine works on the subject include Ricardo R. Caillet-Bois, *Las Malvinas: Una tierra argentina* (Bs As, 1944; 2d ed., 1952) and José L. Muñoz Azpiri, *Historia completa de las Malvinas* (3 vols.; Bs As, 1966); the scope of the conflict has been further broadened in Ernesto J. Fitte, *La disputa con Gran Bretaña por las islas del Atlántico Sur* (Bs As, 1968). German influence in Argentina prior to World War II was first exposed in Enrique Dickmann, *La infiltración nazi-fascista en la Argentina* (Bs As, 1939). A journalistic appraisal of Nazi organization and of the failures of United States policy is presented by Saxtone E. Bradford, *The Battle for Buenos Aires* (New York, 1943). Further documentation was published in the famous Bluebook released by the United States Department of State just prior to the 1946 Argentine elections, *Consultation among the American Republics with Respect to the Argentine Situation* (Washington, D.C., 1946), and in Vol. 5 of *Documents on German Foreign Policy, 1918-1945* (11 vols.; Washington, D.C., 1949-60).

VII. BIBLIOGRAPHIES AND CURRENT PERIODICALS

Although Argentine bibliographies on specific topics are too numerous to list here, specialists will want to start with Abel R. Geoghegan, *Bibliografía de bibliografías argentinas* (Bs As, 1970) and also consult appropriate sections from the annual *Handbook of Latin American Studies* (Cambridge, Mass., 1936-51; Gainesville, 1951-); Charles C. Griffin, ed., *Latin America: A Guide to Historical Literature* (Austin, 1971); Robin A. Humphreys, *Latin American History: A Guide to Literature in English** (London & New York, 1958); Arthur E. Gropp, *A Bibliography of Latin American Bibliographies* (Metuchen, N. J., 1968); Cecil R. Jones, *A Bibliography of Latin American Bibliographies* (Baltimore, 1922; 2d ed., Washington, D.C., 1942; reprint, 1969); Harvard University, Bureau for Economic Research,

* For subsequent English materials see the Latin American section of the American Historical Association, *Guide to Historical Literature* (New York, 1961) and the American Universities Field Staff, *A Select Bibliography*, ed. by Ted C. Grondahl and T. D. Long, *Supplement on Latin America* (New York, 1960, 1965, 1967; Hanover, N.H., 1969).

The Economic Literature of Latin America (2 vols.; Cambridge, Mass., 1935-36); Tom B. Jones, *et al.*, *A Bibliography on South American Economic Affairs: Articles in Nineteenth-Century Periodicals* (Minneapolis, 1955); Charles T. Nisbet, *Latin American Economic Development: A Selected Bibliography* (Los Angeles, 1970); Julian H. Steward, *Handbook of South American Indians* (6 vols. & index; Washington, D.C., 1946-59): Ralph S. Boggs, *Bibliography of Latin American Folklore* (New York, 1940); Timothy J. O'Leary, *Ethnographic Bibliography of South America* (New Haven, 1963); Pan American Union, *Diccionario de la literatura latinoamericana*, Vol. IV, *Argentina* (2 parts; Washington, D.C., 1960-61); David W. and Virginia R. Foster, *Research Guide to Argentine Literature* (Metuchen, N. J., 1970); Edwin M. Borchard, *Guide to the Law and Legal Literature of Argentina, Brazil and Chile* (Washington, D.C., 1917) and a companion volume by Helen F. Clagett, *A Guide to the Law and Legal Literature of Argentina, 1917-1946* (Washington, D.C., 1948); James B. Childs, ed., *A Guide to the Official Publications of the Other American Republics*, Vol. I., *Argentina* (Washington, D.C., 1945), Rosa Quintero Mesa, *Latin American Serial Documents: A Holdings* List (19 vols.; Ann Arbor, 1969-), Vol. V, *Argentina* (forthcoming); and the various annual UNESCO publications, such as the *International Bibliography of Social and Cultural Anthropology, of Economics, of Political Science, and of Sociology.* Also helpful are the book review sections or research inventories of the *Hispanic American Historical Review* (Baltimore, 1918-22; Durham, 1926-, quarterly); *Inter-American Review of Bibliography* (Washington, D.C., 1951-, quarterly); *Journal of Inter-American Studies* (Gainesville, 1959-1964; Coral Gables, 1965-, quarterly); *Journal of Latin American Studies* (Cambridge, Eng., 1969-, semiannual); *Caravelle: Cahier du monde hispanique et luso-brésilien* (Toulouse, 1963-, semiannual); *Aportes* (Paris, 1966-, quarterly); and *Latin American Research Review* (Austin, 1965-, issued every four months).

To follow the current bibliography on Argentine materials is a trying task, although Josefa E. Sabor, "La bibliografía general argentina en curso de publicación," *Handbook of Latin American Studies*, Vol 25, 1963, pp. 374-81, has cast much light on the subject. The most useful aids in tracing book publications include the recently established *Los Libros*, published by Editorial Galerna (Bs As, 1969-, monthly); *Fichero Bibliográfico Hispanoamericano: Catálogo trimestral de toda clase de libros publicados en las Américas en español* (New York, 1961-, quarterly); *Bibliografía Argentina de Artes y Letras* (Bs As, 1959-, quarterly); *Biblos* (Bs As, 1941-66, irregular); *Bibliograma* (Bs As, 1953-57, 1962-, irregular); and the periodic catalogues issued by major publishing houses such as Lajouane, El Ateneo, and Hachette, and bookstores such as Fernández Blanco, Fernando García Cambeiro, Librería del Plata, and Librería Pardo. Valuable assistance in locating the more ephemeral periodical literature can be found in the co-operative efforts by the Columbus Memorial Library, *Index to Latin American Periodicals* (Boston, 1961-62; Metuchen, N.J., 1963-, quarterly); the retrospective material found in Columbus Memorial Library, *Index to Latin American Periodical Literature, 1929-1960* (8 vols.; Boston, 1962), and *1961-1965* (2 vols.; Boston, 1968); in Steven M. Chiarno, *Latin American Newspapers in United States Libraries* (Austin, 1969); in Irene Zimmerman, *A Guide to Current Latin American Periodicals* (Gainesville, 1961); and in Agencia "Los Diarios," *Guía Publicitaria* (Bs As, 1939; various eds.).

There is little coverage of Argentine news items in the United States press beyond occasional articles in the *New York Times* or the *Christian Science Monitor*. Somewhat better coverage appears in *Visión* (Mexico, D.F., 1951-, fortnightly); *The Economist para América Latina* (London, 1967-, fortnightly); and *Latin America* (London, 1967-, weekly). Until 1965 a monthly summary of recent developments selected from the Latin American press appeared in the *Hispanic American Report* (Stanford, 1948-65, formerly *Hispanic World Report*).

Argentine newspapers justly enjoy a high reputation for coverage and cultural leadership. *La Prensa* and *La Nación*, established in 1869 and 1870 respectively, are the conservative deans of the more than twenty daily newspapers presently published in the city of Buenos Aires. For rapid overseas distribution, *La Nación* prints a weekly airmail edition each Monday. Other significant porteño papers include *La Razón* and *Clarín*, and, for the English community, *The Buenos Aires Herald*. Outstanding among the provincial papers are *La Capital* in Rosario, *El Día* in La Plata, *Los Principios* in Córdoba, *La Gaceta* in Tucumán, and *Los Andes* in Mendoza.

For current economic information on Argentina there are numerous important journals: *Anales de la Sociedad Rural Argentina* (Bs As, 1867-, monthly); *Análisis* (Bs As, 1961-, weekly), with emphasis on stock market developments; *Anuario de la Economía Argentina* (Bs As, 1962-, annual), issued by the Consejo Técnico de Inversiones in English and Spanish editions; *Boletín de la Bolsa de Comercio* (Bs As, 1852-; new series, 1905-67, weekly; new series, 1967-, daily); Argentine government publications such as Banco Central, *Boletín Estadístico* (Bs As, 1937-; new series, Jan. 1958-, monthly), and Instituto nacional de estadística y censos, *Boletín Mensual* (Bs As, 1920-; new series, Jan. 1956-, monthly); Techint, or Companía Técnica Internacional, *Boletín Informativo* (Bs As, 1959-61, fortnightly; 1961-, monthly); *Business Conditions in Argentina* (Bs As, 1918-67, quarterly; 1968-, monthly), a summary issued by the banking firm of Ernesto Tornquist & Cía; *Business Trends* (Bs As, 1964-, weekly), issued by the Consejo Técnico de Inversiones in English and Spanish editions; *Comments on Argentine Trade* (Bs As, 1921-, monthly), published by the United States Chamber of Commerce in Argentina; *Competencia* (Bs As, 1967-, fortnightly) published by *Primera Plana; Desarrollo Económico* (Bs As, 1961-, quarterly), a substantial scholarly journal published by the Instituto de Desarrollo Económico y Social; *Economic Survey* (Bs As, 1941-51, 1956-, weekly); *El Economista* (Bs As, 1950-, weekly); *Información* (Bs As, 1930-, monthly), filled with corporation and fiscal data; *Mercado* (Bs As, 1969-, weekly), a general business review; *Nivel de la Economía Argentina* (Bs As, 1962-, annual or biannual, irregular), issued by the Italian firm, FIAT; *Panorama de la Economía* (Bs As, 1957-, quarterly); *Primera Plana* (Bs As, 1962-68, weekly; reissued as *Periscopio*, 1968-70, weekly; recommenced as *Primera Plana*, Sept. 8, 1970-, weekly); *Pulso* (Bs As, 1966-, weekly), issued by Análisis and similar in appeal; *The Review of the River Plate* (Bs As, 1891-, currently issued every ten days), the principal British shipping and trade journal; *Revista de Administración y Economía* (Bs As, 1970-, quarterly), issued by the Instituto para el Desarrollo de Ejecutivos en la Argentina; *Revista de Economía* (Bs As, 1969-, quarterly), published by the Asociación de Economistas Argentinos; *The Situation in Argentina* (Bs As, 1925-, monthly), issued by the First National Bank of Boston; and *Veritas* (Bs As, 1931-50, 1956-, monthly). In an effort to stimulate tourism, the Secretaria de Estado de Difusión y Turismo has recently begun publication of *Argentina* (Bs As, 1969-, monthly), a glossily illustrated magazine with English and Spanish text. More scholarly and theoretical and less current in their approach are the university publications: *Económica* (La Plata, 1954-66, semiannual; 1966-, issued every four months, delayed); *Revista de Ciencias Económicas* (Bs As, 1913-, quarterly, irregular, various changes in title); *Revista de Economía y Estadística* (Córdoba, 1939-54, 1957-, quarterly); *Revista de la Facultad de Ciencias Económicas* (Mendoza, 1949-, quarterly), *Revista del Instituto de Investigaciones Económicas* (Rosario, 1957-, quarterly); *Estudios Económicos* (Bahía Blanca, 1962-, semiannual).

The historical journals, almost entirely devoted to colonial and early national studies, are largely supported by the universities: *Anuario del Departamento de Historia* (Córdoba, 1963-, irregular, delayed); *Anuario del Instituto de Investigaciones Históricas* (Rosario, 1953-, irregular); *Boletín del Instituto de Historia Argentina "Doctor Emilio Ravignani"* (Bs As, 1922-45, 1956-, irregular; formerly *Boletín del Instituto de Investigaciones Históricas*); *Revista de Historia Americana y Argentina* (Mendoza, 1949,

1956-, annual, irregular, delayed); *Revista de la Junta de Estudios Históricos de Mendoza* (Mendoza,1935-40, 1961-, irregular, delayed); *Revisión Histórica* (Tucumán, 1960-, bimonthly); *Trabajos y Comunicaciones* (La Plata, 1942-, irregular); *Revista del Instituto de Historia del Derecho* (Bs As, 1949-, annual); and the recently launched *Investigaciones y Ensayos* (Bs As, 1966-, semiannual), published by the Academia Nacional de la Historia. Two significant private efforts which have now drawn to a close include the fifty issues of *Historia* (Bs As, 1955-1968, quarterly) and the seventy-five issues of *Crónica Histórica Argentina* (Bs As, 1968-69, weekly). Another series on historical topics is currently being published by the Centro Editor de América Latina, *Polémica* (Bs As, 1970-, weekly). The popularization of history has been carried forward successfully under the direction of Félix Luna in *Todo Es Historia* (Bs As, 1967-, monthly). In the social sciences one can turn to the *Revista Argentina de Ciencia Política* (Bs As, 1960-, semiannual) and *Revista Latino-Americana de Sociología* (Bs As, 1965-, issued every four months). For information on legislation and articles on political and legal matters, one should consult the *Boletín de la Biblioteca del Congreso de la Nación* (Bs As, 1918-30, 1932-43, 1946-48, 1956-, irregular) and *Revista de Legislación Ordenada* (Bs As, 1961-, fortnightly).

A number of excellent magazines keep the general public informed on the arts, literature, social sciences, and cultural developments: *Atlántida: Ilustración Argentina* (Bs As, 1918-, monthly); *Criterio* (Bs As, 1928-, currently fortnightly); *Cursos y Conferencias* (Bs As, 1931-, bimonthly, delayed); *Dinámica Social* (Bs As, 1950-, monthly), directed to economists and political scientists; *Diógenes* (Bs As, 1952-, monthly), featuring philosophy and translations from foreign magazines; *Ficción: Revista-libro bimestral* (Bs As, 1956-, currently bimonthly); *Histonium* (Bs As, 1939-, monthly); the popularized *Panorama* (Bs As, 1963-, monthly); the masterful political satire, *Tía Vicenta* (Bs As, 1957-66, fortnightly), which has now been replaced by *María Belem* (Bs As, 1966-, fortnightly); and, of course, the principal literary review, *Sur* (Bs As, 1931-, bimonthly). The universities also publish important journals with cultural or humanistic tendencies: *Revista de la Universidad* (La Plata, 1957-, quarterly); *Humanidades* (La Plata, 1921-, irregular); *Cuadernos de Historia del Arte* (Mendoza, 1961-, irregular); *Humanitas* (Tucumán, 1953-, annual, irregular); *Revista de la Universidad de Buenos Aires* (Bs As, 1904-31, 1943-53, 1956-, quarterly, irregular); *Revista de la Universidad Nacional de Córdoba* (Córdoba, 1914-, quarterly, irregular); *Nordeste* (Resistencia, 1960-, semi-annual); *Universidad* (Santa Fe, 1935-, quarterly); and for the anthropologists, *Runa: Archivo para las ciencias del hombre* (Bs As, 1948-, irregular) and *Revista del instituto de antropología* (Córdoba, 1960-, annual, delayed). The

Unión de Universidades de América Latina has recently shifted its quarterly review, *Universidades,* from Mexico City to Buenos Aires (2d series, 1960-). Outstanding reviews of the fine arts include *Ars: Revista de arte* (Bs As, 1940-, monthly, irregular) and *Lyra* (Bs As, 1943-, quarterly, irregular). The Ministry of Education in La Plata publishes the leading educational journal in the country, *Revista de Educación,* initiated by Sarmiento in 1858 (La Plata, new series, 1956-, varyingly as monthly, bimonthly, or quarterly publication).

Tables and Graph

Province	Capital	Area (In Sq. Mi.)	Population	Density (Per Sq. Mi.)
FEDERAL DISTRICT (INCLUDING THE ISLAND OF MARTÍN GARCÍA)		77	2,972,453	38,600
1. BUENOS AIRES	La Plata	118,800	8,774,529	74
2. CATAMARCA	Catamarca	38,500	172,323	4.5
3. CÓRDOBA	Córdoba	65,200	2,060,065	37
4. CORRIENTES	Corrientes	34,500	564,147	16
5. CHACO	Resistencia	38,400	566,613	15
6. CHUBUT	Rawson	86,700	189,920	2.2
7. ENTRE RÍOS	Paraná	29,400	811,691	28
8. FORMOSA	Formosa	27,800	234,075	8.4
9. JUJUY	Jujuy	20,500	302,436	15
10. LA PAMPA	Santa Rosa	55,400	172,029	3.1
11. LA RIOJA	La Rioja	35,600	136,237	3.8
12. MENDOZA	Mendoza	58,200	973,075	17
13. MISIONES	Posadas	11,500	443,020	38
14. NEUQUÉN	Neuquén	36,300	154,570	4.3
15. RÍO NEGRO	Viedma	78,400	262,622	3.4
16. SALTA	Salta	59,600	509,803	8.5
17. SAN JUAN	San Juan	33,200	384,284	12
18. SAN LUIS	San Luis	29,600	183,460	6.2
19. SANTA CRUZ	Río Gallegos	94,100	84,457	0.9
20. SANTA FE	Santa Fe	51,300	2,135,583	42
21. SANTIAGO DEL ESTERO	Santiago del Estero	52,200	495,419	9.5
22. TUCUMÁN	Tucumán	8,700	765,962	88
Territory				
TIERRA DEL FUEGO, ANTARCTICA, and SOUTH ATLANTIC ISLANDS	Ushuaia	490,000	15,658	—

2. ARGENTINE POPULATION GROWTH AND RATIO OF URBAN TO RURAL POPULATION

Year	Total Population	Urban (In Towns over 2,000)	Rural
1600	350,000 (est.)	—	—
1700	350,000 (est.)	—	—
1750	400,000 (est.)	—	—
1810	500,000 (est.)	—	—
1869	1,800,000 (1st Census)	25%	75%
1895	4,000,000 (2nd Census)	37	63
1914	8,000,000 (3rd Census)	53	47
1947	16,000,000 (4th Census)	63	37
1960	20,000,000 (5th Census)	74	26
1970	23,400,000	75 (est.)	25 (est.)

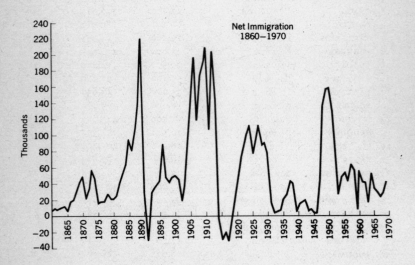

Net Immigration
1860–1970

3. EXPORT TRADE BY MAJOR PRODUCTS*

YEARS	ANNUAL AVERAGE VALUE (In Millions of Pesos)	PERCENTAGES		
		Livestock Products	Agricultural Products	Other
1871-74	95	95%	—	5%
1875-79	106	93	2%	5
1880-84	139	89	7	4
1885-89	209	81	16	3
1890-94	233	66	29	5
1895-99	299	64	31	5
1900-04	499	49	46	5
1905-09	761	39	58	3
1910-14	980	45	51	4
1915-19	1,608	55	39	6
1920-24	1,897	37	58	5
1925-29	2,126	37	59	4
1930-34	1,340	35	60	5
1935-39	1,702	37	57	6
1940-44	1,847	56	26	18
1945-49	4,207	43	50	7
1950-54	6,077	48	43	9
1955-58	18,941	52	40	8
1959	78,377	53	43	4
1960	89,212	48	47	5
1961	79,640	54	40	6
1962	136,181	45	50	5
1963	187,870	49	39	12
1964	196,166	42	49	9
1965	245,990	38	55	7
1966	316,176	43	49	8
1967	462,873	45	45	10
1968	478,179	41	43	16
1969	564,213	43	42	15

* Argentina, Instituto nacional de estadística y censo, *Boletín Trimestral*; and FIAT, Oficina técnica, *Nivel de la Economía Argentina*.

4. ARGENTINE FOREIGN TRADE*
(In Millions of Dollars at Fixed Value of 1960 Prices)

Year	Export	Import	Balance
1935	$1,131.3	$ 765.1	$366.2
1936	1,164.9	733.5	431.4
1937	1,638.8	1,027.3	611.5
1938	1,046.6	1,133.7	(—) 87.1
1939	1,144.0	893.8	250.2
1940	1,007.5	892.0	115.5
1941	964.8	684.2	280.6
1942	942.7	595.1	347.6
1943	1,089.8	425.8	664.0
1944	1,215.0	473.1	741.9
1945	1,282.8	536.0	746.8
1946	1,791.6	1,029.6	762.0
1947	2,002.9	1,965.9	37.0
1948	1,863.5	1,821.8	41.7
1949	1,126.4	1,293.8	(—) 167.4
1950	1,354.5	1,212.8	141.7
1951	1,218.1	1,541.9	(—) 323.8
1952	737.2	1,264.0	(—) 526.8
1953	1,221.6	863.3	358.3
1954	1,112.2	1,060.7	51.5
1955	1,002.8	1,266.3	(—) 263.5
1956	988.3	1,180.7	(—) 192.4
1957	991.7	1,333.1	(—) 341.4
1958	996.9	1,236.3	(—) 239.4
1959	1,001.6	984.6	17.0
1960	1,079.2	1,249.3	(—) 170.1
1961	968.0	1,466.3	(—) 498.3
1962	1,217.2	1,357.9	(—) 140.7
1963	1,370.6	984.6	386.0
1964	1,413.2	1,079.4	333.8
1965	1,467.0	1,177.4	289.6
1966	1,514.4	1,068.7	445.7
1967	1,389.5	1,039.4	350.1
1968	1,267.7	1,083.6	184.1
1969	1,436.8	1,404.7	32.1

* TECHINT, Oficina del *Boletín Informativo*.

5. PERCENTAGES OF THE GROSS NATIONAL PRODUCT CONTRIBUTED
BY MAJOR SECTORS OF THE ECONOMY*
(In Percentages of 1960 Prices)

Year	Crop Farming	Livestock	Manufacturing	Construction	Services	Other
1935	16%	11%	26%	3%	42%	2%
1936	14	12	27	3	43	1
1937	14	11	26	4	43	2
1938	12	11	28	4	43	2
1939	14	11	28	4	42	1
1940	13	11	28	3	43	2
1941	15	12	28	3	41	1
1942	14	11	29	3	41	2
1943	12	12	30	4	41	1
1944	14	11	30	4	39	2
1945	11	11	30	4	42	2
1946	11	11	30	4	43	1
1947	11	10	31	3	44	1
1948	10	9	30	4	45	2
1949	9	9	29	5	46	2
1950	9	9	29	5	46	2
1951	10	9	28	5	46	2
1952	8	9	30	5	46	2
1953	12	9	28	5	44	2
1954	11	9	29	4	45	2
1955	11	9	30	4	45	1
1956	10	8	31	4	45	2
1957	10	8	32	4	45	1
1958	10	7	33	5	44	1
1959	10	8	32	4	45	1
1960	10	7	32	5	45	1
1961	9	6	33	5	45	2
1962	10	6	32	4	46	2
1963	10	7	31	4	46	2
1964	10	7	34	3	44	2
1965	9	6	35	4	44	2
1966	8	7	35	4	44	2
1967	8	7	35	4	44	2
1968	8	7	35	4	44	2
1969	8	7	35	5	43	2

* Argentina, Banco Central, *Boletín Estadístico*, supplement No. 6, June 1966.
Post-1965 figures based on calculations by Aurora Ravina de Luzzi from Banco
Central sources.

6. COST OF LIVING INDEX FOR THE CITY OF BUENOS AIRES[*]
(1960 = 100)

Year	Annual Average	Jan.	Apr.	Jul.	Oct.
1943	2.9	2.9	3.0	2.8	2.8
1944	2.9	2.9	2.8	2.9	2.9
1945	3.5	3.2	3.5	3.5	3.5
1946	4.1	3.9	4.0	4.1	4.2
1947	4.6	4.2	4.5	4.7	4.7
1948	5.2	4.8	4.9	5.2	5.5
1949	6.9	5.9	6.6	7.0	7.4
1950	8.6	7.7	8.1	8.7	9.4
1951	11.7	9.5	10.6	11.9	13.1
1952	16.3	14.9	16.4	16.3	17.0
1953	17.0	16.9	17.0	16.8	16.6
1954	17.6	16.6	17.0	17.6	18.7
1955	19.8	19.2	19.6	19.8	20.0
1956	22.4	20.9	21.4	23.0	23.3
1957	28.0	24.4	26.2	28.4	30.2
1958	36.8	30.2	32.4	37.4	41.0
1959	78.7	55.0	70.0	84.4	89.7
1960	100.2	96.8	99.1	100.9	100.2
1961	113.7	103.1	108.4	115.6	119.4
1962	145.7	124.9	132.3	151.5	161.0
1963	180.7	163.4	175.4	180.1	189.4
1964	220.7	210.0	215.8	219.9	229.9
1965	283.8	240.0	260.3	288.8	307.3
1966	374.9	336.6	358.8	371.4	393.6
1967	483.7	426.5	450.6	498.4	516.8
1968	562.1	550.3	549.8	552.0	571.6
1969	604.7	595.6	594.8	600.3	616.1
1970	686.9	634.6	656.5	674.4	732.3
1971		808.5	851.9		

[*] Argentina, Instituto nacional de estadística y censo, *Costo del nivel en la Capital Federal*, February 1963, pp. 45-51, and *Boletín Trimestral*.

7. EXCHANGE RATE OF THE ARGENTINE PESO TO THE
UNITED STATES DOLLAR*

Year	Official Controlled Exchange	Controlled Free Exchange (Average for Year)	Free Exchange Rate (Average for Year)
1940	4.23	—	4.37
1941	4.23	—	4.24
1942	4.23	—	4.23
1943	4.23	—	4.08
1944	4.23	—	4.02
1945	4.23	—	4.03
1946	4.23	4.09	5.13
1947	4.23	4.08	4.53
1948	4.23	4.45	6.98
1949	6.09	5.87	11.71
1950	6.57	10.72	15.99
1951	7.50	14.22	23.74
1952	7.50	14.05	22.94
1953	7.50	13.98	22.50
1954	7.50	13.98	25.39
1955	9.25	—	30.48
1956	18.00	—	35.56
1957	18.00	—	39.62
1958	18.00	—	48.04
1959	—	—	79.19
1960	—	—	82.94
1961	—	—	82.83
1962	—	—	113.73
1963	—	—	138.29
1964	—	—	139.88
1965	—	—	168.49
1966	—	—	207.45
1967	—	—	331.13
1968	—	—	350.00
1969	—	—	350.00
1970 (after June 18)	—	—	400.00

* Argentina, Banco Central, *Boletín Estadístico*.

Index